P9-EEI-407

WHO KNOWS

WHO KNOWS

From Quine to a Feminist Empiricism

LYNN HANKINSON NELSON

TEMPLE UNIVERSITY PRESS
Philadelphia

Q
175
.N387

Temple University Press, Philadelphia 19122
Copyright © 1990 by Lynn Hankinson Nelson. All rights reserved
Published 1990
Printed in the United States of America

The paper used in this publication meets the minimum requirements of American
National Standard for Information Sciences—Permanence of Paper for Printed Library
Materials, ANSI Z39.48-1984

Library of Congress Cataloging-in-Publication Data
    Nelson, Lynn Hankinson, 1948–
        Who knows : from Quine to a feminist empiricism / Lynn Hankinson
    Nelson.
            p.   cm.
        Includes bibliographic references.
        ISBN 0-87722-647-4 (alk. paper)
            1. Science—Philosophy. 2. Feminism—Philosophy. 3. Quine, W.
    V. (Willard Van Orman)—Contributions in philosophy. I. Title.
    Q175.N386   1990
    501—dc20   89-5173
                                                            CIP

For my daughter, Rebecca Watson, for a Mother's Day long ago,
and Jack Nelson, who knows who knows

The scientific system, ontology and all, is a conceptual bridge of our own making.

—W. V. Quine

As long as their situation is apprehended as natural, inevitable, and inescapable, women's consciousness of themselves . . . is not yet feminist consciousness. . . . Feminist consciousness is the apprehension of possibility.

—S. Bartky

Contents

Acknowledgments

I T IS A CENTRAL THESIS of this work that in the primary sense it is
communities, rather than individuals, who know. Some of those in
my communities who have helped me to know are Hugues Leblanc,
Barbara Brownstein, Peter Roeper, Marilyn Frye, Fred Herzon, Sibyl
Cohen, Elizabeth Potter, Donald Campbell, Robert Schneider, David
Welker, Christine Gray, and my parents, Virginia and Donald Hankinson.
Special thanks are due to Kathryn Addelson, C. Dyke, and Jack Nelson,
who read many versions and significantly influenced the final one, and
who encouraged me to persevere.

This work has also benefited from comments and suggestions of members of departments to whom I have presented parts of it: the philosophy
departments at Temple University, Lehigh University, Lafayette Univer-
sity, and the University of Minnesota-Duluth; the Women's Studies programs at the University of Pittsburgh and the University of Minnesota-
Duluth; and the Center for Philosophy of Science at the University of
Pittsburgh. I have also benefited from the comments and the support of
members of the Society for Women in Philosophy and because Alison
Jaggar graciously invited me to participate in the first Douglass Seminar
in Women's Studies.

My editor, Jane Cullen, displayed more patience and confidence than
any author has a right to expect.

I do not know how to thank my daughter, Rebecca Watson, or hus-
band, Jack Nelson, whose love and encouragement made this work possible.

WHO KNOWS

Reopening a Discussion

The empiricist-derived epistemology that has directed most social and natural scientific inquiry for the last three centuries explicitly holds that historical social relations can only distort our "natural", trans-historical abilities to arrive at reliable beliefs. . . . From this perspective can emerge only bizarre accounts of [feminist inquiry].

—Sandra Harding

THIS BOOK IS an attempt to clear obstacles to several discussions. It attempts to reopen or redirect, among feminists, a discussion of empiricism, and to facilitate, among scientists and philosophers of science, a serious discussion of feminist criticisms of science. Its main objective is to encourage further dialogue between these two communities about the nature of science. The obstacles to these discussions are several, but the largest is surely that most scientists and philosophers of science are empiricists and the issues raised in and by feminist science criticism seem, to many feminists and empiricists, to presuppose the abandonment of empiricism. One fundamental task in furthering a discussion between feminists and empiricists about the nature of science is ascertaining what it is that these communities actually disagree about, and to what extent these communities have been talking past one another. I use and build from the work of W. V. Quine to explore these issues.

In broad (and blurred) strokes, feminist scholars and scientists have, in the past fifteen years, extended their study and criticism to the sciences, epistemology, and the philosophy of science. It is now not uncommon in feminist science criticism for empiricism to be characterized as an inherently flawed doctrine, a doctrine that underwrites or propounds an errone-

3

ous view of the world, of evidence, and of theory formation.[1] The doctrine has been argued to permeate western science to a degree that makes it unlikely that much can be achieved by discussing issues raised by feminist science criticism with practicing scientists or philosophers of science.[2] Moreover, some of the alternatives to empiricism being called for or developed within feminist discussions of epistemology dictate that it is not only difficult but on some level impossible to discuss epistemological concerns, as seen by feminists, with empiricists. Communication fails for want of a common ground.[3]

Many practicing scientists and philosophers of science, on the other hand, may well have failed to notice that feminist scholars and scientists have been discussing science, and that some have now abandoned hope of engendering a fruitful dialogue. This is in part because feminist science criticism has developed largely within the feminist community where time and space to develop and explore views relevant to feminist concerns has been available. It was a necessary and fruitful time (and the initial forays into the larger scientific and philosophic discussions about science were often something less than encouraging). This is not, however, the only reason that feminist science criticism has not received serious and extended attention in scientists' and philosophers' discussions of science; nor is it the most interesting reason from the point of view of this discussion.

Some scientists and philosophers have known there is a conversation about "gender and science" going on, but their views about science, and specifically their understanding of empiricist tenets and of current empiricist accounts of science, have led them to think there is something akin to a category mistake at work. And it would be less than forthright not to say that some scientists and philosophers of science have known of the conversation and have simply not been interested in it. The source of that indifference, at least the source that is interesting given that dogmatism and apathy are not, is apparently an assumption that feminist criticism has few or no implications for the soundness of our current understandings of science or current scientific practice.

In brief, feminist science criticism has now reaped the benefits of two and a half decades of feminist scholarship and has passed through many preliminary discussions and revisions to which the wider community has not been privy. Thus, the wider community has largely failed to note, or to understand, the now full-blown attacks on western science that are being put forth as antiempiricist positions.

In what follows, I argue that although there is no need to abandon empiricism as the foundation of science, both an empirically sound understanding of science and the science we should work to bring about will need to incorporate key insights of feminist criticisms of science. The science we should work to bring about will be different from the conception many scientists and philosophers have about science, and it will be different from science as it is actually practiced, just as these are already different from one another. Unlike the science community's present conception of science, the new science will incorporate values. Unlike much of the present practice of science in which values *are* incorporated and we simply deny that they are, the incorporation and infusion of values will be self-conscious and subject to critical scrutiny. I will also argue that the science we should work to bring about is foreshadowed in what feminist science critics and scientists are currently doing. Thus, I am committed to the view that feminist criticism challenges what we think science is, justly criticizes science as it is, and leads to a conception of how science could and should be. The most fundamental reasons for so characterizing the implications of feminist criticism is that the body of criticism is itself properly construed as *within* science. So, I am also committed to the view that those who are interested in getting things right cannot ignore this body of criticism.

As an attempt to get discussion started or redirected, this book is addressed to feminists and to scientists and to philosophers of science, and generally to all those who are interested in partaking in what we should hope will be an ongoing and increasingly expansive conversation about science. Consequently, almost every reader will find some of the ground covered familiar and perhaps some discussions superficial.

Readers will also find that the issues I discuss are limited. I take what may be described as a "high" philosophical road, addressing topics like the relationship between theories and experience, between common sense and science, between metaphysics and science, and between epistemology and science. Despite what philosophers long thought, attention to topics like these is not all we need to understand science, either as it is or as how it might be better. But it is part of what we need. Nor is such attention a substitute for social and historical studies of science communities, or studies of the social and political contexts within which scientific knowledge develops. The topics I will explore are merely one aspect of the work to be done in understanding science as it is, thus enabling us to see how it can be better.

But these topics are also more than a supplement to these other investigations. All of these other ways of investigating science would themselves be impossible (at the very least, they would not warrant our attention) without an understanding of what is to count as evidence—for these accounts of the factors underlying and shaping the directions of scientific inquiry are purportedly well-supported accounts of these things, that is, they are understood to be accounts for which there is evidence. Thus, they must presume an account of evidence. Empiricism, which is, at bottom, a theory of evidence, is one way of underwriting them. And as a theory of *evidence*, empiricism is far from bankrupt.

Feminism and Epistemology

An ability to see present states of affairs as alterable and to envision alternatives is, as Sandra Bartky points out,[4] a fundamental feature of feminist thinking. Nowhere has this ability enabled and promised more revolutionary insights than in feminist approaches to science. To those familiar with feminist science criticism, it might seem anachronistic or reactionary to undertake a serious consideration of feminism and empiricism and to suggest that radical alternatives to common views about science will emerge through such a consideration. Recent feminist discussions of science and epistemology have, for the most part, concluded or assumed that it is not possible or desirable to reconcile feminist science criticism with empiricism.[5]

This is not surprising. At best, the frameworks outlined and criticized in recent feminist discussions as the possible bases for a "feminist empiricism" have been naïve, incorporating views of knowers and of science that are severely challenged by the focuses and conclusions of feminist science criticism and, before this, by debates in mainstream and Marxist philosophy of science, and in the social sciences.[6]

More interestingly, the "feminist empiricism" sketched in feminist discussions appears self-defeating, either because it incorporates views of knowers and of knowing that cannot accommodate the focuses of feminist science criticism,[7] or because, as Sandra Harding has recently noted, the framework she outlines as "feminist empiricism" appears to "deeply subvert empiricism".[8]

But it is time to reopen, or at least to redirect, a sustained discussion of feminism and empiricism. In Chapter One I lay out an understanding of empiricism that will shape the larger discussion and, after doing so, I offer some quite specific reasons for reopening the discussion. The most pragmatic of these, however, can be stated without those details. The point of feminist science criticism must, in the end, be to change science, and changing science requires changing the practice of scientists. Hence scientists must be brought into the dialogue. Since scientists are empiricists, that dialogue will have to make room, at least in the beginning, for empiricists and for, at least as a topic of discussion, empiricism. In short, the project on which feminist science critics are embarked requires, if it is to have any chance of success, the cooperation and, therefore, as a first step toward cooperation, the engagement of scientists. Science as currently practiced is too entrenched, too pervasive, and too successful to be simply abandoned. The initial goal of this hoped-for engagement should be to gain a central place for feminist voices in those conversations about science which shape scientific practices and our understandings of those practices.

Nor is there reason to think that claiming a place in those conversations requires giving up the valuable insights into science that feminist scientists and scholars are providing. If I am correct, a sophisticated feminist empiricism will enable more radical insights into science than feminists or empiricists might have thought, and we will explore some alternatives that emerge when trends in feminist criticism and contemporary empiricist philosophy of science are allowed to illuminate each other.

The ensuing discussion will be reactionary neither in rationale nor in conclusions. Though I believe that empiricism warrants deeper consideration than it is now accorded in feminist science criticism, I do not take the views underlying the feminist move away from empiricism as obstacles to be overcome in developing a feminist empiricism. Rather, they are indications of what an adequate empiricism must be like.

In the course of the larger discussion, I will be suggesting some alternatives to current approaches to the "epistemology question" in feminism.[9] The first alternative has to do with the view of empiricism at work in most feminist discussions of epistemology and science. At its most serious, contemporary empiricism represents a far more radical departure from traditional and positivist empiricism than has been taken into account in feminist criticisms of empiricism. The task of reconciling feminist science criticism with empiricism is very different once we stop identifying empiricism with logical positivism or with its most immediate heir, the "postlogical" positivist tradition represented by Carl Hempel, Ernest Nagel, and Rudolf Carnap.[10]

A second tenet of the discussion is that the more radical of feminist insights into the sciences—and, in particular, those that have been understood to incorporate or force "antiempiricist" formulations or solutions—need to be incorporated in any sound and meaningful empiricist account of science. This suggests the view that antiempiricist frameworks can be avoided, and that the most radical and valuable implications of feminist science criticism need not be lost in a sufficiently rich empiricist account of science.

A third alternative is related to the issue of "antiempiricist" epistemologies, and I regard it as crucial. I will argue that there is no need to assume an "epistemological chasm" between feminist scholars and scientists, and empiricist philosophers and scientists (or nonfeminists generally)—that is, there is no need to assume or imply that feminists know things that empiricists (and nonfeminists generally) *cannot know*. In fact, I will urge, we should entertain serious doubts that epistemological chasms of the sort are even coherent.

Of equal importance, to assume an epistemological chasm between feminists and nonfeminists (or to offer explanations for feminists' claims that imply that there is such a chasm) requires that we assume science is precisely what we are coming to see that science is *not:* a static entity that is autonomous from our common-sense, social, and political experiences, including those of gender. It is to assume, among other things, that feminist scientists and science critics are not engaged in science.

The lack of unbridgeable epistemological chasms, or of the assumption of them, suggests a different task for feminist epistemology than that for which feminist standpoint epistemologies have been developed, for the latter assume and explain such chasms. Hence, this discussion is addressed to empiricists no less than it is to feminists, for I believe that nonfeminists (or men) can *come to see* what feminist perspectives have made visible.

This is not to deny the uniqueness or the revolutionary nature of feminist insights. As long as experiences are fundamentally divided by sex/gender[11] and political position, feminist perspectives will contribute unique and necessary insights into the nature of things, including the nature of science. I am insisting that these insights have a connection with evidence and that they can be shared.

It is also not to deny that it may require a revolution in some standards of evidence for holders of those standards to come to know what feminists know. But the revolution need not be based on faith. Rational, critical discussion of standards of evidence is possible. (So Kuhn is wrong if he denies that possibility.[12])

Finally, I will argue for a perhaps uncommon view of the relation between epistemology and science. As a theory about how we go about theorizing, the role of an epistemology is, of course, explanatory and, in the very limited sense outlined below, an epistemology plays a justificatory role. But for reasons that will emerge in the larger discussion, I do not believe that an epistemology is, or could be, *outside* of science broadly construed—outside, that is, the theories and practices it explains. Recent developments in philosophy of science and feminist scholarship, as well as the history of epistemology, indicate that an epistemology and the theories it explains will be radically interdependent. Moreover, the "justification" of theories and claims requires much more than an appeal to a going epistemology, although such appeals will also be made. Theories, including epistemologies, are justified, when they are, on the basis of their coherence with our experience.

These views distinguish what I demand of an epistemology from those views that seek or demand a noncircular (and perhaps foundationalist) relationship between an account of how we know and our going theories. Sandra Harding, for example, maintains that "no conceptual system can provide the justificatory grounds for itself" and that to "avoid vicious circularity, justificatory grounds always must be found outside the conceptual system one is trying to justify".[13] I doubt that there are such grounds. But I also doubt that the "circularity" involved, what I have called a "radical interdependence", has to be vicious. This is in part because I do not demand that an epistemology justify our theorizing and theories.

I bring to this work a basic assumption: that the core of empiricism is a theory of *evidence* for which there is currently no viable alternative. Beyond that core (and only, of course, until such time as we find it necessary to abandon it) any so-called "dogmas of empiricism" are signs that things have gone off track.[14] I will not argue for this assumption. I will argue that a feminist empiricism, a view of science that can account for the obvious success of science in explaining and predicting experience and can encompass feminist insights into the relationships between sex/gender, politics, and science, is a viable and powerful option.

Philosophy of Science, Boundaries, and Quine

Traditional philosophy of science has demanded and been granted rigid boundaries between epistemology, metaphysics, science, methodology, and values—including political values and practices. But in the last three decades, research into the assumptions, theories, and practices of the sciences, and the social and political contexts in which science communities are located, has demonstrated interrelationships between all of the activities the traditional view wanted to keep separate.

The relationships have proved to be neither unidirectional nor superficial. Social and political concerns and contexts have been found to play a significant role in shaping the directions of scientific interest and research: the questions addressed, methodologies adopted, and the hypotheses and theories accepted and rejected.[15] It has also become increasingly clear how extensively the theories, research programs, and

methodologies we consider or adopt in the sciences shape, in turn, our
social, political, and moral perspectives and experiences.[16]

The establishment of all these relationships represents a devastating
challenge to the view that science is a practice or set of practices somehow
removed and distinguishable from other practices and belief systems.[17] In
brief, the research of the last three decades has led many of us to see that
knowledge is of a piece, is value laden, and is one with science broadly
construed. Given what Kathryn Addelson calls the "cognitive authority"
science and scientists enjoy,[18] and the relationships that are being exposed
between science and social and political contexts, it is heartening that
science is coming to be recognized as a political force within our larger
community.

The focuses and findings of feminist science criticism have contributed
extensively to these views of knowledge and science, and provoked specific
questions for philosophy of science. In exploring some questions raised
by feminist criticism for empiricist accounts of science, I will pay particular
attention to one of the more prolific, important, and controversial of
contemporary empiricists, W. V. Quine.

I chose to reexamine Quine's account of science in the light of feminist
criticism for a number of reasons. First, some of the more controversial
aspects of Quine's work are, arguably at least, the logical synthesis of
some central tenets of empiricism and twentieth-century developments in
science and philosophy of science.[19] His work is therefore an appropriate
choice for exploring the questions raised by feminist science criticism for
empiricist accounts of science.

Quine's influence in the empiricist tradition in philosophy of science
would be hard to overestimate. As Noam Chomsky, one of his more
outspoken critics, maintains, Quine "has set the agenda for Anglo-American philosophy and beyond since 1950. . . . In major areas of philosophy
you have to begin by considering his formulation of the issues—whatever
your judgment of them happens to be".[20]

It is, on my view, of equal significance that although Quine is the heir
apparent of the "postlogical" positivist tradition, his view of science avoids
the polarization that has resulted from the work and legacies of two other
major traditions in empiricist philosophy of science—what have come to
be viewed as the Hempel/Nagel and the Kuhn/Hanson/Lakatos traditions—and that it avoids some of the problems each encountered.[21]

Feminist science critics have noted some of the problems that the
Hempel/Nagel tradition would encounter in attempting to encompass the
focuses of feminist science criticism.[22] The problems stem in large part
from the tradition's almost exclusive focus on science as a body of theories

(themselves thought of as sets of sentences with a certain logical structure), and on the centrality granted to what has come to be known as "the logic of justification". Within philosophy of science, Quine is largely responsible for exposing the inadequacies of the Hempel/Nagel view of science as I will outline in Chapters Two and Three.

Work in the second tradition, and most clearly as characterized by Kuhn's work, also challenges the focuses of the first tradition and the picture of science these focuses presuppose and support. One of the consequences of Kuhn's emphasis on the history of actual sciences rather than the logic of idealized science is the illumination of the role of the sociology of science communities in determining the directions of scientific inquiry. Kuhn's accounts of normal science and scientific revolutions raise serious questions about the adequacy of viewing science as a body of theories, and of focusing, to the exclusion of broader considerations, on the logic of justification. But I will explore what I think are some fundamental problems in the picture of science drawn by, or attributed to, Kuhn and some specific problems the focuses and legacy of his approach to science pose for feminist science criticism and for those interested in understanding that body of criticism.

I will argue that Quine's advances on some aspects of each of these traditions are among the first steps, though far from the last, that need to be taken in developing a fruitful philosophy of science. In particular, his views challenge the alleged dichotomy that *either* knowledge is passively discovered *or* it is "socially constructed" (or "culturally determined") with little or no constraint imposed on it by "the world". His constellation of views does not involve the alleged relativism of Kuhn, and it offers a much more sophisticated view of science, evidence, inquiry, theory formation, and testing than does the Hempel/Nagel view. And, of course, Quine's work demonstrates that empiricist philosophy of science did not end with either positivism or Kuhn. This last point is too often overlooked.

There are also direct parallels between Quine's view of science and issues raised in and by feminist science criticism. The most important is that Quine has long challenged the boundaries between science, metaphysics, methodology, and epistemology, boundaries specifically and implicitly challenged in feminist criticism, and he has recently addressed the relationship between science and values.[23] His view of science is almost (but not quite) without boundaries, and this most clearly distinguishes his positions and conclusions from those developed and reached in the two other traditions in empiricist philosophy of science. I exploit Quine's challenges to the proponents of clear boundaries while also arguing that feminist science criticism indicates that the boundary he claims is real, that between science and values, and, in particular, science and politics is no more real than those he exposes as false. The collapse of that boundary has far-reaching consequences.

There is more to be gained from attention to Quine's focuses and positions. First, his work is relevant to my argument that the characterization of empiricism with which many nonempiricists are working needs to be updated and deepened. Empirical philosophy of science has undergone radical changes in the past thirty years. As explicated and defended by Quine, basic empiricist tenets turn out to be complex, requiring a more subtle and sophisticated understanding than they are often accorded in criticisms of empiricism. Quine's empiricism does show the marks of the skepticism evident in the tradition that precedes it, a tradition that includes Hume, Hempel, and Kuhn. But I will argue that much of this skepticism is avoided if we adopt a communal rather than an individualistic view of knowledge and knowers. And despite the continuities between Quine's positions and some earlier empiricist accounts, it will be clear that more than centuries separate Hume and Quine, and more than decades Quine and logical positivism. The differences turn out to be important to the question of whether a feminist empiricism, an empiricism shaped by feminist insights into science, is possible.

Indeed, there is support (if not progenitors) in Quine's positions for several important feminist claims about science. Quine's positions indicate that some issues raised in feminist science criticism at least parallel ongoing issues and problems in the development of an empiricist account of science: the relationship between metaphysics and "good" science; that between canons of evidence, epistemology, and other theories; and that between the larger social context and the questions and theories developed in science communities.

Though many of these issues are fundamentally recast and radicalized in feminist science criticism, the parallels with Quine's challenges to positivist positions further strengthen the case for feminist positions and for the possibility that a feminist empiricism can be developed.

Finally, I use aspects of Quine's work to develop arguments against the view that there is, or could be, anything like an epistemological chasm between feminist science critics, and empiricist philosophers and scientists—that feminists know things empiricists *cannot* come to know. Those aspects of Quine's account of science that would preclude epistemological chasms, are, I argue, supported by the very development and directions of feminist science criticism—a development that would be hard if not impossible to explain *without* something like Quine's views.

Several of these points suggest a basic circularity in my approach, and indeed there is one. I use a number of Quine's positions to argue that some moves, which can and need to be further expanded or recast to accommodate feminist insights, have already proved necessary (or at least Quine thinks so) within empiricist philosophy of science—thus strengthening the case for several important feminist positions. I use aspects of feminist criticism to support a number of Quine's views, including those views that I use to strengthen the feminist case.

Those who object to circular arguments may find my approach troublesome, but objections to circular arguments lose their plausibility when the circle becomes sufficiently large and dialectical, when it is self-reconstructing and self-critical. In such a case, we are engaged in a different sort of enterprise than the sort for which the search for a foundation is reasonable—if, indeed, it ever is. It will be a central argument of this discussion that we are within science, broadly construed, when we criticize aspects of it (however large) and attempt to reconstruct them. A large number of going theories and some understanding of what is to count as evidence make such criticism and reconstruction possible.

Moreover, in connecting and entwining the bits and pieces of the larger scheme, we often simply allow to unfold what is already there—and that is all I am attempting to do.

Two qualifications about my use of Quine are in order. I have no reason to think that Quine is a feminist—or to put things in more Quinean terms, to think that Quine would assent to the sentence "I am a feminist". But this has more to do with what Quine believes about his beliefs than it does with Quine's beliefs about science and inquiry. I am not suggesting, not do I believe, that Quine's constellation of views are all we need to bridge the gaps that currently separate feminists and empiricists, and to begin the work of developing a feminist empiricism and a sound and meaningful philosophy of science. But his views give us starting points and springboards that turn out to be enormously helpful.

The second qualification is this. That we can get help from Quine is not an indication that feminist science critics are not challenging fundamentally some of what many of us have thought science is. Quine is no ordinary empiricist. The interplay of feminist criticism and his views discloses that science is not the enterprise that many scientists, philosophers, and laypersons currently take it to be, and that it could be better were we to give up some of the myths we have cherished.

In addition, the views of science, inquiry, and epistemology that I will advocate in the course of the discussion do not all coincide with Quine's. I do not think Quine is everywhere right. I do think his views are well worth discussing, are almost never wildly wrongheaded. I will expand upon those views, using the insights provided by feminist science criticism, most notably by arguing that traditional and positivist skepticism, as well as the skepticism Quine himself is sometimes accused of falling into, is avoided when we separate empiricism from individualism, and when we stop attempting to distinguish between "kinds" of knowledge and between our various practices. To stretch one of Quine's metaphors for science, relativism is avoided when we recognize that all of our activities to organize our experiences and all our ways of organizing these, including our political experiences, our physics, our sociology, our experiences of sex/gender, and our values, are a single fabric. All of our views, including those that are political, can be, and I will argue must be, subjected to critical scrutiny itself based on evidence.

Knowers, Knowledge, and Science Communities

The grounds for two related claims emerge in the interplay of feminist criticism and Quine's empiricism, and these invite a reconsideration of "science communities". Neither claim is unique to this discussion. One is that the empiricist commitment to taking individuals to be the acquirers and owners of knowledge is untenable.[24] I use the implications of feminist science criticism as well as central features of Quine's empiricism to argue against the view that "knowers" are individuals and to support the view that knowers are communities. Communities, not individuals, "acquire" and possess knowledge.[25]

Considerations supporting this alternative weave through the discussion and are pulled together in Chapter Six. The issues are complex and important. Both a sound empiricism and a sound feminist philosophy of science depend on the possibility of a life for empiricism without—or "post"—individualism.[26]

The shift in focus from individuals to communities and the considerations that prompt this alternative view of knowers lead rather directly to a reconsideration of the relationship between science and values, including politics. When we recognize that communities are knowledge "acquirers" and give up the long-standing focus on individuals, we find ourselves taking into account the relationship between communities and values. Values emerge within and shape a community's practices and theories, and many of these values are political in nature and consequence.

My second and more general thesis is that we should not lament the lapsing of the traditional boundaries between metaphysics, epistemology, science, methodology, and values, including politics. Rather, accepting science as being value laden allows us to make sense out of both scientific practice and our values and politics. Scrutinizing and evaluating the values, political and otherwise, that are incorporated in our approaches to human and nonhuman nature must, without the assumption of false boundaries, become part and parcel of good scientific practice. And because not anything goes in science, insofar as values, politics, and science are interfused, the same holds of values and political practices. Not all values or value systems, all political views or political practices, are created equal.

If communities acquire knowledge and incorporate values, and good values require and in turn make good science possible, then science communities are far more inclusive than those special communities we associate with white coats and complicated instruments. We find ourselves, again, challenging a traditional boundary: in this case, that alleged to separate science communities and our larger community. Our larger community, including its values and politics, is, in fact, a science community.

This result has clear moral implications. If a science community encompasses all of the activities and practices with which special scientific communities are inextricably related, and if, as feminist criticism indicates, there is no separating science from values, or science from politics, then good science must incorporate the taking of responsibility for the directions and use of knowledge developed and certified in scientific communities,[27] and self-conscious and critical attention to the values incorporated in scientific theorizing.

The lack of a real boundary between scientific communities and our larger community also suggests some specific things about the relationship of feminist science criticism to science. It indicates that it will not do to limit our visions of alternative sciences to "sciences of a future time"—to the kind of science, for example, that would be practiced in a society that encompassed or was shaped by feminist values. And this is the case whether we think of such a science as a "reformed science as usual" or as a "successor science" that is fundamentally different than current science.[28]

If knowledge is of a piece, if it is the property of communities, and if special science communities are inextricably related to and embedded in the practices and beliefs of the larger social and political context, there will be no feminist society without feminist science. Feminist society and feminist science will evolve apiece, if at all. And if these things are true, then it is also true that in every important sense, feminists are now engaging in science.

On one level, we will find that the science in which feminists are engaged is more in keeping with feminist visions of what good science should be like than with what, by and large, science as currently practiced is like. The differences of consequence are that feminists are self-conscious in their inclusion of values and they insist on subjecting values to empirical controls. Recognizing and focusing on the difference, has, however, obscured deeper relationships. Illuminating the continuities between the work in which feminists are engaged and science as it is currently practiced and recognized exposes the fact that science, *as it is,* is not what many of us thought.

Organization of the Discussion

Exegesis has been complicated by the fact that I am not addressing a homogeneous audience. I want to raise doubts about the notion that theoretical standpoints can generate unbridgeable epistemological chasms, and in particular that feminist standpoints can make rational discussion with nonfeminists impossible. But there is little question that feminist discussions tend to take place in an arena with its own history, evolved views, theories, and vocabulary—in short, in an arena that nonfeminists find extremely difficult to enter without assistance.

It is neither possible nor desirable to ignore these barriers to dialogue. Analytic categories that have become possible in feminist scholarship are often foreign to contemporary empiricism or regarded by empiricists as irrelevant to an account of science. They allow, however, for unique and important insights into science. Consequently, I have spent more time outlining issues in feminist science criticism than those familiar with that criticism may require.

For those readers, I recommend the concluding sections of Chapters Four and Five in which I relate the issues in feminist criticism outlined in earlier sections to issues in empiricist philosophy of science and, ultimately, to Quine's positions and consider their implications.

I use Chapter One to lay out some of the basic building blocks of the larger discussion: the specific understanding of empiricism I bring to the discussion and some issues in feminist science criticism that pose problems for current empiricist accounts of science. In the final section of the chapter I use these building blocks to offer specific reasons as to why a sustained discussion of feminist empiricism is worth engaging in.

I do not presume the reader's familiarity with Quine's work. Chapter Two is devoted to explicating some of the more important background to the issues Quine addresses, and, in particular, to outlining some of the issues that interested the two dominant traditions in "postlogical" positivist philosophy of science: the Hempel/Nagel and Kuhn/Lakatos traditions. The legacies of these two traditions for current thinking about science are also discussed to lay the groundwork for the discussion of feminist sci nce criticism. Chapter Three is devoted to exploring features of Quine's view of science and to relating specific positions and strands in his work to positions taken in these other two traditions, in particular, those positions we will use when we consider issues in feminist science criticism.

Readers familiar with recent philosophy of science and Quine's work may want to skim these chapters, but I do not recommend that they be skipped altogether. This is particularly true of Chapter Three. Quine's work is vast, controversial, and, in my view, often misunderstood. The overview and discussion are not exhaustive or intended to be; they focus on some issues of long-standing interest in the philosophy of science that are relevant to issues in feminist criticism. Some of Quine's positions, for example, concerning the relationship between metaphysics and science, the alleged distinction between science and "common sense", and the appropriate task and role of epistemology, are significantly different from those advocated by those in the two other traditions, and significantly different from the positions attributed to empiricists by their critics (including, unfortunately, the positions frequently attributed to Quine). So, the issues considered in the chapter are central to the question of whether a feminist empiricism can be developed.

In Chapter Six I continue to explore the interplay of feminist science criticism and Quine's views of empiricism and of science, and I discuss the intriguing question "who knows?" It becomes clear in this chapter and in Chapter Five that the project of reconciling feminism and a sufficiently rich empiricism is not impossible. It also becomes apparent that encompassing the focuses of feminist science criticism will require that some aspects of Quine's view of science be revised and others abandoned, and that a central issue is individualism. If Quine's positions do represent the logical synthesis of basic empiricist tenets and twentieth-century developments in science and philosophy of science, then the revisions suggested by feminist criticism have wide applicability.

In Chapter Seven I argue that the covenant we have inherited from Descartes, an agreement to bifurcate knowledge into "knowledge of facts" and "values" and, when doing science, to concern ourselves only with the former, is, at the very least, no longer useful—even as a "noble lie". Maintaining the charade that science and values are distinct only insures that the values and politics we bring into the laboratory will not be acknowledged and subjected to scrutiny.

Exegesis has also been complicated by the fact that I am concerned to illuminate relationships and to undermine alleged boundaries that preclude understanding. To capture—at least not to lose—the complexity and richness of some of the relationships that feminists and Quine have exposed often requires forsaking linear explication, for many of the relationships at issue are not linear.

It will be clear that there are issues relevant to a discussion of feminism and empiricism that are beyond the scope of this discussion, and that many of the arguments I offer are not definitive. Nevertheless, I am not troubled by either of these things. This discussion is an attempt to contribute to a more fruitful dialogue about feminism and empiricism by exploring some alternatives to empiricist positions as these are suggested by feminist science criticism, suggesting alternatives to some feminist approaches to epistemology, and allowing alternatives to emerge in the interplay of the recent history of feminist science criticism and empiricist philosophy of science. As I noted earlier, the discussion remains at the level of talking about science as an activity in which theories are generated, in the course of which ontologies and standards of evidence are adopted, and so on. The discussion will not, however, further the case for viewing science as a static or autonomous enterprise or as a body of knowledge. Indeed, the issues we will consider indicate that such views of science are untenable.

It is, to borrow an insight from C. Dyke, an attempt, building on the work of others, to contribute to "[an advancing of] matters for a time"[29] and I have noted, it is primarily concerned with clearing obstacles. It is not, again borrowing from Dyke, an attempt at "final analysis".[30] Science, unlike religion, neither promises nor lends itself to "final analysis"—an important insight underlying Quine's view of science and his break with positivism, and a lesson to be learned from the very existence and development of feminist science criticism.

I am aware that feminists and empiricists may have doubts about my use of Quine to attempt to clear obstacles and bring things into relief. To paraphrase Evelyn Fox Keller, I only ask that readers consider whether the approach I take sheds light on those things I want to see better,[31] and whether seeing those things better can further dialogue and understanding. My training in philosophy shapes how I see the issues that I want to see better and how I approach them. I do not apologize for this; I use it, aware that philosophy of science represents only one of many discourses about science.

But it is a discourse, as will emerge in the course of discussion, that those with an interest in science cannot afford to ignore, for it has shaped how many scientists view science and, thus, scientific practice. As Quine paraphrases Wittgenstein's insight, "we can kick away our ladder only after we have climbed it".[32] As the discussion has already implied, I am convinced that feminist criticism is, itself, within science, both narrowly and broadly construed, and that recognizing this enables valuable insights into the nature of science.

My hope is that the discussion will prompt others to enter into and advance a dialogue about feminism and empiricism so that alternatives feminists envision for our sciences and for our understandings of science can be understood, debated, and some formulation of them ultimately shared, for a time at least, by our largest science community—our community as a whole. For these things to occur, an ongoing dialogue between feminists, empiricist scientists and philosophers, and others who study and have an interest in the sciences is imperative. We have, I will argue, no reason to think that there are epistemological barriers to that dialogue. Indeed, if we take seriously what we have learned in the last several decades—if, in the end, knowledge is seamless and our largest community constitutes a science community—there can be no insurmountable barriers to it.

The impetus for empiricist scientists and philosophers to engage in such a dialogue is clear-cut. If current empiricist accounts of science are incomplete or distorted, or current scientific practices flawed, surely empiricists want to know this. For empiricists, evidence and experience matter because getting things right matters. Moreover, empiricists need to be particularly wary of any alleged a priori reasons for not taking feminist science criticism seriously.

There are also important reasons for feminists to engage in the dialogue. One of the more important is that a mark of meaningful inquiry is the ability to convince others that the inquiry is worth undertaking. To be sure, and regrettably, it is not always possible to convince others of the worth of a worthwhile project. Further, the fault is often not with those who envision the project or with the methods they use to convey their visions. The world includes the dogmatic and the apathetic.

But it remains the case that scientific and political revolutions occur only if those with revolutionary visions are able to convey their insights to others in ways that make it possible for others to come, eventually, to share them. The new revolution in science that feminists envision could be, as feminists know, as important to the future of our world as any in history. But there are no revolutions without followers.

CHAPTER ONE

Empiricism and Feminist Science Criticism

Those who create and specify reality also specify the conditions under which it may be viewed and verified. Truth or its perception becomes contingent on being male. This was assured, since women were excluded from the public world, from the creation of recorded reality, and from education, for the last 4,000 years.

—Ruth Bleier

As a theory of evidence . . . empiricism remains with us.

—W. V. Quine

I N AN IMPORTANT SENSE, just about everyone is an empiricist. We believe that our theories confront the world, and are developed and modified in accordance with our experiences of it. Most of the time, for most of us, this thesis of empiricism, though perhaps a "milk toast" version of empiricism, is uncontroversial. The practice of justifying and judging claims to know by reference to experience, however loose, enables us to distinguish claims that warrant serious consideration from those that do not. Most of us—at least in our less philosophical moments—engage in the practice.

Indeed, unless we are Cartesians or idealists, this first thesis is basic to our way of dealing with the world. That there is a world that shapes and constrains what it is reasonable to believe, and that it does so by impinging on our sensory receptors, is a hypothesis woven through most of our going beliefs, theories, and practices, and with good reason: it makes the most sense of what we experience. Indeed, as we shall see, there are reasons to think that there probably is no logically coherent way to *doubt* the thesis, despite some valiant attempts in the history of philosophy to do so. And, of course, the thesis is enormously useful. It enables us to survive.

But although the thesis may not require defending, I want to note two things about its role in empiricist accounts of science that distinguish such accounts from alternative epistemologies. The first is that these accounts give "the world" a larger role in shaping and constraining our theorizing than, say, those working in the sociology of knowledge and other areas who minimize (and, in some cases, deny) that role.[1]

Second, the considerations that mitigate against coherently doubting the thesis will prove important to the accounts of knowers, evidence, and science communities that we will explore in later chapters and important to the demands appropriately made of an epistemology, a theory about how we go about theorizing. Some of these considerations will emerge shortly as we consider the second core thesis of empiricism—to those who endorse it, a refinement of the first thesis, giving that thesis its content and force.

Empiricism

A second, and more specific and fundamental, thesis about evidence is usually at issue when empiricism is at issue. This discussion, like most discussions of empiricism, will take empiricism to be a theory that embraces not only the first thesis but the more contentious thesis that our experiences of the world are, in the end, sensory experiences, so that *all* evidence for science is, in the end, sensory evidence.

These two theses, one uncontroversial, the other contentious, are the core of empiricism as I will discuss and advocate it. They mark empiricism as a theory of evidence and distinguish it from other such theories.[2]

Empiricism's status as a theory of evidence depends on these two theses, what I hereafter refer to as empiricism's "core". Its status also depends on our ability to begin with this core and build an account of science that is commensurate with our experiences of science, with science broadly construed to include all of our attempts to explain and predict our experiences—a construal I will use Quine's positions to defend in later discussion. There have been, of course, a number of empiricist accounts of science, some better than others. But I draw attention to the distinction between empiricism, which is a theory of evidence, and the accounts of science that have been built on it.

In maintaining that all evidence for science is, in the end, sensory evidence, empiricists are also on solid ground. According to the information the neurosciences provide us, our sensory receptors are our only point of contact with the external world.

Nonetheless, the second thesis, as I have noted, is the contentious one. There are some who grant that our sensory receptors are our contact with the world but deny that the information so provided has much if anything to do with the stories we tell about how things are. And there are some who view the appeal to neuroscience as involving a vicious circularity.

In addition, the stipulation is itself qualified by some contemporary empiricists, and the qualification sharply distinguishes their accounts of sensory experience and the nature of the evidence for our theories from the accounts argued for or assumed in traditional and positivist empiricism. We will need to get more specific about how contemporary empiricists understand the second thesis in order to see, somewhat more precisely, what it is that empiricists and critics of empiricism disagree about.

Although contemporary empiricists maintain that all evidence is sensory evidence, some, including Quine, whose views in this regard I will later support and use, also insist that sensory experiences are not, and cannot be, foundational. Quine maintains that our sensory experiences are themselves shaped and mediated—indeed they are made *coherent*—by numerous specific theories that are themselves embodied in language.

> Impressed with the fact that we know external things only mediately through our senses, philosophers from Berkeley onward have undertaken to strip away the physicalistic conjectures and bare the sense data. Yet even as we try to recapture the data, in all their innocence of interpretation, we find ourselves depending upon sidelong glances into natural science.
>   . . . the trouble is that immediate experience simply will not, of itself, cohere as an autonomous domain. References to physical things are largely what hold it together. These references are not just inessential vestiges of the initially intersubjective character of language, capable of being weeded out by devising an artificially subjective language for sense data. . . . Conceptualization on any considerable scale is inseparable from language.[3]

Conceptualization is necessary for coherent sensory experience, language is necessary for conceptualization, and language, Quine, among others, argues, is necessarily public.[4]

Thus, Quine specifically rejects the possibility of grounding science in anything like sense datum experience, in pretheoretic or "raw" experience, a grounding the logical positivists envisioned and some undertook to reconstruct by constructing a "sense datum" language. The grounding, and the project of reconstructing it, are, on Quine's view, impossible.[5]

The lack of an extratheoretic or pretheoretic foundation in sensory experience has far-reaching consequences for an empiricist account of science. But neither the lack nor how some contemporary empiricists have dealt with it is always noted by critics of empiricism[6] or by some of its advocates. The lack forces a radically different view of the role of epistemology than that demanded by traditional and positivist empiricist accounts of science,[7] and Quine's view of the relationship between epistemology and science is far removed from the view commonly ascribed to "empiricists".

Traditional and positivist empiricism viewed epistemology, a theory about how we go about theorizing, as "first science": a theory that described the "extrascientific" foundation and provided the "prescientific" justification for science. But Quine recognizes that no account of theorizing, no framework for explaining our theorizing, can provide such a foundation or play such a role. Given the necessity of theory for coherent sensory experience and the understanding that, in the end, whatever evidence we have for science is sensory evidence, there can *be* no such foundation for science. For these and other reasons, Quine maintains that a theory about how we go about theorizing, an epistemology, is firmly *within* science.

We will consider the specifics of Quine's view of epistemology in some detail in subsequent chapters. But I will say some things here about his view of the relationship between epistemology and other theories. The view shapes some of the positions I outline below and use in later discussion.

Quine maintains that our going theories—including what he calls our "common-sense", "scientific", and "philosophical" theories—form a network, together constituting our largest theory of nature. His use of the network metaphor reflects his view that our theories are related; indeed, according to Quine, they show fundamental connections. As part of the network of our going theories, epistemology will be related to and, given the demise of foundationalism, interdependent with our other going theories.

We will have reason to consider the scope and depth of that interdependence in some detail later, but the implications are already somewhat apparent. Empiricists who maintain that there are no extrascientific foundations for science, may, as I have done, use the evidence provided by the neurosciences to support the empiricist thesis that our evidence for science is sensory evidence. We are thus (unabashedly) using the information provided by the sciences as evidence of the nature of evidence—including the evidence for the theories developed in the sciences. As Quine describes the interdependence,

> the crucial insight of empiricism is that any evidence for science has its end points in the senses. This insight remains valid, but it is an insight *which comes after physics, physiology, and psychology, not before.*[8]

> It is by thinking within this unitary conceptual scheme itself, thinking about the processes of the physical world, that we come to appreciate that the world can be evidenced only through stimulation of our senses.[9]

So, on the view of epistemology Quine advocates and I will use in the larger discussion, the relationship between epistemology and the rest of our going theories is one of radical interdependence.

> Epistemology, on this view, is not logically prior somehow to common sense or to the refined common sense which is science; it is part rather of the overall scientific enterprise which Neurath has likened to that of rebuilding a ship while staying afloat in it.[10]

I maintained earlier that the status of empiricism as a theory of evidence depends on our ability to build an account of science from its core: on our ability, beginning with that core, to account for how we go about theorizing. The two theses will also shape the way empiricists go about building that account. One consequence of the first thesis has already been noted: empiricists maintain that "how things are" constrains what it is reasonable to believe. Few of us may be tempted to doubt the claim; it is the extent to which the world constrains our theories and beliefs, and the role attributed to sensory evidence, that usually come into question.

For example, although the question of whether there are (or could be) "social causes" for beliefs and theories has been a controversial one in the social sciences and philosophy of science, it is safe to say that whatever disagreements empiricists have about whether there are (or could be) social causes for belief, they would concur that sociology could not be the *only* cause for reasonable belief. Empiricists believe that it will take more than sociology of knowledge to explain our belief that gravity is real—and to explain why that belief is *better* than its denial—despite the fact that we never experience a world "untheorized" and that we learn theories, themselves embodied in our language and our practices, from others—via, of course, our senses.[11]

This position will be apparent in the approach I take to issues in feminist criticism. I assume that it will take more than sociology of knowledge to explain the claim made by feminist science critics that many theoretical frameworks in the sciences are androcentric, and that androcentrism distorts accounts of "how things are". Certainly it will take more than sociology of knowledge to explain why these feminist claims are *better* than their denials.

So a further and far-reaching consequence of empiricism's core theses is that empiricists are convinced that we can, do, and should distinguish between good theories and bad ones, between good beliefs and bad ones, and that making sense of our ability to do so is one of the important tasks for epistemology.[12] Science, after all, has been successful and so have our "common-sense" dealings with the world. The importance and the possibility of making these distinctions have been consistently maintained in empiricism, distinguishing the latter from accounts of knowing and evidence that are relativistic—both those frameworks that embrace relativism straightforwardly, and any whose inability to give an adequate account of an evidential link between our theories and the world (or that lead to the view that this is an inappropriate task for epistemology[13]) leads to relativism.

But it is probably obvious that empiricists who have given up the dream of grounding science in an extratheoretic foundation of sensory data and who, for this and other reasons, have come to view epistemology as within science, rather than as "first science", are faced with a very different task than their empiricist predecessors. They share with their predecessors the goal of providing an account of how our theories "link up" with the rest of the world that is not relativistic. But contemporary empiricists need to provide such an account without the benefit of a foundation in pretheoretic sensory experience—a foundation that, on earlier empiricist accounts of science, was taken to provide the building blocks, or to serve as the final arbiter, of theories. The first position was advocated by logical positivists; the second, by those working in the "postlogical" positivist tradition represented by Hempel, Carnap, and Nagel.[14]

More specifically, empiricists need an alternative to one long-standing notion of that link: the idea that theories do or should "correspond" to the world, perhaps an intuitive notion, but, for a number of reasons, an extremely problematic one.[15] At least there is a need for an alternative construal of that link if we remain convinced that not all theories and beliefs are created equal, and interested in providing an account of the criteria we use when we distinguish between good theories and bad, that gives a central role to sensory evidence. An alternative to "correspondence" emerges in Quine's work,[16] a position Jack Nelson refers to as "a coherence theory of evidence".[17]

Coherence emerges as an overarching criterion of evidence in Quine's positions and, as explicated and implied in these, it is a dual constraint. Theories and beliefs need to be consistent with our experiences of the world *and* with other going theories.[18] The first constraint distinguishes Quine's criterion of "coherence" from idealist and skeptical "coherence" accounts and, specifically, from "coherence theories of truth". Simply put, the world matters.[19] The second constraint incorporates Quine's view that epistemology is one theory in a larger network of going theories. Because it is, our general and more specific standards of evidence (including, of course, the criterion of coherence) are also within that network and not "first science". The emphasis on the importance of coherence with our going theories also reflects Quine's view, noted above, that our theories show fundamental interconnections.

An empiricist account of science that includes these views cannot maintain anything like a "correspondence theory of truth"—that, roughly speaking, we aim at sentences and theories that "correspond" to "facts" (extralinguistic reality)—although such a theory is not infrequently ascribed to Quine and indiscriminately to "empiricists". (Apparently it is so ascribed because many continue to assume that Tarski's theory of truth is a correspondence theory, and because a correspondence theory is still held or assumed by some empiricists.[20]) We have discussed one issue that raises problems for the notion of "correspondence": the lack of extratheoretic sensory experience of the world, a lack that raises problems for the notion of "fact" that is embedded in the relation of "correspondence". Other issues that raise problems for construing truth as a matter of correspondence will emerge more clearly when we begin to look at Quine's view of science in some detail, but the most important, related to what has been said so far, is that Quine denies the dualism of "organizing scheme" and "that to be organized"—a dualism presupposed in the construal of the relation between theories and the world as one of correspondence.[21]

But we have not said anything directly about the notion of "truth", although the discussion has implied that theories and beliefs that "cohere" with experiences and with our other theories are those we will and should find "acceptable". Is a "theory of truth" implied in the positions outlined or able to be constructed from these? Can we say, and what would it mean to say, given these positions, that a claim is "true"?

One way of talking about the implications of these positions for a theory of "truth" (we will consider others in later chapters) is to consider their implications for skepticism.[22] Given the view that science lacks an extrascientific foundation and a coherence theory of evidence along the lines Quine advocates, one might be tempted to think that skeptical worries about our going theories are warranted—at least that such worries would be reasonable. There are, after all, no "extratheoretic" experiences by which to judge beliefs and theories.

But Quine argues that the very things that we might take as warranting a global skepticism indicate that, in fact, a global skepticism is incoherent. Like foundationalism, a reasonable skepticism about *all* our theories—reasonable in the sense that it is warranted—is possible only if an extratheoretic, or pretheoretic, vantage point is possible. We need only ask ourselves what experiences, what evidence, could prompt a global skepticism, and/or what experiences could resolve it, to see his point.[23]

This does not mean that more "local" skepticisms are not possible or will not be warranted. Science is not static. The network of our going theories, including our methodologies, ontologies, and standards of evidence, continue to evolve as we work to answer the questions posed by our going theories and our experiences of the world. Failures to predict will cause us to make adjustments in some of our going theories and to abandon others. But without experiences or standards of evidence that are extrascientific, understanding science in the broadest sense, that is, as inclusive of all our efforts to organize our experiences, there is nothing to get a global skepticism off the ground. The same reasoning indicates that idealism and at least some antirealist positions appear to be missing (and incapable of being supplemented so as to include) what would be necessary to make them plausible as "world views".

The implications of a coherence theory of evidence for a theory of "truth" and for the role of epistemology are probably obvious. With the exception of its special use as a predicate in a formal metalanguage in which it is applied to sentences in an object language (as Tarski did, in fact, explicate the notion), the predicate 'true' is redundant when we apply it to sentences or claims within our going theories. *We believe to be true what we claim to be true.* Theories of "truth", with the exception of the special theory noted above, disappear. Using the criterion of coherence, itself a dual constraint as Quine explicates it, we can make sense of what it means to say of a belief or theory that it is warranted, and of what it means to say that not all beliefs and theories are equally warranted.[24] But truth, as Quine puts it, is immanent.[25] Thus, the role of an epistemology is explaining how we have gone about constructing our theories. It does not justify these theories.

I will later argue that the necessity of theory for coherent sensory experience, and the several far-reaching consequences of this that I have so far outlined, have a further consequence Quine did not draw but should have: namely, that the empiricist commitment to "individualism", to taking the acquirers of knowledge to be individuals, is, at best, artificial, and, I will argue, it is ultimately untenable.

But in addition to empiricism's core theses, I am sympathetic to others of Quine's positions that have been outlined or implied and we will find these supported by feminist science criticism. Each will receive more extended treatment in later chapters: that our theories are interconnected so that changes in one will reverberate through others, and that these considerations apply to epistemology no less than other theories; that the theorizing some of us do as scientists is not different in kind from the theorizing we do as laypersons or philosophers, and that all of these activities are interconnected; and the view that coherence—to our experiences and others of our theories—is the overarching standard we use in judging whether theories and beliefs are warranted.

There are some general consequences of these positions for our more self-conscious efforts to think about science. First, it is clear that an adequate account of science will be one that, among other things, is capable of explaining our successful theorizing as well as providing explanations for our failures. Insisting on this rules out the conclusions that science is an irrational activity, that most (or all) theory choice is irrational, that our theories bear little or no relation to the world, and that vicious relativism is plausible.

Now it may be that few of us would seriously offer any of these conclusions. (I have grave doubts, in fact, that we could reasonably do so, and for reasons already noted—the most important of which is the lack of extrascientific standards of evidence and the necessity of these for radical skepticism to be plausible.) But insisting that an adequate account of science will be able to explain our success in organizing and predicting our experiences goes deeper than simply insisting that we acknowledge that there have been such successes—and then go on to develop epistemologies and accounts of science that are *unconstrained* by the fact.[26] An adequate account of science will be one that does not (wittingly or otherwise) make those successes look like magic.

Until it is shown that the notion of "successful" theorizing is senseless, it will be a task of any account of science worthy of the description to give an account of how we successfully produce and use theories: how we produce and use those artifacts that bridge our experiences and, as the scope of our theories becomes more general, to bridge other such bridges. This is not the only task of philosophy of science, but it is one task. Because it is, anchoring what we say about how things are, by using, in the end, an evidential link forged by sensory experience and evidence while recognizing that neither is "extrascientific", is crucial.

Further insisting that an adequate account of science be capable of explaining our failures rules out ignoring those situations in which we fail or those that prove problematic—whether they raise problems for our going views about science or for our current epistemology. Currently, empiricist scientists and philosophers find themselves faced with issues that raise problems for both.

Feminist Science Criticism

In the past fifteen years a growing discussion concerned with "sex and science" or "gender and science" has been prompted by criticisms by feminist scientists, philosophers, and scholars of the sciences and of some of our views about science.[27] For many scientists, philosophers, and laypersons, the possibility of there being issues involving sex or gender and science is new.[28] But if we find the analyses exploring such issues to be sound in their approaches and successful in exposing issues that involve sex/gender and science, then empiricists and the rest of us will need to rethink or abandon a number of our views about science. Nor can empiricists assume without looking—on the basis, say, of "what we all *know* about science"—that there could not be such issues. For empiricists, experience and evidence matter. The claims being made will need to be considered.

Feminist science criticism has developed within the larger framework of feminist scholarship. As the research alluded to in the notes and bibliography indicates, we now have reason to believe that the consequences of taking sex/gender seriously may be more far-reaching than was apparent even two decades ago.[29]

I am using the phrase "taking sex/gender seriously" to refer to some general aspects of feminist scholarship: first, the task of uncovering women's experiences, a task that presumes that they may not be reflected in the knowledge we have accumulated to date; second, the task of exploring the ways in which views about sex/gender and views infused with gender categories have been operative and consequential in our intellectual tradition, interacting with the construction and elaboration of theoretical frameworks; and, given each of these, the task of looking at the social arrangements, including the sex/gender arrangements, within which knowledge is developed.[30] The consequences of feminist scholarship are far-reaching. The scholarship indicates that some major theoretical frameworks, both long-standing and current, require substantial revision or need to be replaced by more adequate frameworks. No merely cosmetic alterations in these frameworks, feminist scholarship suggests, will allow us to formulate theories that can hope to adequately account for *human* experience.

Adding and incorporating women's experiences and the practices in which women have engaged if these have been omitted in our accounts of "human experience", redescribing women's activities and experiences if these have been misdescribed, and exploring the relationship between sex/gender, politics, and our philosophic and scientific theorizing that the need for such additions and redescriptions illuminates, must be reasonable goals. Our theories will be empirically sound only if they reflect, derive from, and are capable of explaining human experience.

Nor can this work remain the province of a "special" discipline, its findings not brought to bear on, or reflected in, "mainstream" disciplines. Despite the antiquity and tenacity of the assumption, "human" and "men" are not coextensive categories. Incorporating women's activities, experiences, and perspectives will result in a fuller account of human experience. Moreover, without them, and without our coming to understand how and why they were excluded and the consequences of this, our accounts of human experience and of our theorizing are, at best, incomplete.

I have said that because we want our theories to be empirically sound, it is reasonable to include women's experiences and to uncover the reasons for and the consequences of omitting, misdescribing, and devaluing them. Underlying this claim are several assumptions. These include the assumption that women's experiences and activities may have been different than men's in ways that are relevant to current and traditional theoretical frameworks. Feminist scholars also assume that there is no a priori reason to think that traditional theories either encompass, or provide the basis for theories that will encompass, women's perspectives, and provide empirically sound accounts of women's experiences and activities. And finally, exploring how experiences and views about sex/gender and politics are and have been factors in our theorizing, including our scientific theorizing, is necessary to any account of how we theorize.

These assumptions, however new to some readers, clearly deserve to be taken seriously. There is substantial evidence to suggest that there are fundamental differences in women's and men's experiences in societies in which activities are divided by sex/gender.[31] Further, it is relatively recently that women have been involved in the project of theory building in the western tradition, and even that involvement has been limited in the main to white middle-class women. Finally, many traditional thinkers whose views still shape our ways of organizing things held what we now realize are benighted views about women, about men, about sex/gender, and about sex/gender differences. Areas of fundamental importance have been ignored or devalued in their accounts of human experience, and we also cannot assume that "expunging" the views about women, men, or sex/gender in the theories they offered, or declaring that 'men' can be stretched without distortion to *mean* "women and men", will achieve the task of "humanizing" or degenderizing our intellectual tradition and practices. (These considerations hold, of course, even if we ascribe to a funny theory of language to the effect that when "we" use a word, it "means" what we say it does—a theory of meaning advocated by Lewis Carroll's Humpty Dumpty.) That views about sex/gender and women's exclusion from theory building have had important consequences for other aspects of traditional and contemporary thought is suggested by the references to views about sex/gender in works devoted to the development or elaboration of theoretical frameworks that, to many contemporary thinkers, do not have much to do with sex/gender.

We need to look closer. If those human activities, characteristics, or perspectives identified with women are ignored or devalued in constructing a theoretical framework, then we need to reconsider the framework from a broader perspective, using the knowledge we are gaining about women, about men, about traditional and contemporary thinking about sex/gender, and about the consequences of divisions in experience by sex/gender. If contemporary frameworks incorporate categories and emphases that continue to omit or devalue women's experiences, then these frameworks need to be reconsidered. It may well be, as feminist scholars who have begun these tasks have come to believe, that incorporating women's experiences and bringing the category of "sex/gender" to bear on traditional and current frameworks will result in our finding that many of these frameworks are not incomplete, but fundamentally distorted.[32] Further feminist scholarship indicates that we will learn a lot about how we go about organizing our experiences and will find that relationships exist between practices and experiences that we did not, before feminist criticism, recognize as related.

Now, there is simply no reason, before looking at the evidence, to assume that these considerations lose their force when we come to the "threshold" of science—either in the narrower sense of our most systematic and specialized efforts to construct theories, or in the broader sense of all such efforts. Moreover, feminist science criticism indicates that these considerations do not, in fact, lose their force.

In the course of this discussion we will consider some interesting aspects of the social organization of science communities.[33] These features of science communities indicate that these communities are not sealed off from the social and political context of our larger community and that the view that they have a detached or insulated position has precluded us from asking some important questions about them and their relationship to our larger community.

We will find, for example, that the social organization of many science communities reflects our larger community in incorporating what Kathryn Addelson calls "divisions in cognitive labor and cognitive authority".[34] They also reflect the larger community in the fact that women are generally at the lower end of the hierarchies in labor and authority. We will consider the claims made by feminists and others that these divisions, and the divisions in "cognitive labor and authority" that divide science communities and our larger community, have epistemological consequences.[35] They have, feminist science critics argue, a bearing on the directions and the content of the knowledge developed in scientific communities.

We will also find androcentric perspectives and feminist perspectives at work in various sciences. It will emerge that these perspectives are consequential for the content, directions, and methodologies of research programs and theoretical frameworks. We will find that in a current debate in the biological sciences, western political categories and experiences are consequential for the theoretical models and frameworks advocated by those on both sides of the debate, and that there are deep and important differences in the theoretical frameworks at issue. Of most significance for current accounts of science, we will find that sex/gender and politics are factors not only in what our current standards would lead us to classify as "bad science", but that they are consequential factors in theories and theorizing that cannot be so characterized.

The prospects raised by these issues for new insights into our scientific projects are exciting. But the focuses and claims of feminist science criticism raise several immediate and problematic questions for empiricists. Here I will say some things about these questions and it will be clear, as feminists have noted, that these distinguishable questions are related in the following way: *these are questions* because of certain deeply related views about science, views that have found their clearest statement in empiricist accounts of science. Following Harding, I here divide the questions facing empiricists into three general kinds;[36] later I will argue that each involves a connection between the social identity of scientists and the content of science.

The first question that feminist science criticism raises is how sex/gender could be relevant to science. Within the empiricist framework (at least, the contemporary framework), there is no straightforward way to accommodate issues deriving from the facts that persons are sexed and gendered and that experiences in our larger community are fundamentally differentiated by sex/gender. The accounts given by most contemporary empiricists of "knowers" and of "science" do not include reference to the fact that persons are sexed and gendered, because empiricists have not considered sex/gender to be a variable or factor of epistemological consequence—as a factor that could somehow make a difference to the content of theories and would need to be incorporated in an account of how we go about constructing and evaluating theories.[37] But the presence of feminist and androcentric perspectives in the sciences indicates that sex/gender is, at this time, such a factor, that experiences of and views about sex/gender have a bearing on theorizing in science communities.[38]

A second question (more correctly, a cluster of questions) is prompted by the fact that within empiricist accounts of science, it is not clear how issues having to do with political context could be relevant to science—at least to *good* science. So among other questions, empiricists are faced with the question of whether it is reasonable to consider criticisms of the sciences, or of views about what science is like, if these criticisms were initiated and became possible because of politics in western society. And feminist science criticism is, of course, fundamentally related to feminist politics. Assuming that the rationality of science resides in part in its theories being open to criticism and in the various methods employed to invite criticism,[39] are some criticisms, nonetheless, appropriately ruled out? Are some criticisms suspect, and if they are (or if we regard them as such), what is it that undermines their credibility?

Several philosophers and scientists have suggested that feminist criticisms of the sciences are regarded as suspect, and that this is because the notion of a perspective that has political origins *and* is objective is difficult to countenance.[40] Advocacy, involvement, and engagement are standardly taken to impair or preclude objectivity—a view, as we will explore later, that Quine and other empiricists advocate or imply.[41]

As Harding notes, the issue of the relationship between advocacy and objectivity is not new.[42] There have been those like Marx and contemporary feminists who have maintained that political advocacy or position could provide an epistemological advantage;[43] there are others, many of them empiricists, who have argued that social and political contexts cannot serve as an explanation (or at least not a good one) for *reasonable* belief, maintaining that such factors could only degrade the epistemological competence of an agent.[44] Sociologists of knowledge have, of course, developed social/historical causal accounts of belief production. But unlike those who hold one or the other of the positions just outlined, the question of distinguishing "good" beliefs from "bad" beliefs is often treated as an inappropriate activity by sociologists of knowledge.[45] Some advocates and critics of sociology of knowledge argue that the framework can provide only functionalist and/or relativist accounts of belief production;[46] many of us find functionalist and relativist accounts wholly inadequate when they present themselves as epistemologies.[47] Certainly, empiricists find such accounts inadequate and for reasons we considered in the previous section: experience indicates that some theories *are* better than others, and an account of the epistemology of science should be able to accommodate this. Most feminists would also find functionalist and relativist accounts of knowledge inadequate,[48] and I have suggested that these accounts are inadequate not only in terms of the political problems they engender but for what can be recognized as clearly epistemological reasons.

At least since the development within the philosophy of science of the "postlogical" positivist research program focusing on the logical form of theories and on the logic of justification, many scientists and philosophers have assumed that science and social/political context are, and should be, distinct domains. (Ironically, of course, the original positivist manifestos were themselves explicitly political.[49]) Minimally, the alleged distinction between a "context of discovery" (the ways in which theories are generated) and a "context of justification" (the ways in which theories are tested), and the development of a program for studying the logic of the latter, has made it seem to many empiricist scientists and philosophers that paying attention to the relationship between social/political context and science was unnecessary.[50] If there was bias at work in science, the testing of theories and the demands of intersubjectivity would weed that bias out.

Though few philosophers of science or scientists actually talk about a "context of discovery" and a "context of justification" any longer, apparently many remain convinced that focusing on the logic of testing theories is adequate for characterizing and studying the epistemology of science. This is evidenced by the continuing lack of attention in mainstream philosophy of science to the factors that contribute to the development and directions of scientific knowledge, a topic we will explore in the next chapter.

There are notable exceptions to the general lack of attention. One exception is Quine's proposal that epistemology be "naturalized" and, specifically, that it be pursued in empirical psychology, a position we will consider in some detail in Chapter Six.[51] Another exception is some of the work in "evolutionary epistemology".[52] But although both of these projects approach epistemology as the task of finding out how we come to have the beliefs we do and assume that good theories no less than bad require explaining, neither addresses the role that our experiences of sex/gender and politics might play in shaping knowledge. More to the point, neither incorporates categories that could accommodate such things as factors—at least not in *good* theorizing.

In light of all this, and bearing in mind that the rationality of science is partly a function of its being open to criticism, should empiricists consider the issues that feminists are raising about the sciences? Prima facie, the outcome of considering these criticisms would seem to be that, whatever their origins, these criticisms will enhance our sciences and our understanding of science, or we will find them to be off the mark or vacuous. If they are on the mark, then, of course, the question of their origins and the inability of current views to accommodate such origins will need to be addressed. We will need to find a way to account for the connections between sex/gender and science, and politics and science, that, unlike current empiricist accounts of science, does not assume that such factors are either irrelevant or inherently distorting.[53]

Could we be worse off for having considered criticisms that have been initiated, or have become possible, because of changes in political context, and that are motivated by political concerns? So far, it does not seem that "objectivity" is at risk. But this may be because I have only scratched the surface and I have not taken objectivity to mean more than "veridical". As several feminist science critics have argued, it may be that advocacy or engagement presents special problems within an empiricist framework because the content of "objectivity", as empiricists understand it, is shaped in large part by what empiricists have taken "the knower" to "be"—an individual who, at some level, knows autonomously.[54] In addition, empiricists have long been skeptical about the possibility that values, including political values, can be subjected to empirical controls and evaluated, a skepticism we will also have reason to explore.

A third and related question provoked by feminist science criticism is how social arrangements in and/or outside science communities could have a bearing on the content of science. With the exception of the work done by Kuhn, Lakatos, and others who have undertaken social studies of science, and that done by Marxist science critics, those concerned with the philosophy of science, including the epistemology of science, have not focused on the effect that the social organization of science communities might have on the directions and development of research and theories. Nor have they explored, in a more general sense, the social arrangements within which scientific knowledge develops.[55]

Further, we will find that the specific concerns feminist science critics are raising about science communities are not addressed in the work of either Kuhn or Lakatos or most social studies of science, and only some have been addressed by Marxist science critics. We will also find, as I noted above, that feminist critics are focusing not only on social arrangements in science communities but on the relationship between these arrangements and those in our larger community—a focus they share with Marxist science critics[56] but that often differs in emphases.[57]

In any event, the mainstream empiricist tradition in philosophy of science has concerned itself with different sorts of questions than those we will consider here. I will not have much to say about the logical forms of theories and explanation, the logic of justification, the empirical status of theoretical entities, and the like—although what I take to be the implications of feminist science criticism will suggest that we should have serious doubts about the exhaustiveness of these categories for an empirically sound epistemology or philosophy of science. On the other hand, some issues that have been explored in empiricist philosophy of science may seem clearly relevant to issues I have outlined—the relation between theory and observation, for example.

But standard treatments of the theory-observation relationship provide no help when we ask how sex/gender might influence observation and/or theory formation—and clearly something to do with sex/gender is at issue when we find ourselves faced with an issue like "androcentrism" in scientific theorizing. Nor do those traditional discussions provide a context for seriously evaluating the claims that the social and political context of our larger community, and the social arrangements within science communities and our larger community, influence either observation or theory formation. In short, the sorts of things that empiricist scientists and philosophers of science have said in the past about science seem of no obvious help in evaluating the charges and questions now being raised about the sciences.

As Sandra Harding and other feminist critics point out, each of the specific questions outlined in this section involves, at one level, the current empiricist view of knowers.[58] Harding has posed the problem this way: if individuals are the acquirers of knowledge, how could sex/gender, political commitment, or the sociology of science communities or our larger community have a bearing on the *content* of science—except as such factors might impair the ability of an observer to be "objective"?[59]

The problem can be restated in terms of the basic and contentious empiricist tenet. If, as empiricists claim, our evidence for science is, in the end, sensory evidence, then it is not immediately clear how the factors feminists are linking to the content of science could be so linked. Because we will find that these factors are at work in *good* science no less than bad, the problem is a pressing one.

We will have reason to return to the topic of the empiricist knower. But on a superficial level, the consideration of at least some feminist criticisms of the sciences—those that seek to uncover androcentrism, for example—should present no special problems for empiricists. If there is bias about, empiricists would want it exposed. If there is not, the charges of bias still need to be heard and refuted.

Moreover, empiricists are not wholly without starting points. The past five decades have led to an increasing awareness of the multiplicity and complexity of the factors relevant to our most rigorous and systematic theorizing.[60] The work of Kuhn, Lakatos, and Marxist science critics, and social and historical studies of science, have already indicated the need to expand our view of the epistemology of science to include more than the logical form of completed theories.

It will be a contention of later chapters that Quine's work indicates that we can accommodate some of the factors illuminated in this other work and still maintain basic empiricist assumptions, including empiricism's core theses. We will not, however, be working within a view of science that is common. More specifically, we will be working with a view of science that denies the boundaries many views of science insist on between science, on the one hand, and metaphysics, common sense, and epistemology, on the other.

But we will also find that the focuses and findings of feminist science criticism strain Quine's account of science in fundamental ways and indicate the need for some fundamental changes in empiricist accounts of science and in our views about what science encompasses. The changes will not require the jettisoning of the empiricist account of evidence and, indeed, some will support a number of Quine's specific positions. But the changes called for by feminist criticism will, so to speak, turn things on their head.

A Feminist Empiricism

The questions feminist science criticism poses for empiricism that I have outlined (and some that I have not) have been noted and discussed by feminist science critics.[61] The problems have been understood by some of these critics as indications that an alternative, and specifically feminist, epistemology is needed if the claims made within feminist science criticism and other areas of feminist scholarship are to be accommodated (and, as some would have it, justified). I have indicated that I am not convinced that feminist insights into science are irreconcilable with empiricism. I have also indicated that I think there are important reasons to reopen or redirect a sustained discussion about feminism and empiricism. I can now offer those reasons and qualify the project I am undertaking here. I begin with the latter.

Beyond some basic empiricist tenets, I am not concerned with preserving the details of any current empiricist account of science. I have begun with Quine's account for reasons I outlined in the Introduction, and these will become clearer as the larger discussion progresses.

But we should expect that an empiricist account of science that evolves in response to feminist insights into science and incorporates these will be significantly different in its categories, focuses, and emphases from any current empiricist account of science. Some of what needs to be changed or recast emerges in the ensuing discussion. We should also expect that the directions of research will increasingly reflect feminists' participation in science and that our accounts of science will evolve in response to that participation and criticism. What I hope, as I have said, is that we will eventually develop a view of science that can account for the obvious success of science and can encompass feminist insights into relationships between sex/gender, politics, and science.

I also leave some aspects of Quine's account of science unquestioned that may eventually need to be revised or abandoned. We need somewhere to begin, we need, so to speak, to climb the ladder, and Quine's account of science is as rich as any empiricist account of science and more congenial than most to important issues in feminist criticism. The basis for that congeniality turns out to be worth exploring, for it removes some of what feminists and empiricists thought were obstacles to an important discussion and provides some clues into what an adequate understanding of science will need to incorporate.

The project I undertake here also does not include the critical evaluation of all those frameworks that are being developed or offered as alternatives to empiricism. Justifying an epistemology does not require ruling out all alternatives, real or imagined. I am interested in actually beginning the work of developing a feminist empiricism, not clearing the table of alternatives.

But my discussion will directly engage issues in feminist science criticism, including issues that have led to the exploration and development of alternative epistemologies. Some points of engagement are probably obvious by now to those familiar with feminist criticism. In the context of arguing that feminist empiricism is a real and important option, I will specifically address the concerns of those who have thought it impossible or unpromising.

As I see things, part of the task will be to show that there is a distinction between empiricism as a theory of evidence and the empiricist accounts of science that have incorporated and been built from that theory. The ensuing discussion will testify to the soundness of that distinction. It will, as a whole, also support my contention that feminist criticisms of empiricism are frequently directed at empiricist accounts of science and not the theory of evidence, that many of these criticisms are sound if we ignore the changes in empiricism that Quine has brought about or advocated, and that some are sound even when we take his views into account. In the end, it is the theory of evidence that I am interested in maintaining, along with those aspects of Quine's views that are sound and can help us to do so.

Obviously, I will also need to show that aspects of current empiricist accounts of science that are unable to accommodate issues in feminist criticism are not, in fact, necessary consequences of the empiricist account of evidence. The most important issues in this regard are individualism, and what feminist criticism indicates is a fundamental connectedness between science communities and our larger community—in particular, the politics, including sex/gender arrangements, of that community.[62] Again, it will be the discussion as a whole that shows that we can be empiricists without being individualists, and that viewing knowledge as a piece is compatible with a sufficiently rich empiricism.

Some of what I advocate will be directly relevant to alternatives to empiricism that embrace the view that knowledge is "socially constructed". I will insist that social experience, including the learning and use of public theories, practices, and standards of evidence, are necessary and relevant to all of our theorizing—including that done in scientific communities. There is also no question that one implication of feminist criticism is that *who* is theorizing matters, and that the issue as it emerges in feminist criticism clearly involves social and political experiences—including, fundamentally, experiences of sex/gender. Thus, I will be arguing that science is a process *with subjects,* and that it bears the signatures of those subjects, or—more correctly—of their experiences, including their experiences of sex/gender and politics. And finally, on the view of science I am urging, neither theories nor objects are "discovered". The former are constructed, the latter posited within that process, and the process is subject to the constraints imposed by experience. Knowledge, I will urge, is social in every sense, is constructed by us, and it is constrained by our experiences.

But in specific discussions and in the way the general discussion goes, I will be urging that the stronger claims of sociology of knowledge are relativistic and that, at this time, relativism is unwarranted. My general argument for that conclusion will be that alternative epistemologies that are relativistic are inadequate—not just for reasons we would normally construe as political, but also for reasons that are clearly epistemological.[63]

Not all alternatives to empiricism embrace relativism. One epistemology currently being explored by feminist critics, feminist standpoint epistemology, specifically eschews relativism and for reasons very much in keeping with those I have outlined: namely, that we can and should distinguish between beliefs and theories that are warranted and those that are not.[64] Standpoint epistemologies begin from Marx's insight that class divisions have epistemological consequences, and with his "meta-theoretical" claim that seeing how things really are in a class society is a vantage point available only to members of the oppressed class and achieved (when it is) through political struggle.[65] Feminist standpoint epistemologies build from this insight to explain (and, on some accounts, to justify) feminists' claims.

It is probably clear to those familiar with feminist standpoint epistemologies that I share a number of views and goals with those working to develop them: that relativism can be avoided; that, at this time, feminists have an epistemological advantage; that the advantage is grounded in experience; and that the differences in standards of evidence, going theories, and categories that exist between feminists and nonfeminists will ultimately be explained in terms of divisions in experiences by sex/gender and politics.

But feminist standpoint epistemologies are regarded by those developing them as "antiempiricist", and those aspects of these epistemologies that are (or that are understood to be) "antiempiricist" will not receive direct attention in my discussion until much later. This is because, in addition to the views noted above, I share with standpoint epistemologists a view implied in their work: namely, that an epistemology that focuses on individuals is inadequate, and certainly inadequate to the task of explaining how feminists have come to know what they have about western society, including its sciences. As I have noted, I will urge that knowledge is constructed and possessed by groups, and as I see things, by communities. From this point of view, standpoint epistemologies are not antiempiricist because they eschew individualism, although this is how their antiempiricism is frequently understood. If I am correct, one can be an empiricist without being an individualist.

But, I agree that, as currently conceived and as being developed, standpoint epistemologies are antiempiricist. They are so, on my view, because they incorporate something like the "meta-theoretical" claim noted above:[66] that those engaged in political struggle against the divisions and oppression in a society have an epistemological advantage. Here I will only note two concerns. The second will receive more attention later, the first will not.

The first concern is that using standpoint epistemology to explain feminist claims about science involves the use of a framework less established, and, more importantly, perhaps less able to be straightforwardly established, than at least some of the claims the framework is supposed to explain. Feminists have shown that many research programs, assumptions, and theoretical frameworks in the sciences are androcentric. But, to rephrase a question recently posed by Sandra Harding, who, with others, has been involved in exploring and developing feminist standpoint epistemology: who but the already convinced will grant the meta-theoretical claim noted above, or the standards of evidence that the claim presumes or incorporates?[67] If we can explain how feminists know what they do without depending on a claim less straightforwardly able to be established than what feminists know, we are in a position to argue that feminist criticism is itself *within* science—and this allows us to see that science is different from what many of us thought. I will support this view of feminist science criticism and explore it implications for what science is throughout the discussion.[68]

The second concern has to do with what I take to be the more clearly antiempiricist feature of standpoint epistemologies than their denial of individualism. The meta-theoretical claim with which standpoint epistemologies begin assumes or posits an epistemological chasm between feminists and nonfeminists that is, on my view, far too wide and, of more importance, perhaps by hypothesis (or because of how it is explained by the meta-theoretical claim), *unbridgeable*. I have serious doubts that there can be epistemological chasms (whether these are alleged "incommensurabilities" or "standpoints")—that is, whether there are things one group can know and another cannot know. My doubts are not prompted by political concerns, although the assumption of an epistemological chasm between feminists and nonfeminists does raise problems for feminist politics. They are grounded in reasons that are more clearly epistemological.

In several contexts in the ensuing discussion, I will argue against the possibility of the epistemological chasms apparently assumed and explained by standpoint epistemologies.

In the Introduction I urged that feminists need to engage other scientists so that we can begin the work of changing our views about science, thus making it possible to change some of the practices of science. Finding a way to engage scientists in conversation is among the more important reasons to reconsider a feminist empiricism. But it should by now be clear that it is not the only reason for reconsidering that project. I am not recommending that we consider or strive to develop a feminist empiricism simply because it will enable conversation. Empiricism has more going for it than the fact that scientists are empiricists.

Feminist science criticism often presumes, and needs to presume, that there is a framework in place, or one forthcoming, that allows for the doing of things that can be done, or that are at least recognized as *goals,* in an account of science that has developed along the lines I have outlined and will explore. We need to be able to ground claims to know in experience, and our accounts of experience and of evidence must preclude relativism. We need to explicate criteria that will enable us to distinguish reasonable claims and good theories from bad ones. We need to make explicit the relationships that exist between the theorizing some of us do in scientific communities and the going theories, practices, and experiences in our larger community—not just in cases involving bad science, but in cases where that charge is inappropriate (for example, feminist science criticism). We need to make use of the views that standards of evidence are inextricably related to our going theories, that they can be discussed, and that they can and do change as our theories change. So there are a number of reasons to explore a framework that is committed to these views.

Relatedly, it is of consequence that despite the gaps that currently separate many scientists and feminist science critics, these groups share a basic commitment to taking evidence seriously. Both believe that it is possible and desirable to "get things right"—a goal relativists (however romantic) and the apathetic do not even acknowledge, far less share. It is precisely those commitments that can, on my view, help to eventually bridge the gaps that currently exist between feminists and empiricists, and science and our larger community will be the better for it.

CHAPTER TWO

Autonomy, Objectivity, and Incommensurability

Theoretical science deliberately neglects the immediate values of things, so that the statements of science often appear to be only tenuously relevant to the familiar events and qualities of daily life.

—Ernest Nagel

As in political revolutions, so in paradigm choice—there is no standard higher than the assent of the relevant community.

—Thomas S. Kuhn

THIS CHAPTER IS DEVOTED to exploring the context and background within which Quine developed his philosophy of science and epistemology. The field of philosophy of science was, and in important respects still is, sharply divided into two schools of thinking about science, schools shaped by the "Hempel/Nagel tradition"[1] and a tradition (or cluster of traditions) represented by the work of Kuhn, Hanson, and Lakatos.

Here I will outline some of the specific issues each tradition addressed—in particular, those over which they disagreed—and use the discussion to explore a polarization in thinking about science to which their disagreements contributed. That polarization, I will suggest in the last section of this chapter, continues to shape a good deal of current thinking about science. Thus, it shapes the background against which feminist science criticism is offered and, to some extent, it shapes that criticism.

The overview provided here is not exhaustive of the important contributions made by these traditions. I am interested in exploring issues that we will find addressed in Quine's work and at issue in feminist criticism.

43

The most central of these issues turns out to be the alleged "autonomy" of science. For ironically, despite their apparent incompatibility, both the Hempel/Nagel and Kuhnian traditions share this assumption and so does a good deal of the current work that has evolved from them. The assumption, we shall see, has far-reaching consequences.

Hempel and Nagel:
Science as a Body of Knowledge

The history of empiricist philosophy of science since logical positivism is largely the history of research programs it spawned—in particular, of one that is its intellectual heir and one that arose in reaction to it. The first is exemplified in the work of Hempel and Nagel, and the second, in that of Kuhn, Hanson, and Lakatos. Though many specific goals of the logical positivist program are apparently abandoned by these two later traditions, some central assumptions underlying logical positivism continue to shape the issues that concern both.

The logical positivists had been committed to an inductivist account of science: an account in which direct evidence provided by the senses in "observation" was taken to be the origin and foundation of the generalizations that are, or are incorporated in, the hypotheses, laws, and theories of science.[2] Inductivism was, at bottom, an account of the connection between theories and factual evidence—an account of the "empirical basis" of science. Understanding theories to be sets of sentences, logical positivists set out to show how these could be simple constructions from sense data.

On the positivists' view, securing the connection between theories and sense data required that science be rid of anything that could not be traced (eventually) to direct sensory evidence and the use of induction. Thus, they were concerned to draw distinctions between science and metaphysics, and between science and values. A sense/nonsense distinction was introduced to demarcate science from both.

The "verification theory of meaning" developed in logical positivism provided the criterion for distinguishing sense from nonsense—that is, for distinguishing science from both metaphysics and values—and for making explicit the connection between theories and sensory evidence. The meaning of a sentence, according to the theory, was its method of verification. If the empirical conditions that would verify a sentence could not be specified, the sentence was "meaningless". Metaphysical statements and ethical statements appeared to be banished from science. The "meaningfulness" of mathematical and logical sentences, on the other hand, was salvaged by drawing a further distinction, one between sentences whose truth or falsity was a matter of the "meanings" of their terms and not a matter of fact (analytic sentences), and those that were true or false on the basis of matters of fact (synthetic sentences). As analytic sentences, mathematical and logical sentences, though not empirical, were meaningful.

The logical positivists' program required that the inductivist account could be spelled out: that how hypotheses and theories were constructions from sense data could be shown. It further required that the empirical conditions that would verify an individual sentence could be specified. And it required that the science/metaphysics and science/values distinctions could be maintained.

It is tempting to say of the immediate heirs of the program that what they really want *is* logical positivism. Hempel and Nagel are interested in explicating a connection between theories and sensory evidence using something akin to "straightforward observation". They also share the positivists' assumption that insuring the empirical basis of science requires separating the latter from metaphysics and values. They are interested in maintaining the "meaningfulness" of mathematical and logical statements. And like logical positivism, this "postlogical" positivist approach to science places great emphasis on the logical structure of science: the nature of laws and theories, their relation to each other and to observation, and the nature of explanation.

But Hempel and Nagel also recognize that not all of the logical positivist program can be accomplished—at least not in the ways the positivists thought.

The problems raised by the verification theory of meaning—not least among them, the problem of what the notion of "meaning" comes to— lead those in this later tradition to at least deemphasize the logical positivist insistence that the "meaning" of a sentence can be equated with a method of verification.[3] But the verification theory allowed for things that Hempel and Nagel still want. Rather than specifying what is to count as the "meaning" of a sentence, Hempel specifies the conditions for determining whether a sentence is "cognitively significant". The criteria save precisely the sense/nonsense distinction designed to abolish metaphysics and values from science.

The criteria allow only those sentences that can in principle be tested by empirical evidence, as well as mathematical and logical sentences, into the body of scientific knowledge. Moreover, something called "empirical meaning" is salvaged in the end. As Hempel advocates the criteria, sentences have "empirical meaning" only if they can be tested (at least in principle) by evidence.

> It is a basic principle of contemporary empiricism that *a sentence makes a cognitively significant assertion,* and thus can be said to be either true or false, if and only if either (1) it is analytic or contradictory . . . or else (2) it is capable, at least potentially, of test by experiential evidence—in which case it is said to have *empirical meaning or significance. . . .*
>
> How this general conception of cognitively significant discourse led to the rejection, as devoid of logical and empirical meaning, of various formulations in speculative metaphysics, and even of certain hypotheses offered within empirical science, is too well known to require recounting. I think that the general intent of the empiricist criterion of meaning is basically sound.[4]

Far more definitive than the apparent abandonment of the verification theory of meaning is Hempel's and Nagel's abandonment of inductivism. Three issues lead them to give up the project of providing an inductivist account of the generation of hypothesis and theories: the long-standing "problem of induction", the recognition among some including Hempel that we do not "observe everything" but observe things that prior questions suggest are important,[5] and what had come to be recognized as the inability to construct a "sense datum" language—the language that was to capture (or at least to reconstruct) the "pretheoretical observation" that figured in the inductivist account as the "origin" of science.[6]

Thus, for Hempel, Nagel, and others in the "postlogical" positivist tradition, the connection between scientific theories and sensory evidence needs to be provided by something other than an ability to couch all empirically meaningful statements in some sort of phenomenological (sense datum) language. But the solution to the problem of explicating that connection turned out to be more complicated than replacing "the verification theory of meaning" with "criteria of cognitive significance".

As a first step in forging the connection, a distinction is introduced between a "context of discovery"—the generation of theories and hypotheses, and a "context of justification"—the testing of theories. The problems positivists encountered with specifying the logic of the first context lead their heirs to seek the connection between science and sensory evidence in the latter "context", in the ways theories are tested and justified. The epistemology of science is to involve, then, the context of justification.

The shift in focus requires that the various things an inductivist epistemology of science was to provide can be compensated for. The "objectivity" of science needs to be somehow grounded in the manner in which theories are tested, and the "context of discovery" needs to be shown to be irrelevant to the *content* of science—thus, of no epistemological consequence.

Hempel outlines an understanding of science that underlies and shapes the work undertaken in the tradition. Three related views emerge as basic to that understanding: that science is primarily concerned with explanation, that a specification of explanation (what will count as an explanation and what explanation is) involves a specification of the logical relationships between sentences, and that the connection between the laws, theories, or generalizations of science and "the world" is via sentences that have specifiable and testable "empirical content". This view of the connection between theories and evidence is clear in Hempel's account of scientific explanation.

> To explain the phenomena in the world of our experience, to answer the question "why?" rather than only the question "what?" is one of the foremost objectives of empirical science.[7]

> Let us now abstract some general characteristics of scientific explanation. We divide an explanation into two major constituents, the *explanandum* and the *explanans*. By the explanandum, we understand the sentence describing the phenomenon to be explained; by the explanans, the class of those sentences which are adduced to account for the phenomenon.
>
> The explanandum must be a logical consequence of [must be logically deducible from] the explanans. . . .
>
> The explanans must contain general laws, and these must actually be required for the derivation of the explanandum. . . .
>
> *The explanans must have empirical content; i.e., it must be capable, at least in principle, of test by experiment or observation.* . . .
>
> The sentences constituting the explanans must be true.[8]

Nagel echoes Hempel in maintaining that explanation is the goal of science and that an explanation is a set of sentences that meets certain conditions, the most central of which is that the set is somehow controlled by "factual evidence". Nagel's characterization of science as a "body of knowledge" is more explicit than some others, but the view is implicit in all the work of the movement.

> It is undoubtedly the case that the sciences are organized bodies of knowledge and that in all of them a classification of their materials into significant types or kinds . . . is an indispensable task.
>
> It is the desire for explanations which are at once systematic and controllable by factual evidence that generates science. . . .
>
> To explain [is] to establish some relation of dependence between

propositions superficially unrelated, to exhibit systematic connections between apparently miscellaneous items of information . . . [these] are distinctive marks of scientific inquiry.[9]

So, for those in the movement, understanding science involves the exploration and formalization of the logical relationships between sentences, themselves distinctive to and constitutive of the body of knowledge that *is* science, and specifying the relationship of those sentences to factual evidence—specifying, that is, the "empirical basis" of science.[10]

The emphasis on logic is reflected in the tradition's work to develop a canonical form of science. Hempel and Nagel characterize theories as sets of sentences with a particular logical structure.[11]

> Formally, a scientific theory may be considered as a set of sentences expressed in terms of a specific vocabulary. . . . many of the sentences of a theory are derivable from others by means of the principles of deductive logic. . . .
> The classical paradigms of deductive systems of this kind are the axiomatizations of various mathematical theories . . . ; but by now, a number of theories in empirical science have . . . been put into axiomatic form, or approximations thereof.[12]

> A scientific theory . . . is often suggested by materials of familiar experience or by certain features noted in other theories. . . . Nevertheless, the nonlogical terms of a theory can always be disassociated from the concepts and images that normally accompany them by ignoring the latter, so that attention is directed exclusively to the logical relations in which the terms stand to one another. When this is done, and when a theory is carefully codified, so that it acquires the form of a deductive system . . . the fundamental assumptions of the theory formulate nothing but an abstract relational structure.[13]

And ultimately it is in logical relationships that those in the tradition look to establish the connection between science and sensory evidence. Breaking with logical positivists, Hempel maintains that "scientific knowledge" is not, in fact, "the product of induction". Rather, it is the product of the empirical testing of hypotheses. "Scientific knowledge is not arrived at by applying such an inductive inference procedure to antecedently collected data . . . [but] by inventing hypotheses as tentative answers to a problem under study, and then subjecting these to empirical test".[14] The various emphases of the tradition come together in the account developed of what Hempel calls "empirical testing". Providing an account of the connection between the sentences of science and factual evidence is understood to involve the specification of the "logic of justification"—a logic those in the tradition are convinced can be laid out, and one in which the testing of theories by reference to sensory evidence will be central.

Hempel takes the specific task in providing an account of how scientific knowledge is developed—of the logic of justification—to be that of providing a "theory of confirmation". Confirming hypotheses by observation, he argues, insures that those hypotheses admitted into the "body of scientific knowledge" are connected to evidence.

> The establishment of a general theory of confirmation may well be regarded as one of the most urgent desiderata of the present methodology of empirical science. . . . [It] is a necessary condition for an adequate solution of various fundamental problems concerning the logical structure of scientific procedure. . . .
>
> What determines the soundness of a hypothesis is not the way it is arrived at . . . but the way it stands up when tested, *i.e.* when confronted with relevant observation data. Accordingly, the quest for rules of induction in the original sense of canons of scientific discovery, has to be replaced, in the logic of science, by the quest for general objective criteria. . . . [That is] whether . . . and, if possible, . . . to what degree, a hypothesis *H* may be said to be corroborated by a given body of evidence *E*.[15]

In keeping with the underlying view of science that characterizes the movement, Hempel's theory of confirmation specifies the logical relationships that obtain between kinds of sentence; these relationships insure the connection between a hypothesis and what he calls above "a body of evidence".

> We turn to a closer scrutiny of the reasoning on which scientific tests are based and of the conclusions that may be drawn from their outcomes. . . . [W]e will use the word "hypothesis" to refer to whatever statement is under test. . . .
>
> [T]he test implications of a hypothesis are normally of a conditional character: they tell us that *under specified test conditions,* an outcome of a certain kind will follow. Statements to this effect can be put into the following explicitly conditional form:
>
> If conditions of kind *C* are realized, then an event of kind *E* will occur. . . .
>
> [S]uch test implications are thus [of] the form of if-then sentences.[16]

I want to consider briefly the general features of Hempel's account of the relation of confirmation, the relation which, he maintains, anchors scientific knowledge to evidence. It will be helpful to outline some parallels

and differences between his account of "the logic of justification" and
that developed by Karl Popper. The reason for considering Hempel's
account alongside that developed by Popper is that Popper sees a fundamental problem underlying both his and Hempel's account of the "logic
of justification".

Like those in the tradition we are considering, Popper argues that how
hypotheses and theories are generated is irrelevant to the epistemology of
science.[17] But there is a basic difference in the accounts of justification
that he and Hempel develop. Popper emphasizes the logic of "falsification" rather than that of "confirmation", thus making use of a stronger
logical relationship: a generalization can never be proven by a single
observation (or any finite number of observations), but it can be "falsified"
by a single observation.[18] Popper also uses "falsifiability" as a criterion
for demarcating "scientific" theories from "pseudo-scientific" theories,
wanting, like Hempel, to illuminate the relation of science to factual
evidence—a relation Hempel tries to forge by laying out criteria for
cognitively significant sentences.[19]

For Popper, the "testing" of theories or hypotheses is primarily an
attempt to falsify the latter.

> We say that a theory is falsified only if we have accepted basic
> statements which contradict it. . . . [But] a few stray statements
> contradicting a theory will hardly induce us to reject it as falsified. We
> shall take it as falsified only if we discover a *reproducible effect* which
> refutes the theory.[20]

Despite the difference in focus, Popper shares a basic assumption with
Hempel: that providing what Popper calls "a logical analysis of scientific
knowledge" is providing an account of the relation of science to evidence—of illuminating the "empirical basis" of science. Arguing that how
a hypothesis suggests itself to a person is a matter for empirical psychology
rather than epistemology, Popper maintains that "the task of the logic of
knowledge . . . consists solely in investigating the methods employed in
those systematic tests to which every new idea must be subjected if it is
to be seriously entertained."[21]

But Hempel's and Popper's accounts of the "logic of knowledge"
share a fundamental problem—and, ironically, the problem is related to
one they recognize as devastating to the positivists' attempt to develop
an inductivist account of science: namely, the problem of explicating
"observation" such that the latter is clearly demarcated from theory.
Observation, on Hempel's and Popper's accounts, is to be the "arbiter"
of theories, establishing that science is grounded in factual evidence.

Having learned from the troubles that beset the positivists in their attempt to relate "observations" themselves to hypotheses and theories, Hempel and Popper replace the elusive and problematic "observation" with "observation sentences" (Popper calls them "basic sentences"). It is the latter, on both their accounts, that "record observations" and anchor the edifice of scientific knowledge—complete with its generalizations and its theories incorporating "unobservable" and "theoretical" entities—to sensory evidence. Provided the logical relationship of such sentences to a hypothesis is of the correct sort (and that relationship receives detailed analysis in Hempel's and Popper's work), observation sentences confirm or falsify the hypothesis. So both need to explicate the notion of an observation sentence that can, in fact, "anchor" science to sensory evidence.

In his account of the relation of confirmation, Hempel characterizes observation sentences as sentences that "describe evidence", and the sticky problem of relating "observation" to "the sentences of science" is apparently forestalled by the construal of the relationship between evidence and theory as itself a relationship between sentences. Hempel makes the move directly. "As construed by Nicod", he maintains,

> confirmation was conceived of as a semantical relation obtaining
> between certain extra-linguistic objects on one hand and certain
> sentences on the other. It is possible, however, *to construe confirmation*
> *in an alternative fashion as a relation between two sentences,* one
> describing the evidence, the other expressing the hypothesis.[22]

As Hempel describes them, observation sentences would appear to be the public analogues of sensory experience, close enough to the latter to connect science to factual evidence, but public enough to avoid the threat of solipsism and subjectivism, which long beset empiricism and was exacerbated by the privacy of sense data and observation. In insisting that observation sentences are public, Hempel insures that such sentences are intersubjectively verifiable.

In his explication of observation sentences, a concern to establish the intersubjectivity of these sentences and their connection with basic sensory evidence is clear. One of the things required for the sentences and the logic of confirmation is an "ideal" language of science.

> The evidence adduced in support of a scientific hypothesis or theory
> consists, in the last analysis, in data accessible to what is loosely called
> direct observation, and such data are expressible in the form of
> "observation reports". In view of this consideration, we shall restrict the

evidence sentences which form the domain of the relation of
confirmation *to sentences of the character of observation reports.*

> . . . we shall assume *that we are given a well-determined "language of
> science"*, in terms of which all sentences under consideration . . . are
> formulated. We shall further assume that this language contains, among
> other terms, a *clearly delimited "observational vocabulary"* which
> consists of terms designating more or less *directly observable* attributes
> of things and events. . . .
>
> [Then] an observation sentence [is] a sentence which either asserts or
> denies that a given object has a certain observable property.[23]

Hempel further requires that an "observation sentence" bear the relationship to a hypothesis such that it "would confirm [the hypothesis] . . . if
. . . available",[24] and his account of the logical relationships required for
the relation of confirmation is detailed and sophisticated. But getting to
the bottom of what Hempel means by "sentences of the character of
observation reports" is another and more difficult matter.

For one thing, despite the fact that he discusses these sentences as
reports of "data accessible to what is loosely called direct observation",
it is obvious that Hempel cannot be claiming that observation sentences
report *sense data.*[25] He claims that an observation sentence "describes
a possible outcome of *the accepted observational technique; it asserts
something that might conceivably be established "by means of those
techniques".*[26] He also maintains that what is necessary for a sentence to
serve as an observation sentence, a sentence suitable for the testing of a
hypothesis, is that certain specified techniques of observation have been
"agreed upon", that we have been "given a well-determined language of
science" including a "clearly delimited observational vocabulary".[27] So
he is being careful to distinguish observation sentences from subjective
experience. The sentences that would meet these criteria are public.

However, Hempel also maintains in the passage just quoted that the
relevant observations will be of *"directly observable* attributes of things
or events", attempting to characterize the testing of hypotheses and theories as something akin to bringing "straightforward observation" to bear
on them. His care in presenting an account of observation sentences
reflects the fact that he is offering the account at a time when a growing
literature illuminates the difficulty of distinguishing "observation sentences" from "theoretical" sentences, a literature we will discuss in more
detail as we consider the second tradition.[28] In short, Hempel is attempting
to walk a fine line.

He has, on the one hand, clearly abandoned the positivist's goal of grounding science in sense data or a sense data language. But he never really succeeds in explicating his replacement notions of "directly observable attributes" and "observational vocabulary" in a way that does not make use of already established theories about the general kind and nature of the denizens of the universe. The bottom line is that if observation sentences are couched in publicly accepted language (using "agreed-on techniques") in which publicly recognized objects and named attributes are posited and ascribed, then such sentences certainly do *not* report observations that are "untainted" by theory of any sort. All sorts of theoretical constraints are at work.

Popper is also careful in his explication of observation sentences, sentences he calls "basic statements" and maintains can falsify hypotheses and theories. He explicitly distinguishes such sentences from the subjective experience of an observer, arguing against what he terms a pervasive "psychologism" in traditional and positivist empiricism's attention to "observation". (Popper claims, in fact, that the traditional "problem of induction" is based, in part, on the "psychologism" incorporated in traditional and positivist empiricism.[29])

Basic statements, according to Popper, "are . . . in the material mode of speech—statements asserting that an observable event is occurring in a certain individual region of space and time".[30] As Hempel also insists of observation sentences, Popper insists that the determination of which sentences are "basic" statements is a public decision. Popper's basic statements are "accepted as [basic statements] . . . [as] the result of a decision or agreement"; they are, in his words, "conventions".[31]

Now, Hempel is confident that the relation of confirmation "grounds" scientific knowledge in sensory experience. When he acknowledges in the following passage that a confirming observation cannot provide "conclusive proof" for a hypothesis, he is making a logical point. He is not questioning the status of the observation sentence as a direct report of evidence.

> A favorable outcome . . . cannot provide conclusive proof for a
> hypothesis, but only more or less strong evidential support or
> confirmation. *How strongly a hypothesis is supported by a given body
> of evidence* depends on various characteristics of the evidence [its extent
> and character and the resulting strength of support it gives].[32]

Popper, however, sees the problem. He acknowledges that his account of basic statements indicates that the specification and determination of such sentences presume a larger theoretical system. Indeed, the usefulness of basic statements as potential falsifiers of a theory is underwritten in Popper's account by the conformity of such sentences to public standards of evidence as much as it is by their "basic-ness".

Thus, Popper is not optimistic at all about the "soundness" of the empirical *foundation* provided by such sentences. To use his words, science "rises, as it were, above a swamp".

> The analogy [between judicial decisions] and that by which we decide basic statements is clear. [The analogy] throws light . . . on [the] relativity [of basic statements] and the way they depend upon questions raised by the theory. [*The acceptance of basic statements*] *is part of the application of a theoretical system; and it is only this application which makes any further applications of the theoretical system possible.*
>
> The empirical basis of objective science has thus nothing "absolute" about it. Science does not rest upon rock bottom. The bold structure of its theories rises, as it were, above a swamp. It is like a building erected on piles. The piles are driven down from above into the swamp, but not down to any natural or "given" base; and when we cease our attempts to drive our piles into a deeper layer, it is not because we have reached firm ground. We simply stop when we are satisfied that they are firm enough to carry the structure, at least for the time being.[33]

Again, Hempel does not accept this radically nonfoundationalist view of science. But it is difficult to see how he can avoid it or something like it.

And there are problems facing Hempel and Nagel (and, in some cases, Popper) in addition to those which Popper recognizes as compromising the "foundation" and connection with evidence that observation sentences are to provide for science. As we noted earlier, Hempel and Nagel (and Popper) have written off the "context of discovery". The emphasis on the "relation of confirmation", on providing a model of explanation, and on developing the canonical form of science are not paralleled with a curiosity about where, to use the language of the tradition, the "relevant propositions" come from, whose logical structure and relationships we need to pay attention to when constructing an account of the development of scientific knowledge. Nor do those in the tradition consider, other than in a cursory way, the possibility that factors in the "context of discovery", factors relevant or contributing to the generation of hypotheses and theories, might have implications for the content of science.

So Hempel and Nagel need to explain—at least their account of the epistemology of science needs to show—why the manner in which theories and hypotheses are generated and the language of science is arrived at is not relevant to the *epistemology* of science: why none of these factors are relevant to the content of scientific theories.

One argument for disregarding the context of discovery is offered repeatedly by Hempel and Nagel: namely, that there is no *method* by which we arrive at hypotheses and theories. At least part of their argument for the lack of what they call a "method of discovery" involves their belief that there are no "rules of induction". Convinced that the study of science is a study of the *logic* of scientific knowledge—and convinced that because an inductivist account of the development of scientific knowledge is impossible, *any* attempt to give an account of the generation of hypotheses is impossible—the tradition writes off how hypotheses are arrived at. It is in the context of justification that scientific method has its home.

> Induction is sometimes conceived as a method that leads, by means of mechanically applicable rules, from observed facts to corresponding general principles. . . .
> [But] there are . . . no generally applicable "rules of induction", by which hypotheses or theories can be mechanically derived or inferred from empirical data. The transition from data to theory requires creative imagination. Scientific hypotheses and theories are not *derived* from observed facts, but *invented* to account for them.[34]

In addition, Hempel recognizes that "collecting evidence" presupposes a prior question or tentative hypothesis, and this furthers his argument that induction is not the way in which we arrive at hypotheses and theories.

> In the discussion of scientific method, the concept of relevant evidence plays an important part. And while certain inductivist accounts . . . seem to assume that relevant evidence . . . can be collected . . . prior to the formulation of any hypothesis . . . it should be clear that . . . it is the hypothesis which determines what kind of data or evidence is relevant for it.[35]

Similarly, maintaining that there is no method or logic relevant to discovery—no method or logic to the generation of theories and hypotheses, Nagel defines "scientific method", the method that "produces" scientific knowledge, as the testing of hypotheses that have (somehow) been arrived at.

> There are no rules of discovery and invention for science, any more than there are such rules in the arts.[36]

> The practice of scientific method is the persistent critique of arguments, in the light of tried canons for judging the reliability of the procedures by which evidential data are obtained, and for assessing the probative force of the evidence on which conclusions are based.[37]

But neither the lack of "mechanical rules of induction" nor the persistent critique of arguments does, of itself, guarantee the kind or degree of "objectivity" that those in the tradition want to be able to claim for scientific knowledge. Other assumptions and arguments further their case for why it is not necessary to pay attention to how theories are generated in developing an account of the epistemology of science.

Among the most important arguments are those that stress science's basic differences from "common sense". Nagel distinguishes common sense and science in terms of the close connection that obtains between science and "factual evidence" and the absence of (or lack of insistence on) a connection with evidence in "common-sense" dealings with the world.

> The difference [between science and common sense] can be expressed by the dictum that the conclusions of science, unlike common-sense beliefs, are the products of scientific method. . . .
>
> Implicit in the contrasts [between common sense and science] . . . is the important difference that derives from the deliberate policy of science to expose its cognitive claims to the repeated challenge of critically probative observational data, procured under carefully controlled conditions. . . . Accordingly, the difference between cognitive claims of science and common-sense, which stems from the fact that the former are the products of scientific method, does not connote that the former are invariably true. It does imply that common-sense beliefs are usually accepted without a critical evaluation of the evidence available.[38]

But Nagel is convinced that "common-sense beliefs" and "scientific knowledge" are also distinct in a deeper sense. He argues that there is a distinction in the *content* of common-sense belief and scientific knowledge, and the distinction can be used to underwrite science's objectivity. In a word, science is not concerned with events or things about which "biases and prejudices" might play a role. "The dictum that the conclusions of science, unlike common-sense beliefs, are the products of scientific method", he argues,

> should not be misconstrued. It must not be understood, for example . . . as claiming that the practice of scientific method effectively eliminates every form of personal bias or source of error . . . no such assurance can in fact be given.[39]

> [But] common-sense knowledge is largely concerned with the impact of events upon matters of special value to men [*sic*]; theoretical science is in general not so provincial. . . . *theoretical science deliberately neglects the immediate values of things, so that the statements of science often*

appear to be only tenuously relevant to the familiar events and qualities of daily life.[40]

So a further reason why the "context of discovery" is not scrutinized—and, more importantly, why it does not need to be—is the assumption that there is little reason to think that "biases" or "prejudices" will infect scientific knowledge. For one thing, the latter is "only tenuously" relevant to the familiar events of "daily life" and to those things of "special value". Thus, there is little reason to worry that hypotheses and theories in science will reflect the biases of individual scientists, although, as Nagel notes, there is no guarantee of this. Like much of the work in the tradition, Nagel's examples of hypotheses and theories come primarily from the natural sciences, and this no doubt contributes to these views.[41]

In addition, Hempel and Nagel stress the intersubjectivity of scientific knowledge, relating objectivity directly to that intersubjectivity. Hempel reiterates Nagel's point that individual preference will not make a difference in the application of scientific method. (Intersubjectivity, as we have seen, is also a central figure of Hempel's account of observation sentences.)

> Science aims at knowledge that is *objective* in the sense of being intersubjectively certifiable, independently of individual opinion or preference, on the basis of data obtainable by suitable experiments or observations. This requires that the terms used in formulating scientific statements have clearly specified meanings and be understood in the same sense by all who use them.[42]

Other reasons why factors relevant to the context of discovery are ignored in the tradition are less a matter of conscious argument, or a consequence of the tradition's focus on the natural sciences. There are reasons that lie in the definition those in the tradition give to science and to "scientific knowledge". Both, on Hempel's view, are constituted by just the sets of sentences that have "passed through" the "ways of validation"—on his account, the ways of "confirmation".

> Let us . . . [consider] first, if only in brief and sketchy outline, *the way in which objective scientific knowledge is arrived at*. We may leave aside here the question of *ways of discovery;* . . . for our purposes it will suffice to consider the scientific *ways of validation; i.e.,* the manner in which empirical science goes about examining a proposed new hypothesis and determines whether it is to be accepted or rejected.[43]

Relatedly, as Hempel's condition for objectivity makes clear, the logic of confirmation is applicable only to hypotheses and theories that are *completed* in important ways.

A precise definition of confirmation requires reference to some definite
"language of science", in which all observation reports and all
hypotheses under consideration are assumed to be formulated, and
whose logical structure is supposed to be precisely determined.[44]

As we noted in discussing Hempel's account of observation sentences,
how we have arrived at the "definite language of science"—the questions
we found worthy of attention, the hypotheses we constructed to answer
them, the objects and relationships posited in theories, hypotheses, laws,
and observations—is not relevant to the study of the logic of science or,
therefore, the epistemology of science.

And, finally, because the relation of confirmation is defined as a *logical*
relationship, there is little or no room to introduce a reasonable worry
that an individual scientist might make a difference (except by making a
mistake or being dishonest) in whether a hypothesis or theory survives
testing.

In his [*sic*] endeavor to find a solution to his problem, the scientist may
give free rein to his imagination, and the course of his creative thinking
may be influenced even by scientifically questionable notions. . . . Yet,
scientific objectivity is safeguarded by the principle that while hypotheses
and theories may be freely invented and *proposed* in science, they can be
accepted into the body of scientific knowledge only if they pass critical
scrutiny, which includes in particular the checking of suitable test
implications by careful observation or experiment.[45]

Thus, in the end, science's "objectivity" is underwritten by various
things that insure its intersubjectivity, the remoteness of the body of
scientific knowledge to things we "value", and the fact that the method
for insuring that hypotheses are commensurate with evidence is the application of logical principles.

We should note one additional assumption that appears to be a factor
underlying the tradition's emphases. Underlying Hempel's and Nagel's
apparent lack of interest in the context of discovery may be the more
general view that science can be completed, and that there is a determinate
set of sentences that will constitute the body of science at the end of
inquiry. Given this view of science, *the only* effect the context of discovery
can have is on when and how parts of that final body of science are
discovered. Various factors may hasten or retard the discovery and com-
pletion of particular sciences, but the filter of the context of justification
assures us, insofar as it is reasonable to ask for assurances, that only what
is part of the final corpus of science is accepted into our growing body of
knowledge. Of course, the view that there is a complete and unique end

to inquiry must be rejected if alternative theories, commensurate with our experiences, are possible, and if the hypotheses and theories that figure in the context of justification reflect social and political beliefs and experiences that are not subjected to scrutiny on the grounds that they are *not* factors in scientific theorizing. We will later return to these issues.

One further and important consequence of the focus and claims of the tradition needs to be noted. Hempel's accounts of the logic of confirmation and of "cognitively significant sentences" assume, indeed they *require*, that single sentences have their own "empirical content": some specifiable "experiential evidence" that will count for them and some specifiable evidence that will count against them. If single sentences do not have such specifiable "empirical content" in isolation from a larger theoretical system, then, of course, Hempel's account of the "empirical basis" of science, relying as it does on such sentences, is doubly compromised. The first problem is, as we noted and Popper addressed, that observation sentences as described cannot be extricated from a going system of thought. The second problem involves isolating the conditions under which it would be appropriate to assert and deny single sentences from a larger theoretical system.

Perhaps the most lasting of this tradition's specific contributions are Hempel's model of explanation,[46] Hempel's and Nagel's work on the paradoxes of confirmation,[47] Tarski's semantic account of truth,[48] and the work to develop first-order quantification as the canonical form of science. Although the problem of induction, a central concern of this movement and of traditional empiricism, is of continued interest, it is currently being treated in rather new ways.[49] And a number of potential and related problems have emerged in the tradition's solutions to the tasks it set itself.

The first is the question of whether an emphasis on justificatory procedures can provide an adequate account of the *epistemology* of science— whether, for example, it is important to be able to provide an account of where the "completed" language of science, not to mention its questions and hypotheses, has come from. A second is whether observation sentences can be demarcated from theoretical sentences. A third is whether even sentences "about" so-called singular facts have their "own" empirical content. A fourth is whether science is, in fact, without metaphysical commitments or values. A fifth, related to several of these, is whether scientific knowledge is "objective" in the sense construed by those in the tradition: is it anchored in "direct" sensory evidence via the logic of justification, and is it "autonomous" from "those matters of special value to men [*sic*]"? A sixth is whether there is an end—and a *unique* end—to science, for that assumption is necessary to the viability of the assumption that the "context of discovery" is irrelevant to the content of science.

The underlying view that characterizes this tradition and its predecessors has disappeared as an identifiable research program—the view that the primary business of philosophy of science is to understand the logical structure of science, with science viewed as a completed set of sentences, rather than as an evolving and intertwined corpus of theories and practices. But the legacy of this tradition and the legacy of a tradition that arose in reaction to it are very much with us.

Kuhn: Science as an Activity

Those working in the second tradition we will consider see some fundamental problems in the account of science we have just explored.[50] Emphasizing the importance of understanding how theories are adopted, evolve, and die, philosophers, historians of science, sociologists of knowledge, and social scientists have focused on the history of actual sciences and the actual practices of science communities rather than the formal structure of idealized (and almost never realized) "completed" science.[51] It used to be said that it is the "context of discovery" rather than the "context of justification" that is emphasized in the work of what I am calling a "tradition", and that this shift in emphasis most clearly distinguishes this body of work in rationale and conclusions from the Hempel/Nagel tradition.

It is more correct to say that the work done by Kuhn, Hanson, and Lakatos, and in recent historical and social studies of science, challenges the view that we can ignore all of the factors regarded as aspects of the context of discovery—and, specifically, the social arrangements and practices that characterize science communities—and still construct an adequate account of the epistemology of science. Kuhn and Lakatos focus on the ways that the acceptance or rejection of theories, and indeed their content, are to a significant degree a function of membership, education, and practices in science communities. Hanson's work indicates that observation is fundamentally shaped by theory,[52] and it is an important aspect of Kuhn's account of scientific revolutions and the central role he gives the sociology of science communities in determining the outcomes of these.

In the end, science is understood and studied as an activity in this second tradition, and the work done to analyze the activity suggests that the picture of science Hempel and Nagel provide does not square with the actual process of science—and, of most importance, with how scientific knowledge actually develops and comes to be recognized as knowledge.

In outlining and exploring some of the general features of this approach to science, I will focus on Kuhn's *The Structure of Scientific Revolutions*, a work that has been, and remains, enormously influential. I will not be attempting an exhaustive analysis of Kuhn's work or of its implications; I want to explore those features of his analysis that are relevant to the focuses and positions of the Hempel/Nagel tradition and will concern us when we turn to Quine and to feminist science criticism.

The discussion of Kuhn's analysis will be complicated by the fact that this analysis has been a matter of considerable controversy. The controversy is not simply one of agreeing with or disagreeing with Kuhn—although among those who agree about what he said there is enormous controversy about whether he was right. A more fundamental controversy, and the one relevant here, concerns the issue of determining what Kuhn's analysis of sciences comes to—and specifically, what it implies about the epistemology of science.

In part, the controversy is fueled by the differences in interests, categories, and methodologies that separate the approaches taken to science by "mainstream" philosophers of science, on the one hand, and social scientists and historians, on the other—and these groups typically (deeply) disagree about the content of Kuhn's views, as well as about both their soundness and their implications.[53] The problem is exacerbated by the fact that Kuhn's analysis is not appropriately characterized as "simply" philosophy of science as that is understood by philosophers of science, or "simply" a study of the sociology of science. It contains elements and categories recognizable to those working in each of these traditions—most fundamentally, because Kuhn's account of the epistemology of science gives the sociology of science communities a central role.

But the controversy is also due to the nature of what Kuhn *did* say and *how* he said it. Kuhn often says what appear to be different things about notions that are both unique and fundamental to his analysis—the most important issue in this regard being his notion of a "paradigm".[54] Given the central role of such notions in Kuhn's analysis, it is not surprising that there is substantial disagreement concerning what his analysis indicates about the epistemology of science.

We will not be able, of course, to consider all the ways that Kuhn is understood—even all the ways that Kuhn has explained what he said in his now classic work, or what he meant.[55] There is little question that Kuhn speaks of things like science, paradigms, and scientific revolutions in multiple and distinguishable ways. Each of these is described and characterized in his work in terms of the psychology of individual scientists, in terms of the sociology of science communities, and in terms of "world views" and sets of rules that are not reducible to either psychology or sociology, but discernible (or able to be abstracted or reconstructed) from a consideration of these.[56] And as we shall see, it is not clear that what Kuhn has to say about things like paradigms from the point of view of each of these perspectives is completely compatible with what he has to say from the others.

Moreover, although I do not want to "pigeonhole" Kuhn, I do want to use aspects of his work to illuminate a basic view of science that underlies and emerges in his analysis, for that view (or ones similar to it) remains enormously influential. I am not claiming (or convinced) that it is the "only view" of science to be found in Kuhn's work. I am convinced that it is one view of science to be discerned there. At the very least, it is the "Kuhn" (if not the Kuhn) whose views about science are often at work in current discussions about what science is. Most of the discussion of this section will be devoted to exploring Kuhn's notion of a paradigm and his account of normal science as these illuminate the central role of sociology in determining scientific knowledge. I will also use some of the features Kuhn attributes to normal science to briefly sketch some important features of his account of scientific revolutions, a topic to which we will return in later chapters.

The fundamental insights underlying Kuhn's analysis are that science is an activity and that the sociology of science communities plays a major role in determining that activity—thus, as I noted above, it plays a major role in determining the development and directions of "scientific knowledge". Kuhn also maintains that the forging and testing of the connection between theories and the world, so central to the Hempel/Nagel view of science and to textbook accounts of science, are not what "drive" normal (noncrisis and nonrevolutionary) science, or constitute the "doing of science". Nor, on Kuhn's account, are empirical evidence and the logic of science what determine the outcomes of scientific revolutions.

What drives, underlies, and determines normal science and revolutionary science, thus what determines the knowledge that is recognized as scientific knowledge, are the practices of science communities.

Things may appear clear, but they become difficult. One faces two general problems in attempting to outline Kuhn's arguments for the conclusion. The first I have already noted: there are three ways that Kuhn talks about paradigms, outlined earlier, and there is a question of how these go together. Things are further complicated because, by Kuhn's own account, he has discussed paradigms as two different kinds of thing: one, in which a paradigm is an exemplar, dominates his analysis of normal science, and the other, in which a paradigm is a disciplinary matrix, dominates his analysis of crises and revolutions in science. Obviously we will not be able to disentangle all this. I will be primarily concerned to get to the bottom line of Kuhn's arguments for the dominant role of sociology in determining what science is and the content of scientific knowledge, and to outline the major steps that lead him to the conclusion.

A second problem further complicates the project of outlining Kuhn's arguments. In making a case for the centrality of sociology as the determining factor in normal and revolutionary science, Kuhn takes great pains to downplay the role of things like "rules" and theories in shaping or guiding normal science, or in determining the outcome of scientific revolutions. But it is not clear whether science does or really could operate in the almost total absence of things like rules, including methodological principles and theories. Though I share the worries some have expressed about this aspect of Kuhn's analysis, I will tackle the issue only briefly in the discussion of his account of normal science, but return to it in Chapter Five, where we will consider his account of revolutionary science.[57]

Kuhn begins to build a case for viewing science as an activity in the way he initially defines a "paradigm" and in his account of the role paradigms play in what he calls "normal [nonrevolutionary] science":

> "Normal science" means research firmly based upon one or more past scientific achievements, achievements that some particular scientific community acknowledges for a time as supplying the foundation for future practice. . . .
> I mean to suggest that some accepted examples of actual scientific practice—examples which include law, theory, application and instrumentation together—provide models from which spring particular coherent traditions for scientific research.[58]

> [In a science, a paradigm] is like an accepted judicial decision in the common law, it is an object for further articulation and specification under new or more stringent conditions.[59]

> Closely examined, . . . [normal science] seems [to be] an attempt to force nature into the preformed and relatively inflexible box that the paradigm supplies.[60]

There are several features in this description of normal science that are in sharp contrast with the view of science we found in the work of Hempel and Nagel. The most obvious difference has already been noted: Kuhn focuses on science as an "activity" rather than as the "product" of an activity—hence his characterization of normal science as "research" and his initial characterization of "paradigms" as "achievements". Kuhn's remarks also suggest that science is a community's activities, and that these are shaped by an "achievement".

We are also alerted by Kuhn's initial description of normal science that the study of the history of science and science communities indicates that scientists are not (normally) engaged in "testing theories" so as to falsify or confirm them, as Popper, and Hempel and Nagel, respectively, characterize "scientific method". Rather than "testing" the "paradigm", the activity of normal science, as Kuhn describes it, consists of forcing nature to fit the boxes the paradigm supplies. A paradigm (and we have only noted so far that it is first characterized as an "achievement") leaves enough problems to support the research of a community that is itself dedicated to its "articulation". In addition, of course, although Kuhn has mentioned that theories are included in paradigms, it is as an achievement or "accepted example" that a paradigm underwrites the community's activity. The emphasis on paradigms as achievements rather than as theories is fundamental to Kuhn's analysis of normal science, as we will see shortly.

Kuhn goes on to characterize the problem-solving activity he calls "normal science" somewhat more specifically. The "research problems" that constitute the activity of normal science are themselves determined (or made available) by the paradigm (or by prior research within the science community, which was itself based on the paradigm). And again Kuhn stresses that the "problems" with which normal science concerns itself are not "tests" of the paradigm, let alone attempts at discovery.

> Perhaps the most striking feature of . . . normal research problems . . . is how little they aim to produce major novelties, conceptual or phenomenal. Though [the] outcome of [normal research] can be anticipated [given the paradigm], often in detail so great that what remains to be known is itself uninteresting, the way to achieve that outcome remains very much in doubt.
>
> Bringing a normal research problem to a conclusion is achieving the anticipated in a new way, and it requires the solution of all sorts of complex instrumental, conceptual, and mathematical puzzles. The man [*sic*] who succeeds proves himself an expert puzzle solver.[61]

We have gone as far as we can in explicating Kuhn's view of normal science without tackling the notion of paradigm at work in these passages. Unfortunately, as I noted earlier, Kuhn's explication of the notion is far from clear. But we will need to get as clear as we can about what a paradigm is, for it is a paradigm—and/or at least scientists' allegiance to it—that underwrites and shapes the research of a normal science community, and that is at issue during crisis.

When paradigms are introduced in Kuhn's analysis, they are characterized as achievements that a science community's practices are focused on "articulating". But here things get hazy, for it is not clear how an achievement is "articulated". We normally think of achievements as the sort of things that are praised, studied, used as an example for future achievements, but it strains the usual sense of "achievement" to discuss "articulating" them. Kuhn denies that the paradigm is a "model" in our normal sense of the term, in the sense closest to "example".[62]

In a postscript to the second edition of *The Structure of Scientific Revolutions* Kuhn notes that he uses the term "paradigm" in two senses in the work. One of these uses is that of an "exemplar", and this is the sense I am exploring, because it is the most central, for reasons that will become clear, in Kuhn's account of normal science. In his account of revolutionary science Kuhn's "paradigms" are somewhat different; during crisis, a "paradigm"—at least the one being challenged—clearly incorporates more than an achievement and Kuhn describes it as a disciplinary matrix, as I earlier noted.[63]

As we consider Kuhn's description of normal science in more detail, it is clear that a special sort of "problem solving" virtually exhausts a science community's activity: namely, puzzle solving. So our question about paradigms can be made more specific: how does "an achievement" generate puzzles? Kuhn is quite clear that a paradigm does generate these. "One of the things a scientific community acquires with a paradigm is a *criterion* for choosing problems that, while the paradigm is taken for granted, can be assumed to have solutions".[64] If we look closely at Kuhn's initial discussion of paradigms, we find that, in addition to their designation as "achievements", paradigms are characterized as "akin to judicial decisions", as "foundations" for future practice, as "examples" of scientific practice, and as *"including law, theory, application and instrumentation"*.

The addition of the latter, at least the understanding that things like judicial decisions have implications because of their position in a context—only because they are not, ultimately, "closed curves in space"—helps with seeing how "achievements" might imply, or make explicit, criteria for the future activity of a community—and, in particular, for the kind of rigidly determined "puzzle-solving" activity Kuhn describes as normal science.[65] According to Kuhn, puzzle solving is an activity in which, on the basis of a paradigm, one can both recognize a puzzle and assume it has a solution. Something like theory and methodology (puzzle-solving rules, if you will) must be at least implied in or by the achievement.

Perhaps we can tentatively conclude that paradigms, as "concrete models", imply basic assumptions about what there is, how its study is to be approached, and the problems that remain to be worked out. And Kuhn does discuss such assumptions. He calls them "rules"; and he characterizes these as scientists' "commitments". But Kuhn's account of the rules "at work" in normal science does not suggest that these are what actually determine the activity of normal science.

Kuhn first notes that, like the solution to a puzzle, a proposed "solution" to a research problem is a solution only if, both as a solution and as attained, it is in keeping with something like an "established viewpoint" or "preconception" set by the paradigm. So the first sort of rule implied by a paradigm is an "established viewpoint", itself the most general criterion used to judge puzzle solving.[66]

In addition to this rule, Kuhn maintains there are additional rules—more correctly, there *can* be such additional rules—and that these are often displayed by historical study.

> The most obvious and probably the most binding is exemplified by . . . generalizations. These are explicit statements of scientific law and about scientific concepts and theories. . . .
>
> Rules like these are, however, neither the only nor even the most interesting variety *displayed by historical study*. At a level lower or more concrete than that of laws and theories, there is, for example, *a multitude of commitments* to preferred types of instrumentation and to the ways in which accepted instruments may legitimately be employed. . . .
>
> Less local and temporary, though still not unchanging characteristics of science, are the higher level, quasi-metaphysical commitments that *historical study so regularly displays*.
>
> Finally, at a still higher level, there is *another set of commitments without which no man [sic] is a scientist*. The scientist must, for example, be concerned to understand the world and to extend the precision and scope with which it has been ordered. . . .
>
> The existence of *this strong network of commitments*—conceptual, theoretical, instrumental, and methodological—is a principal source of the metaphor that relates normal science to puzzle-solving. . . . it provides rules that *tell the practitioner of a mature specialty what both the world and his [sic] science are like*.[67]

But in the end, a paradigm, and not rules, more fundamentally shapes the community's activity. For Kuhn claims that although rules like these may shape how puzzles are approached (what research is undertaken) and what constitutes a solution to a research problem, they are at best tacitly understood by scientists. They may be implied by the paradigm and spelled out in science textbooks, but the knowledge required to "practice" in the science community for which the paradigm is the impetus and foundation is, Kuhn claims, often implicit.[68] Indeed, according to Kuhn, normal science can proceed *without rules* as long as there is a paradigm—but not vice versa.[69]

Finally, as these passages indicate, Kuhn frequently states that the rules are displayed in historical study. Unfortunately, his references to historical study occur in the same passages in which the rules are also described as being the *commitments* of scientists, and in which they are characterized as the *criteria* by which solutions to research problems are, in fact, solutions. Thus, as I noted at the outset of the discussion, Kuhn gives us distinct (and perhaps incompatible) ways of thinking about these rules, about their relationship to the paradigm, and about their role: they are scientists' *commitments,* they are *criteria* which determine what "doing science" *is,* and they are displayed in *historical* study of the community's *behavior.*

But what we *can* be sure of is that Kuhn views the rules "at work" in normal science as *distinct from* the paradigm, the concrete achievement that underwrites the community's practices. He views the knowledge scientists have of these rules to be, for the most part, tacit.

> Scientists work from models acquired through education and through subsequent exposure to the literature often *without quite knowing or needing to know what characteristics have given these models the status of community paradigms.* And because they do so, they need no full set of rules.
> ... That scientists do not usually ask or debate what makes a particular problem or solution legitimate tempts us to suppose that, at least intuitively, they know the answer. But it may only indicate that neither the question or the answer is felt to be relevant to their research. Paradigms may be prior to, more binding, and more complete than any set of rules for research that could be unequivocally abstracted from them.
> *One is at liberty to suppose that somewhere along the way the scientist has intuitively abstracted rules of the game for himself [sic], but there is little reason to believe it.*[70]

So, perhaps, and despite his use of the term "commitment" in another passage to describe what he calls "the rules of the game" in the passage just quoted, scientists engaged in normal science are not really *aware* of the rules they are following.

Indeed, Kuhn goes further in minimizing the role of such rules in normal science. Not only do scientists not know the rules or worry about them, Kuhn tells us there may not *be* any rules. And here clearly, despite discussing "rules" as "commitments" earlier, Kuhn must be using "rules" in the common sense of "rules of the game" rather than (at least exclusively) as the "commitments" of scientists. "The coherence displayed by the research tradition in which [scientists] participate may not imply even the existence of an underlying body of rules that additional historical or philosophical investigation might uncover."[71] Indeed, if there are rules (or if rules are needed), these, Kuhn maintains, will usually "emerge" only when the status of a paradigm is uncertain.

> *Normal science can proceed without rules only so long as the relevant scientific community accepts without question the particular problem-solutions already accepted.* Rules should therefore become important and the characteristic unconcern about them should vanish whenever paradigms or models are felt to be insecure. That is, moreover, exactly what does occur.[72]

But, in the end, it is not clear that even paradigms are the things on which to focus to understand the bottom line of Kuhn's view of normal science. It may be that the paradigm that underwrites a normal science tradition (whether we are to understand it as "just" an achievement, or as a cluster of commitments) is recognizable only in retrospect or during crisis. (Indeed, as we will see, at least revolutions are recognized and/or reconstructed in retrospect, according to Kuhn.[73]) So, perhaps Kuhn's view is something like this: in the transition from prescience to science, and from revolutionary science to normal science, the "practices", the activities, of a science community change, and later the historian or philosopher abstracts or reconstructs the commitments scientists apparently "had", the rules they were actually following—but were not particularly curious about. I will not push this interpretation of Kuhn's analysis of normal science (for one thing, taken strongly, it makes scientists appear to behave very strangely). But the following, which is related to it, captures the more basic and important insights of his account of the epistemology of science.

Science communities, according to Kuhn, are "rigid" and "close knit".[74] The practices of normal science are "coherent", and he finds them purposeful and structured. Indeed, he describes these practices as "highly determined".[75] The puzzles of normal science are set by a paradigm, and the ways these can be solved and what will count as a solution are also "set". Thus, what will count as *doing science* is rigidly set.

But, given the view of rules and paradigms outlined above, the rules that determine puzzle solutions are "abstracted" from the achievement, and, more often than not, this is done retrospectively by historians and philosophers. Scientists are largely unaware of the rules and unconcerned about them. If they do articulate these rules, including theory, methodology, quasi-metaphysical commitments, and the like, it is in times of crisis. Given the view that there may be no rules, and that if there are, scientists do not "know" them or indicate concern over knowing them until crisis emerges, what is the source, the basis, of the "rigidity", "coherence", and highly structured activity that Kuhn describes as normal science?

The answer must lie in the *sociology* of the science community. That this is what Kuhn has in mind is supported not only by his minimizing of the role of any rules at work in normal science and his work to distinguish the paradigm from such rules, but also by his account of the education of the scientist. This last, as Kuhn describes it, does not involve (at least not centrally) an imparting of "theory"; indeed, if it does include the latter, it is only in a minimal and peripheral sense.[76] Science education— the education of those who are learning to be members of a science community, not the education we receive as children and undergraduates from science textbooks—consists of the learning of those *practices* that themselves *define* the science community and therefore define what it is to be a member of that community. It is the learning to "do" science, and it is only in the "doing" in accordance with the community's ways of doing things, that one is a member of the community—and, therefore, *a scientist*.

Kuhn's description of what he terms the "professional initiation" of scientists stresses this learning to "do", and the use of the term "initiation" is further indication that he views the result of science education to be *community membership*, rather than a commitment to an achievement or a "disciplinary matrix", let alone a commitment to a "theory".

> Scientists, it should already be clear, never learn concepts, laws, and theories in the abstract and by themselves. Instead, these intellectual tools are from the start encountered in a historically and pedagogically prior unit that displays them with and through their applications. . . . They (the applications) are not there merely as embroidery or even as documentation. On the contrary, the process of learning a theory depends upon the study of applications, including practice problem-solving both with a pencil and paper and with instruments in the laboratory. . . . [*The student*] *learns* less from the incomplete though

sometimes helpful definitions in his [*sic*] text than *by observing and participating in the application of these concepts to problem-solution.*[77]

There are clear implications for how scientific knowledge develops and is "certified" as knowledge when science is progressing "normally". Scientific knowledge consists of solutions to research puzzles, and the practices of a community and the standards of the community determine what counts as a problem and what counts as a solution. In short, a science community is a *self-regulating* and *closed* system.

> One of the things a scientific community acquires with a paradigm is a criterion for choosing problems that, while the paradigm is taken for granted, can be assumed to have solutions. To a great extent these are *the only problems that the community will admit as scientific or encourage its members to undertake.* . . . A paradigm can, for that matter, insulate the community from those socially important problems that are not reducible to the puzzle form, because they cannot be stated in terms of the conceptual and instrumental tools the paradigm supplies.[78]

The role the science community plays in determining the directions and development of scientific knowledge is thrown into even starker relief in Kuhn's account of scientific revolutions.

Revolutions in science (that is, paradigm shifts) are inevitable, according to Kuhn, because the rigid, detailed, puzzle-solving activity of normal science will eventually produce enough anomalies to deeply trouble scientists, causing them to reflect on the paradigm that underwrites their work and eventually to cast around (unconsciously perhaps) for alternatives.[79] Indeed, Kuhn argues, such crises are inevitable because no theory will be "complete" and the rigid, detailed activities of the community will produce anomalies. When there are enough, a crisis will ensue.[80]

The "crisis" is intensified when a "rival paradigm" (or something that can lead to one) "emerges", as Kuhn describes it, "all at once, sometimes in the middle of the night, in the mind of a man [*sic*] deeply immersed in crisis".[81] The crisis is resolved—that is, a revolution occurs—when enough scientists "convert" to the new paradigm.[82] Kuhn uses the term 'conversion' to underscore his contention that the switch in allegiance—at the time at which that switch actually occurs—is not a "rational" decision. That is, the decision, on his view, is not based on evidence or on the comparative soundness of the rival paradigms—indeed, it could *not* be based on either of these given his analysis.

To understand Kuhn's reasons for characterizing revolutions as conversions, and to further illuminate the priority he gives to the sociology of the community in determining the outcome of scientific revolutions (these two things are at bottom one view), we can begin with the analogy Kuhn draws between political revolutions and scientific revolutions.

Like a political revolution, a revolution in science, according to Kuhn, throws literally everything "up for grabs".

> Why should a change of paradigm be called a revolution? . . .
>
> Political revolutions aim to change political institutions in ways that those institutions themselves prohibit. . . . [Eventually] the society is divided into competing camps or parties, one seeking to defend the old institutional constellation, the others seeking to institute some new one. And once that polarization has occurred, *political recourse fails*. Because they differ about the institutional matrix within which political change is to be achieved and evaluated, *because they acknowledge no supra-institutional framework for the adjudication of revolutionary difference, the parties to a revolutionary conflict must finally resort to the techniques of mass persuasion.*
>
> . . . the historical study of paradigm change reveals very similar characteristics in the evolution of the sciences. . . . *the choice [between competing paradigms] is not and can not be determined by the evaluative procedures of normal science, for these depend in part upon a particular paradigm, and that paradigm is at issue.* When paradigms enter, as they must, into a debate about paradigm choice, their role is necessarily circular. Each group uses its own paradigm to argue in that paradigm's defense.[83]

The parallel Kuhn wants to draw is clear. Like political revolutions, there are "no higher standards" to which to appeal in scientific revolutions. Indeed, Kuhn apparently believes there is *nothing* that can be appealed to except the paradigms at issue—and these will not settle matters—and the *members* of the community. In scientific revolutions, what we would construe as *epistemological* recourse fails.

The paradigms at issue—the old, now well articulated, and the new as yet comparatively unarticulated—can play only a circular role.[84] Each incorporates (implicitly at least) a distinct world view, irreconcilable with the other. Moreover, each incorporates a distinct conception of what *science is.* Here, in his discussion of crisis states and revolutions, it is clear that the paradigms Kuhn takes to be at issue do incorporate metaphysical commitments, theories, and methodological prescriptions, whether scientists "know" these or are in a position to articulate them, and these constitute the world views at issue—and, thus, the world.

> The differences between successive paradigms are both necessary and irreconcilable. . . . [*They*] *tell us different things about the population of*

the universe and about that population's behavior. . . . But paradigms
differ in more than substance, for they are directed not only to nature
but also back upon the science that produced them. They are the source
of the methods, problem-field, and standards of solution accepted by
any mature scientific community.[85]

Kuhn's case for the circular role paradigms play, and for the minimal
(or nonexistent) role the "world" can play to resolve the crisis, is built in
part on Hanson's work to show that observation is theory laden and
Kuhn's analysis of the history of science. Both lead Kuhn to maintain that
it would be impossible to choose between competing paradigms on the
basis of observation or evidence. A paradigm, as he puts it above, determines the population of the universe. After a revolution, scientists "see"
things that a now discarded paradigm did not allow for.

Indeed, at one point Kuhn describes the scientist who has traversed a
revolution in science, who has switched "paradigms", as responding to
"a different world":

> Paradigm changes do cause scientists to see the world of their research-
> engagement differently. In so far as their only recourse to that world is
> through what they see and do, we may want to say that after a
> revolution scientists are responding to a different world.[86]

Now, there is an important ambiguity here concerning "the world" at
stake. In this passage it is described by Kuhn both as a "world of . . .
research engagement" and simply "a world". His view, outlined earlier,
that there is no "higher authority" to be appealed to in order to resolve
a crisis between competing paradigms, and the contributing view that the
metaphysical commitments of each paradigm determine the "population
of the universe", suggest that the limited sense implied in the phrase
"world of research engagement" is *not* really the sense of "world" that
Kuhn has in mind. Moreover, he is not claiming that scientists' *interpretation* of the world is at issue. He denies that a distinction can be drawn
between something like an "interpretation of the world" and the world—
and precisely because there is no "higher" or external authority upon
which that distinction could be based. Thus, it must be *the world* that is
at issue, as I will argue below.

> With scientific observation . . . the scientist can have no recourse above
> or beyond what he [*sic*] sees with his eyes and instruments. If there were
> some higher authority by recourse to which his vision might be shown
> to have shifted, then that authority would itself become the source of his
> data.[87]

The circular role paradigms play in crisis is also underscored by the fact, noted above, that paradigms, as they figure in Kuhn's account of crisis and revolution, include metaphysical commitments, methodological commitments, theory—in short, the "rules" so carefully distinguished from paradigms in his account of normal science. It is as a "disciplinary matrix" that a paradigm competes with another, which is also a "matrix" of commitments—although the "rules" determined by the new paradigm will really emerge only later in the behaviors of scientists. Finally, as Kuhn's drawing of a parallel between scientific and political revolutions suggests, part of that disciplinary matrix is a view about what science *is*— thus, the lack of a "higher authority" in terms of understandings of scientific method and so on.

Now if, as Kuhn claims, the paradigms at stake are self-contained, "world" determining, and determining of what counts as science, and if competing paradigms are also irreconcilable, then the weight of the course of events during crisis, like the course of normal science, could be carried only by the sociology of the community: by techniques of persuasion and professional pressure within the community, rather than by anything like rational comparison of paradigms.[88] That sort of comparison, for the reasons outlined above, is *impossible*.

Hence, revolutions in science force or incorporate epistemological chasms, incommensurabilities, and the chasms make epistemological recourse impossible. The crisis can be resolved only by "conversion".

We need to disentangle the specific claims underlying Kuhn's conclusion that a conversion is the only way for the crisis to be resolved and, thus, that sociology determines the outcome of scientific revolutions.

The first is a claim that the world (or evidence of it?) cannot help to settle things. "The world" (or, our observation of it?) is shaped by a paradigm. (Kuhn, I think, tends to the first in each case.[89]) There are "quasi-metaphysical commitments" that determine the "world's population", and the paradigm as a whole shapes observation. Indeed, Kuhn maintains, the paradigm is constitutive of nature.[90] Paradigms, he notes, "provide *all* phenomena except anomalies with a theory-determined place in the scientist's field of vision".[91] Thus, in the end, *each world shaped by a paradigm is, itself, a closed system.*

Nor, in resolving the crisis, is an appeal possible to the theories involved or standards of evidence. (Indeed, in describing one revolution, Kuhn maintains that "the data changed".[92]) Theories and standards of evidence are part of each paradigm—thus, they are at issue—and there are apparently no *other* theories or beliefs beyond those in dispute that can be brought to bear on the situation and used to resolve it. Thus, Kuhn claims, there is no higher theoretical authority. *Each paradigm is itself a closed system.*

Moreover, there really is nowhere else to look but to one's colleagues, for it is the practices of a science community that determine what "doing science" is. This view clearly emerges in Kuhn's account of normal science and since in revolutionary science the new paradigm will not be articulated (or reconstructed) for some time, one's colleagues during crisis and in the period just following a revolution are the only remaining "candidates" for the factors that determine the outcome of the revolution and the practices following it. Moreover, it is by being a member of such a community that one does science, and is a scientist, at all. There is, given these features of Kuhn's picture of science, no wider community to be appealed to. *Each science community is a closed system.*[93]

Finally, when faced with two rival paradigms, one old and one new, it is rather like having two books—and *only* these books—to choose between. But you have only read one, and only recently with any thoroughness. Nor is is possible to read the one not yet read in order to decide which to keep. The new paradigm will not be articulated until a research tradition based on it is under way. The new "theory" and the articulation and justification of the methodology it implies will emerge only *after* the revolution has occurred, only after the relevant science community has undergone a "conversion" of sorts *and the behavior of the community has changed.* When the "rules" do appear (in the work of historians or philosophers of science, and science textbooks), they will rationally reconstruct the conversion, the revolution.[94] Scientists may not (probably will not) abstract the rules that their behavior implies until crisis.

In the end, then, it is this series of "closed systems" that prompt the view that competing paradigms are incommensurable—and, therefore, that sociology, and only sociology, carries the day.

> Like the choice between competing political institutions, that between
> competing paradigms proves to be a choice between incompatible modes
> of life. . . . As in political revolutions, so in paradigm choice—there is
> no standard higher than the assent of the relevant community.[95]

We are now in a position to summarize some fundamental contrasts between Kuhn's view of science and the view underlying Hempel's and Nagel's work, contrasts that are often taken to imply that Kuhn's account of science challenges every aspect of the "postlogical" positivist tradition.

First, Kuhn explicitly links the justification of paradigms, those things that underwrite normal science and are at stake in crisis and overturned in revolutions, to factors Hempel and Nagel consider relevant to the context of discovery and, as such, unimportant to the development and justification of scientific knowledge. Sociology, rather than theory, persuasion rather than the testing of theories, are the important factors in normal and revolutionary science. Indeed, the "justification" of something like a theory is not an issue until crisis, and there is no possibility of comparing the "theories" at issue to each other—or to "observation".

More generally, of course, Kuhn views and studies science as an activity rather than a "body of knowledge", and the activity he finds is very different from the "scientific method" Hempel and Nagel claim produces "scientific knowledge". Rather than testing the paradigm,[96] normal science is the detailed and rigorous work to fit nature to the paradigm, to solve puzzles. The paradigm is accepted—and, perhaps, if there is any role for them, something like theories are accepted, too—at least they, like other rules, may be articulated and defended during crisis and/or "reconstructed" in retrospect. And so it appears that Hempel and Nagel are engaged in precisely the "rational reconstruction" Kuhn claims historians of science and philosophers engage in.

We have also noted that Kuhn like Hanson, whose work he uses,[97] stresses problems with one tenet of the account of justification developed by Hempel and Nagel: the demarcation between observation and theory as this demarcation is attempted in Hempel's explication of "observation sentences" and of the relation of confirmation. Kuhn and Hanson see the problem that Popper saw, but they take the implications of the connection between observations and a going system much further. Kuhn maintains that the paradigm determines *the world* within which scientists work.

Now, without the demarcation between observation and theory, and so, without a demarcation between observation statements and theoretical statements, and with the specific manner of its breakdown—the work of Hanson and Kuhn which indicates that observation is, in fact, "theory laden"—the "base line" statement of evidence, the observation statement, empiricism's "final arbiter" of theories, seems to Kuhn to vanish.

> During revolutions, scientists see new and different things when looking with familiar instruments in places they have looked before. *It is rather as if the professional community has been suddenly transported to another planet.* . . . In so far as their only recourse to that world [the world of their research engagement] is through what they see and do, we may want to say that after a revolution scientists are responding to a different world. . . .[98]

> Can it conceivably be an accident, for example, that Western astronomers first saw change in the previously immutable heavens

during the half century after Copernicus' new paradigm was first
proposed? The Chinese, whose cosmological beliefs did not preclude
celestial change, had recorded the appearance of many new stars in the
heavens at a much earlier date. Also, even without the aid of a
telescope, the Chinese had systematically recorded the appearance of
sunspots centuries before these were seen by Galileo and his
contemporaries.[99]

With the apparent demise of the nontheoretical "observation sentence"
and with the incorporation of "metaphysical commitments" in the "rules"
that tacitly underlie the practice of the community (at least such commitments can be discerned in scientists' behavior retrospectively), the link
between theories and the world, understood by empiricists to be sensory
evidence, seems to many (including Kuhn in some moods) to vanish in
Kuhn's account of science.[100]

Indeed, research into the history of specific sciences and Kuhn's accounts of normal and revolutionary science have led some to question
whether the notion of scientific progress, in the sense of steady accumula-
tion and systematization of important "truths" about the world, makes
sense, and to question whether "theories" could be or are actually constrained by "the world". Kuhn himself specifically denies that scientific
knowledge grows cumulatively, and his notion of the incommensurability
of competing paradigms makes such cumulative progress impossible.[101]
Obviously, Kuhn and others who have built on his analysis and conclusions have had also, at least implicitly, to concern themselves with what
the notion of "truth" comes to. Kuhn insists that his accounts of normal
and revolutionary science do not result in a relativist account of science,
or in skepticism about the rationality of scientific revolutions, but not all
philosophers and social scientists have been so convinced.[102] What
emerges clearly in the positions we have considered is that truth is community bound and community determined.

In the end, neither the "logic" of science, nor an attempt to test
"hypotheses" by observation, nor the world generates and shapes scientific knowledge or determines the outcome of the revolutions. Scientific
knowledge, research puzzle solutions in the main, is generated by the
activities of a community—activities that are themselves shaped by a
paradigm (and perhaps tacit rules). What counts as knowledge—specifically, what counts as the solution to a problem or the solution to crisis—
is indeed intersubjective, as Hempel and Nagel thought. But it is *relative
to and determined by a community*. There are no standards of evidence
to which one can appeal that are not paradigm bound and community

relative. And, according to Kuhn and others, "there is no standard higher than the assent of the relevant community".[103]

An Autonomous Science: A Legacy of Polarization

It would be hard to overestimate the legacies of the two traditions we have considered. The first tradition articulates and supports views about science that are found in the textbooks that, from early ages through undergraduate courses, educate most of us about science. Although few of us may actually think of science as a body of sentences or theories, or as a complete and completed account of how things are, some important consequences of the emphasis on science as a "body of knowledge" and of other positions the "postlogical" positivists advocated have persisted.

One is a picture of science as "a process without a subject"[104]—a picture badly named since the view originated in an account that had, in fact, little if anything to do with "process", as we have seen. But the view is generally understood to mean that the identities of scientists and the factors, including social context, leading to or causing their adoption of theories are of little or no relevance to the development and directions of scientific knowledge. And that view endures. As J. J. Davies advocates the view many of us were taught, "Science is a structure built upon facts".[105]

Although Hempel and Nagel deny that science is *built* (using induction) from "facts", their faith that testing theories by "observation sentences" justifies scientific knowledge, as well as their criteria for disallowing hypotheses and sentences that are metaphysical or have to do with values, seems to insure that science is *grounded* in facts. Because they view science as consisting of just those theories that have passed tests based on observation, science is grounded in sensory evidence. And, in the end, scientific method—an exercise governed by logic and the demand for intersubjectivity—insures that the identities and "subjective interests" of scientists will not be reflected in the content of science. As Hempel maintains,

> Science aims at knowledge that is *objective* in the sense of being
> intersubjectively verifiable, independently of individual opinion or
> preference, on the basis of data obtainable by suitable experiments or
> observations.[106]

Contributing to the view that science is a "process without a subject" and to the faith that scientific method is capable of "weeding out" bad

theories, there is also an implicit view in Hempel's account of the epistemology of science that the "questions" to which scientists address themselves are "self-announcing". Where the ideal language of science that
Hempel discusses, the objects that figure in the theories of science, or the
questions and events scientists think need attention and explaining—
where all these come from is not scrutinized by Hempel and Nagel.
Nor, would it appear, given the several views outlined above, that such
questions are a matter of concern or relevant to the epistemology of
science. In addition, as we earlier noted, Hempel and Nagel may also
assume that there is one unique story to be discovered—an additional
reason why how hypotheses and theories are arrived at is not of consequence.

But the view that how the language and theories of science are arrived
at is not a matter of concern is fueled by more than the assumptions that
questions and evidence are "self-announcing" or that there is a unique
end to inquiry. It is also fueled by a view clearly expressed by Nagel
and underlying the emphases and focuses of the tradition. Science is
autonomous. Not only does science address itself to questions that "present" themselves, these questions are usually not about things we value.
For all these reasons, science is regulated by a logic internal to it.

The picture of an autonomous, self-regulating, self-critical, and non-
subjective set of practices that produce "objective" knowledge continues
to shape science's self-image and, therefore, the practice of science. For it
works to justify what Kathryn Addelson calls the "cognitive authority"
granted to science and claimed by science as its due,[107] a topic to which
we will turn in a later chapter.

Consider the "attitude" attributed by one writer to Galileo. The attitude is one that, for many, including scientists, characterizes scientists
and underwrites their cognitive authority. In a word, scientists are "not
interested" in anything but getting to the truth. The view echoes Nagel's
claim that attention to evidence is what distinguishes science from common sense.

> It was not so much the observations and experiments which Galileo
> made that caused the break with tradition as his *attitude* to them. For
> him, the facts based on them were treated as facts, and not related to
> some preconceived idea.[108]

Popper's scientist, like Hempel's and Nagel's, is not, of course, a collector
of facts without reference to preconceptions. But she or he is also blessed
with a highly developed critical streak, another common feature of prevalent views about science. Hypotheses in science,

these marvelously imaginative and bold conjectures or "anticipations" of ours, are carefully and soberly controlled by systematic tests. Once put forward, none of our "anticipations" are dogmatically upheld. Our method of research is not to defend them, in order to prove how right we are. On the contrary, we try to overthrow them.

   . . . it is not his [*sic*] *possession* of knowledge, of irrefutable truth, that makes the man [*sic*] of science, but his [*sic*] persistent and recklessly critical *quest* for truth.[109]

Finally, the view of science as a process without a subject—or at least, a highly "disengaged" subject so that, with few exceptions, who she or he is does not matter—leads to or presupposes a particular view of "objectivity": the latter is achieved only when "a subject" and "a subject's values" do not influence unduly or determine the development of scientific knowledge. Scientific knowledge, the knowledge gained through the most systematic and rigorous testing of hypotheses and theories, is of the sort that all observers would "see" the soundness of it—regardless of differences in background or interests, and with the exceptions of the difference that science education or mistakes might make.

It was *not*, after all, really very difficult for Kuhn to turn things around.

Having uncovered the lack of anything like the testing of theories or search for new knowledge (other than puzzle solutions) in normal science, drawing on the evidence that indicated that it was impossible to demarcate observation from theory, finding the incorporation of tacit metaphysical commitments in science, and bringing all of these together along with what he perceived to be the *insulation* of science communities, Kuhn concludes that competing paradigms are incommensurable and that sociology carries the day in determining the outcomes of scientific revolutions. Kuhn's analysis of science is generally understood to challenge virtually every feature of the Hempel/Nagel view.

But it doesn't. It is the flip side of the Hempel/Nagel view. It is the consequence of assuming that science is remote from common sense, that science communities are self-contained and self-regulating, although *also* recognizing that those aspects of Hempel's and Nagel's conception of science that were to insure objectivity and a connection with evidence are *untenable*. Thus, the only authority there *could* be on what constitutes "good science" and knowledge is Kuhn's science community—for it is as isolated as Nagel's "body of scientific knowledge" from "those things men [*sic*] value" and common sense and, thus, it is the sole arbiter of truth.

Consider how "incommensurability" is made less shocking when we remember that Kuhn, like Hempel and Nagel, distinguishes science from common sense by portraying science communities as fundamentally self-regulating. Advocates of competing and "incommensurable" paradigms can serve on the same university committees, meaningfully discuss funding issues, work together in social and political contexts, discuss retirement plans, and have each other to dinner, all without any noticeable lapses in the conversation. In other words, the incommensurability is limited to science very narrowly defined. Were this not so, Kuhn's view would be contradicted by Galileo's ability to converse with the church authorities on a wide variety of topics, including which end of a telescope one looks through and what the likelihood of the torture instruments' being used is.

With the assumption that science communities are *autonomous*, what appears to determine the directions of normal science are the self-regulating practices of such communities, practices that are shaped by allegiance to paradigms. With it, what appears to determine the outcome of a revolution in science is the sociology of these communities. There is no wider community, and a paradigm, itself viewed as incorporating a *total* world view, will reign or be overthrown on the basis of the consent of the community's members.

In short, when the barriers that Hempel and Nagel tried to build to separate science from metaphysics, and observation from theory, came down, and when it turned out that scientists do not behave in ways that are in keeping with the picture Hempel and Nagel drew, it was, ironically, on the basis of an assumption that he *shared* with Hempel and Nagel that Kuhn came to the view that scientific revolutions are conversions.

Incommensurability is the price we have to pay for viewing science as an "autonomous" enterprise.

Is the view that science is autonomous relevant to a continuing polarization in thinking about science? Does it underlie two apparently incompatible views of the epistemology of science and approaches to studying science? Does the assumption lead some currently engaged in historical and social studies of science, frameworks for which Kuhn's analysis is the progenitor, to the view that because scientific knowledge is "socially constructed", "the natural world has a small or non-existent role in the construction of scientific knowledge"?[110]

Does it simultaneously underwrite the view, still held by many scientists, philosophers, and laypersons, that science is a process without a subject—that something in the nature of evidence and the logic of science determines the way scientific knowledge develops?

I think so. Our exploration of how the view that science is autonomous works to polarize thinking about science will be indirect. We will, for most of the balance of the larger discussion, be concerned with two approaches to science that deny that science is autonomous: Quine's account of science, and the views of science emerging in and implied by feminist science criticism. Each avoids embracing either of the conclusions just outlined. And in each, knowledge is recognized as socially con-structed—*and* constrained by evidence.

We will begin with Quine.

CHAPTER THREE

Quine: Science (Almost) without Boundaries

Our one serious conceptual scheme is the inclusive, evolving one of
science, which we inherit and, in our several small ways, help to
improve.

—W. V. Quine

THE HARDEST PART of talking about Quine is beginning to talk
about Quine. Quine's views, to use one of his favorite metaphors,
are best thought of as forming a network and, as Richard Schuldenfrei notes, they incorporate "a world view".[1] This makes it difficult
to isolate particular aspects of Quine's work without reference to the
larger picture.

In addition, although there are relationships between Quine's specific
positions, these do not include or build from a foundation. Even the most
pervasive aspect of his work, a commitment to empiricism, is closely
connected to twentieth-century developments in science and philosophy
of science, and best understood when considered in the larger context of
other of his positions. In approaching the constellation of his views, we
do well to use his insight that "we [always] begin in the middle".[2]

I will begin with what Quine would call "aerial reconnaissance",
laying out some of the larger features of what Schuldenfrei calls "Quine's
world view" so that I can refer to these when exploring specifics. As
Quine says of the role theoretical discourse plays in aiding understanding
of less cohesive and less obviously theoretical "low level" discourse,

We would not find our way across the ground but for the aerial
reconnaissance. On the ground we cannot see the woods for the trees.

Theory brings system; system is simplicity; and simplicity is
psychologically imperative.[3]

The first thing aerial reconnaissance reveals is that there is system to
"Quine's world view", what I will call his "philosophy of science", and
that the network metaphor is an apt way of characterizing its structure.
Its aptness goes deeper than the lack of Cartesian-like foundations, and
the interrelationships between specific positions, in Quine's work. Quine
views his own account of science as one developing firmly *within* science.

> Our talk of external things, our very notion of things, is just a
> conceptual apparatus that helps us to foresee and control the triggering
> of our sensory receptors in the light of previous triggering of our sensory
> receptors. The triggering, first and last, is all we have to go on.
>
> In saying this I too am talking of external things, namely, people and
> their nerve endings. Thus what I am saying applies in particular to what
> I am saying, and is not meant as skeptical. There is nothing we can be
> more confident of than external things—some of them, anyway—other
> people, sticks, stones. But there remains the fact—a fact of science
> itself—that science is a conceptual bridge of our own making, linking
> sensory stimulation to sensory stimulation.[4]

As I briefly sketched in Chapter One, the network metaphor reflects
Quine's general account of the epistemological enterprise. With science
broadly construed to include "common-sense theorizing" (on Quine's
view, this is primarily theorizing about physical objects) as well as scientific and philosophical theorizing, Quine maintains that an account of
that theorizing, a theory of theorizing, will be within the framework of
science, and that it will make use of other going theories. The view
that science and epistemology are interdependent represents the most
fundamental difference between Quine's understandings of epistemology
and science, and the views that characterized empiricism through the
"postlogical" positivist tradition.

> It would be unwarranted rationalism to suppose that we can stake out
> the business of science in advance of pursuing science and arriving at a
> certain body of scientific theory.[5]

> The crucial insight of empiricism is that any evidence for science has its
> end points in the senses. This insight remains valid, but it is an insight
> *which comes after* physics, physiology, and psychology, not before.
>   . . . we accept this circularity, simply recognizing that the science of
> science is a science.[6]

In short, "justification" of our beliefs and theories is not going to be
supplied from outside of science. Quine's naturalized epistemology is a

consequence of his rejection of foundationalism. We must, according to
Quine, presume that most of our beliefs are true. Given this, the task of
epistemology is discovering how the beliefs we have are acquired. On
Quine's view, this, in the end, is a task for natural science.

Quine is more specific, as the following passage indicates, about where
and how epistemological questions should be pursued. The study of how
we go about theorizing, how we go about constructing theories given the
information our senses provide, should, on his view, be conducted within
empirical psychology. The proposal represents a further break with postlogical positivist philosophy of science: Quine, unlike Hempel and Nagel
(and Popper), does not write off the "context of discovery".

> The setting is . . . the physical world, seen in terms of the global science
> to which, with minor variations, we all subscribe. Amid all this there are
> our sensory receptors and the bodies near and far whose emanations
> impinge on our receptors. Epistemology, for me, or what comes nearest
> to it, is the study of how we animals can have contrived that very
> science, given just that sketchy neural input.[7]

As I noted in earlier discussion, Quine relates the shift to a naturalized
epistemology to the impossibility of coherent pretheoretic sensory experience, an impossibility that, in turn, makes an extrascientific foundation for
science impossible. Even a "rational reconstruction" of a "sense datum"
language, Quine maintains, would be dependent "upon sidelong glances
into natural science".[8]

> Philosophers have rightly despaired of translating everything into
> observational and logico-mathematical terms. . . . And the impossibility
> of that sort of epistemological reduction dissipated the last advantage
> that rational reconstruction [of our theorizing] seemed to have over
> psychology. . . . epistemology still goes on, though in a new setting and
> a clarified status. . . .
>   The old epistemology aspired to contain, in a sense, natural science;
> it would construct it somehow from sense data. Epistemology in its new
> setting, conversely, is contained in natural science, as a chapter of
> psychology. But the old containment remains valid too. . . . We are
> studying how the human subject . . . posits bodies and projects his [*sic*]
> physics from his data, and we appreciate that our position in the world
> is just like his. Our very epistemological enterprise, and the psychology
> wherein it is a component chapter, and the whole of natural science
> wherein psychology is a component—all this is our own construction or
> projection from stimulations like those we are meting out to our
> epistemological subject.

There is thus reciprocal containment, though containment in different senses: epistemology in natural science and natural science in epistemology.[9]

What Quine refers to as "the reciprocal containment" of epistemology and science will be explored somewhat in this chapter and his proposal for "naturalizing epistemology" will receive more extended consideration in Chapter Six. Here, I draw attention to the fact, already obvious, that Quine's empiricism is not positivism. Quine explicitly denies that there can be a "first science" and that science is built from "raw" sense data. So, epistemology will be, or will at least include as its primary task, an effort to provide an account of how we go about constructing theories and positing objects, a project abandoned by the postlogical positivist tradition when the project of providing an inductivist account of "discovery" failed.

One is struck early on by Quine's frequent use of metaphor. His account of metaphor sheds light on his view of the relationship between new questions and ongoing inquiry.[10]

Along the philosophical fringes of science we may find reasons to question basic conceptual structures and to grope for ways to refashion them. Old idioms are bound to fail us here, and only metaphor can begin to limn the new order.[11]

This passage suggests that theories, ways of organizing things (including other theories), even when so revolutionary that they require self-conscious recourse to metaphor, emerge from within, indeed are made possible by, ongoing inquiry.[12] In a number of discussions Quine uses a metaphor of Neurath's to describe the relationship between a body of theory that is accepted and new questions, and to underscore the lack of extra-scientific vantage points. Indeed, and of course, these two views are, at bottom, one, although we have not yet considered the details of Quine's arguments for the general insight.

Neurath has likened science to a boat, which, if we are to rebuild it, we must rebuild plank by plank while staying afloat in it.[13]

Our boat stays afloat because at each alteration we keep the bulk of it intact as a going concern. Our words continue to make passable sense because of continuity of change of theory: we warp usage gradually enough to avoid rupture. . . . We are limited in how we can start even if not in where we may end up. To vary Neurath's figure with

Wittgenstein's, we may kick away our ladder only after we have climbed it.[14]

The view that science is a going concern within which new questions emerge, are judged, and addressed, is a fundamental theme in Quine's work and it will prove useful when we turn in later discussion to characterizing the relationship between feminist science criticism and the aspects of science it criticizes. Before then, we will have filled in some of the specific arguments and positions that Quine uses to support the view.

From Ideas to Systems of Sentences

Of the several larger themes that reverberate through the network of Quine's work, the most consequential is empiricism. Quine describes what he calls "the two cardinal tenets of empiricism" as:

> whatever evidence there *is* for science *is* sensory evidence. The other . . .
> is that all inculcation of meanings of words must rest ultimately on
> sensory evidence.[15]

It is clear, as noted earlier, that Quine views empiricism as fundamentally a theory of evidence. Note also the sparseness of empiricism's core assumptions as Quine understands these; on the surface at least, there is far less to empiricism than is generally attributed to it. There are, for example, none of the so-called dogmas that critics of empiricism and some empiricists view as constitutive of or necessary to empiricism.[16]

The third point to note is that Quine's formulation of the two tenets of empiricism is somewhat cryptic. It is clear, for example, that Hume would have accepted the tenets but would have understood them differently. It is also clear that the connection between, say, sensory evidence and high-energy physics is not without need of more explication.

In another discussion Quine enumerates what he calls the "five milestones of empiricism"[17] and provides some filling out of his views of empiricism and science, and of the continuities and discontinuities between these and traditional, and logical and postlogical positivist, empiricism.

The first and second "milestones" Quine cites are earlier developments in empiricism; the third is a shift for which he credits Duhem; and the fourth and fifth are shifts for which he is at least partly responsible. The last three remain controversial. As we follow Quine's arguments for the shifts, his metaphor of science as a "network" gains content, and the shape of the network, as Quine sees it, begins to emerge.

The first empiricist "advance" cited by Quine is the move from a focus on "ideas" to words. Quine notes that Locke's "*idea* idea itself measures up poorly to empiricist standards".[18] The shift from ideas to words also serves as a bulwark against one source of skepticism facing the empiricist who begins with "ideas": the problems she or he encounters attempting to answer questions like "Where do our ideas come from?" or "How do we know that our ideas reflect a world that is independent of and causes them?"[19]

Something like these questions (Berkeley's answer to which put him well outside anything empiricism's theory of evidence could account for, albeit illuminating an important problem) always threatened to dissolve into the more vicious "Where do *my* ideas come from?" Briefly put, then, the move from ideas to words makes respectable (in keeping with empiricism's account of evidence) and public (given the specific threat of skepticism that the solipsism of the empiricist knower provokes) what it is that needs to be related to the world—what has empirical content. Language, unlike ideas, is public.

That ideas are not public is sufficient reason for moving to words. Quine, however, has other reasons for rejecting the "idea" idea. He finds the identity conditions for mental entities, including ideas, fuzzy at best. And he is, in his own words, "as much of a behaviorist as anyone in his [*sic*] right mind would be". If he thought we really needed ideas as the building blocks of thought (and thus of theories), Quine would work hard to clarify the identity conditions and so on for ideas. But we don't, and he doesn't.

Those who do not share Quine's qualms about mental entities in general and ideas in particular do strive to make these notions clear. Issues of ontological admissibility aside, it remains an interesting question whether a theory of thought can be built on necessarily private objects and still avoid the skepticism threatened by conjoining empiricism and individualism. This issue will continue to reappear in the course of this discussion and is addressed directly in Chapter Six.

Quine notes that the focus on words was superseded by a second shift: from terms (words) to sentences, a shift he attributes to Bentham's notion of contextual definition.[20] Words were no longer viewed as the bearers of meaning; they were recognized to have the meaning they did because of their role in sentences. Quine regards this shift as "less sudden" than the Copernican revolution, but no less a "shift of center" in empiricism.[21]

Some of the consequences are evident from our exploration of the

Hempel/Nagel tradition. The focus on sentences permits many of the developments that emerge in logical positivist and postlogical positivist research: Tarski's theory of truth, the Hempel/Nagel model of explanation, the study of the logic of theories and of justification, and the work to develop first-order quantification as a canonical form for science.

In addition, the focus has enabled Quine to maintain that "beliefs" can be discerned and individuated in terms of behaviors. Ascertaining a person's belief (including one's own) can become a matter of seeing whether one assents to a dissent from a sentence. For Quine, of course, the notion of "meaning" at work in this second shift (that sentences, and not words, are the bearers thereof) is not understood in terms of abstract objects or "mental entities". The meaning of sentences, as is evident in what Quine calls "the second tenet of empiricism", is their empirical content—a notion to which we now turn.

This second shift was eventually superseded with a change in focus from individual sentences to systems of sentences, or at least so Quine, who draws on the work of Duhem, would have it. The shift in focus as Quine understands and advocates it significantly distinguishes his views from those of Hempel and Nagel.

The first difference (and it underlies the others) is that Hempel and Nagel assume that individual sentences (observation sentences, for example) have their "own" specifiable "empirical content"—a list of sensory stimulations by virtue of which they can "stand alone" to judge theories and function in explanations.[22]

Quine denies that most single sentences have empirical content in isolation from a going body of theory.

> The typical statement about bodies has no fund of experiential implications it can call its own. A substantial mass of theory, taken together, will commonly have experiential implications; this is how we make verifiable predictions.[23]

> Statements about bodies, common-sense or recondite, commonly make little or no empirical sense except as bits of a collectively significant containing system. Various statements can surely be supplanted by their negations, without conflict with any possible sensory contingency, provided that we revise other portions of our science in compensatory ways. Science is empirically underdetermined: there is slack.[24]

Popper, we have seen, also recognizes that "observation sentences" (which he calls "basic statements") are relative to a theoretical system; this leads him to the skepticism reflected in his metaphor of science as an edifice

"that rises above a swamp". Quine does not share Popper's skepticism—
at least he does not share the same kind of skepticism. One source of the
difference is the way Quine understands "systems of sentences".

For Quine, the "systems of sentences" that have empirical content are
not particular theories. Rather, he argues, in the end, it is the network of
all our theories that has empirical content, a view of empirical meaning
he refers to as "holism". Quine's reasons for maintaining that it is our
theories as a whole that have empirical content are his views that our going
theories show fundamental connections and that they are interdependent.

Quine uses an arch metaphor to describe the network.

> Theory may be deliberate, as in a chapter on chemistry, or it may be
> second nature, as is the immemorial doctrine of ordinary enduring
> middle-sized objects. In either case, theory causes a sharing, by
> sentences, of sensory supports. In an arch, an overhead block is
> supported immediately by other overhead blocks, and ultimately by all
> the base blocks collectively and none individually; and so it is with
> sentences, when theoretically fitted.
>
> What comes of the association of sentences with sentences is a vast
> verbal structure which, primarily as a whole, is multifariously linked to
> non-verbal stimulation. . . . In an obvious way this structure of
> interconnected sentences is a single connected fabric including all
> sciences, and indeed everything we ever say about the world; for the
> logical truths at least, and no doubt many more commonplace sentences,
> too, are germane to all topics and thus provide connections.[25]

And so, according to Quine, it is as a "whole" that our theories
confront the world: "our statements about the external world face the
tribunal of sense experience not individually but only as a corporate
body".[26] In fact, Quine maintains, smaller "blocks" of theory are usually
necessary to our judgment of a single sentence. Although it is as a whole
that our theories in fact "face the world", it is also true that, given
recalcitrant experience, less than wholesale adjustments are required.
Indeed, as the discussion of Chapter One implied, Quine maintains that
there is no possibility of a "wholesale" rejection of the network. Thus, in
a recent paper he refers to the shift in focus from individual sentences to
systems of sentences as "a moderate or relative holism".[27]

> Some middle-sized scrap of theory usually will embody all the
> connections that are likely to affect our adjudication of a given
> sentence.[28]

> It is an uninteresting legalism . . . to think of our scientific system of the

world as involved *en bloc* in every prediction. More modest chunks suffice, and so may be ascribed their independent empirical meaning, nearly enough, since some vagueness in meaning must be allowed for in any event.[29]

The move to focusing on systems of sentences incorporates two far-reaching conclusions that together recast the notion of "empirical content" that Hempel and Nagel use to delineate the logic of justification. The first conclusion involves the empirical meaning of sentences, and it is part of what leads to the second—Quine's claim that it is the whole of science that has empirical meaning.

What is important is that we cease to demand or expect of a scientific sentence that it have its own separable empirical meaning.[30]

What I am . . . urging is that even in taking the statement as a unit we have drawn our grid too finely. *The unit of empirical significance is the whole of science.*[31]

Another and consequential break with the views of Hempel and Nagel, and with those of Kuhn, is reflected in the passage quoted above in which Quine describes science as a "single fabric". The "whole of science", according to Quine, incorporates more than scientific theories; as he notes in the passage the fabric includes "everything we ever say about the world". We will return, often, to this view, for it permits Quine to avoid a number of problems that Kuhn, Hempel, and Nagel encounter. What we have not yet addressed is what the notions of "observation" and the testing of theories come to, given the shift in focus from individual sentences to systems of sentences. And with the exception of noting earlier that Quine maintains a coherence theory of evidence and outlining the latter, we have not yet explored that notion of evidence in terms of the shifts outlined so far.

The fourth "advance" in Quine's litany is related to the shift to holism.[32] Not only are systems of sentences to be viewed as the bearers of empirical meaning, but, Quine maintains, all sentences within the system are to be regarded in a somewhat uniform way—specifically, as empirical.

This claim represents another far-reaching break with positivist and postlogical positivist views. In these traditions the "meaningfulness" of mathematical and logical sentences is insured, despite the fact that these sentences are viewed to be "non-empirical", by understanding them to be "analytic"—true by virtue of their "meaning" and without reference to "facts". But Quine argues that the proposed distinction between analytic sentences (those without empirical content) and synthetic sentences (those with empirical content) is a false distinction.[33]

In "Two Dogmas of Empiricism" Quine sets out to show that the notion of "analyticity" relies, in the end, on the notion of synonymy, which, he argues, is as unclarified and problematic as analyticity is without it.[34] This problem and the relationship between those sentences viewed to be "analytic" and other sentences lead Quine to argue that all sentences both organize and share empirical content. All, in varying degrees, share the tasks that had been understood to be the separate provinces of analytic and synthetic sentences.[35]

The collapse of the analytic/synthetic distinction, and the resulting view that all meaningful sentences have empirical content, have several consequences.[36] For one thing, all sentences, including logical and mathematical truths, are, on this view, subject to revision.

> It is misleading to speak of the empirical content of an individual statement—especially [as in the case of logical statements] if it is a statement at all remote from the experiential periphery of the field.
>
> Furthermore it becomes folly to seek a boundary between synthetic statements, which hold contingently on experience, and analytic statements, which hold come what may. Any statement can be held true come what may, if we make drastic enough adjustments elsewhere in the system. . . . by the same token, no statement is immune to revision.[37]

Quine attributes several structural features to the network of going theories that give content to and limit what some have understood to be a skepticism, or a pragmatism that actually represents a "skeptical retreat", implicit in his rejection of the analytic/synthetic distinction.[38]

First, not all sentences, according to Quine, are equally likely to be revised. Some sentences in the network are less likely to be revised because they are more "embedded" in the network (logical and mathematical truths, for example); others are less likely to be revised because they are closest to the "periphery" of sensory stimulation, and we are less likely to get them wrong.[39]

In the case of mathematical and logical truths, there are two aspects to Quine's notion of "embeddedness": logical and mathematical statements, and Quine also includes theoretical statements of physics and ontology in this category, are less likely to be challenged by recalcitrant experience because they are further from the periphery of sensory experience and do not have any particular sensory stimulations associated with them; second, these sentences are interwoven throughout our going theories so that the mutual support they share with other sentences is pronounced.

> A recalcitrant experience can, I have argued, be accommodated by any of various alternative reevaluations in various alternative quarters of the total system . . . but . . . our natural tendency to disturb the total system as little as possible would lead us to focus our revisions upon these specific sentences [about physical objects]. [Highly theoretical statements of physics or logic or ontology] may be thought of as relatively centrally located within the total network, meaning merely that little preferential connection with any particular sense data obtrudes itself.[40]

The embeddedness of mathematical and logical sentences in the network of our theories, as well as that of the sentences of theoretical physics and ontology, renders these sentences a special but not a "nonempirical" status. Revising them would reverberate through the network, and this, together with their distance from sensory experience, makes it less likely that we will do so.

Quine's insistence that all sentences are empirical is relevant to a question of current interest in feminist science criticism as to whether mathematics and logic are "pure" of any content that could be affected or determined by social or political factors. This question is part of what is at issue in what I will call, paraphrasing Sandra Harding, "the physics question" in feminism,[41] a question posed more by traditional scientists than feminists. "How could", some ask, "physics be affected by politics?" Quine's argument against the analytic/synthetic distinction is increasingly cited in feminist criticism[42] because of its implications for the status of mathematical and logical sentences. But the argument is also relevant to the question of the special status of physics. I will not address that issue in detail until Chapter Five, but note here that Quine's insistence that it is the whole of science that has empirical significance, and that all our theories are connected and interdependent, makes the granting to physics (or mathematics or whatever) any special or isolated status dubious indeed.

Here I will note some general consequences and important features of Quine's argument against the analytic/synthetic distinction. The first general point to note is that Quine's view of mathematics and logic is not skeptical. Nor is it "pragmatic" *if* we understand pragmatism as a skeptical position. What Sandra Harding and others describe as "Quine's turn to pragmatism"[43] (Quine also uses the term[44]) is not correctly construed as the view that "the most we can ask is that theories work *because* we no longer believe of our going theories, or seek in our efforts to refine or construct new ones, that these are, or will be, *true*". Quine has not given up talking about "true theories" as the goal (achievable goal) of our theorizing; and relatedly, his understanding of "pragmatism" is more subtle.[45]

Quine's "pragmatism" builds, among other things, from his view of science as a bridge of our own making between sensory stimulations (a view to which we shortly give content), from his view that there are no extratheoretical standpoints, and from his view (related to each of these) that truth is "immanent".[46] The last two positions indicate that we cannot coherently take on the project of Descartes' First Meditation, and this includes a thoroughgoing skepticism about mathematics and logic. Moreover, as I noted in the overview of empiricism in Chapter One, and as the discussion of this chapter will explore in some detail, Quine maintains that there is no point of view from which we could decide to adopt "pragmatism" as a *replacement* for "truth". What needs replacing, Quine argues, is the correspondence theory of truth: the view that there is a "correspondence" between our theories and extralinguistic reality. That notion of truth, as I noted earlier, is specifically rejected by Quine.[47] Thus, the most apt description of Quine's account of "truth" is a "disappearance" theory of truth.

> The scientific system, ontology and all, is a conceptual bridge of our own making, linking sensory stimulation to sensory stimulation.
>
> But I also [have an] unswerving belief in external things—people, nerve endings, sticks, stones. . . . Now how is all this robust realism to be reconciled with the barren scene that I have just been depicting? The answer is naturalism: the recognition that it is within science itself, and not in some prior philosophy, that reality is to be identified and described.
>
> . . . it is a confusion to suppose that we can stand aloof and recognize all the alternative ontologies as true in their several ways. . . . It is a confusion of truth with evidential support. *Truth is immanent, and there is no higher.* We must speak from within a theory, albeit any of various.[48]

There are other consequences of Quine's argument against the analytic/synthetic distinction. The collapse of the distinction challenges the "verification" theory of meaning, and relatedly, the "criterion of cognitive significance", which Hempel wanted to apply to single sentences. As Quine argues in "Two Dogmas of Empiricism", the two dogmas, the analytic/synthetic distinction and the verification theory of meaning, are, in the end, one view: namely, that we can talk about the empirical content of *single sentences*.

The one dogma clearly supports the other this way: as long as it is taken
to be significant in general to speak of the confirmation and infirmation
of a statement, it seems significant to speak also of a limiting kind of
statement which is vacuously confirmed, *ipso facto,* come what may;
and such a statement is analytic.

The two dogmas are, indeed, at root identical.[49]

So, the collapse also challenges the related distinction the logical
positivists and Hempel drew between metaphysical sentences and empirical sentences—a distinction that was understood to distinguish meaningful (empirical) sentences from meaningless (metaphysical) sentences.

On Quine's account (with, it turns out, one very important exception),
there are no sentences without empirical content—or at least no sentence
that is embedded in a theory is without such content. In addition, we will
see that Quine maintains that metaphysics is inseparable from science,
that it is part and parcel of doing science.

Now, few scientists and philosophers worry any longer about the
"meaninglessness" of "metaphysical statements". (The example that purportedly propelled the positivists into the position that metaphysical statements are "meaningless" was "the Absolute enters into, but is itself
incapable of change"—small wonder that it struck them as meaningless.)

But the legacy of the metaphysical/empirical distinction remains in two
current, and apparently incompatible, views of the relationship between
science and metaphysics that we considered in Chapter Two, although I
have suggested that Kuhn's view may, in fact, represent something more
like the "flip side" of the positivist's view. On the one hand, as Kathryn
Addelson points out, scientists are still loath to acknowledge that research
programs or methodologies presume or incorporate metaphysical commitments.[50] Kuhn, on the other hand, argues that metaphysical assumptions are within science (at least they can be abstracted from normal
science and are at issue in scientific revolutions), but that they are hidden
or tacit until crisis. When the latter occurs, these commitments, even if
elucidated, are not able to be evaluated. I think Quine avoids both the
mystification of the first view and the skepticism of the second. We will
consider his understanding of the relationship of metaphysics to science
in a later section of this chapter.

The fifth advance enumerated by Quine is a move to what he calls
"epistemological naturalism", a position I have had reason to note in
several contexts. With the shift to holism, the collapse of the analytic/
synthetic distinction, and the view that physical-object ontology is our
conceptual first (a position outlined below), Quine argues that the dream

of epistemology as "first science" must be given up and epistemology recognized as part of science.[51] As noted earlier, Quine suggests that our epistemological questions be pursued in neuroscience.

The break with Popper's understanding of epistemology is clear. Like Quine, Popper relegated questions about "discovery" (which he called "questions of fact")—how we come to posit objects and construct theories—to empirical psychology. But Popper also specifically distinguished that project from the epistemology of science, which was, on his view, the study of the logic of justification of theories.

Hempel and Nagel also specifically rule out, as relevant to an account of science, most centrally an account of the connection between theories and sensory evidence, the kinds of question that Quine thinks epistemology should pursue. Quine is not willing to write off these questions; nor is it clear how, given his views, the alleged distinction between two such "contexts" of science can be drawn.

We now have an overview of the general shifts in empiricism and philosophy of science that Quine advocates. Although systems of sentences—indeed, the whole of science, rather than individual sentences, are recognized as the vehicles of "empirical content" (the latter having replaced words, and words having replaced Lockian and Humean ideas), the continuity with traditional empiricism remains in the view that, in the end, empirical evidence is sensory stimulations. This is not a "first principle" of "first science", but a fact of science itself.

Missing from Quine's empiricism is the question "Where do our ideas come from?" Gone, too, is the search by a "first science" for the foundations of science. Epistemology and philosophy (and, Quine maintains, "philosophy of science is philosophy enough") are recognized and pursued as part of empirical science.

Equally decisive is the break with the postlogical positivist and Kuhnian view that science, in the narrow sense, is autonomous. We have begun to see that Quine views the "fabric of science", our theory of nature, as inclusive of "everything we ever say about the world".

Rubbing Out Boundaries

A pervasive aspect of Quine's work is beginning to emerge: his persistent interest in "rubbing out boundaries".[52] In the largest sense, Quine denies that we can distinguish "the objects we talk about" from "the ways we talk about them". And so, he rejects the view that metaphysics and epistemology are activities separable from each other, and from serious science.[53]

In this section I discuss Quine's challenges to several long-standing and interconnected boundaries: the alleged distinctions between metaphysics and science, between theoretical sentences and observation sentences, between metaphysics and epistemology, and between either of these and science. His arguments against these boundaries give content to the general views I have so far outlined, and we will later find the boundaries to be at issue in feminist science criticism.

Quine is not, of course, alone in challenging the boundary between metaphysics and science, although the general view that metaphysics and epistemology are not separable from each other or science to which his challenge contributes are not common. Many philosophers of science are also no longer committed to the theory/observation distinction—at least not as philosophers of science and scientists once tried to draw it.

But Quine's challenges to these distinctions are different from other challenges, and so are the consequences he draws from their collapse. I will be specifically concerned to explore alternative views of how and why the boundaries collapse to Kuhn's views, and to lay out, in general terms, an alternative view of the consequences. We will use these alternatives when considering issues raised by feminist science criticism.

My discussion of these rather "thick" and interconnected issues—the alleged boundaries between metaphysics and science, between theoretical statements and observation statements, and between metaphysics and epistemology—will not do justice to Quine's arguments; the latter have more resonance than it will be possible to capture here. It will be sufficient for our purposes to lay out alternatives to positions we explored in the previous chapter, and to explore the source of the differences.

So, I will specifically shape the discussion of these boundaries to reintroduce and explore, now with the benefit of some content, Quine's denial of another alleged "boundary": the boundary between "science" (narrowly construed) and "common-sense" and philosophical theorizing. The view of science as (with one exception) without boundaries, as inclusive of almost all of our efforts to organize our experiences, is the most important and far-reaching of the differences between Quine's view of science and others we have considered, and it is fundamentally related to how he views the collapse of the other boundaries we will consider. And it is because Quine denies that science is autonomous, that is is distinct from things like common sense and metaphysics, that he is able to avoid at least some of the skepticism others have fallen into (or have been accused of falling into) as the boundaries between science and other things were recognized as untenable. The exception, the boundary he does not challenge, to which we will turn at the end of this chapter and often in the balance of the larger discussion, is a big one: the alleged boundary between science and values.

METAPHYSICS AND SCIENCE

Quine says many things about ontology, the heart of metaphysics, but perhaps the best place to begin is with a relatively early discussion, his "On What There Is".[54] The thrust of the discussion is, in fact, epistemological rather than metaphysical, reflecting its fundamental argument: that it is impossible to discuss "ontology" (what there is) without discussing "theory" (what we say there is). As Quine has put things more recently, "ontological questions [are] meaningless when taken absolutely".[55] Ontological questions, he argues, are always relative to some theory—or, as he sometimes says, to some "set of coordinates" or "background theory", itself taken at "face value". Moreover, Quine maintains, ontologies are always propounded *in theorizing;* they are not established, discovered, or posited prior to that activity.[56] So, readers who turn to "On What There Is" to find out what there is (or what Quine thinks there is) ought to be disappointed.

The answer, Quine tells us at the outset, to the question "What is there?" is "Everything". There are two (partially) separate theses underlying the answer. The first is that we cannot separate ontology from ideology. There are no bare particulars or things "in themselves". The second is that the only answer to "What is there?" is what this or that theory says there is.

This statement of "what there is" also does not make or allow for distinctions among kinds or degrees of existence. Quine's account of existence is unequivocal. There are no objects that "subsist", and of current interest in some areas of philosophy, there are no "possible objects". And a more general consequence of the statement of what there is, is that there is not a special class of "theoretical entities" to be distinguished from "real entities". The objects that figure in our ways of organizing things are, given Quine's account of ontology, both theoretical and real.

The statement of what there is is meant to convince or remind us of the scope and importance of our common-sense "there is" idiom. The objects we are committed to are the objects we say there are, and the "there is" idiom, Quine maintains in another discussion, is involved in all of our dealings with the world.

We can locate objectual quantification in our own language because we grow up using those very words: if not the actual quantifier, then words like "exists" and "there is" by which they come to be explained to us.[57]

Our ontic commitments are not restricted, of course, to sentences that include the "there is" idiom. Many sentences carry ontic commitment although they do not include the words "there is" or "exists"—"That house is red" or "Mary is upset", for example, which commit us, respectively, to a house and to Mary (but not to redness or upsets).

Following Russell,[58] Quine maintains that we can always expose the ontic commitments we honor by rendering our sentences in first-order quantification theory, a language that includes the quantifier, itself the logical equivalent of "there is". Thus, we are always in a position to find out what, in the way of ontology, a theory commits us to.[59]

> We now have a more explicit standard whereby to decide what ontology a given theory or form of discourse is committed to: a theory is committed to those and only those entities to which the bound variables of the theory must be capable of referring in order that the affirmations made in the theory be true.[60]

What we gain from rendering a theory in first-order quantification is the means of discovering our metaphysical commitments—at least insofar as the latter are ontic commitments, commitments about what things there are. Such commitments are exposed when we look to the bound variables of that quantification, to what the domain of a theory contains.

> We commit ourselves to an ontology containing numbers when we say there are prime numbers larger than a million; we commit ourselves to an ontology containing centaurs when we say there are centaurs; and we commit ourselves to an ontology containing Pegasus when we say Pegasus is.[61]

This is not to say that logic, as it is here being used, tells us what there is. Logic is being used to reveal those commitments already contained in a theory.

> We're checking not on existence, but on imputations of existence: on what a theory says exists.[62]

> Now how are we to adjudicate among rival ontologies? . . . We look to bound variables in connection with ontology not in order to know what there is, but in order to know what a given remark or doctrine, ours or someone else's, *says* there is; and this much is quite properly a problem of language. But what there is is another question.[63]

Now, Quine claims there is "no more to be said" in explicating the notion of existence. The "there is" idiom of everyday language and the rendering of what we say in existentially quantified sentences constitute the explication of "existence".

> I mean "exists" to cover all there is, and such of course if the force of the quantifier.[64]

> Existence *is* what existential quantification expresses. There are things of kind F if and only if $(\exists x)$ Fx. . . . It is unreasonable to ask for an explication of existence in simpler terms. An explication of general existence is a forlorn cause.[65]

What, then, is metaphysics? It is certainly not the study of "being, qua being" of Aristotle's *Metaphysics*. There is, according to Quine, no such subject matter. Nor is there a study of "what there is" independent of, or prior to, theorizing. Ontology shows itself in what we are willing to quantify over—in what, when we symbolize our sentences in quantification form, we are willing to accept.

So, what is the relationship of metaphysics to science? The answer, given the views I have outlined, is, of course, that science is *permeated* with metaphysics and metaphysics is *part* of science. Our metaphysical or ontic commitments are not "free floating" or lurking in the background; nor are they hidden (views that Kuhn, among others, implies). Nor, in what now looks to be a view deeply related to Kuhn's, are they *avoidable,* as the logical positivists and Hempel had hoped. Ontic commitments permeate *all* our theories, including scientific theories. Moreover, as we will see in a discussion of reductionism later in this chapter, even what Quine calls "the highly theoretical statements of ontology" most deeply embedded in the network of theories are sentences of what our *going theories commit us to*. We can reveal a *general* metaphysical commitment to how things happen by looking at our theories in the way Quine has suggested.

Alternatively said, it is nonsense to talk of picking an ontology. Rather, we build a theory and accept the ontology it brings with it, pending the evolving of a better theory. The work of science, that is, of rational inquiry, is the work of theorizing: of building, composing, and evaluating theories. The result is a theory we are willing to accept and live with, for the moment at least, and an ontology the theory commits us to. We are not, nor could we ever be, in a position "outside theory", looking to see *what* there is so we can then talk *about* it. We may in light of future results withdraw our ontic commitment to subatomic particles—even, as

Quine notes, to physical objects.[66] But this would come about *within* the process of constructing and evaluating theories, within science broadly construed.

Of course, one way of evaluating a theory (but only a less than all-embracing theory) is to see what ontic commitment it carries with it and whether its objects are congenial with our broader theories. Our broader theory or views do indicate some criteria, or at least Quine thinks they do, that make some ontic commitments more suspect than others. These criteria include simplicity and clarity of identity criteria. So, for example, Quine is loath to accept a theory that commits us to propositions or attributes because (in no special order) these alleged entities have no clear identity criteria; they make for a more complicated ontology; and there are no or insufficient counterbalancing benefits to be obtained by countenancing such entities.

Thus, ontological decisions can and should be made, and some will be important (for example, whether we "admit" into our overall ontology mental entities like "intentions" or platonic entities like "meanings"). But the more general and far-reaching consequence of the views considered in this section is that making such decisions is *part and parcel* of evaluating and selecting theories, not antecedent to that activity. Thus, Quine would argue that the criteria he suggests should be used to evaluate ontologies have themselves evolved within science. Our current broadest theory brings with it an ontology that includes trees and water, as well as molecules and subatomic particles, but not, or so Quine would have it, "meanings", "attributes", or mental entities as traditionally understood. On the other hand, it does include objects that are not physical—classes or sets, for example—for our going theories require mathematics, and mathematics needs classes. So not only does science incorporate metaphysics, it can lead to good metaphysics—to ontologies that help us to better organize things and to the rejection of those that do not.

COMMON SENSE, SCIENCE, AND EPISTEMOLOGY

One of Quine's arguments against the possibility of "absolute" ontological decisions, of determining what there is in isolation from what to say about it, will allow us to begin to explore his view that the "fabric of science" is inclusive of all of our theorizing.[67] A central feature of the argument is the claim that one ontology, physical-object ontology, is fundamental to all our theorizing.

In *Word and Object* and "Posits and Reality" Quine argues that physical-object ontology is our "conceptual first" and that the ontology is highly theoretical. Part of his argument for the primacy of physical-object ontology is the view that sensory experience will not of itself "hold together", and that physical-object ontology, which we learn as we learn language, is what permits coherent experience.[68] Physical objects are the "basics" of the conceptual scheme into which we are socially inculcated as children.

Quine also argues that the introduction to physical objects is, itself, inseparable from the learning of physical-object *theory*. In describing how a child learns language, Quine argues that the grasping or getting on to physical-object ontology *without* having grasped physical-object *theory* is impossible.

> We in our maturity have come to look upon the child's mother as an integral body who, in an irregular closed orbit, revisits the child from time to time; and to look upon red in a radically different way, viz., as scattered about. . . . But the mother [and] red . . . are for the infant all of a type: each is just a history of sporadic encounter, a scattered portion of what goes on. . . .
>
> It is only when the child has got on to the full and proper use of *individuative* terms like "apple" that he [*sic*] can properly be said to have taken to using terms as terms, and speaking of objects. . . . To learn "apple" it is not sufficient to learn how much of what goes on counts as apple; we must learn how much counts as *an* apple, and how much as another. Such terms possess built-in-modes of individuation. . . .
>
> Only at this stage does it begin to make sense to wonder whether the apple now in one's hand is the apple noticed yesterday.[69]

It is in the learning of the "mechanics of individuation", of the difference between mass terms and single terms, of that between the latter and general terms, and of the scheme of enduring physical objects that a child actually acquires the ontology of physical objects. The child, according to Quine,

> can never fully master "apple" in its individuative use, except as he [*sic*] gets on with the scheme of enduring and recurrent physical objects. . . . Until individuation emerges, the child can scarcely be said to have general or singular terms, there being no express talk of objects. . . . [The mastering of individuation] is a major step in acquiring the conceptual scheme we all know so well. *For it is on achieving this step, and only then, that there can be any general talk of objects as such.*[70]

This specific argument about the relationship between physical-object theory and physical-object ontology is generalized by Quine to all ontologies. All ontologies are theoretical; all are propounded *in theories*. We do not, for example, first posit molecules and then decide what to *say* about molecules. Our positing of molecules is inseparable from what we say of them and from the theorizing in which we posit them as a way of organizing experience and other theories.

There is, according to Quine, as I noted at the outset of this section, no sense to be made of a distinction between the objects we talk about and the ways we talk about them. So, if ontic commitments are, as he argues, embedded in our theories, so, too, are the ways we individuate objects and the relationships we posit between them.

> One tends to imagine that when someone propounds a theory concerning some sort of objects, our understanding of what he [*sic*] is saying will have two phases: first we must understand what the objects are, and second we must understand what the theory says about them. . . .
>
> [Yet] . . . our understanding of "what the objects are" awaits the second phase. . . . We do not learn first what to talk about and then what to say about it.[71]

Two other features of physical-object ontology are relevant to Quine's denial of a boundary between common-sense theorizing and scientific theorizing. Quine argues that the ontology of "middle-sized enduring objects" is not only necessary for making sense (if indeed we can make sense) of the alleged ontology of sense data. The ontology is also the basis of our "scientific" ontologies—those, for example, of unobservable objects.

Scientific ontologies, Quine argues, are dependent on physical-object ontology in fundamental ways. One aspect of that dependency is that our evidence for unobservable objects is indirect; it consists in their bearing on observable reality.

> According to physics, my desk is, for all its seeming fixity and solidity, a swarm of vibrating molecules. . . . no glimpse is to be had of the separate molecules of the desk; they are, we are told, too small.
>
> Lacking such experience, what evidence can the physicist muster for his [*sic*] doctrine of molecules? His answer is that there is a convergence of indirect evidence, drawn from such varied phenomena as expansion, heat conduction. . . . Any defense of [the molecular doctrine] has to do . . . with its indirect bearing on observable reality.[72]

A second aspect of the dependency of scientific ontologies on physical-object ontology is that scientific ontologies are posited by analogy to our conceptually first ontology, physical-object ontology. The things we say of such unobservable objects tend to be, Quine notes in a passage cited below, "framed" and "phrased" in the terms we use to talk about physical objects.

Third, though our more esoteric ontologies enable us to organize a more general account that integrates phenomena that, within physical-object theory, are dissimilar, these ontologies have the status they do only because of their relationship to physical objects. Thus, Quine remarks that sentences about molecules are "gibberish by themselves", their significance depends on their being part of a larger, inclusive theory of nature. Without reference to a larger system that includes physical objects, molecules (and other unobservable objects)

> lose even the dignity of inferred or hypothetical entities. . . . The very sentences which seem to propound them are gibberish by themselves, and indirectly significant only as contributory clauses of an inclusive system which does also treat of the real. The molecular physicist is, like all of us, concerned with commonplace reality, and merely finds that he [*sic*] can simplify his laws by positing an esoteric supplement to the esoteric universe.[73]

Finally, Quine argues that the interrelationships that exist between the three general levels of ontology, sense data, common sense, and scientific, indicate that no one of these levels is *epistemologically* privileged.

> Sense data [*if they are to be posited at all*] are *evidentially* fundamental: every man [*sic*] is beholden to his senses for every hint of bodies. The physical particles are *naturally* fundamental in this kind of way: laws of behavior of those particles afford, so far as we know, the simplest formulation of a general theory of what happens. Common-sense bodies, finally, are *conceptually* fundamental: *it is by reference to them that the very notions of reality and evidence are acquired, and that the concepts which have to do with physical particles or even with sense data tend to be framed and phrased.*[74]

> Bodies are assumed, yes; they are the things, first and foremost. Beyond them there is a succession of dwindling analogies.[75]

At least so says our present best theory of the world.

Although physical objects have a special place in our network of theories, a "base line" on Quine's view that enables us, by analogy, to posit objects that are unobservable and to be *warranted* in doing so, physical objects are not the extratheoretic "foundation" of science. Physical objects, as we have seen, are themselves highly theoretical. Moreover, that physical objects have the role of a "base line" in our theorizing is a consequence of our current view of the world, *not* a precursor to it.

One final aspect of the special place physical objects have in our conceptual scheme is alluded to in Quine's remark, in the passage quoted above, that "the very notions of reality and evidence" are acquired through our dealings with these objects. His view of a basic relationship between physical-object ontology and our notions of evidence is clearer, in an argument in which he claims that, given the current state of science, it is neither possible nor desirable to doubt physical-object ontology— whether on the basis of an allegedly "more fundamental" ontology of sense data, or on the basis of subatomic particles posited in physics, or on the grounds that we are not "sure enough" of the evidence for physical objects.[76]

Recognizing, for example, that from the point of view of molecular theory, physical objects are "just posits" that help us to organize what we experience is, Quine argues, to recognize that the point holds for *all* objects—including molecules. Not only do we acquire the notion of evidence in our dealings with physical objects, but common-sense theory which, on Quine's view, is primarily theorizing about physical objects, gives the notions of evidence and reality *content*.

Alternatively said, when we recognize that our evidence for physical objects is that they help us to organize our experiences and to predict future experiences, we recognize *the nature of evidence for all objects and theories*.

> We cannot properly represent man [*sic*] as inventing a myth of physical objects to fit past and present sense data, for past ones are lost except to memory; and memory, far from being a straightforward register of past sense data, usually depends on past posits of physical objects. . . .
>
> Having noticed that man [*sic*] has no evidence for the existence of bodies beyond the fact that their assumption helps him organize experience, we should [do] well, instead of disclaiming evidence for the existence of bodies, to conclude: *such, then, at bottom, is what evidence is, both for ordinary bodies and for molecules.*[77]

In the end, then, our most general standards of evidence and, indeed, the notion of evidence itself, emerge from our common-sense dealings with physical objects.

> On the face of it there is a certain verbal perversity in the idea that ordinary talk of familiar physical things is not in large part understood

as it stands, or that the familiar physical things are not real, or that evidence for their reality needs to be uncovered. For surely the key words "understood", "real", and "evidence" here are too ill-defined to stand up under such punishment. We should only be depriving them of the very denotations to which they mainly owe such sense as they make to us. . . . The familiar material objects may not be all that is real, but there are admirable examples.[78]

Quine's argument has far-reaching consequences. It indicates that standards of evidence are not "pretheoretic" but emerge *within* theorizing—and first, with common-sense theorizing. Such standards emerge concomitantly within the business of constructing bridges between our experiences. Thus, epistemology and metaphysics are fundamentally related—and *part* of science.

As an empiricist I continue to think of the conceptual scheme of science as a tool, ultimately, for predicting future experience in the light of past experience. Physical objects are conceptually imported into the situation as convenient intermediaries—not by definition in terms of experience, but simply as irreducible posits. . . .
Positing does not stop with macroscopic physical objects. Objects at the atomic level are posited to make the laws of macroscopic objects, and ultimately the laws of experience, simpler and more manageable.[79]

Here, the pragmatism in Quine's view of science is clearly obvious, but again, it is not correctly construed as a retreat from assuming our going theories are *true*.

Ontology, of any sort, is constrained by theory. To call a posit a posit is not to patronize it. . . .
Everything to which we concede existence is a posit from the standpoint of a description of the theory-building process, and simultaneously real from the standpoint of the theory that is being built. Nor let us look down on the standpoint of the theory as make-believe; for we can never do better than occupy the standpoint of some theory or other, the best we can muster at the time.[80]

We have focused on Quine's views about ontology in order to explore some long-standing distinctions, and several things have emerged. One is the reliance of "scientific objects" and those objects that have figured in attempts to reconstruct a foundation for common-sense ontology (sense data) on what Quine argues is a very comfortable and necessary "home base" in common-sense (physical-object) ontology. Ultimately, the mutual dependency of our various "levels" of theorizing was thrown into relief. Physics, though dependent on common-sense theory, also underwrites the latter and allows us to talk in more general terms about what happens at the level of physical objects. The relationship between the two "levels" of theorizing of common sense and science is one of mutual dependence.

> Our one serious conceptual scheme is the inclusive, evolving one of science, which we inherit and, in our several small ways, help to improve.[81]

A second thing to emerge in the fundamental connection between the notion of evidence and common-sense theorizing about physical objects is the relationship between standards of evidence and going theories. Such standards are adopted concomitantly with theorizing. This connection indicates, again, that there can be no "first science", no epistemological foundation for science that underwrites and is epistemologically prior to the doing of science. Our common-sense theorizing is itself highly theoretical, and there is no "sub-basement" to it. And a more general consequence of these views concerns the nature of evidence: our evidence for physical objects—that they enable us to organize our experiences— is, Quine maintains, what evidence comes to.

A third position to emerge is a general one about ontology. Objects are posited to organize experience and our success in doing that constitutes the evidence we have for objects. In addition, there are no "absolute" ontological decisions. We do not discover objects and then theorize about them. Ontologies are propounded in, and evaluated within, theories. A fourth position to emerge is the specific one we set out to explore: Quine's account of the relationship between metaphysics and science. All of our theories, Quine argues, contain metaphysical commitments; these can be ascertained by formalizing a theory and looking at the required values of the bound variables. Even our most general ontological commitments can be exposed by looking at the body of our theories and seeing what these commit us to.

As we have seen, Quine is not alone in maintaining the general position that science incorporates metaphysical commitments. Others in the empiricist tradition, the logical positivists and their immediate heirs, tried to separate science from such commitments, but Kuhn argues that science includes such commitments. However, Quine's account of the relationship between metaphysics and science is fundamentally different from Kuhn's. For Quine, metaphysical commitments are not pernicious— at least they need not be—and they can be and should be evaluated. The point is that such commitments are incorporated in theories. Even our larger commitments (to the existence of individual objects, for example) are not free floating. They are incorporated in the larger body of our going theories.

There is a moral to be drawn here. It is apparently the attempt to separate science from metaphysics that leads to the view that when we recognize metaphysical commitments in science, something is "wrong", or science is not rational, since such commitments "shouldn't be in science" because they can't be evaluated, they are not subject to empirical constraints.

Conversely, if despite all evidence to the contrary we remain committed to the view that science and metaphysics really *are* separate (or that they *could be*), we effectively preclude the evaluation of the metaphysical commitments our theories *do embody*. When we are faced with Kuhn's study of science communities and scientific revolutions, and other studies of science that expose the presence and consequences of metaphysical commitments, a skepticism about the rationality of theory choice or scientific practice may appear warranted. Quine's arguments indicate that such skepticism is not warranted.

And there is more to be gained by recognizing that there is no separating science from metaphysics. Quine's arguments suggest that science can lead to *better* metaphysics, provided we give up several myths: that objects are "discovered" and subsequently theorized about, rather than posited in the process of theorizing; that we can separate what we talk about (the objects) from our ways of talking about them; that ontology is *more* than a way of bridging our experiences; and that because objects are "posits" and different theories may incorporate different ontological commitments, theories cannot be compared, and/or do not reflect—or face—experience.

We have also explored some of what leads Quine to claim that science is inclusive of all our theorizing—the fundamental relationships he exposes between common-sense theorizing (at least physical-object theorizing) and scientific theorizing. And his argument that a theory (on his view, physical-object theory) is fundamental to our positing of other ontologies, together with the impossibility of "nontheoretical" ontology, suggests that there is no observation pure of theory (at least not at the level at which "ontology" is involved).[82]

To further the cases for the theory-dependence of observation and for the fundamental relationship between science in the narrow sense and other theorizing, we will need to talk more about theories. The discussion of "ontology", though useful in illuminating some relationships, has also been somewhat strange. For reasons we have considered, Quine maintains that there are no questions about "what there is" prior to or separable from the activity of theorizing, from the construction and refinement of theories.

THEORY AND OBSERVATION

In "Facts of the Matter" Quine notes that "ontology is not what mainly matters".[83] Putting together the various views we have considered so far, it is clearly theories that mainly matter. It is also clear from the discussion so far that Quine views theories as artifacts we produce and use to bridge our experiences and, as the scope of our theories becomes more general, to bridge other such bridges. And, on Quine's view, it is *collectively*, as a whole, that these artifacts bridge sensory stimulations and explain and organize experience. This is a consequence of holism, Quine's insistence that it is the whole of science—including common sense—that has empirical meaning.

Although Quine often focuses on the "fabric of science"—the network of theories we produce—science, in both the narrow and broadest sense, is not, on his view, *theories,* but the activity of constructing these. The activity includes, as the discussion of the previous section indicates, the positing of objects in the course of theory construction, the adoption of standards of evidence, and the evaluation of theories.

We can also say somewhat more specifically that Quine views theories as sets of sentences.[84]

> What sort of thing is a scientific theory? It is an idea, one might
> naturally say, or a complex of ideas. But the most practical way of
> coming to grips with ideas, and usually the only way, is by way of the
> words that express them. What to look for in the way of theories, then,
> are the sentences that express them.[85]

Quine's construal of theories as sets of sentences is consonant with his view that theorizing is fundamentally public, and it reflects the view, also discussed earlier, that the "smallest unit of empirical content" is a system of sentences. It is not because "ideas" would introduce subjective elements that they are eschewed for talk of sentences. The emphasis on linguistic entities, words initially and eventually sentences, is due to two factors: the difficulty in identifying "ideas",[86] and Quine's claim that it is only because of public language and theorizing that coherent experience is possible and anything like the "having" of "ideas" is possible. Thus, his remark above that "little can be done in the way of tracking thought processes except when we put words to them".

Earlier, in the context of outlining the shifts in focus Quine advocates, I noted that we would need to consider what, if anything, the notion of "observation sentences" would come to, given the views that systems of sentences have empirical content and that epistemology is the study, within science, of how we go about constructing theories. We were left, that is, with the general question of how, given these views, theories "face", or link up with, the world, a connection the postlogical positivist tradition forged with "observation sentences", and Quine discusses in terms of "empirical content".

It is worth repeating as we begin to explore Quine's account of empirical content that we are not just discussing scientific theories in the narrow sense. We have considered some of the relationships Quine maintains hold between scientific theorizing and common-sense theorizing in our discussion of what he has to say about ontology. Quine also claims that there are fundamental relationships between the goals and methods of what he views as three levels of theorizing.

Science in the narrow sense, is, Quine maintains, "self-conscious common sense", and philosophy "in turn, . . . as an effort to get clearer on things, is not to be distinguished in essential points of purpose and method from good and bad science".[87] Each activity attempts to make our experiences cohere, by providing bridges between them through the construction of theories.[88] Such efforts to bridge experience and other such bridges, become, respectively, more self-conscious and more systematic as they progress from common sense, to science, to philosophy. The extent of the differences between common sense, science and philosophy, on this view, are degrees of systemization and "self-consciousness".

I noted earlier that Quine also argues that all of our sentences show interconnections (he refers to their "interanimation" in one discussion[89]), and that they, and the theories they compose, are interdependent. Theories share empirical content, which is Quine's account of "the relation of scientific theory to sensory evidence".[90]

> What comes of the association of sentences with sentences is a vast verbal structure which, primarily as a whole, is multifariously linked to non-verbal stimulation.[91]

It is the "link"—its nature and its "forging"—to which we will now turn.

It is an obvious consequence of several arguments that we have considered that there are no observations outside theory, and no sentences that are not theoretical. The relevant positions (which are, of course, related) are the primacy of physical-object ontology, the impossibility of coherent sensory experience without theory, and the impossibility of ontology without theory.

Further, it is an obvious consequence of holism and the grounds for it (the lack of specifiable empirical content for most single sentences and the interconnectedness of sentences and, therefore, of theories) that sentences do not have empirical content in isolation from, or "independently" of, some number of others. (We can think, for example, of the principles of individuation necessary for even a rather "simple" sentence about physical objects as this becomes clear when we think about a child learning language.)

Nevertheless, Quine maintains that we can make sense of classifying some sentences as "observation sentences" and that we can characterize the use of these sentences as bringing experience to bear on theories.[92] But the "connection" between theories and experience that Quine outlines is fundamentally different from what Hempel and Nagel hoped for, and Kuhn despaired of. I will begin with Quine's account of the sentences he classifies as "observation sentences". I will then outline the nature of the connection they provide and conclude with Quine's account of the degree of evidential support our theories can enjoy.

Quine argues that although most single sentences do not have their own empirical content—content in isolation from a going body of theory—some sentences (occasion sentences) can be singled out and their empirical content roughly specified—by reference *to a community of speakers*. These sentences, Quine argues, can be classified as "observation sentences", for their stimulus conditions can be specified relevant to that community.

The relevant sentences, according to Quine, will be close to the "periphery of the network"—that is, they will be more obviously connected to publicly observable things and less likely to be affected by the presence or absence of collateral information. As such, the sentences will be such that most members of the relevant language community will assent to them in the *presence* of rather specific circumstances, and dissent from them in the *absence* of these. We must be able to specify both the conditions for assent and the conditions for dissent. The sentences Quine has in mind are not "standing sentences"; they are occasion sentences, sentences that will be assented to or dissented from only in relation to present and appropriate stimulation.[93]

> The less susceptible the stimulus meaning of an occasion sentence is to the influences of collateral information, the less absurdity there is in thinking of the stimulus meaning of the sentence as the meaning of the sentence. Occasion sentences whose stimulus meanings vary none under

the influence of collateral information may naturally be called *observation sentences,* and their stimulus meanings may without fear of contradiction be said to do full justice to their meanings.[94]

It is interesting to note that what we have dredged out, a notion of degree of observationality, is not beyond cleaning up and rendering respectable. . . . the observation sentences as we have identified them are just the occasion sentences on which there is pretty sure to be firm agreement on the part of well-placed observers. Thus they are just the sentences on which a scientist will tend to fall back when pressed by doubting colleagues.[95]

Now the sentences Quine is calling "observation sentences" are clearly *theoretical.* They do not have empirical content in isolation from a body of theory, but their "stimulus conditions", the empirical conditions under which members of a community will assent to them and dissent from them, can be specified.[96] The notion of "collateral information" (that such information does not play a role in the community's decision) has to do with the stimulus conditions; it is not the claim that these sentences have empirical meaning in isolation from a body of theory.

The sentences that would meet the criteria Quine outlines are also not necessarily "low-level", that is less theoretical, sentences, although Quine's use of the term 'periphery' to describe an "edge" of the "network of theories" might be construed to mean that only our most "basic" sentences about physical objects "face" experience. Depending on how we specify the community, the sentences that can serve as observation sentences are not restricted. There will be sentences that meet the conditions that are of a highly theoretical nature, for the relevant community can be restricted to a community of specialists.[97]

Despite their theoretical nature, observation sentences can be used, Quine argues, to give content to the claim that our theories are constrained by sensory experience. A theory will imply a number of observation conditionals, sentences of the form "Where there's smoke, there's fire", which predict that under certain conditions, certain consequences will follow.[98] Testing a theory becomes a matter of the testing of these observational conditionals in relation to the stimulus conditions that a relevant community recognizes.

The problem of relating theory to sensory stimulation may now be put less forbiddingly as that of relating theory formulations to observation sentences. In this we have a head start in that we recognize the observation sentences to be theory-laden. What this means is that terms embedded in observation sentences recur in the theory formulations.

What qualifies a sentence as observational is not a lack of such terms,
but just that the sentence taken as an undivided whole commands assent
consistently or dissent consistently when the same global sensory
stimulation is repeated.[99]

Again, an observation sentence does not have empirical content in isolation from a body of theory; nor can we use such sentences to conclusively
affirm or falsify a theory. When a prediction misfires, it will not be
clear which of the sentences of the embedding theory is the problem. In
addition, we can always adjust various aspects of our theory in subtle
ways in order to accommodate the apparent slippage with experience.

But holism and the demise of foundationalism change the nature of
the connection observation sentences can provide between experience and
theory. In short, we are no longer considering a relationship between *one*
theory and *the world*, for a consequence of the views that it is the system
of our theories that has empirical content and that there are no extratheoretical experiences is a coherence theory of evidence. And this account of
evidence incorporates a different construal of each part of the theory/
world connection.

I will begin with "the world" side. Although we can focus on an
individual theory and ascertain observational conditionals it implies, we
are not using these to test the theory by reference to *the world*, but by
reference to its coherence with our *other going theories* and with our
experiences. Experiences, for Quine, are at bottom the firings of our
sensory receptors, but we do not, of course, consciously "experience"
those firings.[100] We experience the world through the lens of our going
theories.

In terms of the other side of the connection, the "one theory" that
figures in the accounts of Hempel and Nagel, or the "one paradigm" that
figures in Kuhn's account, any such theory must also be compatible with
others of our going theories. (That is, although paradigms, on Kuhn's
account, are "all encompassing", this, as I suggested in Chapter Two,
requires the view that science communities are completely isolated entities.
Scientists who disagree about theories do not disagree with each other
about *everything*.) This means that any part of the larger network of our
going theories that is relevant (other scientific theories, logic, common-
sense theories, and so forth) can be brought to bear—indeed, *will* be—in
the appraisal of a theory by means of observational conditionals.

Thus, in the end, though we have salvaged the notion of an "observation sentence", we have moved quite far from the view of individual
predictions—or individual sentences—as the bearers of empirical meaning

and, therefore, as the testing ground of theories. We have also moved far from the view that individual theories stand alone. And we are certainly not demanding of a theory that it "correspond" to "the world". We are trying to see if what a theory implies in the way of observation coheres with our experiences, with the understanding that observation, and experience generally, are shaped by a going body of theory. When the nature and the role of observation sentences are so understood, skepticism about the ability to bring sensory evidence to bear on a theory dissipates. We judge theories by reference to their coherence with our sensory experiences and our other theories. What we cannot do—as Kuhn also saw—is bring a world "untheorized" to bear on any theory.

So the connection established between theories and evidence by these observation sentences is not the same connection sought or denied by more traditional philosophers of science. But neither is the "result". Quine argues that all of our theories are and will be underdetermined by the evidence we have or will have for them. This includes, Quine argues, our sentences about "ordinary" physical objects.

> The truths that can be said even in common-sense terms about ordinary things *are themselves* . . . *far in excess of any available data.* [There is a] basic indeterminacy: . . . events are less than determined by our surface irritations. This remains true even if we include all past, present, and future irritations of all the far-flung surfaces of mankind [*sic*] and probably even if we throw in an in fact unachieved ideal organon of scientific method besides. . . .
>
> Considered relative to our surface irritations, which exhaust our clues to an external world, molecules and their extraordinary ilk are thus much on a par with the most ordinary physical objects. The incompleteness of determination of molecular behavior by the behavior of ordinary things is hence only incidental to this more basic indeterminacy: *both* sorts of events are less than determined by our surface irritations.[101]

Perhaps the most straightforward way to render Quine's point about the degree of evidential support theories do and could enjoy would be to begin with something other than physical-object theory. If we begin with something like quantum theory Quine's claim about "under-determination" will, I think, be recognized as unproblematic.

Most of us have little or no trouble recognizing that the things we say in quantum theory, the generalizations we make, the objects we posit, and so on, exceed *all* the evidence for that theory. That is, we can easily conceive of there being alternative theories that though incompatible with quantum theory, are nevertheless commensurate with *all* the evidence we currently have for quantum theory. We can conceive of the possibility that we would eventually give up quantum theory for another theory that is incompatible with our present theory, but in keeping with all the evidence we currently have.[102] The point is one about *evidence*. Quantum theory is *underdetermined* by all the evidence we have for it.

Given the current stage of quantum theory, to say that it is underdetermined by the evidence is not controversial. But in the passage quoted above, Quine is making the point that the most commonplace things we say and take for granted—about, for example, physical objects—are no more determined by the evidence we have for them, or will, than are the sentences of quantum theory. It is conceivable that alternatives to our talk of physical objects, though incompatible with physical-object theory, could nevertheless be commensurate with *all* the evidence we have for physical objects. It is also conceivable that at a future time (and despite its current primacy) we will give up physical-object theory and adopt another theory, incompatible with our current theory, but commensurate with most of the evidence we currently have for the latter.

In short, there is "play"—or to use Quine's word, there is "slack"[103]— between even the *whole* of our network of theories and *all* of our sensory experiences.

Moreover, as Quine notes at the end of that passage, the relationship of evidence to theories, the underdetermination of the latter by the former, will not be altered by more inquiry, or even an "ideal" scientific method rigorously adhered to.

> Even if we by-pass such troubles [as are raised by assuming a final organon of scientific method] by identifying truth somewhat fancifully with the ideal result of applying scientific method outright to the whole future totality of surface irritations, still there is trouble in the imputation of uniqueness ("the *ideal* result"). . . . we have no reason to suppose that man's [*sic*] surface irritations even unto eternity admit of any one systematization that is scientifically better or simpler than all possible others. It seems likelier, if only on account of symmetries or dualities, that countless alternatives would be tied for first place. Scientific method is the way to truth, but it affords, even in principle, no unique definition of truth.[104]

Underdetermination, on this view, is a basic fact about the relationship between the things we say and the evidence we can have for saying them. There is no unique way of organizing our experiences commensurate with all the evidence we have, or will have.

Given the view that our sentences share sensory support and are, thus, fundamentally interdependent, and the views that all the sentences within the network are theoretical (the consequence of our discussion of physical-object theory), that all are subject to revision (a consequence of the collapse of the analytic/synthetic distinction), and that all sentences (even our most basic) are underdetermined by sensory evidence, on what does the "network" of our going theories rest? Have we worked ourselves into a position where skepticism about our theories or our theorizing is reasonable? The answer, on Quine's view, is "no", at least not skepticism of the ordinary variety.

I will outline, very briefly, the last of the pieces we will need to contrast the view of science that emerges in the positions I have outlined with those of positivism (in its early and later varieties) and those of Kuhn—in particular, the contrast with the view, common to both of these accounts, that science is autonomous.

We might think it plausible, given various issues and positions we considered in this and the preceding chapter, to view science with some skepticism—even to consider the possibility that all of our going theories might be wrong. Sandra Harding, reflecting on what she takes to be the implications of Kuhn's work, does indeed pose a skeptical question about science. The history of science, she suggests, indicates that it is reasonable to ask if we might eventually give up science. "As Kuhn pointed out, paradigmatic theories in particular areas of inquiry eventually wear out as fruitful guides to research. Shouldn't this also be true for science as a whole?"[105]

If we build on the positions of Quine's that I have outlined, the answer to Harding's question is, I think, an emphatic "no". Some of what makes the question dubious can be laid out straightforwardly.

In the first place, Harding, like Kuhn, is focusing here on science in the narrow sense, and not in the broader sense that Quine's arguments make compelling. Moreover, her question is about the methods of research and inquiry that *currently* characterize science communities. But the boundary allegedly separating the theories, methods, and goals of inquiry engaged in within these special communities from those of common-sense theorizing is, in several respects, a false boundary. The theorizing engaged in in the most esoteric fields of science shares a mutual dependency with common-sense theorizing. Thus, there is no sense to be made of doubting all of science in the narrow sense, *without doubting it all*. In addition, science in both the narrow and the broader sense is not the static entity the question presupposes. It is evolving constantly—a fact that *prompted* the question.

So perhaps the question should be recast to something like: "Couldn't it be that constructing theories, in the course of which we posit objects and develop standards of evidence, and using such theories to organize and predict our experiences, will eventually 'wear out' as a fruitful guide to experience?" Currently, this, and nothing else, is constitutive of science.

The flip side of the question (and it is the flip side and not a different question) is: "If we know that all our theories are underdetermined by the evidence we have for them, and that paradigmatic theories eventually fail and are replaced (I assume the sense of 'wearing out' Harding is using), isn't it reasonable to consider the possibility (or, more strongly, isn't it reasonable to *assume*) that all of our current theories are *false*?"

The most straightforward way of dealing with questions like these is to begin by asking ourselves just where we "could be" in the sense of an epistemological vantage point to ask whether all our theories could be "wrong"—or whether it could turn out (eventually) that we will give up "science". We must be asking these questions from *within* the same network of theories we are questioning, for the latter is the source of our very notions of evidence, reality, "wrong", and so on.

Moreover, even if these are coherent questions, the suggested answers are unwarranted. It is our own thinking about things, using the very notions of evidence and of objects (including ourselves) and an epistemology (which, in the case of empiricism, maintains that our only evidence for what happens is afforded by our sensory receptors through which we learn language, hear others' reports and theories, read theories, and ultimately have coherent experience), that has apparently led us to questioning the strength and the nature of the evidence we can have for what we say. We have arrived at the conclusion that our "truths" about ordinary things are underdetermined precisely by relying on some of what, for now, we *know*. The history of science, complete with its now discarded theories and revolutions, indicates that predictions can fail, and that when they do, theories will (eventually) wither—we will give them up. Skepticism, ironically, depends on our recognizing that there *is* a connection between experience and theories.[106]

So, the response to skepticism of the sort the above questions imply, is, I think, something like Quine's—again, with the understanding that Quine is discussing science in the inclusive sense.

> Radical skepticism . . . is not of itself incoherent. Science is vulnerable to illusion on its own showing . . . and the skeptic may be seen merely as overreacting when he [*sic*] repudiates science across the board.
> Experience might still take a turn that would justify . . . doubts about external objects. Our success in predicting observations might fall off sharply, and concomitantly with this we might begin to be somewhat

successful in basing predictions upon dreams or reveries. At that point
we might reasonably doubt our theory of nature in even fairly broad
outlines. *But our doubts would still be immanent, and of a piece with
the scientific endeavor.*[107]

Thus, the last of the three boundaries we set out to discuss, and
perhaps the most central of these, has collapsed: the alleged boundary
between epistemology and science. An epistemology (whether empiricism
or something else), a theory of theorizing, can emerge only *within science,*
within our attempts to explain things—in this case, in our attempts to
explain our explaining. Any skepticism that is warranted will be warranted by evidence (however much that evidence conflicts with how we
expected things to go), and the dependence of a reasonable skepticism on
evidence indicates that skepticism cannot be wholesale, however broad.

We should expect, then, given the history of science and our current
account of the strength of the evidence we can have for any theory, that
science will continue to evolve—constantly responding to what is going
on within science, broadly construed, and our experiences.

Could all the theories we now hold be replaced eventually? Certainly.
But not at once. And not on the basis of something "other than" science—
with the understanding that even our understanding of what science *is,*
and the more specific methods we have used to explain and predict
experience, have, and will continue to, evolve.

Reductionism

No discussion of empiricism would be complete without a discussion of
reductionism—or at least so criticisms of empiricism would imply. Logical
positivism and the postlogical positivist tradition have long been associated with two "isms"—materialism and "reductionism"—although the
latter term is used to refer to what are, in fact, distinguishable positions.[108]
Both "isms" have been ascribed to Quine, although it is not always clear
what kind of reductionism writers have in mind.

Sandra Harding recently described Quine's views as ones many theorists find "still far too reductionist".

> Quine recommended substituting pragmatic and behaviorist questions
> for the traditional philosophical ones, replacing what he thought were
> undesirable philosophical preoccupations with what he thought were
> desirable scientific ones. We can appreciate the pragmatic tendencies in
> his thinking without having to agree to his behaviorism—to his program

for replacing philosophy with what appears to many theorists as a still
far too reductionist and obsessively empiricist social science.[109]

It should by now be clear that Quine explicitly rejects one kind of
reductionism long associated with the positivist and postlogical tradition,
as he describes it:

> that to each statement . . . there is associated a unique range of possible
> sensory events such that the occurrence of any of them would add to the
> likelihood of truth of the statement, and that there is associated also
> another unique range of possible sensory events whose occurrence would
> detract from that likelihood.[110]

The rejection of reductionism so understood is just the third of the five
shifts outlined earlier that Quine advocates.[111] It is a consequence of the
demise of the view that individual sentences have empirical content, a
denial that is also a death knell to the analytic/synthetic distinction.

Because Quine is increasingly cited in feminist criticism and other
criticism as representing something like the "natural end point" of empiricism,[112] and empiricism is so generally associated with "reductionism" by
its critics, it is worth spending time to consider the relationship between
empiricism, or, more correctly, an empiricist account of science, and
"reductionism". I will explore Quine's metaphysics in this section, and
what I think is the interesting kind of reductionism that might be at issue
in his account of science. I will offer some reasons why it is plausible to
distinguish the latter kind of reductionism, perhaps appropriately attributed to Quine, from another and stronger reductionist approach frequently ascribed to empiricism per se. It will at least emerge that empiricism and one strong version of reductionism are separable. The discussion
will also enable us to consider Quine's view of "mental objects" and his
advocacy of behaviorism, the source of the charge that his account of
science is reductionist and perhaps of the charge that his "social science"
is "obsessively empiricist". His views about "mental objects" are among
those we will need to be clear about when we later consider his proposal
that epistemology be "naturalized" and the tenability of the view that the
primary epistemological agents are individuals.

PHYSICALISM

Quine's metaphysics has been described, by Richard Schuldenfrei among
others, as materialism.[113] Quine is not a materialist. He subscribes to a
physicalist metaphysics, and the difference between the two positions is

important and relevant to how some of his positions are to be understood, and to understanding the relationship of empiricism to one kind of reductionism.

In a recent paper, Quine offers a formulation of physicalism that, although related to an earlier position, is also something of a revision. He characterizes the current formulation as "incomplete" because it relies on a specification of predicates that are not yet available, a specification, which our current understandings of "what happens" suggest, will be supplied (if they become available) by physics.

Quine begins the discussion by reconsidering his earlier formulation of physicalism:

> The physicalist does not insist on an exclusively corporeal ontology. He [*sic*] is content to declare bodies to be *fundamental* to nature in somewhat this sense: there is no difference *in the world* without a difference in states of bodies.[114]

Since the notion of physical difference does not apply to mathematical objects like classes, these objects can be part of our overall ontology without challenging the physicalist ontology. But even this earlier formulation of physicalism is not materialism, allowing as it does, for mathematical objects.

Given the shift in physics from particle models to field theory, Quine argues that the basic notion of physical difference (the core of physicalism) needs to be recast, for the explicit link with physical-object ontology (and, therefore, with "states of bodies") has been severed in what Quine refers to as our "most refined" theory—our most general account of what happens.

Nevertheless, Quine maintains, though materialism will not do as a general view about what counts as a factual matter, physicalism, suitably rethought, will. Specifically, physicalism will still allow for the notion of physical difference:

> What now of physicalism? To profess materialism after all this, would seem grotesquely inappropriate; but physicalism, reasonably reformulated, retains its vigor and validation.
> ... What now is the claim of physicalism? Simply that there is no difference in matters of fact without a difference in the fulfillment of the physical-state predicates by space-time [or "place-time"] regions.[115]

This formulation of physicalism is intended as an account of what counts as "facts of the matter". Physical difference is physical change and only physical change counts as "a difference in facts of the matter"; only physical states count as "facts of the matter".

Quine's metaphysics is not materialism, but we can ask whether his understanding of physicalism comes only to the ruling out of "nonphysical entities" that are alleged to "make a difference", and no more than this. If it is only the latter, then unless we are committed to the existence of nonphysical entities (soul, for example) that affect the way things go, the thesis is minimal and, for many of us, uncontroversial. A more contentious issue is whether physicalism so understood is a reductionist thesis of the strong sort advocated by those who envisioned a "unity of science": whether, as Wartofsky explicates reductionism, it entails that all theories are, in principle, "able to be translated into a canonical reduction language—presumably either that of sense data or of physical things in space and time".[116]

It is clear from earlier discussion that Quine does not hold the view that theories or sentences about physical objects can be translated into a sense data language, and the notion of "physical things", he argues above, has given way to the fulfillment of physical-state predicates by place-time regions. So, in part, the answer to the question of whether Quine's formulation of physicalism is a reductionist thesis of the strong sort Wartofsky describes will depend on whether it is a consequence of physicalism that in order for something to "count" as an object or an event, it must, in principle, be able to be couched in terms of the fulfillment of physical-state predicates by place-time regions—or in terms of whatever it is that our science of the time suggests is the most basic way of discussing physical states and events.

Whether we would regard an affirmative answer to the latter as an indication that physicalism is a "reductionist" thesis will depend on how we construe the "in principle" clause. Some things are clear, however. The issue of *explanation*— that the most basic ways of describing physical states and events "explains" the rest of what we say—is not a view that can be ascribed to Quine. Given Quine's account of empirical meaning, it is the whole of science that *explains*, that bridges sensory stimulations; each part of the fabric, on his view, is supported by the rest. If, as Quine maintains, sentences about molecules are "gibberish" in isolation from a body of theory about macroscopic physical objects, one cannot replace physical-object talk with molecule, or place-time, talk. Finally, in considering whether physicalism is a reductionist thesis, we will need to consider what, if any, notion of "translation" is at issue or implied by Quine's views.

These questions are not easy, and here I will only outline some aspects of Quine's work that are relevant to the kinds of concern currently being raised by critics of empiricism, including feminist science critics. We can begin by noting the central role granted to physics in Quine's account of "facts of the matter". The emphasis on physical-state predicates and place-time regions as the criterion for "facts", and not on, say, molecules, cells, biological processes, and social groups, suggests the view that at whatever level we are describing change or states—in sociology, chemistry, biology, and so forth—to count as a "fact", the description and explanation of factual change or state needs to be able to be expressed— *eventually,* at least in principle—in some system that, in turn, can be expressed—*eventually,* at least in principle—in terms of the fulfillment of place-time regions. (The "in principle" twice is meant to underscore that we might not be talented enough, or *interested* enough, to undertake the "reduction".) But unless we can make sense of that kind of specification of the alleged state or change we are positing or considering, Quine's formulation of physicalism maintains that we do not have a "fact of the matter" at hand.

So understood, physicalism might come to little more than that, for example, it would be surprising if at a fictional "end of inquiry" in which we understood all of physics, we found ourselves unable, *in principle,* to predict chemistry.[117] Given our current descriptions of these sciences, that outcome seems highly unlikely.

If physicalism is the latter, it might be the reflection of what is a psychologically compelling view given our current view that things are "made up" of other things, and that the different sciences study different levels of that "make up": namely, that some part of science (that might, at some future time, be something other than physics) "underwrites" the rest.

In terms of the issue of whether "translation" is involved in this understanding of physicalism (for reductionism, in Wartofsky's account, which I used above, and as commonly understood, is an issue about translation and metaphysics[118]), we can also consider Quine's account of the canonical notation of theories. Our "most serious" and inclusive theory of the world, Quine maintains, will be, by current lights, a first-order theory—a theory able to be formalized in first-order quantification.

> Taking the canonical notation thus austerely . . . we have just these basic constructions: predication, universal quantification, and the truth functions. . . . What . . . confronts us as a scheme for systems of the world is that structure so well understood by present day logicians, the logic of quantification of calculus of predicates. . . .
> Not that the idioms thus renounced are supposed to be unneeded in the market place or the laboratory. . . . The doctrine is only that such a canonical idiom can be abstracted and then adhered to in the statement

of one's scientific theory. The doctrine is that all traits of reality worthy of the name can be set down in an idiom of this austere form if in any idiom.[119]

Our theories, referred to in these passages as our "systems of the world", can be rendered in first-order quantification, and the universe of discourse will be discrete objects. Are we to understand that in our most serious theory, a theory that "legitimates" by underwriting the rest, these objects will be place-time regions? Are the predicates of "the system of the world" (or of "that statement of one's scientific theory") the predicates for whose specification we will turn to physics?

The foregoing might be taken as an indication that physicalism is, at bottom, a commitment to a strong version of reductionism, but we have considered a number of Quine's positions that indicate he does not hold the view that we can "reduce" or translate talk on one level, which involves one set of objects, into talk of another set of objects, in order to find a resting place in something like *the most real* objects.

First, Quine denies that physical-object ontology is "unreal", or able to be doubted on the basis of ontologies of unobservables (subatomic particles or any other object posited in physics)— or that it could be *replaced* by these. Rather, he maintains that our ontologies of subatomic particles (and the point would hold for place-time regions) are no more or less real than the ontology of middle-size physical objects. Indeed, he argues that scientific ontologies are *dependent* on physical-object ontology in important ways.

A second reason for doubting that Quine has any particular universe of discourse in mind for an overall "system of the world", as those advocating a strong thesis of reductionism do, are his general views about ontology. Though he has sometimes turned to what he calls "reductive reinterpretation", exploring cases in which we can reinterpret an ontology by identifying it with another,[120] Quine notes in the passage I have just cited that the "idioms . . . renounced" when a theory is formalized "are not unneeded in the market place or the laboratory". And in a passage immediately following it, he is more specific about the "ontological questions" that remain after one has arrived at a "canonical form".

> Once we have said of a proposed theory that its constructions are to be predication, quantification, and the truth functions, we have settled just the logic of the theory.
> Questions then remain not only of its vocabulary of general terms, but also of its universe of discourse: the range of values of its variables of quantification. The very meaningfulness of quantification would seem

to presuppose some notion as to what objects are to count as values of variables.

Complete explicitness on this point is rendered unnecessary, however, by the fact that our quantifications usually depend for their truth upon only rather special denizens of a universe that admits of variation in other respects.[121]

In the last remark Quine is alluding to a view of ontology that we have discussed in some detail: namely, that there are no "absolute" ontological questions. Questions of "what there is" are always relevant to a background theory, and any particular "theory form" can be interpreted "anew" by picking a new universe of discourse over which to quantify.[122] In short, the relationship between ontology and theory does not allow for the notion that we pick out an ontology (or discover one) and *then* decide what to say about the objects (then proceed to theorize about them). In addition, Quine maintains that ontologies are not really what matter. What really matters are theories, those things we construct to bridge sensory stimulations, in the course of which we posit objects.

So clearly physicalism cannot represent a commitment to what there is (or "really" is), for example, the fulfillment of physical-state predicates by place-time regions, that is *prior to* or independent of what our going theories *say* there is. Nor does it entail that ontologies other than that of physics are unreal.

However, we can say some additional things about the kind of ontology presumed by Quine's account of the canonical notation of theories that are relevant to current concerns. It is clear that if theories must be of the sort that they can be rendered in first-order quantification, Quine is committed to the view that our "scientific" theory, our most inclusive theory, will incorporate an ontology of discrete entities. (And perhaps the latter will include events, if "event" is not understood as a primitive term but used to refer to the "material content of any portion of space time",[123] Quine's most general account of "an object".) And given that view of the canonical form of theories, we might ask whether such an "austere" form would or could "capture" all that we want to capture of what goes on. For example, would a first-order theory of the sort outlined "capture" causation? And of relevance to issues currently of importance in the biological sciences, would such an austere form "capture" biological processes?[124]

If we are tempted to answer "no" to these last questions, then we are brought back to our earlier question of whether we would find it surprising if we could know "all there was to know" about physics and not be able to predict, for instance, biology. Moreover, so far at least, physicalism does not seem to entail (although Quine may indeed envision such a project) that we would be interested (if, indeed, it were possible) in "reductively *reinterpreting*" the objects, events, and processes talked about in various theories (in evolutionary biology, for example) in the terms of our current physics. It is perfectly compatible with physicalism itself and others of Quine's positions, that although physicalism maintains there are "facts of the matter" in biological processes only if these involve the fulfillment of physical state predicates by place-time regions, we *need* biology, complete with its ontology of genes, cells, and processes, and the relations posited in biological theories, to state some of what happens.

Moreover, there is no reason not to have *all* of that. Given Quine's account of what is to count as "facts of the matter", the issue is: can biology be "legitimized", that is underwritten, by, for example, physics— at this time, our most basic understanding of what happens? This is not the claim that physics explains biology, since it is as a whole that our theories explain. So it would seem that the "underwriting" posited here would not be problematic.

To further explicate the notion of underwriting involved, I will next consider some of Quine's more controversial views, those concerning "mental objects". His views about these illuminate some of what is at issue (or might be) when reductionism of the sort I have been discussing is at issue.

MENTAL OBJECTS

One aspect of Quine's views that leads Schuldenfrei and others to describe his metaphysics as "materialist" and "reductionist" are his views about "mental objects". Schuldenfrei, for example, describes what he calls Quine's "world view" as

> an anti-Cartesian materialist view. It is anti-Cartesian materialism
> because it asserts, first, that there is fundamentally only one kind of
> entity in the world, and that kind is the kind studied by natural
> scientists—physical objects; and, second, that there is only one kind of
> knowledge in the world, and it is the kind that natural scientists have.[125]

We have considered issues relevant to the second view Schuldenfrei attributes to Quine, a view about knowledge and "natural scientists". Schuldenfrei's account of Quine's epistemology is at least misleading, and unless he means that "common sense" and philosophical theorizing *are* "that kind" of "knowing", the account as stated is just wrong. Quine denies there are distinctions between common-sense knowledge and the knowledge developed in the natural sciences.[126]

Also misleading is Schuldenfrei's use of a distinction between metaphysics and epistemology as if Quine would recognize a distinction between (or prioritize) metaphysical views and views about epistemology. We have seen that the distinction is untenable given a number of Quine's positions.

Of more relevance to the issue of reductionism and empiricism is Schuldenfrei's claim about "Quine's metaphysics" and, in particular, the view of mental objects he attributes to Quine, a view perhaps also underlying Harding's remark that Quine's view is "obsessively empiricist". Schuldenfrei states that in Quine's positions,

> Sentences have replaced thoughts and dispositions to assent have replaced belief.[127]

> [Quine's claim that there is only one kind of entity in the world and that it is the kind studied by natural scientists—physical objects] conflicts with the claims . . . that there are minds, thoughts, ideas . . . over and above those which can be dealt with within the framework of physical objects. What is useful in talk about such entities Quine believes can be captured by behavioristic psychology—which he sees as the physics of people.[128]

It is tempting to accept the quip that "Quine's philosophy of mind is only skin deep". But the quip is unfair. We need to consider the issues that prompt Schuldenfrei and others to attribute a denial of thoughts, ideas, and beliefs to Quine, or lead them to argue that Quine *replaces* these notions with sentences and dispositions or "reduces" these to behaviors[129]—particularly when the views so ascribed are also assumed to be inevitable consequences of empiricism.

I noted earlier that Quine has declined to grant ontological status to "mental objects" and that he interprets the mental idiom in behaviorist terms. But there are problems in taking his view of "persons", or "minds", or "mental objects" to be "materialist".

For one thing, although Quine argues that we should not acknowledge one class of so-called mental objects, "meanings", this is not a decision prompted by a commitment to a physicalist metaphysics. The inclusion of "meanings" (either as "mental objects" as we are discussing, or as "abstract objects") would not challenge the physicalist account of what happens any more than the inclusion of classes does, as long as "meanings" are not taken to be the sort of things that can bring about a change in the "facts of the matter". The point is that Quine's argument against including "meanings" in our overall ontology is based on the impossibility of giving clear identity criteria for "meanings",[130] and his belief that we can get along quite nicely without them—unlike classes that do have clear identity criteria and without which we cannot do.

Quine has also consistently maintained that the objects posited in mentalistic idiom—ideas, beliefs, and the like—are an appropriate subject of *study,* but they are as yet too unclarified to be used in explanations. We want (or would accept) a theory that legitimates (that is, underwrites) belief talk, or some of it, in the sense I discussed in the previous section. But, for a number of reasons, Quine apparently thinks we cannot have it. The reasons include the fact that there is not a "logic of belief", a way of individuating beliefs using mentalistic idiom, a way of generalizing about them (except in a most rudimentary way), or a way of predicting them— some of what Quine views to be the perhaps insurmountable difficulties of developing an "intensional logic", a topic he explores in a number of discussions.[131]

Thus, Quine recommends that "beliefs" and the like be studied, and he suggests that behaviors are a public and intersubjective way of *determining* and *individuating* them— not that behaviors *are* mental states or should (or could) *replace* mental states (whatever "mental states" turn out to be). Nor does he, as some argue, "write off" "mental objects" as unimportant.[132] We can, on his view, keep and use belief talk to the extent that behaviors legitimate it by allowing us to individuate beliefs—this means keeping some, but not all, psychology.

> My position is that the notions of thought and belief are very worthy objects of philosophical and scientific clarification and analysis, and that they are in equal measure very ill suited for use as instruments of philosophical and scientific clarification and analysis.[133]

Apparently, it is Quine's interpretation of mental idiom in behaviorist terms that leads Schuldenfrei and others to characterize his views (or empiricism generally) as denying the existence of things like ideas. What Quine denies is that there are nonphysical, mental "entities". Quine also makes it clear in his discussion of physicalism and in a recent response to Schuldenfrei[134] that stimulus-response behaviorism may not, in the end, do all that we want, but that some sort of behaviorist psychology will. (As I noted earlier, Quine describes himself as being as much of a behaviorist as "anyone in his [*sic*] right mind would be.") "What it is we want", on Quine's view, is a way of attributing and individuating "mental states" like beliefs. "Behaviors" are a means of doing these things, but they are neither *identical with* the objects discussed in mental idiom nor *explanatory* of them on his view.

In his discussion of physicalism, Quine hints at the implications for psychology of a physicalist metaphysics. It is clear that, on his view, the neurosciences, and not behaviorist psychology, are the places in which *explanations* of mental states should be sought. If the notion of "mental state" is to be an object of study for the neurosciences, then it is also clear that Quine's notion of these states is that they are physical states. Schuldenfrei is certainly correct that Quine is not a dualist.

> Mental states and events do not reduce to behavior, nor are they explained by behavior. They are explained by neurology, when they are explained. But their behavioral adjuncts serve to specify them objectively. When we talk of mental states or events subject to behavioral criteria, we can rest assured that we are not just bandying words; there is a physical fact of the matter, a fact ultimately of elementary physical states.
> ... Causal explanations of psychology are to be sought in physiology, of physiology in biology, of biology in chemistry, and of chemistry in physics—in the elementary physical states.[135]

But it is just as clear that this is not a materialist view of "minds". Minds are not being discussed *as* "physical objects", nor does Quine equate the objects we talk about in mental idiom with the brain, with brain states, or with the subatomic particles of the brain. Nor does he suggest a reduction of the "mind" to subatomic particles or physical-state predicates. In fact, it is not clear that a list of "correlations"—a one-to-one mapping of behaviors and neurophysiological events—will ever be forthcoming.

So, at least in the case of "mental states", a commitment to physicalism does not involve (at least it does not entail) a commitment to the "reducibility" of one ontology into the more fundamental ontology of place-time regions. Quine advocates that we use behaviors to ascertain mental states and, in so doing, know at least in terms of behaviors that they can be underwritten—in principle—by our most general account of what happens.

> To repudiate mental entities is not to deny that we sense or even that we are conscious; it is merely to report and try to describe these facts without assuming entities of a mental kind.[136]

So far, the views we have considered come to the following: there is no difference in mental states without a difference in physical states (or without a difference in the fulfillment of the physical-state predicates, and so forth). In other words, people are not magic. They are physical objects in a physical world. If they undergo change or it makes sense to talk about them in terms of a "state", we are positing a physical change in the first case, a physical state in the second.

But questions remain that are relevant to the issue of reductionism. The account Quine gives of the "casual explanations" to be sought for "mental states" in a passage above—in which he maintains that these explanations are to be sought in physiology, and explanations for the latter are to be sought in biology, and so on—does raise the question of what the notion of "explanation" is that is at work here. I suggested earlier, and reiterate the suggestion in this context, that physicalism and this particular claim about the explanation of "mental states" might be the view that, in the end, it is the possibility (whether or not we try it) of explaining mental states and events in neurophysiology, and the latter in biology, and so on, that *underwrites* our talk of "ideas" and "beliefs". If the notion of "explanation" is simply the view that this sort of "reductive reinterpretation" would finance our talk of mental states, then unless we are dualists or committed to the view that mental states are not appropriately ascribed to individuals,[137] the reinterpretation so envisioned need not be troublesome. More specifically, it does not commit us to the view that mental states are not real or that they are unimportant.

Moreover, though my interpretation of Quine's notion of reductionism may be (from some points of view) a too charitable one, I noted earlier that it is likely that the more general conclusion about mental states that Quine tends to is that, in fact, they will *not* be so underwritten—that is, in the end, things like molecules and beliefs are different.

The point can be made this way. When we are considering this sense of "explanation", the sense in which it is an issue of underwriting or legitimizing another level of discourse in terms of a current understanding of the most basic stuff things are "made up of", molecules are unproblematic. They are able to be individuated, and they are clearly physical stuff. Whether or not we do undertake "underwriting" molecules, the "in principle" possibility that physicalism entails is that we can say that what goes on that involves molecules is not magic.

Beliefs, however, are perhaps, on Quine's view, different. It may be that Quine does not think that kind of underwriting will, in fact, be possible, and for the reasons outlined above, to do with the lack of a logic of belief. So the kind of "causal explanation" Quine projects, again assuming it is one that involves "underwriting", is probably one he does not think can be pulled off. His move to talking about behaviors, again not as replacements for beliefs or reductions of the latter to behaviors, but as a way of individuating at least some beliefs, may reflect his pessimism about that underwriting.

Two last points about what Quine calls "the physicalist thesis" should be noted. The first is that Quine would argue that this metaphysical commitment, a general statement of ontology, emerges from and *is contained within* our going theories, with the exception, of course, of any that posit nonphysical entities that are alleged to make a difference. Quine insists that metaphysics and science are inseparable.

The second and related point is that physicalism is, of course, an empirical hypothesis, and not above revision.[138] If changes in our theories require that it be given up, it will be.

A last point about reductionism (or rather the mention of a cluster of issues) is also warranted. I have tried, by implication at least, to separate from the pack of "reductionisms" currently at issue in a number of contexts a kind of "reductionism" that does not entail that physics is "paradigmatic" in several senses: that does not entail that all things that are to count as explanations must "look like" the explanations we find in classical physics—that is, that all explanations must incorporate laws, or the positing of hierarchical and linear relationships among discrete entities. Nor does the view I have explicated entail that the only objects and/or relations that are real are those we need in physics.

The sense of reductionism I think is appropriately ascribed to Quine is this. If, à la George Burns, you were going to create a fish ex nihilio, you would create subatomic particles (or building blocks of some sort)[139] and from the molecules and proteins and cells and. . . . And when you were done with all this, you would have a fish. There is nothing left out. You would not (could not) create all of physics and chemistry and all the other denizens of the universe and this fish—and still be free to decide how fish will *behave*. Physics is not insolatable. The basic stuff, its nature, settles issues about what will and will not happen at "higher levels"—but this does not mean that studying quarks is an efficient way of learning about fish; nor is studying fish an efficient way of learning about quarks. But truths about each are not independent of truths about the other. I am stressing relationships again.

It is compatible with this understanding of reductionism that what is to be gained in the way of advancing our understanding of our world by trying to "underwrite" the ontologies, relationships, and processes in, for example, the biological sciences, with talk of "place-time" regions and physical-state predicates is an enhancement of our understanding of the most general and basic picture of things—with the understanding that *the full picture, understanding, and explanation of what happens will be inclusive,* paraphrasing Quine, *of everything we say at every level.*

If I have missed or blurred subtleties that others find at stake even in terms of the sense of reductionism I have outlined, then the foregoing can be interpreted as a suggestion that when we refer to a view or a project as "reductionist" (whether pejoratively or as a way of praising it), we need to be as clear as we can about what we think is at stake. If we take reductionism to be *the same as* empiricism (whatever that would mean), or a commitment to "linear explanations" rather than holistic approaches, or a commitment to eternal objects rather than processes, or a commitment to deterministic explanations rather than something else that in some (or many) contexts (evolutionary theory, quantum theory, and so forth) is more appropriate, then we need to say so—and as clearly as we can.

A Remaining Boundary

In his autobiography[140] Quine muses about what he calls his "disdain of conceptual [boundaries]", a disdain evidenced in a number of the arguments we have considered in this chapter.

> My love of earthly boundaries . . . stacks up oddly with my disdain of conceptual ones. My challenge of the boundary between analytic and synthetic statements is notorious, and I have been at pains to blur the boundaries between natural science, mathematics, and philosophy.[141]

So it is interesting that Quine's work to rub out boundaries so carefully forged and tenaciously defended by traditional empiricism and the earlier and later phases of the positivist tradition never included a challenge to the alleged boundary between science and values. It is particularly interesting, given that Quine maintains that there is no "natural" boundary between common-sense theorizing and science in the narrow sense, or between either and philosophical thinking. Clearly, our common-sense dealings with the world, including those involving physical objects, are permeated with values, and one major area of philosophical thinking has, from the beginning, been a concern with values. But Quine incorporates within the area of philosophy he calls "scientific philosophy" and describes himself as engaged in only those studies of moral and analytic values that are "of an analytic cast . . . and apt to offer little in the way of inspiration or consolation",[142] and we have seen that his account of common-sense theory focuses on our theorizing about physical objects.

Indeed, Quine proclaims the boundary between science and values as strongly as he questions virtually every other boundary separating science from other things, while he also notes that our initial learning of values and of the appropriate use of value terms takes place at the *same time* that we are learning about physical objects.

> Scientific theory stands proudly and notoriously aloof from value judgments.[143]

> I think that what sets morals apart from scientific theory is a substantive point of modern scientific theory itself: a scientific doctrine as to the origins and basis of morality. Science sees the moral law no longer as coeval with the cosmos, but as the work of society. Therefore science addresses itself to the origins of the moral law, among other things, *but does not incorporate its content.* This divorce of science from moral values is a sophisticated manifestation, reflecting no significant quirk in language learning.[144]

However, in a more recent discussion devoted exclusively to exploring the nature of values, Quine argues there is one "legitimate mixture of ethics and science", one that, he states, "somewhat mitigates the methodological predicament of ethics".[145] The methodological predicament of ethics, on Quine's view, is that although scientific theories are constrained and sustained by what he calls "empirical controls", there are no such constraints on values. We can talk of objectivity in terms of science—of beliefs and theories being more or less warranted than others—but the notion of "objectivity" does not, on Quine's view, similarly apply to moral values.

> Scientific theories . . . are sustained by empirical controls, partial and devious though they be. It is a bitter irony that *so vital a matter as the difference between good and evil should have no comparable claim to objectivity.* No wonder there have been efforts since earliest times to work a justification of moral values into the fabric of what might pass for factual science.[146]

According to Quine, the legitimate mixture that can somewhat mitigate ethics' predicament would be the importation into ethical reasoning of a method used in science: specifically, the reducing of some axioms to others to show that the resulting statement is one already accepted. In the case of ethical axioms, the method can be used to show that the values that can be deduced from the axiom one wants accepted are themselves already recognized as valuable.[147]

There is, however, one other "mixing" of science and values that Quine himself engages in in several discussions,[148] and it is alluded to (as legitimate) in the passage quoted above in which Quine maintains that science does, in fact, get into the business of explaining the *origins* of moral values. For his own part, Quine seems to hold the views that although values are social, they are derivatively so[149] for they are probably grounded in natural selection and inherited by individuals; and the view that all societies share similar interests and concerns, and so do most of their members, so that moral conflicts are not frequent and the lack of a way of resolving them is not a pressing matter.[150]

Implicit in these views is an assumption that an evolutionary explanation is a satisfactory way of assuring ourselves that the values a society incorporates are "sound". (That is, such values have evolved by "natural selection"; how could they be bad?) These several views, and the assumption, are clear in various of Quine's discussions.

> Normally and typically there is agreement in the community as to what is to count as morally good; for morality, like language itself, is a community matter.[151]

> [While my account of how we are trained in terms of moral behavior] represents each of us as pursuing exclusively his [*sic*] own private satisfactions . . . [t]hanks to the moral values that have been trained into us . . . plus any innate moral beginnings that there may have been, there is no clash of interests as we pursue our separate ways. Our scales of values blend in social harmony.[152]

> [Such traits] as fellow feeling and altruistic inclinations have surely been favored by natural selection, being favorable to survival of society. People are thus born with a moral head start. This, and not training, is probably the main reason for there being widespread agreement on basic moral issues, even among very dissimilar peoples.[153]

> Moral values may be expected to vary less radically than language from one society to another, even when the societies are isolated. True, there are societies whose bans and licenses boggle our sheltered imaginations. But we can expect a common core, since the most basic problems of societies are bound to run to type. Morality touches the common lot of mankind [*sic*].[154]

As is clear in these passages, there is no small amount of tension between Quine's characterization of values as a "community matter" and as socially inculcated, and his view that values are inherited by individuals, chosen by natural selection, and social only in a "derivative sense". The specific issue (or hornet's nets of issues) concerning whether values are "traits" (let alone whether *traits* are genetically determined and selected for by natural selection), or whether values are inherently social, is one I will not address here, although we will return to it in later discussion. The issues that will concern us in the next two chapters, and again in the last, though related to these issues, can be talked about more generally as involving the alleged boundary between science and values.

One issue concerns a view clearly implied by Quine, and widely held, that there is no adjudicating values—no judging them in the way that "scientific claims" (I am using the latter in the broad sense) can be judged and adjudicated by reference to *evidence*. The basis for Quine's skepticism (and, I suspect, for the skepticism others feel), is the view that values (with the exception of his own discussion of natural selection) are ungrounded—and unable *to be* grounded— in how things *are*. Thus, Quine states above that moral claims have no "comparable claim to objectivity"—comparable, that is, to the claims available to science—because values are not subject to "empirical controls".

But the exception is a very telling one in terms of the boundary alleged to be real between science and values. Contrary to what Quine maintains in the passage quoted above, his appeal to natural selection, indeed any use of science, to *explain* the origins of values does not keep science out of the business of values. It results precisely in the "incorporation of values" into the "content of science". A "value judgment" on "values" *is issued within* science. Values, assumed by Quine to be cross-cultural and, for the most part, uncontroversial, when they are also argued to be the "product" of natural selection, are *good*. Under the rubric of natural selection, they provide for survival, and they meet the common needs of societies, and of humankind.

In later discussion, I will support the *spirit* of Quine's use of science, of the knowledge we acquire about how things are being brought to bear on moral, social, and political values. That project *must*, I will urge, be undertaken. But that sort of project involves science (in both the narrow and inclusive sense) far more deeply in the business of values than Quine acknowledges, and we have to be quite self-conscious about what we are doing when we get into the business of "explaining" values. The use of natural selection, as Quine and others use it, to explain values, would justify *any* moral values we could provide an evolutionary explanation for. Moreover, of course, Quine's *use* of science to underwrite values suggests that values are "objective" in a way that Quine maintains elsewhere values cannot be.

The "moral" of this short story is one we will return to frequently, but it can be outlined briefly here. As long as we attempt to separate values from science as Quine claims they should be separated—at least, he maintains science should stand "aloof" from them—then, however precariously or inconsistently we manage to keep them separated (or define them as such), Quine is probably right about values. If values remain separated from what we can ascertain about how things *are*, if we advocate them or praise them or adopt them without reference to what we come to know about how things are, there's nothing "objective" about them. If left unevaluated, they become incorporated in the content of science, and then ideology has a field day—particularly when we continue to declare that they are *not* so incorporated.

But the separation is unnecessary, and as Quine's own use of natural selection indicates, it is also pernicious if science is going to get into the business of explaining the origins of values while also declaring itself "aloof". As we shall see, a number of sciences have long been trying to walk that impossible tightrope.

So, we will need to talk about the other side of the boundary— the one Quine, among others, so desperately wants to hold on to and proclaims as if we all know it is so: that science does not itself incorporate values, that it stands "aloof" from values, and that values are not incorporated in its content. That, as the research of the last three decades indicates, and we will discuss in the next two chapters, is just false. The overthrow of this "boundary", a last mile Quine might have walked, is one we will need to come back to, and we will need to begin to walk it.

Science without Boundaries—Except One

We can now briefly summarize the basic differences and continuities between Quine's view of science and the views that characterize the two traditions we considered in the previous chapter, views that, I have argued, continue to shape two current discourses about science, one engaged in by many philosophers of science and scientists, the other underlying the categories and assumptions incorporated in a number of social studies of science.

Quine, like Kuhn, rejects the rigidity and naïvetè of the Hempel/Nagel approach to science, with its clear distinctions between observation sentences and theoretical sentences, between a context of discovery and a context of justification, between analytic sentences and synthetic sentences, and between metaphysics and science.

Quine also addresses a number of the questions Kuhn addresses: the relationship between a current conceptual framework (including theories and logical truths) and observation, the ways theories are adopted, the relationship between standards of evidence and going theories, and the fact that standards of evidence, theories, and "truth", are *community-bound*. The need for a more expansive and realistic account of the epistemology of science that Kuhn and others have illuminated is reflected in Quine's attention to science as a process, rather than simply a product, and in his refusal to write off what had been bracketed by Hempel, Nagel, and Popper as "the context of discovery". (As we have begun to consider and will return to in Chapter Five, Kuhn's account of how new paradigms come into being also precludes any serious analysis of that process. He describes new paradigms as mysteriously emerging "all at once, sometimes in the middle of the night, in the mind of a man [*sic*] deeply immersed in crisis", and concludes, "What the nature of that stage is . . . may remain . . . permanently inscrutable".[155]) But Quine's approaches to these traditional and current issues, and his conclusions, are quite different from Kuhn's. In short, though science is not a process without a subject, though the "product" of the process is a bridge of our own making, science, on Quine's account, is constrained by experience.

Like Hempel and Nagel in whose tradition he is clearly working, Quine also focuses on the "product" of the process. He also takes the "product" of science to be theories, and construes these as sets of sentences. And like Hempel, Nagel, and Kuhn, he is concerned with the connection between theories and sensory evidence, an account that Kuhn apparently despaired of giving on the basis of his study of scientific communities and revolutions, the theory-ladenness of observation, and the untenability of various positivist positions.

It is here, in terms of the issue of "empirical content", the relation of theories to experience, that Quine's views are most clearly distinguishable from the work of both of these traditions, and it is in terms of this issues that his views illuminate the significant, and ironic, overlap between what seem on the surface to be incompatible approaches in the views of science advocated by Hempel, Nagel, and Kuhn.

First, because the relationship to be accounted for is reconstrued by Quine to be a connection between almost *all* the ways we organize things and our *experiences,* because it is not construed as a connection between *a* theory and *the* world, the fact that scientific observations are theory-laden does not constitute the problem it does for Hempel and Nagel, or provoke the skepticism it does in Kuhn's analysis. For one thing, given Quine's arguments about the necessity of public theory for coherent experience, we never experience a world "untheorized". There is no sense to be made of asking whether our theories correspond to such a thing. We are interested in constructing theories that allow us to bridge our experiences, that are coherent with these and with each other.

As it turns out, some theories we construct are better than others, and some fail—and the latter is, of course, why the revolutions Kuhn discusses occur at all. They are prompted by precisely the connection Quine claims does hold, and Kuhn also recognizes when he is discussing normal science: our experiences can indicate (and do) when a theory's predictions fail. But it is from *within* science, broadly construed, from within the process of doing science, that the failure occurs and that is is recognized. This is not a failure of science. It is a success of science.

Thus, Kuhn has made it clear that we must take account of the process of science, but it is also clear that from the perspective afforded by Quine's positions the process looks neither like the rationally reconstructed account Hempel and Nagel offer, nor like a process driven solely by sociology. Science in the narrow and broadest sense produces an evolving corpus of theories, and neither the work that yields and evaluates these theories nor the theories are the isolated product or process described by these two traditions. Science is not autonomous.

With the exception of the boundary between science and values, Quine's account of science is without boundaries. Common sense, science, and philosophy are all theoretical, related to one another, interdependent, and evolving. In terms of the theoretical frameworks of common sense, science, and philosophy, Quine says

> these three types of priority must not be viewed as somehow
> determining three competing, self-sufficient, conceptual schemes. Our
> one serious conceptual scheme is the inclusive, evolving one of science,
> which we inherit and, in our several small ways, help to improve.[156]

We will find Quine's arguments against the boundaries discussed in this chapter supported by feminist science criticism and of particular help in discussing issues raised in and by that criticism. But it would be hard to overestimate the importance of the boundary Quine does not challenge, or the consequences of its demise. As much as any of the boundaries and distinctions we have discussed, the alleged boundary between science and values will concern us in the balance of the discussion.

For deeply related to Quine's assumptions that moral disagreements are rare and that there is nothing "objective" about values is a question.

Is there—are *we*—the monolithic "we" I've spoken of, as Quine does, in these many pages?

CHAPTER FOUR

Addelson: The Politics of Knowledge

> It is the *unexamined* exercise of cognitive authority within our present social arrangements which is most to be feared.
>
> —Kathryn Addelson

THE THESIS of this chapter is one that underlies all feminist science criticism. It is the thesis that, for now at least, the autonomy of science is a myth and a pernicious one. The autonomy at issue has been discussed in the preceding two chapters: it is the alleged detachment of science (in the narrow sense) from common-sense experience and theory, including social and political arrangements, views, issues, and values.

From a view of science shaped by Quine's positions, I am tempted to think that an "autonomous" science would be impossible at any time. But this might be due to a paucity in my ability to imagine. In any event, it is our science as it is, and our society as it is, that matter. It is in terms of these that the myth of science's detachment and insulation from the social and political context of our larger community has—in whatever sense one finds these distinctions useful—epistemological, social, moral, and political implications. In a different kind of society the myth's implications might not span these categories. But in our society they do.

If science is not so detached, if the norm governing science is not being lived up to, then another norm linking autonomy and science needs to be scrutinized: that science should not be interfered with or answerable to the larger community, that scientists must be allowed to pursue "knowledge for its own sake". The latter norm, which constrains the larger community and insulates science from a range of criticism, has been justified on the basis of the view that science is living up to the first norm.

In its thesis, this chapter overlaps with all that follow. But its subject matter is specific. We will consider one area of interest to feminist science critics: the ways in which what Kathryn Addelson calls "cognitive labor" and "cognitive authority" are organized, divided, and institutionalized within scientific communities and our larger community.[1] The discussion will contribute part of what we need in order to see some deep and consequential relationships that exist between science and our other practices and experiences, and to begin to consider the epistemological and political consequences of those relationships.

We will explore two aspects of the social arrangements within which scientific knowledge develops that feminist science critics are interested in exposing and/or problematizing: first, the hierarchial divisions in cognitive labor and authority that many science communities and our community as a whole incorporate and the "cognitive authority" scientists are granted and exercise,[2] and second, within the hierarchies and divisions in scientific communities, the status of women at the "lower" and, in several senses, less powerful positions.[3]

The incorporation of hierarchical divisions in labor and authority in science communities suggests fundamental continuities between these communities and our larger society. But feminist science criticism addressed to these divisions is interested to do more than expose sociological continuities between scientific communities and western society—at least, more than we would expect if we think sociology and epistemology are unrelated. I will use Addelson's notion of "cognitive authority" and her analysis of the divisions in cognitive authority and labor that characterize social arrangements in science communities and our larger society[4] to consider the epistemological and political consequences of these hierarchical divisions.

The divisions in cognitive labor and authority within scientific communities, and those that separate scientists from our larger community, are not new to most of us. Nor are some of us surprised to find women in the lower end of the hierarchies in science communities—although we differ in the reasons we have for not being surprised. But, these divisions have not been noted or addressed in the accounts of science we considered in the preceding two chapters. This is in part because, despite the differences in the views of science underlying these accounts, they share a lack of what would be needed to see that divisions in cognitive labor and authority might have a bearing on scientific knowledge. None of these accounts incorporates what would make it possible to see that such divisions might be of epistemological significance and need to be incorporated in our accounts of scientific theorizing.

Addelson is concerned to problematize the "cognitive authority" scientists enjoy and exercise in our larger community—what she calls "the institution" of science's cognitive authority—and the hierarchical divisions in cognitive labor and authority that characterize scientific communities. She suggests that such divisions do have epistemological consequences: they have a bearing on how and what knowledge develops within science communities and how that knowledge is communicated to and received by the society at large. And she suggests that because the cognitive authority scientists exercise is unscrutinized, it is political.

We will begin with the institution of science's cognitive authority. After laying out some features of Addelson's analysis of that authority and her concerns, we will consider a current research program, E. O. Wilson's Sociobiology. The development and popularity of Sociobiology indicate that concerns about the sources and consequences of the cognitive authority scientists enjoy and exercise are warranted. We will then explore the social arrangements in science communities and those of our larger society that result in a relatively small percentage of our larger community having cognitive authority and an even smaller percentage of women being in that privileged group.

Addelson: Cognitive Authority

In [1983] Addelson deepens the kind of analysis that Kuhn and others have undertaken of the sociology of science communities. Like Kuhn, Addelson approaches science as an activity, and she maintains that the study of the epistemology of science should include the study of the sociology of science communities, the social arrangements in which scientific knowledge develops. But Addelson's analysis differs from Kuhn's and some other recent social studies of science communities in important respects.

Kuhn regards the sociology of science and, therefore, the epistemology of science, as virtually exhausted by the sociology of science communities. These communities, on his view, are "closed systems", and I have urged that this is part of what contributes to his conclusions about scientific revolutions and to the epistemology that his analysis implies. Addelson expands the notion of "the sociology of science"—thus expanding, on her view, the epistemology of science—to include the sociology of the larger community. She is concerned to explore a number of relationships, and specifically, epistemological relationships, that hold between science communities and the larger community.

In addition, whereas Kuhn discusses the cognitive labor in science communities as if the latter is monolithic, Addelson illuminates divisions in "cognitive authority and labor" within these communities. Her analysis suggests that taking account of these divisions is also necessary to understanding the epistemology of science. Her reasons for these conclusions are best explored in terms of her notion of "cognitive authority".

Addelson begins to explicate the notion by discussing the several levels at which the expertise that scientists achieve through education and membership in science communities, combined with a cultural commitment to maintaining the "autonomy of science" (the second of the norms outlined earlier that limits the criticism that science is subject to), result in scientists' having a special sort of authority: an epistemological authority on matters within their fields.[5] Their understandings, Addelson notes, are viewed as the "definitive" understandings—as knowledge.

> The authority of specialists in science is not per se an authority to command obedience from some group of people, or to make decisions on either public policy or private investment. Specialists have, rather, an epistemological or cognitive authority: we take their understanding of factual matters and the nature of the world within their sphere of expertise as knowledge, or as the definitive understanding.[6]

On one level, Addelson notes, it is scientists as a group who are granted this epistemological or cognitive authority. They have the authority to name and to define, to characterize and to explain, the areas of human and nonhuman nature that are their specialties.

> In accord with the norm of the "autonomy of science", researchers develop hypotheses and theories, discover laws, define problems and solutions, criticize and falsify beliefs, make scientific revolutions. They have the authority to do that on matters in their professional specialty.[7]

And, in addition to the authority they have as members of specific disciplines, Addelson reminds us that scientists have an authority that is not limited to their ability to define problems and solutions within science communities. They have what she calls an "external authority",[8] and that authority is a feature of our larger community.

Scientists, and especially senior researchers, are granted and exercise a cognitive authority to shape the larger community's understanding of nature, including human nature. In exercising this authority, scientists can and do shape social and political policy based on the understandings of nature they "certify" and communicate.

Researchers also exercise cognitive authority outside their professions, for scientific specialists have an authority to define the true nature of the living and nonliving world around us. We are taught their scientific understanding in school. Public and private officials accept it to use in solving political, social, military, and manufacturing problems.[9]

Of great significance, on Addelson's view, as senior researchers communicate their findings to the larger community— indeed, even as they convey research questions and the methodologies they have adopted for approaching these—they simultaneously convey metaphysical commitments.

Scientific authority to define the nature of the world is not limited to the laws and theories printed in boldface sentences in our textbooks. Metaphysical commitments are beliefs about the nature of the living and non-living things of our world and about their relations with us and with each other. In teaching us their scientific specialties, researchers simultaneously teach us these broader understandings.[10]

As an example of the consequences of the metaphysical commitments imparted to our larger community, Addelson cites the revolution in our world view brought about by evolutionary theory and outlines the various ways scientists' understandings of nature are communicated.

The Darwinian revolution . . . changed the metaphysics of a world designed by God in which all creatures were ordered in a chain of being, to a world of natural selection.[11]

Theories and explanations [the conventional understandings among significant communicators in a scientific specialty] are published in journals and presented at conferences. . . . Eventually conventional understandings are ritualized in college texts. . . . Through the textbooks and lectures, and through advice to government and industry, the conventional understandings are passed on to the rest of us as part of the exercise of the specialist's external authority.[12]

Darwin was, of course, consciously advocating a metaphysics. But, Addelson notes, even in cases where scientists regard themselves as committed "only to a *methodological* framework", the metaphysical commitments a methodology implies are conveyed to the larger community as research programs are communicated. And, she maintains, the communication of such commitments has potential consequences for social and political policy.

As an example of the impact a methodological framework adopted in research can have on social and political attitudes and policy, Addelson cites the sharing of a functionalist methodology in the life sciences and social sciences. Drawing on the work of Donna Haraway, who chronicles what Addelson describes as a change in the metaphysics of the biological sciences after World War I,[13] Addelson considers the consequences for the social sciences and social policy of borrowing a functionalist methodology from the biological sciences. Although regarded by social scientists as simply a "methodological framework", Addelson uses Merton's theory of deviance to illustrate a relationship between the methodology and a metaphysics.[14]

> Merton insists that [in adopting a functionalist methodology], he is only borrowing a *methodological framework* from the biological sciences.
> In fact, the framework carries with it a metaphysics—as the change in life sciences reported by Haraway shows. This widespread use of metaphysics confirms its truth, through the internal authority of specialists. It changes dominant world views in a society through the external authority of specialists.[15]

Addelson argues that Merton's critique of an earlier functionalist framework, in which deviance was explained as the malfunctioning of social organization in controlling "original nature" or "biological impulses", involved reformulating, or redefining, the problem of deviance in a significant way.[16] On Merton's account, social structures are not functioning to restrain "original nature"; rather, these structures fail to preclude the sort of social "substructures" to which deviant behaviors are a response. And, as I noted, Merton viewed the functionalist framework he used and publicized as "simply a methodological framework".

But Addelson builds on Kuhn's views to argue that the adoption of a methodology does imply a metaphysics. (Quine, of course, would insist that the adoption of a methodology *commits* us to a metaphysics.) And, she argues, given the external authority scientists enjoy, the adoption of functionalist frameworks in the social sciences had an impact on how social problems were regarded and what came to be viewed as the appropriate methods of "solving" them. The impact, according to Addelson, is directly related to the metaphysical commitments implied in research and communicated through textbooks, journals, and scientific meetings.

When we compare Merton's theory of deviance to the theory he criticized, we are of course comparing frameworks that share a functionalist methodology. But even though they share that general approach, it is clear that they suggest different problems and different solutions. According to the framework Merton adopted, deviance is a response to *malfunctions* of the *social structure*; in the earlier framework deviance represented the malfunction of the social structure in *controlling biology*. Unless the frameworks resulted in the same sorts of suggestions or policies for social change, which Addelson shows was not so,[17] or theories of deviance bear no relation to therapeutic practice and social attitudes and policy, these differences are significant. However those within the research program regard the frameworks—whether they consider them as "only" methodological frameworks or as reflecting the actual metaphysics of the situation—the frameworks convey different views of social reality to the culture at large.[18] And whether we explain deviance as socially caused or biologically caused has, of course, political implications. The Merton example, says Addelson,

> indicates that the cognitive authority of science supported one set of political positions over another by that definition of the human world. *This happened not by abuse of authority but by normal procedures in the normal social arrangement of science.*[19]

Two important points emerge in those we have so far considered: Addelson's argument that methodologies and research questions convey metaphysical commitments, and that it is a feature of science as things normally go that what she terms "the conventional understandings" of specialists, including the metaphysical commitments implied in their approaches, are conveyed to the larger society and impact on social and political attitudes and policy. Addelson suggests that we need to problematize the cognitive authority researchers have—to critically evaluate and scrutinize the ways in which this authority impacts on our views and can lead to or legitimize social and political policy.

Now, many of us would expect that scientific research will or could (eventually) have an impact on the views we in the larger community come to have about how things are—at least that successful research will or might have such an impact. And we would expect that the impact could in some cases be great; for instance it might involve a revolution in world view such as that brought about by evolutionary theory; or, the impact might be more localized—as in the case of a theory of deviance, and like the latter, we might expect areas of research to have an impact on social and political policy. Indeed, we might hope that social and political policy would reflect the current state of scientific knowledge. But Addelson's reasons for maintaining that the cognitive authority scientists exercise needs to be scrutinized are also clear.

First, despite the long-standing view that science does not incorporate metaphysical commitments—or the flip side of the view, that if science does incorporate these, they are somehow hidden or tacit and, thus, beyond elucidation or criticism— metaphysical commitments are conveyed to the larger community with consequences for attitudes and policies even in cases in which scientists deny that they have, in adopting a methodology, committed themselves to a metaphysics. Second, there can be substantial social and political consequences of such commitments, and Haraway's and Addelson's studies of the impact of a functionalist methodology shared by the life sciences and the social sciences indicate that there have been such consequences.[20]

But Addelson goes on to explore a further relationship between science communities and the large community that is relevant both to the general issue of whether the cognitive authority granted to scientists should be scrutinized and to her specific concern with metaphysical commitments. She notes that in many cases the larger social and political context shapes "the problem" to be explained within a research program and/or the approach taken to it. For example, Addelson argues in the case of a "theory of deviance", what are regarded as the problems to be explained— the deviant behaviors—will often be deeply connected to current social and political context.

> Bank robbing, pot smoking, and homosexuality are social problems in the eyes of certain segments of our population, not others. [Becker and other sociologists in the interactionist tradition have argued that] social problems don't exist for the neutral scientific eye to discern, any more than deviance does. Something is a social problem or not depending on one's social position and perspective.[21]

So Addelson suggests that science and the larger social context interact in ways that we are prevented from seeing if we assume that science is detached from social and political context and that research questions "present themselves" without that context being a factor. Moreover, the norm that science must be allowed to proceed without interference from the larger community, that it must proceed autonomously, would make it inappropriate to scrutinize that interaction. In the end, Addelson's analysis of the Merton case suggests that the consequences of such relationships and of the institution of cognitive authority are not only epistemological but also social and political.

What we regard as deviant, and what we regard as the cause of deviance (in this case, sociology or biology), incorporate metaphysical commitments and will have a bearing on social attitudes and on policy that is designed to "manage" or to "fix" what is regarded as a problem. And given the political nature of such solutions, and the politics that are often involved in naming behaviors deviant (homosexual behavior, for example), the external authority exercised by scientists will have social and political consequences. Moreover, because we do not acknowledge that scientific understanding might itself be shaped by current political views and practices, the "naming" of some behaviors as "problems" or "deviant", and the methodology adopted for explaining these, are not subjected to scrutiny.

So, there is reason to look at how questions, metaphysical commitments, and findings are conveyed and become part of the larger community's knowledge and to explore how the cognitive authority granted to scientists allows this group to shape our largest views of reality in ways that, ironically, some of our own views about science *preclude* our questioning or scrutinizing. By portraying science as having a detached position that no human activity can have, we make it inappropriate to ask the critical questions that are appropriately asked of any alleged cognitive authority.

I want to turn to a current example in which all of the issues Addelson raises are at work—with what seems to many to be disastrous consequences. What will emerge is that the consequences are clearly political.

Naming and Explaining Reality: Wilson's Sociobiology

Sociobiology, the discipline pioneered and advocated by E. O. Wilson,[22] is a timely example for considering the issues Addelson raises about the cognitive authority granted to and exercised by scientists. Unless otherwise noted, my discussion will be limited to the discipline promoted by Wilson and others as an explanatory framework for all animal social behavior, including human social behavior, and all social organization, including "the" organization of human societies. The discipline Wilson pioneered is understood by its advocates to complete a "grand synthesis", bringing together behavioral biology and population biology to explain all social behavior and organization and, thus, to synthesize animal sociology, the social sciences, and biology. It is important to distinguish Wilson's Sociobiology from some other research programs and evolutionary frameworks.

There are sociobiologists who do not think the theoretical framework is appropriately extended to the study of human behavior and social organization.[23] There are also evolutionary theorists who argue that the underlying explanatory model of sociobiology—a neo-Darwinian model that posits linear, fine, and continuous variation as the source of evolutionary change—oversimplifies and distorts the complexities of evolutionary processes.[24] Included in the preceding group are geneticists and other biologists who argue that the model of gene action incorporated in Sociobiology is grossly oversimplified and distorting, and that, contrary to what Sociobiologists claim, genes can determine neither behavior nor traits, let alone social organization. Our concern here will be with the work that is based on the core theses of Wilson's Sociobiology.[25]

Both the development and the proliferation of Wilson's Sociobiology are relevant to a number of Addelson's concerns. First, the discipline provides a good example of the "external authority" scientists exercise. Sociobiology is the focus of a current debate (much of it being fought out in the popular press and in books written by Sociobiologists for the layperson), and it has received an enormous amount of publicity.[26] That it has received both the amount and the kind of publicity it has is, in part, a function of the cognitive authority granted to scientists as a group, and to senior researchers in particular. It is also a function of the interest Sociobiologists have in promulgating their theory and claims to the lay public.

It will also be obvious that central factors in the debate over Sociobiology are the metaphysical commitments of the framework, and what those on both sides of the debate recognize to be the social and political implications of those commitments. One of the more far-reaching metaphysical commitments of Sociobiology has already been noted: its commitment to the view that explanations for all human social behavior and social organization will be found in biology. More specifically, Sociobiologists claim that human social behavior is genetically determined and the product of natural selection, and that human social organization reflects this "genetic core".

This large commitment incorporates of course, a second metaphysical commitment: that there are universal (transhistorical and cross-cultural) human behaviors and universal features of human social organization. A third metaphysical commitment of the discipline is that complex behaviors and characteristics are encoded for in genes. A fourth is that this encoding occurs through a long and linear process characterized by very small changes, competition, and selection, to promote "inclusive fitness". A fifth is that social organization is determined by the biology of individuals. Finally, Sociobiology's methodology incorporates a commitment to the view that similarities in human and other animal behaviors and social organization constitute evidence for a "common cause" to those arrangements—specifically, a genetic basis for the behaviors, itself the product of natural selection.[27]

Although the discipline pioneered by Wilson is relatively new, the range of explanations for human behavior and features of human societies that Sociobiologists have offered is already quite extensive and broad. Sociobiologists explain war, male-dominance hierarchies, and aggression, for example, as "fitness-promoting" and the product of natural selection. And those advocating the new discipline claim that its most "impressive successes" are its explanations for "sex" differences, and divisions of labor and power by sex.[28]

That Sociobiology's explanations have clear implications for social and political policy is reflected in the list of things Sociobiologists claim to explain as well as in the interest political and social theorists, feminists, Marxists, and antifeminists have paid to the discipline. But the implications are also reflected in prescriptions some Sociobiologists offer for social policy,[29] and others claim are obvious consequences of the claims Sociobiology makes.

Before we explore Sociobiology in any detail, I want to make clear what my purposes are in considering the discipline. I have no interest in seriously evaluating Wilson's Sociobiology here, and certainly none in debunking it. There are many reasons to think that the discipline is one of the least promising research programs currently being pursued, and its problems have been exposed by biologists, animal sociologists, evolutionary theorists, social scientists, philosophers of science, and feminist and Marxist science critics.[30] Since the discipline has received more than its fair share of favorable and unfavorable publicity, I feel no responsibility to weigh its worth here. There is an ample literature available, some of it supportive and some of it critical. I am using it as a current example of a research program that indicates that the concerns Addelson raises about the institution of science's cognitive authority are warranted: the basis and the consequences of that authority, the metaphysical commitments incorporated in research questions and methodologies, the imparting of such commitments to the larger community, and the implications of these things for social and political attitudes and policy—to which that ample literature is itself pertinent.

I will spend time outlining some of Sociobiology's claims, and some of what other scientists and science critics find problematic about these and with the underlying explanatory model of the discipline.[31] I will also outline some of the debate prompted by the program that centers on the issue of the relationship between politics and science, and, more generally, on the two norms relating autonomy and science: that science is insulated from social and political context and the implications of that view for the apolitical status granted to scientific theorizing and theories, and that science must be allowed to pursue knowledge without interference based on political issues or concerns.

I do so, again, to explore the issue of science's cognitive authority. The controversy surrounding the program, and the sources and nature of that controversy, indicate that the view that science communities are detached or insulated from social and political context is deeply suspect. Nor can we assume that only the social sciences reflect that context. Those who are developing and advocating Sociobiology include evolutionary biologists and geneticists, experimental psychologists, and zoologists. They are members of sciences regarded as tipping far more toward the "hard" and well-insulated sciences. And it will be clear that genteticists, entomologists, and evolutionary biologists, no less than social scientists, are not insulated from social and political context and that their claims can be *political* in nature and in consequence.

Our analysis of this case will also indicate that the assumption that scientific theorizing is so insulated prevents our seeing some of the factors that can be relevant to the acceptance of a theory. Given the current status of Sociobiology's claims about human social behavior and social organization—given, that is, the status of the models of gene action and evolutionary processes incorporated in the theory and the status of the evidence for the claims Sociobiologists make—Sociobiology provides a clear example of how theory acceptance can be related to factors *other than* a theory's "scientific" soundness or gaps in our knowledge that need to be filled. And, finally, Addelson's claim that cognitive authority is political prove warranted when we consider some of Sociobiology's claims and what Sociobiologists claim about the nonpolitical nature of these claims. Their claims, we will see, *are* political in nature and the appeals made by Sociobiologists to both norms linking autonomy and science are part of what contributes to the political nature of those claims.

Finally, although I will not attempt to debunk Sociobiology, I will urge that its proponents are appallingly irresponsible in their exercise of the cognitive authority scientists enjoy. The full-blown argument that such irresponsibility constitutes bad science will take the course of the larger discussion. My main interest here will be establishing the political nature of the research program and supporting Addelson's contention that science's cognitive authority is political and in need of scrutiny.

The core doctrines of Wilson's Sociobiology are commitments to a biological evolution driven by "fitness" considerations, to a cultural evolution determined by biological evolution, and to an "essential genetic core" bequeathed through evolution to each member of a species in order to promote "fitness". According to Sociobiology, the "genetic core" bequeathed to each member of the human species is determining of social behavior and social organization, and it is sex-differentiated.

The Sociobiologist David Barash describes the discipline and the task it sets itself.

> Sociobiology is Wilson's name for what had previously been a loose amalgam of evolutionary theory, ecology and animal behavior. This new discipline has already been spectacularly successful in helping us understand the behavior of animals, but the real excitement and controversy lie ahead, in the ways that sociobiology may be applied to a very important but little-understood primate—ourselves. . . . [Sociobiology] may help us discover our own nature and allow us to eavesdrop on the whispers of biology within us all. . . . [Sociobiology] is concerned less with the behavioral baggage of our primate past than with using the principles of evolution and natural selection to analyze and interpret our present.[32]

Barash describes the "genetic core" each human inherits, its role in determining behavior, and the "central principle" of Sociobiology.

> Core elements are the essential person, an entity bequeathed by evolution to each of us; they are the *us* upon which experience acts.[33]

> Our genes speak to our behavior second hand—through the medium of our bodies. . . . individuals behave, not genes, but the behaviors reflect strategies that the genes have evolved for replicating themselves. . . . Any way you choose to see it, the fact is we tend to do things that maximize our fitness.
> This is the central principle of sociobiology: insofar as a behavior reflects at least some component of gene action, individuals will tend to behave so as to maximize their fitness.[34]

"Fitness" is understood by Sociobiologists as the ability of individuals to reproduce (or to enable their kin to reproduce) and/or (Sociobiologists are not always clear about this, as the passages from Barash's text suggest) the ability of genes to replicate themselves.

Barash, echoing other Sociobiologists,[35] claims that one of the most impressive successes of Sociobiology is its explanations of "sex-differentiated" behaviors and characteristics, and divisions of labor and power by sex in human societies. Indeed, the explanations of sex differences form the cornerstone of Sociobiology, as Barash notes. "Sociobiology", he maintains, "relies heavily upon the biology of male-female differences".[36] We will begin our consideration of the relationship between Sociobiology and politics with the "cornerstone" of the discipline.

The explanations that Sociobiologists offer of sex differences use the central principle Barash outlines, and they proceed like this. Maintaining that there are universals in sex-differentiated behaviors and sex/gender arrangements in human societies, and claiming that these universals are similar to universals in other species, Sociobiologists claim that the "insofar" clause of the central principle outlined by Barash has been fulfilled: the relevant behaviors or arrangements have been shown to reflect some component of gene action. Sociobiologists then offer a story about how the behavior or social arrangement would enable individuals to maximize their fitness (to reproduce the most number of offspring) or would enable the genes of these individuals to replicate themselves, and that story, along with the commitment to inclusive fitness as the "goal" of genes or organisms, constitutes the explanation for why the behavior or characteristic has been genetically encoded and selected for.

Obviously, Sociobiology's explanations for "sex" differences in behaviors and characteristics and for social arrangements that incorporate divisions in labor by sex/gender have implications for current social and political issues and policies. Sociobiologists' awareness of the social and political implications of their explanations is reflected in their books and textbooks. In a textbook described by Wilson as "the best introductory textbook on the subject",[37] Barash muses over whether the term "sexist" applies to Sociobiology's account of female/male differences.

> As we shall see . . . some of sociobiology's most impressive theory and data involve male-female differences. Insofar as some component of these differences shows up in human behavior, then sociobiology could legitimately be considered sexist. . . .
>   [But] the description of male traits and of female traits is not in itself value-laden, so it does not seem useful to employ the pejorative term "sexist".[38]

Despite the disclaimer, two chapters of Barash's *The Whisperings Within* that are devoted to reproduction incorporate the term 'sexism' in their titles. (The first of the two is entitled "Sexism: Strategies of Reproduction, or When Is Beeswax Like a Ferrari?"[39]) Indeed, Barash goes on to note that " 'Mother' Nature" is "the greatest sexist of them all."[40]

> We will explore the biological underpinning . . . and take a hard-headed (and undoubtedly unpopular) look at the evolutionary biology of differences between men and women, including a theory for the biological basis of the double standard.[41]

Sexism, and the injustices, power relationships, and divisions in labor that Barash so glibly glosses over with the description *"the* double standard", are by no means "value-neutral" or nonpolitical. Moreover, to claim that "nature is sexist" is to acknowledge the political implications of one's own claims and that these legitimize those power relationships one is claiming to explain.

And we should note at the outset that neither Barash nor any other Sociobiologist does, in fact, explore the *"biological underpinning"* of such alleged human sex differences, the genetic encoding that Barash claims underlies "the double standard" he purportedly explains as promoting of inclusive fitness. Nor do Sociobiologists explore the *genetic* encoding of *any* human social behavior or way of organizing social life that they explain as fitness promoting.

Sociobiology's explanations make use of the methodology and reasoning outlined earlier, and they proceed at the level I described: find an animal (ducks, bluebirds, or insects will do, but other primates are best) with a behavior that looks like those you attribute to all humans, past and present. Ignore or dismiss exceptions and assume that you know the range, and understand the complexity, of all human behavior and social arrangements.[42] (In defense of the universalizing he engages in about human behavior and societies, Wilson told an interviewer, "I have seen so many societies all over the world, I know what they are like".[43]) Try to establish or assume that the behavior has a genetic basis in other species. If you can then tell a story about why the behavior (or social arrangement based on it) would maximize inclusive fitness, you're done. You have shown the *human* social behavior to be genetically determined, and the product of natural selection.

Barash's Introduction to *The Whispering's Within,* a work written for the lay public, outlines the methodology and a partial list of the behaviors and social arrangements he will explain.

> During this journey, I will be telling many animal stories, providing, perhaps, a somewhat novel perspective on the birds and the bees— stories of rape in ducks, adultery in bluebirds, prostitution in hummingbirds, divorce and lesbian pairing in gulls, even homosexual rape in parasitic worms.
>
> What I hope is that *the animals you'll meet in the following pages will help you know yourself better.* But don't misunderstand; I won't be arguing that just because hairy-nosed wombats do something or other we should be inclined to do the same. The animals we meet may help reveal the way evolution operates on behavior, without necessarily

prescribing the exact form the behavior will take. . . . By watching how evolution operates on the behavior of animals, it is possible we may begin to be able *to identify general principles*. Then, of course, we can take these principles and *try them on ourselves, and if the shoe fits* . . . The *real* subject of this book, then is *human* behavior. . . .[44]

And, as we shall see, Barash does indeed claim that the animals he meets do indicate "general principles" underlying human behavior and he does use these principles to prescribe "correct" human behavior and social arrangements.

In his pioneer work,[45] Wilson announces that Sociobiology promises to replace the social sciences. The new discipline, according to Wilson, will provide biological explanations, specifically genetic explanations, for all human social behaviors and social organization. Interestingly, the pioneer work also included a claim that "early man [sic] was its focus". But the second passage below belies that description.

Sociobiology is defined as *the systematic study of the biological basis of all social behavior*. For the present it focuses on animal societies, their population structure, castes, and communication, together with all of the physiology underlying the social adaptations. But the discipline is also concerned with the social behavior of early man [sic] and the adaptive features of organization in the more primitive contemporary human societies. . . .

It may not be too much to say that sociology and the other social sciences, as well as the humanities, are the last branches of biology waiting to be included in the Modern Synthesis [in which each phenomenon is weighed for its adaptive significance and then related to the basic principles of population genetics].[46]

Chapters 1 and 27 of *Sociobiology, the New Synthesis* included these claims and listed some of the universals in human behavior that Wilson thought Sociobiology could and would explain. The intervening twenty-five chapters were, for the most part, devoted to other species.

Again, it is important to note that Barash and other Sociobiologists, including Wilson in later work, are not just explaining, or concerned to explain, the social behavior of "early man [sic]"; they claim to explain what they allege are *current* and universal sex differences in human behavior and other human social behaviors and features of human societies. The list of explanations Sociobiologists have offered to date includes what they call "male aggressiveness",[47] "male dominance",[48] "male fickleness",[49] "female coyness",[50] and a number of other "sex differences"[51] that lead to and/or underwrite male dominance and male-to-male competition, rape,[52] war,[53] dominance hierarchies, and other alleged universals of human behavior and societies, including racial discrimination.[54]

To appreciate the seriousness of the questions Sociobiology raises about science's cognitive authority and its alleged autonomy from political context, it is important to understand the current status of Sociobiology's claims about human behavior. Some of the problems that other scientists claim are incorporated in Wilson's Sociobiology are specific to it.[55] Questioning the genetic determination of human behavior, critics point out the rapidity with which cultures can change (genetic variation would have to have occurred far too fast to be used in an explanation of the cultural changes), and they point out the variations in and range of human behavior.[56] Historians, anthropologists, and sociologists argue that cross-cultural and historical studies provide ample counterexamples to the "universals" of human social organization and sex-differentiated characteristics and behaviors that Sociobiology purportedly explains as genetically determined and as maximizing fitness.[57] Primatologists and anthropologists also argue that species that do not display the behaviors Sociobiologists want to link to human behavior and explain as fitness maximizing and genetically determined (male dominance and male aggression, for example) are ignored by Sociobiologists, and that Sociobiologists' descriptions of animal behavior and social organization are deeply anthropomorphic, ethnocentric, and sexist.[58]

Further, as I noted earlier, the underlying model of evolutionary processes on which Wilson's Sociobiology builds, a linear building block account,[59] as well as the program's commitments to biological determinism, the genetic determination of complex traits and behaviors, inclusive fitness, and selectionist explanations are matters of considerable debate among evolutionary theorists. There has been and continues to be criticism of the adequacy of the model, and alternative models are being advocated by other scientists.[60]

Finally, Sociobiologists have been faulted for their methods: the methodology of assuming similar causes (that is, genetic bases and natural selection) for what they take to be similar effects (similarities in human and animal behaviors and social organization),[61] for their dismissal of exceptions that do not fit in with their universals,[62] and for the sloppiness of their ontology, which includes such objects as "female coyness", "male fickleness", rabbit "husbands", and "rape" in nonhuman species.[63]

But despite the problems other scientists find in Wilson's Sociobiology, the ongoing debate in the biological sciences concerning the adequacy of the models of gene action and evolutionary process on which it builds, and the lack of evidence at various levels currently available to support its claims about the genetic determination of human behavior, Wilson's Sociobiology has received an enormous amount of favorable publicity in the popular press. At least in part because of the cognitive authority of some of its well-known advocates, and no doubt to that granted to scientists in general, it has been publicized in everything from the *New York Times* [1978], in which it was described as "revolutionary", to an issue of *Reader's Digest* that is estimated to have had a readership of 31 million readers in sixteen languages.

And in keeping with the way that Sociobiologists put forth the theory and their specific claims, Sociobiology has been publicized in the media as successful and complete. Its advocates have published textbooks and numerous books for the layperson that are in no way provisional in tone. The following is from Barash's textbook.[64] It illuminates the political nature of Sociobiology's explanations and a willingness to use cognitive authority to legitimize current political arrangements and practices.

> Because men maximize their fitness differently from women, *it is perfectly good biology* that business and profession taste sweeter to them, while home and child care taste sweeter to women.
> While it may be true that it's "not nice to fool Mother Nature", it can be done. Biology's whispers can be denied, but in most cases at a real cost. . . . Although women who participate in [a system in which mothers are liberated from the social responsibility of child care] may be attracted by the promise of "liberation", they are *in fact simply adopting a male strategy while denying their own. Evolution has designed* male parenting to be on-again, off-again, depending on the benefit to fitness in each case. Cavalier female parenting is *maladaptive* for all mammals; for humans, it may be a socially instituted trap *that is harmful to everyone concerned.*[65]

We should also note that because Sociobiologists grant that what Barash calls the "biological whisperings" can be "denied", they apparently feel they have forestalled any need to explore or discuss counterexamples to their universals. Indeed, their work is full of caveats about the role that culture might play in shaping behavior.

For example, in a tone far different from that which characterizes his later work, Wilson's first work contains the following: "Although [in the human species] the genes have given away most of their sovereignty, they maintain a certain amount of influence in at least the behavioral qualities that underlie variations between cultures".[66] But Sociobiologists are more sure that human "freedom" and flexibility are quite circumscribed and are more willing to claim this, as is reflected in what Barash says above about the "cost" of denying the whispers of biology. You can fool Mother

Nature, but you had better not. And Wilson, in a passage a few paragraphs below the one in which he notes that genes "have given away most of their sovereignty" in determining human behavior, goes on to say, "there is a need for a discipline of *anthropological genetics*. In the interval before we acquire it, it should be possible to characterize the *human biogram* by . . . indirect methods".[67] The indirect methods for establishing a biological basis for human social behaviors that Wilson outlines are precisely of the sort I outlined earlier: he advocates that we construct models from what he calls "the most elementary rules of human behavior" and compare these to "the ethograms of other primate species", and that we study other primates to identify what he calls "basic primate traits that lie beneath the surface".[68]

Ironically, given the storm of controversy that surrounded the publication of *Sociobiology, the New Synthesis,* and the number of works written for the public by Sociobiologists, including Wilson, in which claims are made in anything but a provisional tone about the evolutionary purpose of things like war, and sex differences in power and "roles", Wilson maintains that he does not regard the program as more than a promising research program.[69] He also denies that Sociobiology or his own explanations are political or that they can be used to underwrite any social or political arrangement or policy. He has bitterly responded to the criticisms lodged by other scientists about the social and political implications of the program.[70] Maintaining that his critics are politically motivated, Wilson denies that his views are politically shaped or motivated, that they are political in nature, or that they would, used properly, have political consequences.

> There is no reasonable way that [my] empirical conclusion [that human beings are neither infinitely malleable nor completely fixed] can be construed as a support of the status quo and continued injustice.[71]

> By their own testimony [those scientists who wrote a letter criticizing my book] worked for months on the project. They appear to have been alarmed by the impact a critical success of the book might have on the acceptability of their own political views.[72]

It should be noted that the critics Wilson is referring to did not deny they were politically motivated; nor is it clear that they share his view that political advocacy and objectivity are necessarily exclusive.[73] But these critics of Sociobiology have also been concerned to illuminate what they argue are flaws in Sociobiology's methodology and the lack of evidence for the claims contained in the first and twenty-seventh chapters of Wilson's pioneer work, and contained in subsequent work in Sociobiology, including Wilson's. I have outlined some of these criticisms.

And in weighing the alleged nonpolitical status of Wilson's work, we need to take Wilson's own claims into account, for many of these are quite specific about the genetic determination of human behavior—and the implications of his claims are clearly political. In *On Human Nature*, a book, unlike the pioneer work, that is addressed to the layperson and for which he won a Pulitzer prize, Wilson, like Barash, explains what he claims are sex differences. He states, for example:

> The anatomical difference between the two kinds of sex cell is often extreme. In particular, the human egg is eighty-five thousand times larger than the human sperm. *The consequences of this gametic dimorphism ramify throughout the biology and psychology of human sex.* The most important immediate result is that the female places a greater investment in each of her sex cells. . . . In contrast, a man releases 100 million sperm with each ejaculation. . . .
>
> *The resulting conflict of interest between the sexes is a property of not only human beings but also the majority of animal species. Males are characteristically aggressive*, especially toward one another and most intensely during the breeding season.
>
> *In most species, assertiveness is the most profitable male strategy. . . . It pays males to be aggressive, hasty, fickle, and undiscriminating. In theory it is more profitable for females to be coy*, to hold back until they can identify males with the best genes. In species that rear young, it is also important for the females to select males who are more likely to stay with them after insemination.
>
> *Human beings obey this biological principle faithfully.*[74]

This is certainly not the "middle of the road" thesis concerning the nature-versus-nurture controversy Wilson's response to his critics implies, a thesis he also implies was "deliberately" misunderstood by his critics on the basis of their political views.[75] Nor is Wilson limiting his explanations to "early man [*sic*]". Indeed, it is difficult to imagine how Wilson thought there were no political implications, and, specifically, no justification of the status quo of sex/gender expectations and arrangements, in such statements. It is not just that his claims could be *used* to justify the status quo. The claims themselves *justify* the status quo. Sex-differentiated behaviors, as Wilson and other Sociobiologists see these, and sex/gender arrangements, including expectations and divisions of labor by sex/gender, are argued to be determined by what Wilson calls "biological principles". Barash specifically addresses the dangers of going *against* these principles, but Wilson's claims about biological principles are no less legitimizing of current political attitudes and practices.

The implications of Sociobiology's explanations were understood precisely by the media. The issue of *Time* that covered the program had as its cover caption, "The Sexes: How They Differ and Why" and a picture of female and male puppets controlled by "genes".[76] Nor is it difficult to see in Barash's and Wilson's use of "investment" metaphors to explain "female and male reproductive strategies" how the Sociobiologist Dawkins came to assert: "The female sex is exploited, and the fundamental evolutionary basis for the exploitation is that eggs are larger than sperms".[77] The implications for social and political policy are clear. *Exploitation* of women is *natural*; it is determined by evolution and it promotes *fitness*. Feminists and other "egalitarians" (a term laced through Barash's *The Whisperings Within*) certainly cannot fight the size of eggs and sperms.

A problem is emerging that is serious, and it is directly related to the institution and exercise of cognitive authority. One aspect of the problem is this. If Wilson, Barash, or any other Sociobiologist really does think that sexism, aggression, war, and other objects they purportedly explain on the basis of inclusive fitness could not, or should not, be *justified* by their explanations and/or are not inevitable, then it is appallingly irresponsible not to spend equal time clarifying how this alleged dichotomy between the genetic determination and selectionist explanations they are committed to and the actual possibilities for *different* (non-maladaptive) human behavior can be pulled off. Simply declaring that their explanations do not (or are not meant to) justify current divisions in labor and power, or aggression, or war, or rape, in light of the nature of their claims and explanations, is not enough. Moreover, most Sociobiologists (Wilson's *early* work may be an exception) are not interested in making any such disclaimer's or qualifications, as Barash's warnings about going against nature indicate.

A second problem related to the institution and exercise of cognitive authority involves the relative lack of evidence for the claims Sociobiologists are advancing. Whatever other problems the program has, its evidence for the *genetic* determination of human social behavior and social organization is, as we have seen, at best indirect. But this has not deterred Sociobiologists from writing books for the layperson and textbooks in which claims such as those we have considered here are made and conclusions about appropriate behavior and divisions in labor are offered.

Moreover, the proliferation of Sociobiology has not been limited to what Ruth Bleier calls its "aggressive marketing" by its advocates, or its coverage in the popular press. It has already made its way into the science curriculum of high schools.[78] The film, Sociobiology: Doing What Comes Naturally, and a science curriculum called Exploring Human Nature are now part of many high school curriculi.[79]

Barash's treatment of rape in a textbook now in its second edition is an example of the willingness of Sociobiologists to explore and advocate the implications of their claims in the absence of direct evidence for genetic encoding of human behavior. It is an example that illuminates the political nature of Sociobiology's explanations and the potential consequences of those. And it throws into starkest relief the consequences of granting science an autonomous status. The most sophisticated geneticist or zoologist can, under the guise of science's insulation from political context and the apolitical nature of scientific theorizing, engage in and propound the most unsophisticated social and political theorizing—and, in so doing, legitimize violence against women. Barash's irresponsibility will, I hope, appall readers. But the more far-reaching issue with which we need to contend is that his explanation of rape can be offered as scientific and "value-free" because we grant scientists cognitive authority that we do not scrutinize and insist that scientific theorizing is value-free. Thus, Barash feels free to reject any responsibility for the implications of his claims. He is, on his account, simply telling us how things are.

Against the background of the substantial evidence that rape is an act of *violence* and not sex or a sexually motivated act and of the history of the ways rape and rape victims have been treated legally and socially on the basis of the assumption that rape is sex, Barash proclaims that "rape" occurs throughout nonhuman living nature. He also proclaims that in other species, "rape" is a *reproductive strategy*—a way for males to promote their fitness (reproduce). (I use quotes here because it is not clear that rape *could* occur in any but the human species.[80]) After citing a number of cases of what he names "male sexual aggression for *reproductive rights*" (my emphasis)—all of which involve ducks and other nonhuman species—Barash goes so far as to claim that bees "rape" flowers by "bombarding them with pollen".[81]

As biologist Ruth Bleier remarks, rape begins to sound fairly harmless when one extends the notion to bees and flowers. "By defining the insertion of a pollen tube into a female flower as a rape, Barash begins to set the scene for the naturalness and—yes—the innocence of rape".[82] In accordance with Sociobiology's methodology, having "established" a universal, Barash offers an explanation of rape on the basis of inclusive fitness.

> [In all these cases of nonhuman "rape"] rape appears to be *a fitness-maximizing strategy, attempted when the benefits [from replicating their genes] for the males outweigh the costs.*[83]

Ultimately, for Barash, the appropriate way to think about rape is that it is a *fitness-maximizing strategy*—a way for males to secure their reproductive *rights*.

> Daniel Janzen, one of our most creative ecologists . . . pointed out that even plants "perform courtship displays, rape, promiscuity, and fickleness just as do animals. . . ." Plants that commit rape . . . are following evolutionary strategies that maximize their fitness. And clearly, in neither case do the actors know what they are doing, or why. We human beings like to think we are different. We introspect, we are confident that we know what we are doing, and why. *But we may have to open our minds and admit the possibility that our need to maximize our fitness may be whispering somewhere deep with us and that, know it or not, most of the time we are heeding these whisperings.*[84]

Janzen seems creative indeed. And despite his own half-hearted qualification about the adequacy of using the behavior or mallard ducks (we should add, as that behavior is *named* by Barash) to understand human behavior, Barash does precisely the latter twenty pages later.

> Rape in humans is by no means as simple [as rape among mallard ducks], influenced as it is by an extremely complex overlay of cultural attitudes. Nevertheless, mallard rape and bluebird adultery may have a degree of relevance to human behavior. *Perhaps human rapists, in their own criminally misguided way, are doing the best they can to maximize their fitness. If so, they are not that different from the sexually excluded bachelor mallards.*[85]

The implication of Barash's claims is clear and appalling. We ought to rethink our views about rape—to use his own words, we ought to "open our minds"—because what Barash names "rape" occurs throughout non-human nature and it is possible, using a model of reproduction that sees this as "investment", to tell a story about how "rape" promotes the fitness of other species whose members engage in it. Indeed, it is a way of fulfilling what Barash calls above *"our need"* to maximize "our" fitness.

But Barash is not finished. As a final piece of evidence for the "naturalness" of rape, Barash's *textbook* contains the following general claim, although the empirical study he is no doubt basing it on is not cited: "whether they like to admit it or not, many human males are stimulated by the idea of rape".[86]

Birds do it . . . bees do it . . . many men find it stimulating to think about. . . . Now, *how could rape be bad?*

In a film prepared by two Sociobiologists for use in a high school science curriculum, the implications of Sociobiology for social and political policy are advocated explicitly.

> It's time we started viewing ourselves as having biological, genetic and natural components to our behavior, *and that we start setting up a physical and social world to match those tendencies.*[87]

Of course the first thing to note is that the social world to "match the tendencies" that Sociobiologists regard as "natural" is in some respects already "set up" in societies in which, among other things, women, men, and children are raped (Barash does not talk about how they are often beaten, mutilated, or murdered in the process, or how these things might maximize fitness), and in which some think that "male dominance", male aggression, rape, and war are natural. The further adjustment we could make to "match those tendencies", is, of course, to stop treating things like rape, aggression, war, racial discrimination, male dominance, dominance hierarchies, and so forth, as problems, as socially rather than biologically caused, or as avoidable and contingent features of some human societies. Each of these things has been described as fitness promoting and the product of natural selection by Sociobiologists.[88]

But in recognizing that part of our social world either does "match these tendencies" or is believed to match these by Sociobiologists, the fundamental relationships between Sociobiology and the political and social context of contemporary western societies become clear. These relationships are directly relevant to issues Addelson raises about the cognitive authority granted to scientists.

Science and Social Context

First, Sociobiologists are actively conveying their metaphysical commitments and their findings to the lay public, including high school and college students. Further, like the specific cases Addelson explores, the potential consequences of this research program are political and far-reaching. If Sociobiology is accepted as an explanatory framework for human behavior and social organization, and if the explanations for specific behaviors, social arrangements, and divisions in power that Sociobiologists offer are accepted, the impact on our understandings of ourselves and on social and political policy will be substantial. Sociobiologists offer explanations rooted in "inclusive fitness" for many things we might hope are not inevitable—and Sociobiologists do not have evidence that they are inevitable—and for many things that, although they may be found in contemporary western society (at least something superficially like them), are claimed by other scientists to not be universal, including rape, male aggression, and war. And like Quine's appeal to natural selection as the source of values "we all agree about", the appeal made by Sociobiologists to natural selection *justifies* the behaviors and social arrangements they name, universalize, and allegedly explain.

So there can be no question that the metaphysical commitments of Sociobiology have the potential to impact on social attitudes and policy or that their impact will be political. The program has already had an impact that reflects the implications of its metaphysical commitments and explanations. Sociobiology has been adopted and put to use by conservative right-wing groups[89] as providing the "proof" of the "naturalness" and the explanation of racism and sexism. These groups have recognized Sociobiology's explanations as justifying social and political practices arrangements in western societies.[90]

And although we might not always find it appropriate to hold scientists responsible for how their work is used by others, there is no absolving Sociobiologists of responsibility for the implications of their explanations. It is not possible to separate the social and political implications of those explanations from "the research program *itself*" or the explanations themselves. No such detachment is possible, and it is not argued for by most Sociobiologists. Wilson argues that Sociobiology is apolitical, as I noted earlier, but I have argued that this claim is illegitimate given the content of his claims about human behavior and societies—and the lack of evidence for them. Moreover, most Sociobiologists are well aware of the political implications of their claims and of the metaphysical commitments of the research program, and, as we have seen, they are quite interested in explicating and communicating these. They are certainly not standing "aloof" from values and politics—although they claim to be "just reporting" how things are, however little we may like it.

Barash, for example, dismisses feminists—more correctly, the "straw persons" he characterizes as "feminists" and other "egalitarians".

> It strains belief that around the globe and throughout history women have been the victims of a coordinated and sustained plot by churlish males who have conspired to manipulate the social structure to exploit women by forcing them into unwanted roles.[91]

The ontology and "universals" incorporated in Sociobiology are further indications of deep relationships between the discipline and the social and political context of western societies. As unclarified as they are in Sociobiologists' writings, the relationship of these "universal" "behaviors" and "forms of social organization" to the context of contemporary western societies is clear. Other scientists point out that a little bit of homework reveals that they are universal neither transhistorically nor cross-culturally.[92]

As Bleier and other critics of Sociobiology also note,[93] some of these characteristics, behaviors, and features, though recognizable because of their superficiality and generality to contemporary westerners, are quite strange scientific objects. What, for example, are the behavioral conditions for "female coyness"? The conditions that would not be recognized just in our society but are met in other species, other cultures, other historical periods? Why should we call animal groups with one male "harems"?[94] And what is the sense of 'harem' in this context? Why is a female in any species referred to as "a male's female"?[95] How do genes "intend" anything? How do bees? Such objects and descriptions are undefined and unclarified by Sociobiologists, but the relationship between them and contemporary western thinking and political context is clear enough that many of those accepting or rejecting the program have not needed further clarification.

There are other indications that the relationship between this research program and the social and political context of our larger society runs deep. As we have seen, Sociobiologists have addressed current political issues directly. They have stated that "egalitarian politics" involve "going against nature",[96] and I noted Barash's claim that "mother nature is the greatest sexist of all". Some warn against altering divisions of labor in which women are primarily responsible for childrearing,[97] and Barash describes rapists as being no different from sexually excluded mallards.

The relationships between the objects Sociobiologists posit and explain, and current social and political context, are exactly of the sort that Addelson claims can obtain between research programs and the larger community. Sociobiologists are offering explanations for behaviors, expectations, arrangements, and divisions in labor and power that exist, and are now regarded as problems, within a certain social and political context—a context that includes such features, or something like them—and in which there is currently political and social interest.

THEORY ACCEPTANCE AND SOCIAL CONTEXT

But there is more to learn from this case that is relevant to Addelson's contention that there are deep relationships between science communities and the larger social and political context. Specifically, there is more to be learned about the role that social and political context can play in theory acceptance. Sociobiology has prompted interest and gained wide acceptance in a number of spheres—among scientists from various disciplines, philosophers, political advocates, and high school administrators and science teachers. It has also received more than the usual amount of publicity in the popular press for research programs, and most Sociobiologists, other advocates of the program, and the press put the theory forth as if it is "successful" and "confirmed".

When we look to find the basis for the widespread acceptance of this research program, we find that on "strictly scientific" grounds—on the grounds of the methodological principles currently accepted in the disciplines of evolutionary biology, genetics, theories of social evolution, animal sociology, and the social sciences—the status of Sociobiology is at least controversial. Moreover, even on Sociobiologists' accounts, their evidence for genetic determination of human behavior and social arrangements is indirect.

Now despite these problems, the research program has gained wide acceptance, and many Sociobiologists claim or imply that the theory is confirmed. So, its acceptance must be on the basis of something *other than* its own merits on "strictly scientific grounds". Bleier makes a similar point.

> If this amount of attention, which also includes the continuing production by Sociobiologists of new books that say nothing new and are aimed at the lay public, is being paid to a question with neither intrinsic scientific or intellectual merit nor hope of definitive proof, we can suspect that it is a question of great political, social, or economic merit and most likely all three.[98]

In fact, there are two general candidates for these grounds. One is the current state of science in the narrow sense: the status of alternative theories and research programs, and/or the need for a theoretical framework. The other candidate is the larger social and political context that is already deeply reflected in this research program. Which is the factor underwriting the acceptance of Sociobiology? We can begin with the first candidate.

We know that the provisional acceptance of a theory is not always related to the theory's strength on "strictly scientific" grounds (as was the case, for example, in the initial acceptance of the Copernican theory[99]), and often, as in the case of the Copernican theory, we can point to the "current state of scientific inquiry" to explain, even to justify, the provisional acceptance of a framework for further investigation. These grounds obtain when an earlier or rival framework has been exposed to be bankrupt or rife with problems. In such cases there is good reason, and we can say good "scientific reason"— reasons related to the status of other scientific theories—to begin casting around for viable alternatives.

But this is not the situation that obtains now. Alternative frameworks for explaining what Sociobiology claims to explain are not bankrupt. There are current and promising alternative evolutionary models and alternative accounts of human cultural evolution.[100] And Sociobiology is not, of course, the only alternative to denying that biology has anything to do with human behavior. (The "Sociobiology or else" so often claimed by Sociobiologists is a red herring. The most well-known critics of the program, R. C. Lewontin, Stephen Gould, Ruth Bleier, and Ruth Hubbard, insist that biology is relevant to human behavior. What they deny is that genes determine behavior or traits.) Moreover, the social sciences are not bankrupt. Rather, the evolutionary model on which Sociobiology builds and its explanations depend is one for which many evolutionary theorists are developing alternatives because they have found it inadequate[101] and the universals in behavior and social arrangements that Sociobiology requires are contradicted by current work in anthropology, primatology, sociology, and history.

Finally, of course, many Sociobiologists and advocates of the program are not "provisionally" accepting the framework and working now to develop and confirm it. Many put the framework forward as "successful" and "confirmed". So in looking for the grounds on which this theory has been widely accepted, we find the current social and political concerns and context of our larger society.

The success Sociobiologists have had in promoting their discipline and their explanations, and their willingness to promote the latter and to explore their implications for social policy, suggest that Addelson's concerns about the cognitive authority scientists exercise are warranted. We need to explore the assumption that science is insulated from social and political context, an assumption that underwrites that authority. We need to look at the role that the context plays in shaping the directions of research and the content of theories. We also need to scrutinize how researchers communicate their findings and metaphysical commitments to the larger community, as well as the implications of this communication for social and political attitudes and policy. And we have found that a further relationship can exist between science communities and social and political context. The grounds for theory acceptance can include things other than a theory's acceptability on strictly scientific grounds. Sociobiology is a case in which social and political context and concerns have overcome large deficiencies in a theoretical framework.

What emerges as problematic about the "cognitive authority" scientists are granted and exercise is that the authority is unscrutinized for the most part, and when it is scrutinized, scientists call "foul", appealing to the "autonomy of science"; it is unscrutinized on the basis of the view that scientists are insulated from social and political context—a view deeply suspect in cases like the one we have considered; and because it is unscrutinized, the cognitive authority scientists exercise is political. I want to focus on the last of these problems.

Wilson, Barash, and other Sociobiologists demand that the "autonomy" of science be respected, that they be able to tell us "how things are" even if we do not like it. They demand to be allowed to exercise their cognitive authority without interference based on political views.

They justify these demands by portraying their own research as standing aloof of social and political context, as "value free" and apolitical. The concerns voiced by other scientists and scholars about both the theoretical adequacy and the political implications of Sociobiology are characterized by Sociobiologists as politically motivated attacks on the pursuit of "knowledge for its own sake" and the freedom of scientists to pass that "knowledge" along. The assumption that science is insulated from politics enables Sociobiologists to promote their claims as simply a report of "how things are". But we have found a number of reasons to doubt the insulation of this discipline.

There are deeper problems. Sociobiologists are aware of the nature of the evidence for the claims they make about human social behavior—at best, that evidence is indirect—and they are aware of the implications of their claims—even if, like Wilson, they think one has to misunderstand those claims to use them as a justification of the status quo and/or that Sociobiology is merely a "promising" research program.

If we take into account the enormous work Sociobiologists will need to undertake to clean up and make respectable the ontology they have built and the "sociology" they maintain, that it will take to establish anything like direct evidence for genetic determination of human social behaviors and social organization, and the controversial status of the evolutionary model among other evolutionary biologists and geneticists, the very best one could say—the very best—is that Wilson's *Sociobiology* is a promising hypothesis.

But then we must also say that the cognitive authority granted to Sociobiologists as scientists is political, and their use of it to advertise and promote explanations for views of human behavior that imply the social and political arrangements best suited to that nature—an implication some of them advocate and others know can be misunderstood—is political as well.

The autonomy from politics that Sociobiologists demand as their due is premised on an autonomy that is artificial.

EMPIRICISM, AND METAPHYSICS AND SCIENCE

As Addelson's analysis and our consideration of Sociobiology indicate, scientists communicate metaphysical commitments to our larger community as they communicate their questions, methodologies, and findings. In Chapter Two I outlined some problems that the issue of metaphysics and science raises for views shaped by the Hempel and Nagel tradition. We also considered what Kuhn has said about the role of metaphysical commitments in science. Quine's views concerning the relationship between metaphysics and science are more helpful than either.

Quine shows that metaphysics is not *separable* from serious science, that ontology is deeply embedded in our theories, and that it shows itself in what, when we render a theory in first-order quantification, the domain of our theory includes.[102] He also shows that it is not possible to separate what we talk about (the objects we posit) from the way we talk about them.

The consequence is that we cannot accept a theory and reject the metaphysical commitments it incorporates or dispense with these. Moreover, because metaphysical commitments *can* be exposed and evaluated, good science can be seen to *require* good metaphysics, and to lead to good metaphysics.

Given these views, we would expect to find metaphysical commitments incorporated in theories, methodologies, and questions. And we would expect that in conveying these things, scientists will convey metaphysical commitments. The point is that the issue Addelson and others raise about metaphysical commitments in science is an issue only if scientists refuse to acknowledge that research questions, methodologies, and theories commit us to the metaphysics they incorporate and continue the myth that science is without such commitments, or if we assume, like Kuhn, that metaphysical commitments are beyond elucidation and evaluation—except perhaps in revolutionary science or in retrospect.

Recognizing that we cannot use a theory to organize our experience and be free to reject the metaphysics inherent in it, we can suggest, as an opening response to the issues Addelson raises about metaphysical commitments, that science needs to be demystified. Scientists need to be explicit about the metaphysical commitments incorporated in research questions, methodological commitments, and theories. Sociobiologists, for example, should be expected to be explicit concerning the commitments this theory makes to such objects as "female coyness", and they should be expected to clean that ontology up, being equally explicit about what precisely "coyness" is—the conditions under which it is appropriate to attribute it and those in which it is not, and their grounds for universalizing it across cultures, historical periods, and species. That the commitment to searching for biological explanations for human behaviors and social organization incorporates metaphysical commitments, and that it leads to the methodological commitments outlined earlier, also must be made explicit. And it needs to be made explicit that whatever evidence there is for genetic determination of human social behavior is, at best, indirect. Finally, Sociobiologists need to explain how genes determine complex traits and social arrangements, and why it is not necessary to make use of, or to at least establish that they do not need to make use of, the current research done by historians, anthropologists, primatologists, and sociologists that makes their own sociology and animal sociology appear superficial at best.

Now, ontological house cleaning and the clear statement of a research program's metaphysical commitments do not insure that those metaphysical commitments that reflect political context and experiences will be exposed as doing so, or that metaphysical and methodological commitments will, upon explicit statement, reveal their dubious status. But when we acknowledge that the boundary between science and metaphysics is false, we can at least see that such attention is necessary to and constitutive of good science. When we also recognize that judging ontologies and evaluating a theory or explanation on the basis of standards of ontological clarity, and metaphysical and methodological commitments, are possible, then we can insist that such evaluation be part of our standards for doing good science and be used to evaluate theories and research programs.

So a more sophisticated awareness among scientists and the rest of us of the relationship between theories and metaphysics is called for. Minimally, such awareness would open the door for scrutinizing such commitments and coming to recognize their actual import. Insofar as scientists convey their theories and research at all, Addelson and Quine show that they convey metaphysical commitments. Insofar as Quine and feminist critics show that metaphysical commitments can be elucidated and scrutinized, then it is clear that we can and should *judge* a theory, research program, or methodology on the basis of the metaphysical commitments it incorporates, and on the basis of the standards the advocates of these adhere to. A theory will be only as serious, precise, and worthy of attention as are its metaphysical commitments.

Finally, we have found that Addelson is correct that metaphysical commitments can be shaped by, and shape, social and political views and practices. There are deep connections between the universals Sociobiologists allege and take it upon themselves to explain, and our common-sense ontology, expectations, practices and experiences, including those involving sex/gender and politics.

Hierarchies in Cognitive Authority and Labor

Addelson is also concerned with how social arrangements in science communities affect the development of scientific knowledge. She points out that those within science communities who set the questions to be pursued and determine which understandings are "legitimate" are often a small minority of a research specialty.

> Only some of the many people who work within a research specialty have epistemological authority within it. Barbara Reskin remarks, "The roles of both student and technician are characterized by lower status and by a technical division of labor that allocates scientific creativity and decision making to scientists and laboratory work to those assigned the role of technician or student" [Reskin 1978, p. 20]. The role division justifies assigning credit to the chief investigator, but its most important effect is on communication. Technicians and students work on the chief investigator's problems in ways he or she considers appropriate. . . . They are not among the significant communicators of the specialty.
>
> Researchers who *are* significant communicators set categories for classifying their subjects of study, and they define the meaning of what is taking place.[103]

Addelson notes that cognitive authority is further divided hierarchically according to "prestige". The sciences differ in prestige, and specialties within sciences differ in terms of prestige as well. Addelson maintains that there are epistemological consequences of these various divisions; they can, she argues, determine which understandings are pursued as promising and which are eventually proliferated. The frameworks adopted in research and funded, for example, can be determined by these prestige hierarchies.

> The sciences differ in prestige, physics having more than economics, and both having more than educational psychology. Specialties in a science differ in prestige, experimental having more than clinical psychology for example. Prestige differences affect researchers' judgments on which metaphysical and methodological commitments are to be preferred. . . .
>
> Within specialties, researchers differ in prestige, so that some have access to positions of power while other do not. Some teach in prestigious institutions and train the next generation of successful researchers.[104]

Now, it is reasonable to think that science communities require some divisions of labor, and that some within these communities—because of differences in expertise and focus, in experience and vision, and because of the practices of agencies that fund scientific research[105]—appropriately assume a special position with relation to defining problems, acquiring funding, and communicating information.

We may recognize the efficiency of divisions in cognitive labor, but it is clear that we should explore whether the divisions have epistemological consequences, and whether prestige hierarchies and divisions in cognitive authority have consequences as well. Specifically, the hierarchical nature of divisions in cognitive labor and authority needs to be examined. If social arrangements within scientific communities limit the number of people who define the focus of research programs and convey the findings of research to other scientists and to the public, and if these social arrangements and funding practices work together to determine which understandings come to be regarded as *legitimate* and which are not pursued, then such arrangements need to be scrutinized. They are appropriately considered factors of the epistemology of science.

> The question is not whether top scientists in most fields produce some very good work but rather the more important question of whether other good work, even work critical of the top scientists, is not taken seriously because its proponents are not members of the same powerful networks and so cannot exercise the same cognitive authority. The question is made particularly difficult because, by disregarding or downgrading competing research, the "top scientists" cut off the resources necessary for their competition to develop really good work. In most fields, it is next to impossible to do research without free time, aid from research assistants, secretaries, craftsmen, custodians, and in many cases, access to equipment.[106]

Although Addelson's concerns may be readily acknowledged as relevant to the epistemology of science, they would be understood in a specific way by most empiricists. It would seem to most that no more is at stake here relative to the epistemology of science than "two heads would be better than one" (or lots would be, rather than fewer), and criticism should not be limited.

Indeed, none of the accounts of science we have examined considers how the specific social arrangements incorporated in science communities might have a bearing on the directions of scientific knowledge. Hempel and Nagel assume that the logic of justification (which, on their account, exhausts the logic of science), along with the autonomy of science from common sense, will insure (if we do things right) the objectivity of the knowledge developed in science communities. On these grounds, they write off the issue of how questions, methodologies, or theories are arrived at as irrelevant to the content of science, the body of knowledge that is arrived at through the testing of theories. Though Kuhn recognizes that social arrangements within science communities are fundamental to the epistemology of science, there is nothing in his account of such arrangements to indicate that there are *divisions* in labor, prestige, and authority, or that such divisions could have consequences. Quine apparently assumes that at a given time "we" will agree about the questions worth asking and the standards by which potential answers are to be judged, so he does not consider social arrangements as epistemological factors. But Addelson thinks there is more at stake than that these divisions might limit criticism, as we will consider shortly.

Several other insights emerge in Addelson's attention to these divisions. One is that when we consider how these divisions might be changed, it becomes clear that they are related to factors in the larger context of our society. We can imagine, for example, how cognitive labor might be organized in a society in which hierarchical divisions in labor and authority are not viewed as acceptable ways to organize or divide labor of any sort. We can also imagine that participation in science might not be limited to a small percentage of the population, if educational and funding practices were not shaped by the expectation that only a relative few could engage in science. And we can also see that were participation in science more widespread, scientists would probably not have the status of "autonomous experts". It might be expected that the larger community would partake in decisions concerning which research should be undertaken. We can also recognize that the current emphasis on individual initiative and the current prestige hierarchies (physicists over social scientists, Harvard researchers over virtually everyone else) might be contingent features of science and deeply related to social and political arrangements and practices in western societies.

And, there is evidence to suggest that the current sociology of science is contingent and related to social and political factors in our society. One sort of evidence is the effort to develop widespread participation in science in China.[107] The steps being taken to facilitate this participation suggest that who participates in science is at least in part a function of factors in the larger social and political context.[108] There are also scientists working in Puerto Rico and in Latin America to develop science communities that are more broadly based.[109] These efforts support Addelson's contention that the current sociology of science in western society is not an inevitable feature of science and that it has consequences for the content of science.

Biologist Richard Levins has worked with other scientists to develop science communities in Puerto Rico.[110] On the basis of this effort and his study of the role played by social and political arrangements in determining who engages in science,[111] Levins argues that the relatively small number of scientists in the United States, and the even smaller number of senior researchers, are not due to the nature of inquiry or innate lacks in the intelligence or interest necessary to doing science, but rather to social and political factors. According to Levins, the factors contributing to a small number of scientists in western societies include differential access to education, the assumption among many working in early and middle education and in the society at large that only "the brightest" can be scientists, and the assumptions and practices of those organizations that fund scientific research and education.[112]

Levins maintains that changing the factors that work to discourage interest in science and the assumptions that underlie these factors—for example, that only a relatively few can understand and do science—would probably result in very different social arrangements than those that characterize western science.

> Science [in the United States and other western industrial societies] as it has developed in the past, through recruitment by stringent selection, is a result of the structure of society rather than the nature of knowledge or the nature of discovery. There is at least the potential of an alternative way of developing science as much more of a mass phenomenon.[113]

As evidence for the contingency of the selection procedure, Levins notes the changes in the learning patterns and interests of groups previously excluded from higher education (or thought to be uninterested in it) that came about because of changes in social and political arrangements. He cites the study among prison inmates of law, history, and sociology, the rise of Reconstruction schools dedicated to making knowledge of the classics available to former slaves previously denied access to these, and the recent rise in the number of people studying economics and science in Cuba.[114] As Levins points out, these changes in learning patterns were brought about by changes in social and political context.

> In each of these cases, a very large population suddenly becomes interested in the class of problems that we have been taught is beyond the capacity of the mob, because of the belief that they can cope with it, they can handle it, and that what they do matters. Now what this suggests is at least the plausible possibility of further experimentation in the task of making science broadly accessible—*not simply as a democratic duty, but as a way of making science better.*[115]

Unless we are convinced that only a few can, in fact, be scientists, and that an even smaller number are capable of being "top researchers", Addelson's and Levin's analyses suggest that the current social arrangements in which scientific knowledge develops could be different if other things in the social and political context of western societies changed.

But Levins also maintains in the passage above that science would be *better* were these social arrangements to change, and he is here introducing a new dimension to the issue of divisions in cognitive labor and authority. How could making science more *broadly accessible* make science *better?* Addelson's concerns with divisions in cognitive labor within science communities and about the role that prestige hierarchies and funding practices play in determining which research is pursued and which understandings become accepted and eventually proliferated also suggest the view that the social arrangements of science have a bearing on the content of science.

Levins argues explicitly that divisions in cognitive labor and authority can have a bearing on the directions of research and the content of scientific knowledge. He cites a number of cases in which a narrow focus among researchers and the funders of a project led to problems that would have been avoided if the proposed project had been open to scrutiny and input from a larger segment of the population. He also cites cases in which the current economics of science have determined the research undertaken and the knowledge gained. He notes, for example, that because funding has been made available for research into pesticides, our knowledge of these as well as their use has grown enormously. And, he argues, because those in positions to fund research have not been interested in alternatives, relatively little research has been done into agricultural practices that would not require pesticides. These cases do not indicate that "more heads would be better than fewer". They suggest that *divisions in experience* in some cases, the reliance of research on funding, and the interests of those who can provide funding, can be factors in determining the questions pursued and the knowledge gained.[116] Thus, Levins' examples suggest that social arrangements, including economics, have consequences for the content of science.

We will not consider what appear to be clear consequences of the current divisions in cognitive labor until the next chapter. But the experience of Levins and others who are building science communities in other countries suggest that the factors Addelson draws to our attention are not inevitable features of or "constitutive" of science. Changes in educational practices, in funding practices, and in how we view science—as, for instance, a project that many could and would participate in rather than an activity in which only a few can and will engage—could change the divisions in cognitive labor and authority that currently characterize our society and scientific communities, enable more broadly based criticism, and have an effect on the research undertaken. Of direct relevance to the issues raised by Sociobiology, such changes could alter the status of scientists as "autonomous experts"—a status we have already seen can be consequential for our attitudes and practices and for social and political policy.

Some issues discussed in earlier chapters would allow us to at least begin to think about how social arrangements within science and the larger society could have a bearing on the content of science. If our view of science has developed beyond the positivist and postpositivist visions, if we recognize, for example, that theories are constructed and not "discovered", that all of our ways of organizing things are interconnected, and that all of our theories are underdetermined by the evidence we have for them, then we can also recognize that alternative theories, commensurate with the evidence we have for our current theories, might have become prevalent. To use Quine's term, there is "slack" between everything we say and our evidence for it.

In addition, if Addelson is correct that the directions research takes and the understandings that come to be certified are often a function of the cognitive authority granted to "top researchers" and the prestige granted to some sciences over others (physics, for example, over all others), then we can see that it is possible that some frameworks that have been discarded might have been pursued, given a different way of organizing cognitive labor, different (or no) prestige hierarchies, and different funding practices. It seems clearly plausible, for example, that the prestige of genetics, zoology, etc., over the social sciences is at least part of what enables Sociobiologists to feel warranted in ignoring research in the social sciences that challenges their own claims.

Although each of the accounts of science we have considered presents obstacles to our dealing with divisions in cognitive labor and authority as epistemological issues, it is also clear that not all the questions suggested by our going theories and experiences are pursued in the sciences. Choices are made about which questions warrant attention and about how they should be pursued. There may be many of us convinced, for example, that human biology and evolutionary history have something to do with human behavior (we do not photosynthesize, for example, and we are large enough to be subject to gravity), and we might be interested in pursuing the question of the relationship but think the way it is pursued in Sociobiology is not promising. We could pursue it in a very different way than Sociobiology does—but still in a way commensurate with many of our other going theories.

These two kinds of "slack", one between the body of our theories and the evidence we have for them, the other between the questions we pursue and our going theories, make it possible to see that the current sociology of science, in particular the divisions in cognitive authority and labor, and prestige, could have a bearing on the content of scientific knowledge. Neither of these vitiates the view that theories and beliefs are constrained by experience or that coherence to other theories is the other general standard we use to judge theories. With a going body of theories, although we can imagine that they certainly might have been otherwise (the regularity reflected in Boyle's law might, within an alternative body of theory, appear in a different form), it is also the case that changes will come about through the process of science, with the bulk of theories and standards of evidence left intact. What Addelson's and Levins' analyses suggest is that, given the slack, the process and the factors that determine the directions of scientific knowledge deserve scrutiny.

The directions and content of scientific research and knowledge, their arguments suggest, are not determined solely, nor are they exhausted by, the logic of inquiry, nature, and the current state of scientific knowledge. The slack between theories and evidence, and the recognition that knowledge is socially constructed, allow us to see that social arrangements may also be determinants of the content of science.

Some of us might remain convinced that the directions of scientific knowledge *are* determined by nature and the logic of science, or we might think that there are no divisions in experience deep enough or consequential enough to make a difference, at least not one of consequence, to the content of scientific theorizing. If we think either of these things, then the divisions in cognitive labor within science and in our larger community might strike us as factors of epistemological consequence only insofar as they limit criticism.

So the last of the divisions in cognitive labor and authority we will consider in this chapter—the division by sex/gender— may not seem to be an "epistemological" issue to some readers. In the discussion of the division in the next section I will be concerned to further illuminate relationships between science communities and the larger social and political context—in particular, the continuities involving sex/gender arrangements between our science communities and our larger community. But I will be laying the groundwork for considering the epistemological consequences, the consequences for the content of science, of the several divisions we have considered in this chapter, including, centrally, divisions in cognitive labor and authority by sex/gender.

Women in Science

A second general issue feminist science critics raise about the social arrangements in science communities is the fact that women, for the most part, are in the lower positions in the hierarchies of cognitive labor and authority. The larger social context is mirrored not only in this aspect of the social structure of science communities. It is also reflected in the attitudes of many male scientists. Feminist critics point out that despite the lifting of the formal barriers to the admission of women to graduate programs and science communities and despite the large number of women in science, women as a group remain in less prestigious and less policy-making positions in scientific communities and industrial research, and on science faculties.[117]

Though the formal barriers to the admission of women into doctoral programs and science communities have been lifted, Sandra Harding and other feminist critics cite a number of "informal barriers" that remain. These, they argue, result in a social order in science communities that reflects that of the larger society: a hierarchical order that is dominated by men.[118]

Women's experiences in the sciences are difficult to characterize and, in this and other respects, they are in keeping with the experiences of women in various careers. Scientists differ over the significance of sex/gender to their careers and experiences. Some claim that sex/gender has had nothing to do with their experiences or careers; others claims that it has been a consequential variable.[119] Statistics I will outline indicate that women do face problems in science, and that these problems are specifically related to sex/gender.

And, what emerges in what many scientists say about their experiences and in the statistics we will consider is that women scientists face what feminists call "a glass ceiling":[120] a barrier which the lifting of formal barriers prohibits, but one that remains and shapes and limits careers. The problem (the glass) is that the barriers are often subtle and well hidden.

> I am an experimental psychologist, doing research on vision. The profession has for a long time considered this activity, on the part of my sex, to be an outrageous violation of the social order and against all the laws of nature. . . . I was remarkably naive. Stupid, you might say. Anybody can be president, no? So, anybody can be a scientist. . . . I was not prepared for the discovery that women were not welcome in science, primarily because nobody had told me.
>
> . . . my discovery that women were not welcome in psychology began when I arrived at Harvard, on the first day of class. That day, the entering graduate students had been invited to lunch with one of the star professors in the department. After lunch, he leaned back in his chair, lit his pipe, began to puff, and announced: "Women don't belong in graduate school". The male graduate students, as if by prearranged signal . . . nodded and assented, "yeah".
>
> . . . the male graduate students never were told that they didn't belong. They rapidly became trusted junior partners in the great research firms at Harvard. They were carefully nurtured, groomed, and run. . . . But for the women in my class it was different. We were *shown* we didn't belong. For instance, even though I was first in my class, when I wanted to do my dissertation research, I couldn't get access to the necessary equipment. The excuse was I might break the equipment. This was certainly true. . . . The male graduate students working with it broke it every week; I didn't expect to be different.[121]

Perhaps the most acutely felt problem experienced by scientists who are women is that they cannot be "colleagues" of their male counterparts.

> Scientific meetings, conferences, and conventions are harassing and humiliating for women because women, by and large, cannot have male colleagues. Conversations, social relations, invitations to lunch, and the like are generally viewed as sexual, not professional, encounters if a woman participates in them. It does not cross men's minds that a woman's motivation may be entirely professional.[122]
>
> I had graduated Phi Beta Kappa from Wellesley; had obtained my Ph.D. in psychology at Harvard in two and one half years, ranked first in my graduate class, and I couldn't get a job. . . . at the places where I was being considered for jobs, they were asking me questions like,

"How can a little girl like you teach a great big class of men"? . . . A famous faculty liberal . . . put what I assume was a fatherly hand on my knee, and said in a tone of deep concern, "You ought to get married".[123]

Some scientists claim that although informal barriers are becoming increasingly subtle, they are still at work, and in some fields they are as pervasive and consequential as their less subtle predecessors. They include personal and sexual harassment; discrimination in hiring, in research grants, and in access to technological aids and pay; and frequent references by professors and colleagues to the "inappropriateness" of women in science.[124] They also include the continuing practice among the Ivy League and more prestigious universities of admitting more men than women;[125] the lesser amount of financial aid offered to women in higher education;[126] the lesser number of research grants given to women in the sciences and in engineering; the higher number of teaching assistantships in fields for which research grants will, over the long term, yield the better results from a career standpoint;[127] and other restrictions that women face in higher education.[128]

Many scientists and engineers note that they were ill prepared for the blatant sexism that they find in science communities.[129] The sexism they encounter reflects views in the larger social context, but feminist science critics argue that it is also related to a long-standing view that science is a "masculine" enterprise. Either or both may be at work in the report a dean of a major university gave several years ago to the National Academy of Science. "We have more women than men among the entering graduate students in chemistry this year, and I'm a little worried about the quality of the department."[130] And a number of studies indicate that whatever the specific mechanics involved, women's credentials and achievements within the sciences, as within other fields, will not have what Sandra Harding calls the "reinvestment potential" that men's do.[131] Even when women are able to get the same educational background in terms of institutions attended, class ranking, course background, dissertation topic, and advisers, they are generally not able to "reinvest" these credentials to the degree their male colleagues do.[132] In 1984, the National Academy of Sciences' Committee on Women reported:

This year has brought dramatic gains for American women. The first three female astronauts have flown in space. The endurance and ability of female athletes was recognized by the inclusion of a women's marathon in the Olympic games. . . .
But these women remain the exceptions in a society that still assigns

most of its leadership roles to men, especially in science and engineering. The inequity is widespread: *women Ph.D.'s are half as likely as their male counterparts to be hired for industrial research positions, and those who do obtain employment are only half as likely as men to advance to management positions.* Women also remain *grossly underrepresented on science and engineering facilities:* at M.I.T., for example, the proportion is one in ten.[133]

Where are the women who have earned doctorates in science and engineering if they are not on science faculties, in industrial research, or in management positions in that research? It is not that women are not entering the sciences and engineering. They are and have been for some time. Statistics indicate that there are many *more* women with doctorates in the sciences and engineering than there are in the humanities. In 1982 there were 50,000 women who held doctorates in science and engineering; there were fewer than 20,000 with doctorates in the humanities.[134] This is not what a casual view of the fields would suggest. And the trend toward doctorates in the sciences and engineering has not slowed down among women. In 1985 approximately 4,500 women earned doctoral degrees in the sciences and engineering, compared with 1,500 in the humanities.[135] So where are they?

According to the National Academy of Sciences, women are almost twice as likely as men "to be involved in support activities in research programs, such as performing library services, collecting data, and writing reports".[136] Their research indicated "a continuing strong preference by employers and senior faculty for men over women, regardless of qualifications".[137] The Academy also found that the laws that forbid discrimination in hiring can be gotten around informally, and frequently are.

> A look at the 1970's, when colleges and universities sought to reduce their faculties and budgets because of an anticipated decline in enrollments while also observing the laws that prohibit sex discrimination, is revealing. Women were indeed hired, but mainly for the newly minted "revolving door" or "folding chair" appointments. Their presence in a variety of off-track, junior, and short-term positions has produced a superficial look of equality, quite without substance. *In the 25 leading U.S. universities, women faculty in science and engineering are twice as likely as their male counterparts to be hired for positions without a future.*[138]

Given what we have found to be a prevalent understanding about science—indeed, a view that underwrites its claim to objectivity as the latter has long been defined and defended, namely, that the *particular* identity of the scientist is either irrelevant (with the exception of education) to what the observer would see, or that it would be filtered out through scientific method—what sort of view is operating here?

Some feminists argue that the multifaceted aspects of gender socialization and deep relationships between gender categories and views of science—in particular, those that involve the view that science is masculine and/or a "male enterprise"— combine to provide a network of informal barriers to women's success in many sciences, and to the association of many fields with what are perceived to be "masculine" characteristics.[139]

> In articulating the commonplace that [in the history of our race the equation objective = masculine is a valid one], Simmel steps outside the convention of academic discourse. The historically pervasive association between masculine and objective, more specifically between masculine and scientific, is a topic that academic critics resist taking seriously. Why is that? . . .
>
> The virtual silence of at least the nonfeminist academic community on this subject suggests that the association of masculinity with scientific thought has the status of a myth which either cannot or should not be examined closely. It has simultaneously the air of being "self-evident" and "nonsensical"—the former by virtue of existing in the realm of common knowledge (that is, everyone knows it), and the latter by virtue of lying outside the realm of formal knowledge.[140]

Evelyn Fox Keller's view that the equating of masculinity and science is in the realm of common knowledge is supported by several recent studies of how scientists view their fields and by women's experiences in various sciences.[141]

What is suggested by these studies, by the experiences women report, and by the statistics I have outlined, is that the association of science with "masculinity" is very deep[142] and that some scientists regard the traits necessary for doing science to be in some sense inherently "masculine".[143] Women, as the National Academy of Sciences study indicates, are largely in the sort of handmaiden jobs that characterize women's labor in other fields. Indeed, in an article in *Science* the chairperson of a biophysics department advises biophysicists to hire women as research assistants, precisely on the basis of sex/gender stereotypes and an implicit view that senior researchers will be men.

> The purpose of this assistant is to require daily instruction about what to do. Thus you are inescapably forced to plan for the operation of another pair of hands. The female is better because she will not operate quite as readily on her own, and this is exactly what you want.[144]

Cross-cultural and historical differences in divisions of labor by sex/ gender, in ideas about gender, and in the behaviors women and men exhibit, indicate that "socialization" is a fundamental factor in the differences in behaviors that are highly prized in the "most rigorous" sciences, for example, aggressiveness, disdain for others, and "careful insubordination".[145] There is also a growing body of research that explores the historical and current associations of science with masculinity, the coincidence of the traits regarded as necessary to doing science (at least "hard science") and those associated with masculinity, and the socialization that feminists and others argue underlies current behavioral differences between women and men.[146]

This work is too serious and extensive to be summarized superficially, and the issues we will consider in the balance of the larger discussion do not require it. The positions of women in the lower ends of the hierarchies that characterize science communities and the view among many male scientists, educators, and laypersons that women do not belong in science are additional indications that there are deep relationships between science communities and the larger social context. The questions that will concern us in the balance of the larger discussion involve the *consequences* of these continuities for the *content* of science, and the insights those consequences provide into the epistemology of science.

Epistemology, and the Sociology and Autonomy of Science

We can now ask if the cognitive authority scientists are granted and exercise, the potential impact of that authority, and the various divisions in cognitive authority and labor we have considered, as several among many aspects of the social dynamics of science, should be incorporated within the bounds of inquiry about science, and how they should be characterized. How would including them affect our views about science? What relevance might they have to the epistemology of science? And what do they indicate about the two norms linking autonomy and science?

Obviously, a view that takes science be a body of theories whose statements have a certain logical form, a view along the lines of that held by Hempel, Nagel, and many other empiricists, will not permit the kind of scrutiny that feminist research and other studies of science suggest is warranted.

Addelson suggests that we need to broaden our understandings of the factors that are relevant to the epistemology of science.

Although the "rationality of science" is supposed to lie in the fact that scientific understanding is the most open to criticism of *all* understanding, a crucial area for criticism was ruled out of consideration [by the view of science that many Anglo-American philosophers of science took]: the social arrangements through which scientific understanding is developed and through which cognitive authority of the specialist is exercised. . . .[147]

We should . . . try using the notion of cognitive authority and expanding the range of the criteria of scientific rationality and criticism so that it includes social arrangements within the scientific professions.[148]

On Addelson's view, expanding our accounts of science to include the institution of cognitive authority and expanding the study of science to include the social arrangements in science communities would not consist in politicizing a nonpolitical activity. It would not violate an *actual* division between science and politics. The granting of cognitive authority to scientists, given the views that science is detached and insulated from social and political context and that its autonomy must be maintained, is itself political.

If we expand the range of criticism, I believe that philosophers of science and scientists as well will find themselves advocating change in our social system. This would not result in a sudden illegitimate politicization of science or an opening of the floodgates of irrationality. Quite the contrary. Because they have cognitive authority, our scientists already *are* politicized.[149]

There are, of course, philosophers of science and others who have advocated that the sociology of science communities be incorporated in an account of the epistemology of science. Kuhn, as we have seen, takes the sociology of science to be fundamental to the epistemology of science, but he does not include divisions of labor and authority within his account of science, nor does his analysis permit our encompassing the relationships between science communities and the societies in which they are located.[150] And none of the accounts of science we considered earlier discusses the positions of women in science communities or incorporates anything to suggest that their historical exclusion from, or current positions in the hierarchies of, science might have consequences for scientific practice and knowledge.

Thus, there are large hurdles to be overcome if this broadening of scope for appropriate criticism and evaluation is to be managed. Some of these hurdles are due to the emphases and categories in empiricist philosophy of science and some to prevalent views about science among scientists and laypersons. All are related in some way or other to the issue of science's alleged autonomy from social and political context. The view that scientific theorizing is insulated from that context suggests that the identity of the scientists would not matter to the content of her or his scientific theorizing and that the political implications of scientific claims are not appropriately considered by scientists or appropriately criticized by others.

There are other and related difficulties. The issues we have considered indicate that the social arrangements within and outside science communities, for example, the relatively small number engaged in science, the divisions in cognitive authority and labor, and the divisions in authority and labor by sex/gender, are a function of factors in the larger social and political context. Thus, any scrutiny of the social arrangements in science communities and the cognitive authority scientists exercise would need to encompass those factors that underwrite the current social dynamics of science. We would need to expand the epistemology of science to include social arrangements that characterize not only science communities, but our larger society.

Levins addresses the complexity involved in exploring and developing alternative sciences by changing such factors.

> Now we have the problems of what the obstacles are of learning science
> . . . and this means that once we set an agenda of mobilizing the
> intellectual power of a much broader community, we have to start
> thinking about the nature of the educational process, and going off in a
> lot of directions we know very little about at the present time.
>   What makes the theoretical underpinning a very fruitful one is the
> way in which it opens up exciting possibilities, about which there is
> sufficient positive results at the present time to justify continued
> effort.[151]

So, scrutinizing those social arrangements that characterize cognitive labor would require, as a first step, that we recognize science as a *part of*, and not detached from, our larger community and that we recognize social arrangements, including those shaped by politics and economics, as epistemological factors.

Of the three accounts of science we have considered, only Quine's denies the detachment of science from common sense. Quine argues that there are fundamental connections between common-sense theorizing and scientific theorizing. There are, he maintains, connections between the ontologies of these theories, between their methods, and between their theories.

As we saw earlier, Quine also agrees with Addelson's contention that methodologies and research questions incorporate metaphysical commitments, and that these are communicated when research is communicated. Moreover, neither Quine nor many of the rest of us would deny that the development of a theory in science would have a bearing on common-sense views. On Quine's view, the connection is explicit: our theories form a network, show interconnections, and are fundamentally interdependent. Thus, we should expect that views developed in science would have consequences for common-sense beliefs and theories. But several other issues we have discussed in this chapter are either not explored or explicitly ruled as irrelevant to science, by Quine.

One issue is whether issues in the larger social and political context could affect scientific theories—that is, whether social and political issues could have a bearing on the problems researchers address and on the manner in which they address these problems, an issue brought into stark relief by Sociobiology.

There are two things to note here about Quine's view of science. The first is that although Quine maintains that our theories are related, he does not address the possibility that issues in the larger social community could have a bearing on scientific theories. The network of theories is structured in such a way, on his account, that some theories (and certainly those that "systemize" common sense) are better insulated than lower-level theories.

A second and related issue is that as Quine describes it, "common-sense theory" is trans-historical and virtually exhausted by "physical-object theory". Thus, it is not clear where or how assumptions or theories about sex/gender are to be accommodated within the network of theories. Moreover, Quine maintains that science and values are distinct. And even if we expand his notion of "common-sense theorizing" to include social and political views, including views about sex/gender, the issue remains of whether such views could have an impact on more well-insulated theories—of interest here, the research and theories pursued and developed in science.

Feminists have also illuminated and problematized hierarchical divisions in cognitive labor and authority in science communities, and women's positions in these hierarchies. These issues indicate that Quine's account of science communities is at least superficial and that it is naïve. Addelson's and Levins's arguments suggest that these divisions, and those that separate scientists and the larger community, have a bearing on the content of theories. We have already considered how views about sex/gender are incorporated in one research program, Sociobiology. On some level it is becoming clear that we need to explore relationships between *who* is theorizing and the content of that theorizing as both Addelson and Levins suggest.

Quine obviously does not take this possibility into account except in a very superficial sense. Although he views science as a social and ongoing process and knowledge as a bridge of our making, he apparently assumes that in the relevant community (with the exception of differences in education) we will all, so to speak, see the same thing. On that view, divisions in cognitive authority and the positions of women in science communities would not have consequences for the content of science except insofar as they limit criticism. They would not figure in our accounts of the epistemology of science, our explanations of how current theories have come about. There is, of course, no guarantee that science will not go off the track, but except for differences in education and expertise, *who* is doing the theorizing will not make a difference for the content of science.

The issues we have considered suggest that we need to go deeper. The issues raised by Addelson about science's cognitive authority and the hierarchical social structure within many research programs deserve attention, from several points of view.

For our purposes, they deserve epistemological consideration: how do divisions in cognitive labor and authority affect the development and content of scientific understanding? Is criticism limited within research programs in ways that constrain or shape the understandings of nature that are developed in science? Has the norm of the autonomy of science further limited the criticism science should face, and is the norm itself based on views about science that are untenable? Does the sharing of information between scientists and our larger community proceed in only one way? Do the relationships and the cognitive authority granted to scientists need to be scrutinized? Has the view that science is insulated from politics underwritten the political theorizing engaged in by Sociobiologists, and is it part of what enables such unsophisticated politics to pass as "objective knowledge"?

Women's positions in science also deserve attention, and in ways that legal studies are not likely to provide. We should be concerned when a significant number of practicing scientists believe that only men can do science, whether this is indicated by their saying so or by the statistics indicating that divisions involving sex/gender are at work. We should explore the potential consequences of the views operative in such belief, and we should be suspicious of the claim that this is a trivial dispute without consequence for the content of the theories being put forward by scientists.

We have already considered a research program whose connections

to views about sex/gender are obvious. On the basis of our brief exploration of Sociobiology, both in terms of the content and its acceptance, it
is clear that we need to be very suspicious of the view that social arrangements within science communities and the attitudes of male scientists to
having female colleagues do not have a bearing on the content of theories.

It is certainly plausible that these social arrangements have influenced
the nature of the theories produced and promulgated by these hierarchies
and that our failure to recognize or acknowledge this is itself a political
decision. We need to look closer.

CHAPTER FIVE

Bridges of Our Own Making

> There remains the fact—a fact of science itself—that science is a
> conceptual bridge of our own making.
>
> —W. V. Quine

IVISIONS in cognitive authority and labor in science communities and our larger society involve epistemology only if the identities of scientists make a difference to the content of scientific knowledge—only if who is theorizing has a bearing on the research undertaken, the methodologies adopted, and, ultimately, the content of scientific theories. Unless such connections exist, the divisions are social and political issues, and for some of us they are moral issues. As any or all of these, the divisions rightly claim a place in our accounts of science. But they would not figure in our accounts of the *epistemology* of science. They would not be among the factors included in our account of how theories, including standards of evidence, are generated and the nature of the evidence available for those theories.

We may find it ironic that sexism is a feature of science communities, given that a commitment to subjecting all beliefs to rational criticism is a defining feature of science. We might also find that sexism ironic given the current reluctance of many scientists to acknowledge that sex/gender has anything to do with science. But we may nonetheless be convinced that the sex/gender or political experiences of scientists, or their views about sex/gender and politics, have little to do with what most scientists are trying to find out about the world—and virtually nothing to do with what they find.

We might also believe that if views shaped by social and political practices and experiences, including those of sex/gender, did find their way into research questions, methodologies, and theories in the sciences, these views would be filtered out by the rigors of scientific method and the demand for intersubjectivity. We might regard Wilson's Sociobiology as an unfortunate but rare example of what happens when politics, including the politics of sex/gender, mixes with science. In short, our views about science might commit us to the view that any theory that reflects the sex/gender and/or political experience of scientists is an example of bad science.

Ironically, despite fundamental differences in the three influential accounts of science we considered in earlier chapters, those accounts appear to be in substantial agreement on issues such as these. The Hempel/Nagel, Kuhnian, and Quinean accounts of science recognize science education as the only sociological variable with epistemological force. None of the accounts incorporates, at least straightforwardly, anything that would prompt us to look for connections between the sex/gender and political experiences of scientists, and the understandings of human and nonhuman nature that develop in science communities—at least when things are going right.

But the similarity among the three frameworks turns out to be superficial; the differences, interesting. Despite the obstacles noted in the conclusion of Chapter Four, Quine's advances on the Hempel/Nagel and Kuhnian traditions clear some other important obstacles to recognizing connections between the identities of scientists and the content of science. Quine's positions undermine what has been regarded as a real and necessary dichotomy: *either* knowledge is passively discovered *or* it is "socially constructed" ("or culturally determined") with little or no constraint imposed on it by "the world". Cutting through the alleged dichotomy, Quine maintains that one "scientific fact" to emerge in the last five decades is that science is a bridge of our own making. But he also maintains a coherence theory of evidence, an account in which the bridges we build are constrained by experience. That science is a bridge of our own making does not on Quine's account sever the connection between science and evidence.

Another difference that is relevant to issues involving divisions in cognitive labor and authority is that Quine denies the autonomy of science. He argues that common-sense, scientific, and philosophic theories and theorizing are fundamentally connected and ultimately interdependent. On his view, scientific theorizing systematizes common-sense theorizing, but it is *dependent* on the latter for its own sense, and it is by analogy with our common-sense theories that scientific theories are generated and ontologies are posited. Indeed, Quine maintains that the notion of evidence is itself grounded in our "common-sense" dealings with the world; these experiences and theorizing give the notion of evidence its content.

Finally, Quine maintains that there is no unique story or set of theories that will organize and explain our experiences; alternative theories, commensurate with most of our experiences, are possible. Relatedly, he argues that all of our going scientific theories are (and will always be) underdetermined by the evidence available for them. Science is not, and will not be, complete.

Given a view of science that incorporates these positions, it is possible to recognize that if current divisions in cognitive labor and authority also mirror differences in "common-sense" or "extrascientific" experience, such divisions might have consequences for the content of science—that is, who is theorizing, in terms of common-sense experience, might make a difference to the content of that theorizing. The "slack" between theories and evidence, and the connections between common sense and science, might allow for such an occurrence. I say "might" here because although Quine argues that scientific theories are fundamentally dependent on common-sense theorizing, he also maintains that scientific theories are more "insulated" than common-sense beliefs and theories—a position to which we will return in later discussion.

As the conclusion of the preceding chapter indicated, other of Quine's positions pose obstacles to our being able to accommodate the connections between observers and the content of science that are emerging in feminist criticism. The largest obstacles are his view that the alleged boundary between science and values, including politics, is real, and his apparent assumption that there are no fundamental differences in common-sense experience and theorizing. Both the boundary and the assumption would preclude sex/gender and politics as factors in scientific theorizing.

Issues in Feminist Science Criticism

The issues raised by feminist science criticism that I will consider here indicate that an epistemology that does not recognize that sex/gender and political experience are factors in scientific theorizing is inadequate. They indicate that the directions of scientific research and the content of theories often reflect scientists' experiences of sex/gender and politics.

What some may find most surprising and disturbing, and what is of most significance in terms of the soundness of current views about science, is that feminist criticism indicates that sex/gender and politics are factors not just in cases where the charge of "bad science" is appropriate, as some would say it is of Sociobiology (at least as that charge would currently be understood)—but in cases where the charge is not appropriate. Not only is it not possible to write off all the cases where androcentrism and political experiences are factors in scientific theorizing as unambiguously bad science (again, as the latter charge would currently be construed), but I will argue that feminists' arguments that reveal the role these have played within scientific theorizing are themselves properly construed as being *within* science. Together, these suggest that some of what we have thought about science needs to be abandoned.

ANDROCENTRISM

Feminist science critics claim that in a number of sciences the language used to describe phenomena, the questions pursued, the models adopted, the interpretation of data and observations, and the theoretical frameworks developed reflect the fact that science is and has been dominated by men.[1] These critics claim that androcentrism or "male bias" is evident in many research programs and theoretical frameworks, and that it affects the content of science: its presence leads to faulty methodologies and models, and, ultimately, to partial or distorted accounts of various aspects of human and nonhuman nature.[2]

To focus the discussion on epistemological issues, I will use the term 'androcentrism' rather than 'male bias'. Describing the perspectives at issue as "biased" suggests that scientists could and should be disengaged observers of the world. Although such disengagement has traditionally been associated with objectivity and, thus, with good science, we will find that feminist science criticism raises fundamental questions about these ideals.[3] A second reason for not introducing the notion of bias is that it implies the conscious manipulation of data and theories, and such manipulation, when it occurs, is uninteresting when we are attempting to understand the epistemology of science. The interesting and important cases that we need to consider are precisely those where no scientist is consciously manipulating research questions or data.

There are also reasons for not describing the beliefs, assumptions, and methodologies at issue as "male". The description suggests a universality and connection with biology that cross-cultural and historical studies belie, and our current understandings of various biological processes make quite suspect. The perspectives feminists are uncovering and criticizing as androcentric are straightforwardly connected to contemporary western practices, views, and assumptions to do with sex/gender; they are not universal across cultures or historical periods.[4] In addition, there is currently no evidence for connecting science and male *biology,* and an abundance of evidence to indicate that no such connection could exist. The most obvious evidence against such a connection are cross-cultural and historical differences in views about sex/gender, women's and men's behavior, divisions of labor by sex/gender,[5] and the fact that many contemporary western *women,* and perhaps all of us, hold views shaped by a long androcentric tradition. A final reason that a connection with biology is unlikely is that human biology is itself neither static nor given. Our evolutionary history, the cross-cultural variations in the physical characteristics of women and men, and our current understandings of various biological processes indicate that human biology continuously interacts with and responds to physical and social environments.[6]

The reasonable view, given research of the last three decades, is that "women" and "men" are neither exclusively biological nor exclusively sociological categories, but enormously plastic and complex,[7] historically and culturally relative, and related in a multitude of ways to other cultural categories, practices, and activities.[8] A given "male biology" and "female biology"—and thus any alleged *sex* differences, differences determined by biology, in ways of knowing or organizing experiences—are deeply suspect. This is not to deny that androcentrism reinforces and perpetuates men's domination or to deny that the source of androcentrism is a long history of the domination of western practices and thinking by men. It is to say that there is no evidence that male *biology* is the source of the androcentrism at work in science and an abundance of evidence to suggest that it is not.

Thus, our discussion of androcentrism will focus on "male-centered" methodologies, categories, organizing principles, and theories in various sciences. Following Helen Longino and Ruth Doell and other feminist critics, I distinguish androcentricism and sexism. Longino and Doell describe androcentrism as "the perception of social life from a male point of view with a consequent failure accurately to perceive or describe the activity of women", and sexism as "statements, attitudes, and theories that presuppose, assert, or imply the inferiority of women, the legitimacy of their subordination, or the legitimacy of sex-based prescriptions of social roles and behaviors".[9] I would replace 'male' in the definition of androcentrism with "men's" and relativize the "point of view" to historical periods and specific cultures, for there is enormous variety across these in terms of sex/gender practices.

The first example of androcentrism I will outline involves a methodology. I begin with it because its androcentrism can be recognized straight-forwardly, and feminist criticism indicates it is widely used. A number of research programs and theoretical frameworks have sought and claimed to provide an account of some aspect of *human* experience, but have begun and ended their studies and analyses with *men's* experiences, behaviors, and activities. Typically, the results of these studies are generalized to women or attempts are made to assimilate women into the framework suggested by the initial research. Independent studies of women's experiences, behaviors, or activities are not undertaken to establish that the models suggested by the initial studies provide "norms" that are generalizable. The methodology reflects long-standing assumptions in the western tradition to the effect that men can represent the species and/or that men's behaviors, experiences, and activities provide the "norm" of human experience, and/or that it is to men's experiences and activities that we should look to find and study those things that are "distinctly human". That such assumptions are androcentric is obvious. That androcentrism is problematic, that it leads, among other things, to partial or distorted accounts of how things are, is now obvious to many of us—but, of course, it wasn't always.

As feminist critics point out, the use of the methodology affects the *content* of theories. One consequence of using men's experiences, behaviors, and activities as norms (and it turns out to be one of several) is that this frequently prompts a "woman question". When women are studied and do not fit the original model, scientists, like their forefathers in the western philosophical and theological traditions, frequently conclude that "something is wrong with women". The "woman question" is a further indication of how deeply androcentrism is embedded in western thinking; even faced with recalcitrant data—in this case, the data about women—many scientists have not asked whether men's behavior, activities, or experiences might afford a *partial* account of human experience, or only one of the possible models of human behavior. Other consequences of beginning with or focusing exclusively on men's activities and behavior, particularly visible in anthropology, sociology, and history, are that important areas of social life are completely overlooked, women's activities are subsumed under men's or simply ignored, and the differences between women's and men's positions and experiences are not incorporated in accounts of social life or historical periods, or explored as part of what is needed to understand social dynamics or historical periods.[10]

Feminist scholarship indicates that the methodology of beginning with men's behavior, activities, and experiences is widespread in the social sciences, history, and philosophy.[11] As one example of the methodology, its connections with the woman question, and other of its consequences for the content of theories, feminist critics point to the history of developmental psychology and the accounts of psychological and moral development and maturity offered by major figures in that field. Freud, Erikson, and Kohlberg each constructed a model of "normal" human psychological development based on studies of boys' and men's development.[12] When subsequent studies of women and girls suggested a development that did not fit the original model, Freud concluded that women "fail" to develop normally;[13] studies of women using the model Kohlberg developed of psychological and moral development suggested that women do not reach the "higher stages" of those developments.[14] And although Erikson did note differences in the development of boys and girls, his model of "*human* life stages" was based on boys' and men's development.[15]

The question of whether women's psychological development follows an alternative—*and nondeviant*—course has only recently been pursued by Nancy Chodorow, Carol Gilligan, and other feminist psychologists who are studying women's psychological development and moral reasoning without assuming that models developed using boys and men can provide the "norm" of human psychological and moral development.[16] Based on her studies of women and girls, and her recasting of the studies and results of Kohlberg and other psychologists, Gilligan argues that women's psychological and moral development follows a different course than men's and that comparison of the two models indicates that this development is not a "truncated version" of men's but a different development, suggesting different norms of psychological and moral maturity.[17]

Although Gilligan's work remains controversial, it has illuminated some of the problems engendered by using men to develop theories about humanity, and it reveals the connection between that methodology and "a woman question". Feminist psychologists are not the first to argue, or the first whose studies suggest, that women's psychological and moral development are different from men's;[18] but they are fundamentally recasting those differences and earlier conclusions.

What their work indicates is that there are consequences when studies are shaped by androcentric assumptions and this is made evident when women are studied on their own terms. The knowledge gained by studying women represents more than simply an addition to existing knowledge. Her studies of girls and women prompted Gilligan to argue that neither women's or men's psychological and moral development could be viewed as a "norm", and that a first step in developing an empirically sound account of human psychology and moral maturity and reasoning would be to use each course and model to illuminate and evaluate the other.[19]

So, knowledge about women is prompting a reevaluation of the "normalcy" of men's psychological development and the norms of "psychological maturity" and moral development adopted on the basis of these.[20]

Gilligan and other psychologists are also connecting the hypothesis that psychological development is different for women and men to current research and theoretical work in gender theory, sociology, and object-relations theory to explore the psychosocial factors that might explain each course of development and the fact that there are two.[21] Thus, what many psychologists have understood to be a natural or "inevitable" course of psychological and moral development (when it proceeds normally), and a generalizable model of moral reasoning, may prove to be fundamentally sociological in nature and deeply connected to, among other factors, sex/gender arrangements.[22]

A more general result of Gilligan's work and that of other feminist psychologists and social scientists is the insight gained into factors relevant to scientific theorizing that we had not recognized prior to feminist criticism. Sex/gender is a factor not only in the methodologies, organizing principles, and theories feminists are criticizing, but also in their own approaches. Feminist criticism of androcentric methodologies in the social sciences and the alternative models and theories now being developed are fundamentally related to feminist perspectives on sex/gender arrangements and politics. It is these which have led to a recognition that "male-centered" approaches have consequences for theories.

As I noted above, the work feminists are engaged in in psychology is paralleled in a number of fields. Feminist scientists and scholars in history,[23] anthropology,[24] biology,[25] economics,[26] political science,[27] evolutionary theory,[28] sociology,[29] psychology,[30] philosophy,[31] and literary theory[32] are also exploring the role that emphasis on men's behaviors and activities has played in shaping knowledge, categories, models, and theoretical frameworks previously accepted, and they are challenging all of these.

The other examples of androcentrism we will consider are more complex, and our sense that faulty methodologies and unwarranted assumptions are at work prove more difficult to pin down. Of most significance, drawing a line between "good science" and "bad" only on the basis of androcentrism becomes increasingly more complex. The first examples involve biological research into sex differences and, specifically, alleged sex differences in cognitive abilities and behavior.[33]

In reproductive endocrinology, research into relationships between hormones and the brain, and the effects such interactions have on other organs and behavior, began as efforts to understand the mechanisms—

thought to be hormonal but involving neural events—that regulate ovarian cyclic function.[34] Initial studies conducted using rats suggested that hypothalamic neurons respond cyclically in females, regulating pituitary and gonadal cyclic functions.[35] In male rats the presence of androgens apparently blocks the cyclic responses. Thus, the sex difference suggested by these studies involves the effects of hormones (and specifically, androgens) on fetal brains of rats, and researchers began to talk about the organizing effects that hormones have on hypothalamic neurons of rodent brains in terms of the organizing of "female brains" and "male brains".[36]

Research was subsequently expanded to the study of ovarian cycles in primates and of behavior—initially, rodent behavior. In the studies concerned with behavior, what researchers posited as "female characteristics" and "male characteristics" were correlated with hormonal effects on hypothalamic neurons. One specific characteristic introduced, "male aggressivity", described fighting encounters between male rodents, and it was correlated with androgens.[37]

Eventually, some biologists and psychologists used the model correlating hormones, behavior, and brain organization to look for hormonal and neural bases for what they assumed were *human* sex differences. The questions pursued in these studies include "Why are men aggressive?" and "Why do men and not women do well at and succeed in science?"[38] Neurophysiologist Ruth Bleier describes the working hypotheses of the studies in this way:

> The hypotheses (widely seen as established facts) are that women's lack of androgens may account for their lack of aggressivity and drive for achievement, and that *either hormones or genes or both (or their lack)* have influenced the development of a brain less able to conceptualize visuospatial relations that are basic to mathematical and perhaps other intellectual skills and, therefore, to success in engineering and the sciences and many other fields as well.[39]

Bleier and other feminist critics claim that there are several problems with this research into human sex differences.[40] For one thing, something called "aggressivity" is being correlated with males across species—from rodents to humans—but without clarification of the specific behavioral criteria being used.[41] Nor, in the case of the alleged sex differences to be explained using the model, are the sex differences established—for example, that women *are* less able to conceptualize visuospatial relations and/or less able to successfully engage in science.

Bleier argues that the larger social and political context, and specifically androcentric and sexist assumptions and practices, are underwriting this research into hormonal determinants of alleged sex differences in cognitive abilities and in the behaviors "necessary" to engaging in science.

> The reasoning starts with the observation that women do not share equally with men in positions of leadership, authority, or power and are far from equally represented in industry, business, the university, the arts, engineering, science and other professionals. The suspicion follows, then, that perhaps this situation has less to do with ideologies and institutions, with sex-role stereotyping and channeling from babyhood on, or with conscious or unconscious, legal and illegal discrimination against women in educational and employment opportunities than with women's innate inability to perform equally with men, either because of our naturally nurturant, passive, noncompetitive, and unambitious temperaments or because of biological limitations on the capacities and skills required to achieve in our kind of society.[42]

That social and political contexts are playing a role in shaping the questions pursued suggests itself in the assumptions about individual success, and in the connection assumed between aggression and success, aggression and science, and science and sex/gender, that underlie the research questions. Ethnocentrism is also obvious; cross-cultural and historical variations in the behaviors expected of and exhibited by women and men now documented by anthropologists, sociologists, and historians are ignored. Searching for a biological basis for sex differences in cognitive abilities requires the assumption that such differences are universal.

Bleier argues that there are also fundamental problems with the original research model and the attempts to extrapolate it beyond rodents. She points out that the model correlating hormones and behavior, and hormones and brain differences, in rodents has not been successfully extended even to guinea pigs or primates;[43] that the model is faulty because it assumes a linear relationship between hormones and behavior;[44] that the experimental results allegedly correlating androgens and aggressivity are, so far, contradictory;[45] and that the effects of the experimental environment on animal behavior, like fighting encounters, are not taken into account by researchers.[46]

Now, these problems are interesting because the studies correlating hormones and "female and male" rodent brains have been received with enthusiasm by some psychologists, sociologists, and Sociobiologists and used as the basis for claims about or studies into alleged human sex differences.

> The theory has provided the conceptual framework for theories and beliefs about the sexual differentiation of human brains and,

consequently, of our social roles and behaviors. Though such extrapolations are not usually made by the biologists doing the research, they are made by some, and they have also been uncritically and widely accepted by social scientists and natural scientists in other fields.[47]

The problems underlying and incorporated in the research model lead Bleier to conclude that the widespread acceptance of the "theory", like the questions being pursued, is fundamentally related to social and political context.

Without doubt . . . the subsequent leap from rodents to humans and the popularization of the notion that gender inequalities in status and power rest upon *in utero* hormonally determined differences in temperament and ability reflect and reinforce the ideology that presents as "natural" and "essential" that which is social and political.[48]

Some features of this research support Bleier's contention that social and political context is contributing to the acceptance of and interest in the theory that hormones produce sex-differentiated human brains. The wide range of possibilities being explored as possible sources of women's inferiority (at whatever it is that it takes to do science) is particularly revealing. The range—"either hormones, or genes, or both, or their lack"—suggests the lack of a clear research mandate to prompt the research.[49]

In addition, the problems Bleier cited with the original research model become compounded in its extension to humans. Positing a linear relationship from hormones to neural events to human behavior fails to take into account both the much greater complexity of our brain and the evidence that activities increase and decrease our hormone levels.[50] Moreover, of course, it is fundamentally unclear what the connection is supposed to be between fighting encounters among caged rodents, and the behaviors and characteristics (if, indeed, there is such a list) required for successfully engaging in science. Assumptions about sex/gender, and a correlation between "masculinity" and science, appear to be "filling in" or smoothing over the gaps and problems incorporated in the research model.

Further, whether the alleged human sex differences for which explanations are being sought in hormones and hypothalamic neurons are real is one of the more basic questions to raise about the rationale of this research. But it is not being asked or pursued by many of those proclaiming research results or adopting the theory or research results as the basis for their own work and claims—despite the fact that such sex differences are and have been a matter of considerable controversy among scientists in the relevant fields.[51]

Nevertheless, when we consider this research into hormonal determinants of sex-differentiated brains and behavior and its acceptance in the light of other current research, we find that writing off the studies, hypotheses, or general theory, or the current interest paid to all of these by scientists in various fields, as *only* the result of sexually biased views, or as *conscious* attempts to justify current divisions in power by sex/gender—or, most importantly, as unambiguously "bad science"—is also unwarranted. To make the point, it will be useful to outline another area of current research devoted to finding a biological basis for what are alleged to be sex differences in cognitive abilities.

In neuroendocrinology and empirical psychology there is also current research devoted to explaining "women's lack of success in science" and "men's success". In this research it is assumed that there are sex differences in hemispheric lateralization—differences that are assumed, in turn, to be the result of hormonal differences.[52] Bleier and other feminist critics argue that (currently, at least) there is no larger theoretical framework to warrant this research.

Bleier points out that the central assumption underlying the research to establish a *hormonal basis* for sex-differentiated lateralization is borrowed from a research program in reproductive neuroendocrinology. That research program is attempting to establish that there *are* sex differences in hemispheric lateralization, and it has not done so.[53] But, Bleier notes, the studies allegedly correlating hormones and lateralization are proceeding as if sex differences in lateralization have been established, and results are being published that convey the impression that they have been established.[54]

One popular theory to explain what remains an unestablished sex difference in hemispheric lateralization is based on a sex difference in rodent brains. Two areas of the cortex of male rat brains are 3 percent thicker on the right side than the left side, and this occurs in areas that are linked to the processing of visual information.[55] The areas are not thicker on the right side of female rodent brains. As part of the project of establishing a hormonal basis for human sex-differences in cognitive abilities, researchers are attempting to correlate this thickness with the presence of the hormone testosterone, and what they argue is greater spatial orientation in male rats. They propose that males across species are right-hemisphere dominant and that this is the cause of men's alleged superiority in the cognitive abilities required for science and math.[56]

Bleier argues that there is no theoretical basis for correlating the thicknesses of these areas in rodent brains with lateralization, no other basis for correlating hormones and lateralization, and none, of course, to suggest that male rodents are better at "scientific reasoning" than female rodents (although, as I noted above, some researchers argue that male rats are more spatially oriented than female rats).[57] The only assumption about sex-differentiated brains to have empirical support is that the difference in thickness in the two sides of the rodent brain appears only in male rats.[58]

An additional problem is that those proposing that males are right-hemisphere dominant use as evidence a study of human fetal brains that indicated that two convolutions of the right hemisphere develop several weeks earlier than those of the left hemisphere.[59] But they fail to note in reporting their own research into hormonal differences, differences they want to correlate with lateralization, that this is *not* a sex difference; the convolutions of the right hemisphere appear in *both* female and male fetal brains. Nor do they note that the study they cite involved 507 human fetal brains of 10–44 weeks' gestational age and that the study reported that researchers found *no* significant sex differences.[60]

Indeed, according to Bleier, there are more fundamental problems with all current research devoted to explaining or establishing sex differences in hemispheric lateralization. She claims that there is no larger theoretical framework to account for a relationship between cognitive abilities and lateralization except through the borrowing of untested or unconfirmed hypotheses, and no theoretical framework to suggest, or to provide a way of accounting for, such a connection.

For example, there is no evidence that a correlation would exist between hemispheric lateralization and visuospatial ability, and there is no reason to think, with the possible exception of geometry, that visuospatial ability is a factor in mathematical and/or scientific ability.[61] Given the problems she and other critics have found incorporated in the research questions and models, Bleier claims that current research into sex differences in lateralization and cognitive abilities is underwritten by circular reasoning, and specifically, androcentric and sexist assumptions.

> The assumption is that the (questionable) demonstration of right hemispheric lateralization of visuospatial processing in males accounts for their presumed superiority in visuospatial skills. But no independent evidence supports this assumption. It is a product of circular reasoning: men are superior in visuospatial skills because their right hemispheres are specialized for visuospatial cognitive processing; we know that right hemispheric specialization provides superior visuospatial skills because men have better visuospatial skills than women, who use both hemispheres for visuospatial processing.[62]

Despite the problems Bleier and other critics cite, researchers who began with the question "Why are men better at science and mathematics than women?" are publishing results that once again convey the impression that these other "details" are uncontroversial.[63] Indeed, both the proliferation of studies and the underlying problems with the model linking hormones to sex differences in lateralization have prompted rather severe criticism from other empirical psychologists.[64] Psychologist Marcel Kinsbourne concluded his review of a much-quoted overview of the research into lateralization with the following comment.[65]

> We have seen that the evidence for sex-differential lateralization fails to convince on logical, methodological, and empirical grounds. Is that surprising? Not all the points made in my critique are subtle, and some at least must be obvious to anyone in the field. Why then do reputable investigators persist in ignoring them? Because the study of sex differences is not like the rest of psychology. Under pressure from the gathering momentum of feminism, and perhaps in backlash to it, many investigators seem determined to discover that men and women "really" are different. It seems that if sex differences (e.g., in lateralization) do not exist, then they have to be invented.[66]

An additional problem with the research into sex differences in lateralization is one we encountered in our consideration of research into a hormonal bases for sex-differentiated brains. Research is proceeding and results are being published as if sex differences in cognitive abilities have been established, although, as I have noted, that remains a matter of such considerable controversy that it would require another chapter to outline the claims, the disagreements, the statistics, and the issues. For our purposes, it will suffice to say that there is no general agreement that there are differences in women's and men's cognitive abilities, and that those who maintain that there are disagree about what they are, the degree to which women and men differ, the soundness of isolating sex as a variable, and the role of sociology, and specifically gender socialization and sexism, in causing such differences.[67] Moreover, given the now substantial evidence that the major growth in the human brain occurs *postnatally* and *requires* specific interaction with environmental factors including membership in a sociolinguistic community, the emphasis given to biological factors as determinants of cognitive abilities seems fundamentally misplaced.[68]

And there is a telling indication that something strange is afoot in the research attempting to explain alleged sex differences in cognitive abilities

200 Bridges of Our Own MakingBridges of Our Own Making

on the basis of alleged sex differences in lateralization. Two of the more widely discussed studies that allegedly explain women's "lack of success in science" flatly contradict each other about the source of that lack. One claims that women's inabilities are due to a *lesser degree of lateralization;*[69] the other claims that women's inabilities are due to a *greater degree of lateralization.*[70] In both, what other scientists claim is an "unestablished" object of historical and current interest—"women's inability to do science"—is explained—and, as explained, it is determined by women's biology.[71]

But although there are clear connections between the two areas of research I have outlined and social/political context, there are reasons to think that we need a perspective larger than that of the individual studies and research programs involved to see the role that androcentrism and sexism are playing and to wrestle with the question of whether this research can be correctly characterized as "bad science". Kinsbourne may be correct that faced with the specter of feminism, "otherwise reputable" investigators will throw scientific standards out the window, deliberately ignoring inconsistencies, contradictions, and gaps underlying or incorporated in their research, and if need be, inventing sex differences. And certainly, the reporting of results as if the hypothesis one is borrowing and using to support one's own research has been confirmed when it has not been is at least misleading if not dishonest.[72]

But it is not really plausible to suppose that only a conscious desire to justify men's domination of science or to reaffirm their own sexist views is all that is underwriting this research and leading researchers to continue it. This becomes clear when we ask, "At what point did androcentrism or sexism (or both) step in to underwrite or prompt research that would *otherwise* have been recognized as unwarranted?"

In addressing the question, we need first to note that some of the questions, hypotheses, and models that appear unwarranted when considered in isolation—studies, for example, that attempt to connect hormones with hemispheric lateralization in the absence of evidence that there *are* sex differences in lateralization, or that lateralization would have a bearing on cognitive abilities, or that there are sex differences in cognitive abilities—are strongly connected to other working hypotheses, studies, research programs, and to one another.

At least some of the research devoted to finding hormonal bases for human sex-differentiated brains is based on the model and studies of the effects hormones have on fetal rodent brains, and specifically, on the organizing of what researchers *introduced* as "female brains" and "male brains". And, in fact, one instance of a morphological sex difference has been established in other research devoted to "finding a clear signature of sexual differentiation",[73] and a connection with hormones has been established. The sex difference is in a group of neurons that are necessary for the males of some bird species to sing; a correlation between androgens, and the size of the relevant neurons and of the group of neurons, has been established.[74]

Other research models and programs that contribute to the apparent plausibility of human sex-differentiated brains include the research seeking to establish correlations between lateralization and visuospatial and other cognitive abilities,[75] a number of studies that claim to establish that there are clear differences in the mathematical abilities of girls and boys,[76] the research undertaken in empirical psychology to establish that there are sex differences in hemispheric lateralization,[77] and the correlation found in research in reproductive neuroendocrinology between hormones and thickness in two areas of male rodent brains.[78]

The hypothesis that hormones are linked to "male aggressivity" in human males and those of other species, as it is incorporated in theories in Sociobiology[79] and sociology,[80] is also connected to other current research. As we saw earlier, studies of rodent behavior in reproductive endocrinology linked what researchers called "aggressivity" in male and female rodents (again, on the basis of fighting encounters between caged rodents) to the presence or introduction of androgens.[81] And, as we shall see in the next example of androcentrism we consider, the assumption that males are aggressive spans a number of sciences. It has shaped observations and has been incorporated in theories in primatology, animal sociology, sociology, anthropology, and a theory of human cultural evolution. Finally, we will see that the assumption that there are universal human sex differences, an assumption that underwrites the plausibility of biological determinants of such differences, has until recently, been proclaimed or implied in most major work in anthropology, history, psychology, and sociology. Indeed, Bleier documents a pervasive and conscious borrowing of hypotheses and results between research programs and sciences investigating sex differences.

But the practice of borrowing is *not* a mark of "bad" or "flawed" scientific procedure. Synthesizing and building on the tentative hypotheses, observations, and results of other fields and research has led to great breakthroughs, Darwin's theory of natural selection among them. Moreover, we certainly do not expect each area of research to take place in a vacuum, to begin "from scratch", even were such a thing possible. Nor does good science demand that we pursue only those questions whose legitimacy has been established by the confirmation of some interdependent or higher level hypothesis—particularly when there is an abundance of concurrent research that is connected to what one is exploring.

On the other hand, a *hundred* research projects attempting to establish or explain sex differences, and interconnected and interdependent at various levels, will not add up to *one larger good* research project if each incorporates a wrongheaded assumption. I suggest that there are two perspectives from which the research into sex differences we have considered is wrongheaded and from which androcentrism and sexism emerge as factors incorporated in and underwriting research questions and projects. The first perspective I will outline is a historical and political one.

Feminists and other science critics note persistent themes in the long history of research into sex differences. One is the fascination with establishing or explaining sex differences. From a *consciously* political perspective, one is struck by that fascination and led to ask, "Why are scientists so interested in establishing and/or explaining sex differences?"—particularly when the differences are not related to reproductive functions and we are a species with relatively little sexual dimorphism. A *partial* list of the sex differences scientists have claimed to find includes hormones,[82] genes,[83] evolutionary strategies,[84] "quirks" on the brain,[85] brain morphology,[86] absolute brain weight,[87] the "energy" required for the proper functioning of the uterus,[88] absolute brain size,[89] the relative size of the frontal and parietal lobes,[90] the absolute size of frontal lobes,[91] the ratio of brain size to body height,[92] and the ratio of brain size to body weight.[93]

From an historical perspective that recognizes the social and political contexts within which science is practiced as possible factors in scientific theorizing, one can also see that interest in establishing sex differences intensifies when social movements or debates about women's economic, social, and political position or "roles" are taking place.[94] Third, one notes the *consistency* of the results (although not of the biological explanations, as the list above indicates). Whatever is alleged to be the biological basis for the difference, explanations of sex differences have consistently explained women's inability to engage successfully in *precisely* those activities that are dominated by men, of high cultural value, and that carry "cognitive authority"—including, of course, science.

Fourth, and of particular significance in terms of current research into sex differences, the search for biological determinants for what are alleged to be differences in cognitive abilities persists even as other research *undermines* the rationale of such research and explanations. So the second perspective from which current research into sex differences appears wrongheaded encompasses the current state of science in the narrow sense. Current research into biological determinants of sex differences in cognitive abilities is occurring concomitantly with research into the postnatal growth and development of the structures that *enable* and are required for cognitive functioning, research that makes a biological determination of cognitive abilities deeply suspect. It is also occurring against the background of biological research that indicates that *sex* cannot be used in isolation to establish or explore sex differences, but that any such differences could be reasonably established only if we used more than twenty *other* variables in any such research. And, finally, research into sex differences in cognitive abilities is occurring precisely with the closing of the gaps between girl's and boy's achievements in math and science as educational policies change.[95]

Feminists argue that several themes emerge from a historical and consciously political perspective on research into sex differences. The first passage is from Ruth Bleier; the second from Ruth Hubbard.

> The theme, raised recurrently over the last century, remains frighteningly the same despite enormous advances in general scientific sophistication: Women's efforts to do other than what they are destined to do—by biology, by evolution, by nature and by temperament—threaten the health and survival of the human race.[96]

> For a long time, biologists, anthropologists, psychologists, and physicians have allocated a great deal of attention to the question, *why are males masculine and females feminine?* They have searched busily for *the* answer: just the right ratio of nature to nurture required to produce our present schizophrenic state of affairs. Nature, it appears, works in ways mysterious and widely varying, depending upon which man of science we accept.[97]

Finally, like two current explanations of women's alleged inability to do science—one that women's brains are lateralized to a greater degree than men's, the other that they are less lateralized—the explanations given historically of why women cannot do science or math, or succeed in business, or be educated, or practice medicine, or leave the house . . . not infrequently contradict each other. Women's inferior intellectual abilities have been explained as the result of smaller frontal lobes . . . *and* larger frontal lobes,[98] of smaller "absolute" brain size and/or weight,[99] *and* a brain that is larger or heavier relative to body weight than men's.[100]

Indeed, in the case of the frontal lobe explanation, scientists first claimed that women's inferior intellectual abilities were the result of smaller frontal lobes and subsequently reversed themselves when it was found that women's frontal lobes were larger. In 1895 G. T. W. Patrick took the new data in stride; it had no bearing on his contention that women were intellectually inferior to men and that the explanation for this was to be found in women's brains.

> The frontal region is not, as has been supposed, smaller in woman, but rather larger relatively. But the parietal lobe is somewhat smaller. It is now believed, however, that a preponderance of the frontal region does not imply intellectual superiority, as was formerly supposed, but that the parietal region is really the more important.[101]

Against the background of this history, our inability to pinpoint a specific question as "the place" where androcentrism or sexism rears its head is both more understandable—the web of androcentrism and sexism is tangled indeed—and more illuminating of the complex relationships between science and political context.

One perspective we have used to consider this research is consciously political and historical—but historical in a specific sense: we have not assumed that the history of science has been determined by a logic internal to science. From such a perspective, a clear pattern of interaction between science and politics emerges. As Bleier notes,

> Today, we can see clearly the biases of some of the most reputable scientists working in the middle and late 19th century, a period of turmoil in regard to slavery and women's rights, who found female and "Negro" brains to be inferior and underdeveloped. . . . Stephen Jay Gould has shown how the most prominent brain scientists of the period, obsessed with numbers as indicators of scientific rigor, used craniometry to "confirm all the common prejudices of comfortable white males—that blacks, women, and poor people occupy their subordinate roles by the harsh dictates of nature" (Gould, 1981, p. 74).[102]

I am willing to wager that, after studying the history of research into sex, race, class, and ethnic differences, and the findings that have been proclaimed by scientists, few would remain tempted by the view that science is an autonomous enterprise, disengaged from social and political issues and contexts, or by the view that research into sex differences, as well as race, class, and ethnic differences, is not *political.*

In addition, we have wrestled with the question of whether this research is unambiguously bad science. In doing so, we have focused not only on the individual research programs but judged them on the basis of a broader perspective that took the current state of science, in the narrow sense of science, into account. On the one hand, the broader perspective revealed that the research programs I have outlined are not fruitfully judged in isolation, in which case it might seem that they are easily written off as examples of "bad science". We found the two research programs

we considered to be strongly connected to other research, and this provided some rationale, from *within science,* for them. From this perspective,
writing off the research as clearly "bad science" seems inappropriate.

On the other hand, when the research into sex differences in cognitive
abilities is considered against an even broader background—although still
against the background of other current scientific research—one that
encompasses research into postnatal neurobiological development, the
increasing evidence that we are a species with relatively little sexual
dimorphism, and sociological studies that document that socialization is
a factor in science and math performance, then the rationale for the
substantial body of interdependent research into sex differences in cognitive abilities is questionable indeed. We can say that ignoring the implications of this research and searching for a biological basis for sex differences
are problematic *given the current state of science.* From this perspective,
again using the current state of science, we can also see androcentrism
and sexism as factors underwriting current research.

The bottom line of all this is that although we can distinguish viable
theories/research programs from nonviable ones, there is no magic for-
mula for doing so. Hobbes allegedly said, "The Inn of Evidence has no
signpost". Whether he said it or not, this is surely so. As the last example
illustrates, viable theories, like evidence, are not self-announcing. The
judgments "good science" and "bad science" are warranted not by the
passing or failing of some simple test but by careful, multifaceted evalua-
tions such as those begun here. Moreover, the judgment "bad science",
even after this kind of evaluation, would be better parsed as "initially
promising but nonviable given fuller (but, as always, still incomplete)
investigation".

What may be bothering some readers is that I have not cited the
relationship between social and political context and this research as itself
an indication of "bad science". My reasons for not doing so will emerge
in the final section of this chapter, but one may already be obvious:
namely, the connection itself cannot be assumed to be a criterion of, or
to lead to, bad science. Feminist criticism of this research and of other cases
in which androcentrism and sexism are factors is itself fundamentally
connected to social and political context. For this, and other reasons I
will later explore, a relationship between social and political context
cannot be assumed to be a mark of or to lead to bad science. We will need
to develop a more sophisticated and complex account of the relationship
between science and politics and of "good" science.

The last area of feminist criticism concerned with androcentrism that
we will consider is one aspect of the feminist criticism directed at the

"man, the hunter" theory of human evolution: the criticism directed at an organizing principle incorporated in the theory. Feminists' criticism of the organizing principle provides insight into how subtle and pervasive a factor androcentrism has been in a number of sciences, and how consequential it has been for the content of theories.[103] It also further illuminates the difficulties in writing off any theorizing in which sex/gender and politics are factors as bad science.

Feminists point out that research into animal and human behavior and social organization often incorporates a basic organizing principle that males are socially oriented—their activities skilled and determining of social organization and, in the case of humans, of culture as well, and that females are biologically oriented—their activities "natural", unskilled, and without consequence for the social dynamics of human and animal groups. In models and theories incorporating the organizing principle, females are satellites to male actors who dominate and determine social dynamics.

Feminists argue that the pervasive association of females with reproductive functions that are themselves assumed to be "natural" and without need of analysis or consequence for social dynamics, and the association of males with dominance, aggression, hierarchies, and social dynamics or culture, have had substantial consequences for observations and theories in various sciences.[104]

"Man, the hunter" theory constitutes a particularly useful example of a theory incorporating the organizing principle and the consequences of the principle because the account of human brain and cultural evolution incorporates and builds on theories and observations in other fields.[105] Primatology,[106] anthropology,[107] sociology,[108] and animal sociology[109] are among the fields whose observations and theories were synthesized by "man, the hunter" theorists.

As feminist science critics note, "man, the hunter" theory credits the evolution of *Homo sapiens* to what are assumed to be activities and behaviors engaged in and exhibited by our male ancestors. Within the theory, women appear to have gotten a free "evolutionary ride"—for they were menstruating, childbearing, lactating, and childrearing, and, it is assumed, their behavior and activities were not contributing to the evolution of bipedalist and speaking "man".

Biologist, Ruth Hubbard, outlines the central thesis of "man, the hunter" theory.

> In the myth of Man the hunter, males had to invent not only tools, but also the social organization that allowed them to hunt big animals. They

also had to roam great distances and learn to cope with many and varied circumstances. We are told that this entire constellation of factors stimulated the astonishing and relatively rapid development of his brain that came to distinguish Man from his ape cousins.[110]

Indeed, a "male-driven" evolution does emerge in the accounts offered by "man, the hunter" theorists and its advocates. The first passage is from Washburn and Lancaster's "The Evolution of Hunting", the second from Fox's *Kinship and Marriage,* and the third from Oakley's *Man, the Tool-maker.*

In a very real sense our intellect, interests, emotions, and basic social life—all are evolutionary products of the success of the hunting adaptation. . . . *The biology, psychology, and customs that separate us from apes—all these we owe to the hunters of time past.*[111]

It was the *men* who hunted the game, fought the enemies, and made the decisions.[112]

Human culture in all its diversity is the outcome of the capacity for conceptual thinking, but the leading factors in its development are tradition coupled with invention. The primitive hunter made an implement in a particular fashion largely because as a child he watched his father at work or because he copied the work of a hunter in a neighboring tribe.[113]

As Hubbard remarks about the androcentrism of Oakley's account, "it seems a remarkable feat of clairvoyance to see in such detail what happened some 250,000 years in pre-history, complete with the little boy and his little stone chipping set just like daddy's big one".[114]

In addition to assuming that only our male ancestors hunted, "man, the hunter" theorists and the theory's advocates frequently conclude "with some degree of confidence", as Edward Wilson does below, that early hominids and humans divided labor along the lines of what Wilson elsewhere calls the "classic division of the sexes"—by which he means in ways precisely like those assumed to be characteristic of industrial western societies, and perhaps, at least until recently, ascribed appropriately to the upper classes of those societies.

On this model, our female ancestors remained "at home" taking care of hearth and children; our male ancestors organized hunts, and in so doing, developed language, and social and political organization. Males were also responsible for defending and providing for what "man, the hunter" theorists assume were basically dependent females and young—and, ultimately, men's tool making and need for social organization and planning to facilitate hunting were responsible for the evolution of our brains. Wilson is also sure that males were dominant in early human groups.

> What we can conclude with some degree of confidence is that primitive men lived in small territorial groups, within which males were dominant over females. . . . Sexual selection would tend to be linked with hunting prowess, leadership, skill at tool making, and other visible attributes that contribute to the success of the family and the *male band*.[115]

Feminists argue that there are fundamental problems with this account of human evolution and that these are directly related to androcentric assumptions incorporated within it. For one thing, they argue, we have no reason to assume that our female ancestors were completely occupied with procreation and childrearing activities or that male dominance hierarchies characterized these groups. Some "man, the hunter" theorists and advocates simply assume or declare that males were the hunters and dominant over females and children. Others use the accounts given by anthropologists of contemporary hunter/gatherer societies to support their assumptions about early hominid and human social life. And some of the theory's advocates, including Sociobiologists, use observations and theories in primatology as evidence for early human behavior and social organization.

But feminists in anthropology,[116] primatology,[117] and animal sociology[118] have documented that the social/male, natural/female dichotomy has shaped observations and accounts of social dynamics and behavior in primate groups and contemporary hunter/gatherer societies.[119] In short, what feminist criticism reveals, once again, is a vast feedback system across disciplines, a system reinforcing androcentric assumptions and views, including those incorporated in "man, the hunter" theory.

The consequences of the organizing principle (or more correctly, a cluster of consequences) emerge with force in the light of recent cross-cultural and historical studies and of studies of primate groups that have been done in the past two decades by feminists who are not assuming a social/male, nature/female dichotomy.[120] This body of research indicates, for example, that the assumption that procreative and reproductive activities are "natural" and "unskilled" has led "man, the hunter theorists" as well as sociologists, Sociobiologists, anthropologists, primatologists, animal sociologists, and historians to give what now appear to be distorted accounts of the social dynamics of various human and animal groups.[121] Research and theories incorporating the assumption either misrepresent or miss completely how even so-called reproductive activities interact with productive and other activities; they ignore or fail to recognize variations in procreative and reproductive activities, and, thus, they make it impossible to recognize relationships between these activities and other features of the social and physical environments.[122] Without the assumption that procreation and reproduction are "natural" and unvaried, it is possible to recognize and study fundamental relationships between "reproductive" and "productive" activities and to see that each plays a part in shaping the other.

Some examples will help here. Primatologists long described groups with one male as "harems", and their descriptions of the social dynamics of these groups incorporated all of the controlling and dominance that the notion of a male who has a harem invokes (at least for westerners) and female dependency, sexual availability, function, and powerlessness.[123] The most important feature of the social dynamics of such groups was taken to be the dominant male. Feminist primatologists argue that males in these groups are often more correctly viewed as studs who are largely peripheral to the social dynamics of the groups, dynamics that are primarily centered on and determined by mother/young groups.[124] So, a male-centered approach to animal sociology and behavior has precluded analysis of female behavior and activities—and thus distorted the picture of social dynamics. The assumption of "male dominance" turns out to be significant in shaping models in animal sociology and the "man, the hunter" account of human evolution.

The picture of contemporary hunter/gatherer societies that has been accepted until recently by anthropologists and is now accepted by Sociobiologists also illuminates the depth of the distortion that a social/male, nature/female dichotomy can lead to. Anthropologists long focused on the hunting of animals by the men in these societies and, in effect, wrote off women's gathering activities as unskilled and without important consequence for social dynamics.[125] Their accounts of hunter/gatherer societies also suggested that women are primarily concerned with procreative and reproductive activities, and that this limited their contribution to "productive" activities by keeping them close to home while males hunt. And the assumption that procreative and reproductive activities are themselves "natural" has effectively precluded any analysis of them, their relation to physical and social environments, or the role they might play in determining other social arrangements. The work done in the past fifteen years by feminist anthropologists fundamentally challenges these pictures of social dynamics in hunter/gatherer societies.

Among the differences are the following: women's gathering activities are highly skilled, requiring knowledge of hundreds of plants and other ecological factors, and gathering is most often a fundamentally social, rather than individual and unskilled, activity; women's gathering provides as much as 80 percent of the sustenance for hunter/gatherer groups; in some hunter/gatherer groups, women are as much away from home as their male counterparts and childcare is shared among the group; although there are usually divisions of labor by sex/gender, (including the fact that usually only males hunt), these divisions are often flexible and respond to changes in environmental conditions, including proximity to other groups, settled as opposed to nomadic life, and the influence of missionaries; and finally, women's productive activities apparently *determine* the spacing of children and child care arrangements, rather than vice versa, as anthropologists and Sociobiologists have assumed or argued.[126]

Thus, we can now see that the social/male and nature/female dichotomy is consequential for observations and theories. In evolutionary theory, it precluded analysis of the role that women's reproductive and productive activities would have played in human evolution, and it seems probable that it has distorted accounts of the social dynamics that would have characterized early hominid and human groups. Without the androcentric assumptions, very different accounts of the social dynamics of various cultures and animal groups emerge, and so do the assumptions we would bring to a reconstruction of human evolution.

One alternative, the "woman, the gatherer" theory of human evolution, is being developed by feminists in a number of disciplines, including anthropology and biology. In it, women's activities as gatherers and mothers are assumed to have been central factors leading to tool use, the acquisition of language, and the formation of social groups.[127] Feminists argue that if we assume that the major enduring relationship in early hominid groups was the mother/child relationship, an assumption that is supported by studies of primate groups that are not shaped by the assumption that the activities of males are the most significant, then it is plausible that the "obstetrical dilemma" that resulted in a greater period of dependency for the young, together with the environmental pressures that led to bipedalism, and the importance of women's gathering for themselves and their young, would have placed selection pressure at least equally on females for tool use, language, cooperation, and social organization. "Woman, the gatherer" theorists appeal to primate behavior and social dynamics, and to contemporary hunter/gatherer societies, to support their reconstruction of human evolution. But their observations of primate behavior and their accounts of the social dynamics of contemporary hunter/gatherer societies incorporate the assumption that reproductive activities are neither natural nor unskilled, that women (or females) are productive members of social groups, and that reproductive and productive activities are not invariable or unrelated but interact with one another as well as with social and physical environments.

Without androcentric assumptions, an analysis of women's activities, a recasting of the significance of men's activities, and a very different picture of social dynamics are possible. In reconstructing human evolution, for example, anthropologist Sally Slocum places central emphasis on the selection pressures on female hominids.

> Picture the primate band: each individual gathers its own food, and the major enduring relationship is the mother-infant bond. It is in similar circumstances that we imagine the evolving protohominids. We don't know what started them in the direction of neoteny and increased brain size, but once begun, the trends would prove adaptive. To explain the shift from the primate individual gathering to human food sharing, we cannot simply jump to hunting. Hunting does not explain its own origin. It is much more logical to assume that as the period of infant dependency began to lengthen, *the mothers would begin to increase the scope of their gathering to provide for their still-dependent infants.* The already strong primate mother-infant bond would begin to extend over a longer time period, increasing the depth and scope of social relationships, and giving rise to the first sharing of food.[128]

Ruth Hubbard also claims that androcentrism has led "man, the hunter" theorists to ignore factors important to evolution.

> It is likely that the evolution of speech has been one of the most powerful forces directing our biological, cultural, and social evolution, and it is surprising that its significance has largely been ignored by biologists. But, of course, it does not fit into the androcentric paradigm. No one has ever claimed that women can not talk; so if men are the vanguard of evolution, humans must have evolved through the stereotypically male behaviors of competition, tool use, and hunting.[129]

Feminist criticism of the organizing principle incorporated in "man, the hunter" theory and other theories on which that account of evolution built, and the alternative accounts feminists are developing in primatology, cross-cultural studies, and evolutionary theory are additional indications that sex/gender is a factor in scientific theorizing. Scientists' experiences of and views about sex/gender have had an obvious impact on their assumptions, observations, and theories.

Again, the relationship is evident not only in the male-centered approach and stereotypical views of women and men incorporated in the frameworks feminists are criticizing. It is also evident in feminist approaches. Given the pervasiveness in various sciences of the organizing principle feminists criticize, *and* the support that organizing principle enjoys both because it is shared across sciences and because it precludes the very analysis of females' activities that would challenge it, we cannot simply write off "man, the hunter" theory as "bad science". Its advocates appealed to available research in primatology and anthropology, and the sex differences they assume would have characterized early human groups were also assumed and supported by going theories in history, sociology, biology, and anthropology.

But given this, it is clear that feminists' views about sex/gender and political arrangements are what have enabled their criticism and the alternatives they are proposing. To try to separate feminist criticism of the assumption of male dominance and the centrality of men's activities from feminist politics would be as ludicrous as separating the androcentrism feminists have uncovered in primatology, anthropology, and evolutionary theory from the androcentrism and sexism of the societies in which scientists live. In short, androcentrism and sexism are problems. But we cannot conclude that experiences of sex/gender and political perspectives are inherently distorting of scientific theorizing. Nor given feminist criticism of "man, the hunter" theory and other fields on which it built, can we any longer maintain that sex/gender is not a factor in science. It is a factor, and we will need to find a way to accommodate that fact that does not assume it is a factor only in bad science.

DOMINANCE AND HIERARCHIES

We have seen that a central feature of feminist criticism of models and theories in various sciences is a critique of the centrality of dominance relations in these. Feminists argue that the assumption that dominance hierarchies and male dominance are universal features of human and animal social groups has distorted the accounts scientists have developed of the social dynamics in animal and human groups and of the "man, the hunter" theory of human evolution. The assumption that male dominance is a universal feature of human and animal groups is also incorporated in explanations offered by Sociobiologists; indeed, according to Sociobiologists, male dominance promotes "inclusive fitness".

Recently feminists have extended their criticism of models in which dominance relations are central to models in molecular biology.[130] Biophysicist Evelyn Fox Keller, biologists Ruth Bleier and Ruth Hubbard, and other scientists question the appropriateness of linear and hierarchical causal models in the characterization of biological processes.[131] Feminists who criticize such models are not alone in doing so; a substantial body of criticism of such models has been offered recently by other biologists, geneticists, and philosophers of science.[132]

Some feminist critics also criticize a broader metaphysical commitment among scientists to the universality of linear and hierarchical relationships in human and nonhuman nature, a commitment they claim is reflected in the positing of "laws of nature". And some have turned their attention to exploring the notions of dominance incorporated in the view that the goal of science is "to dominate nature".[133] There are three related aspects of feminist criticism directed at the centrality of notions of dominance in our approaches to nature.

On one level, feminist critics claim that there are connections between western political experience, and models and organizing principles in the biological sciences.[134] Among the models Keller, Bleier, and Hubbard have criticized in this regard are the "master molecule" or "executive DNA" model of cellular development, the model of gene action incorporated in Sociobiology, and all biological determinist arguments that rely on linear and determinist models.[135]

Feminists also claim that political categories and experiences, including those of sex/gender, shape the understanding of the relationship of science to nature that emerged in the scientific revolution and persists in contemporary views. That relationship is often described as one involving, or requiring, dominance and violence; gender categories are also frequently incorporated in those understandings—nature is female, science is male—and violence against women is incorporated as well. The relationship of scientists and science to nature has been described as "rape", "forced penetration", and "domination",[136] and nature is consistently described as a "female" who is "unruly" or "disorderly", and historically as a female whose "secrets" a "masculine science" or male scientist was to expose and tame through "penetration".[137]

Finally, Evelyn Fox Keller claims that the broad metaphysical commitment to "laws of nature" that phenomena "obey" is political in origin and limits our approach to and understandings of natural relationships.

For those tempted by the view that there is a distinction to be drawn between "our language" and something like "what we are describing", or by the view that metaphysical commitments are "free floating" rather than embedded in our models, methodologies, and theories, it will emerge that the issues feminists are raising are not about language or mysterious metaphysical agendas. The commitments to linear and hierarchical relationships, to executives and controllers, and to laws that phenomena obey are incorporated in our theories, methodologies, and models, and a commitment to "dominating nature" is incorporated in many of our scientific practices.[138] We are not discussing language. We are discussing methodologies, theories, and practices in which dominance emerges as a central feature, the appropriateness of these, and their relationship to western political experience.

I will focus here on feminist criticism of linear and hierarchical models in the biological sciences and, specifically, their criticism of the "master molecule" or "executive DNA" theory of gene action.[139] I will limit the discussion to feminists' arguments that claim that these models distort biological processes, but I will first mention one additional aspect of the criticism feminists and others direct at these models.

Feminists argue that linear and hierarchical causal models that posit discrete and executive determinants of biological processes make deterministic models of animal and human behavior and social organization appear far more plausible than they in fact are. Although we will focus on the claim that linear and hierarchical models are related to political experience and distort what are actually far more complex relationships within and between biological entities, organisms, and processes, the implications for biological determinist theories, and feminist concern with the political consequences of these, will also emerge.

The "master molecule" theory of cellular protein development incorporates a commitment to what Ruth Hubbard and other biologists call "genetic reductionism", a commitment that it shares with other theories in the biological sciences.[140] Hubbard uses the phrase 'genetic reductionism' to refer to what are, in fact, a cluster of assumptions: that genes are "irreducible and separate things that determine events",[141] that complex traits are discrete, and that such traits are genetically determined. (We saw in Chapter Four, for example, that Sociobiologists are committed to the view that "male aggressiveness", "male fickleness", and "female coyness" are such traits and that they are genetically determined and promoting of "inclusive fitness".)

Hubbard points out that the views incorporated in genetic reductionism are in keeping with a long-standing assumption that there is a discrete carrier of "traits". She notes that even before the gene was isolated, the term 'gene' was used to refer to a "carrier" presumed to be inheritable and determining of complex characteristics. But, she claims, the metaphysical and methodological commitments of genetic reductionism constitute an inappropriate framework for understanding biological processes.

Hubbard and other critics of this model of gene action argue that the dominant role assigned to genes in the "master molecule" or executive DNA model of cellular development obscures and distorts far more complex relationships involved in that process. For one thing, Hubbard maintains, although genes "impart specificity", models that posit them as "executives" of the organism and biological processes fail to encompass the actions of other molecules, and the effects of the biological environments and processes within these genes act. "Genes (DNA) impart specificity, but so do other molecules (e.g., RNA, proteins, and even carbohydrates and lipids), and so do many *processes* that occur within organisms and in the interactions in which organisms engage with their environments".[142] And in cellular protein synthesis, Hubbard claims, genetic specification cannot be separated and analyzed. Although genes specify the sequence of elements within particular protein molecules, the protein molecules have to "fold up" into three-dimensional configurations, and the particular configuration affects their function.[143] But, Hubbard argues, the patterns of folding are not themselves genetically determined; they are a consequence of the larger biological environment of the organism and the organism's environment.[144]

Moreover, at the much more complex and removed level of behaviors and characteristics, Hubbard claims, the genetic determination incorporated in the "master molecule" theory and biological determinist theories like Sociobiology is impossible. "It is not possible to conclude that DNA controls or programs the many different ways in which proteins participate in the structure and functioning of organisms, not to speak of the many more complex characters of individuals and species."[145]

Ruth Bleier also maintains that it is inappropriate to view genes as "discrete causes" of characteristics and behaviors, and she argues that models that incorporate the view ignore the effects of interactions between genes and the effects of the environment of the organism on gene expression.

> Not only can a complex behavior pattern or a characteristic not be linked to a gene or a gene cluster, there is not even any single cause and effect relationship between a particular gene and a particular anatomical feature, for example between a gene and eye color or body size. Any gene's action or expression is affected, first of all, by its interactions with many other genes . . . and the nature of these interactions is not at all clear. . . . Genes' actions occur only within an environmental milieu and are affected by it. In short, what genes do is only *one part* of the developmental process.[146]

As an example of the various factors involved in biological processes that include gene action, Bleier outlines some of the factors necessary for normal fetal development. In addition to the effects of interaction between genes, Bleier argues that a rather specific maternal environment is *neces-*

sary to that development. Moreover, she claims, there is no way to "tease apart" the genetic component and the environmental component in fetal development.

> The next factor that complicates gene effects on body structure is the uterine environment of the fetus. . . . Fetuses develop within a maternal physiological milieu including salts, fluids, proteins . . . and so on, which are at the same time the milieu within which genes' actions occur that guide the fetus' growth and development. There is no way to tease apart genetic and environmental factors in human development or to know where genetic effects end and environmental ones begin; in fact, this is a meaningless way to view the problem since from conception the relationships between the gene's protein synthesizing activity and the fetus' maternal environment are interdependent.[147]

Thus, according to Hubbard and Bleier, a fundamental problem with the model of gene action incorporated in the "master molecule" theory is that it dichotomizes, and then arranges in hierarchical causal sequences, the discrete "gene" and its alleged discrete effects from the environment of the larger organism—an environment of complex processes.

Evelyn Fox Keller also criticizes the "master molecule" theory. In [1983B], she compares the work of biologist Barbara McClintock, who advocates a more complex and nonlinear model of gene action, with the executive DNA model proposed by Watson and Crick. Keller stresses differences in the methodologies used by McClintock and by Watson and Crick, and she relates these differences to metaphysical commitments. Watson and Crick, she argues, assumed that the relationships involved in cellular protein synthesis were linear and hierarchical, and their model reflected that assumption. Their discovery in 1954 of the double-helical structure of DNA permitted answers to questions about the mechanics of inheritance, but because they assumed that the relationships involved in cellular protein synthesis were linear and hierarchical, the central hypothesis of molecular biology was premised on a "one-way" translation of information.

In [1957] Crick viewed the unidirectional translation of information as the "central dogma" of molecular biology.[148]

> This states that once "information" has passed into protein, *it cannot get out again*. In more detail, the transfer of information from nucleic acid to nucleic acid, or from nucleic acid to protein may be possible, but transfer from protein to protein, or from protein to nucleic acid is impossible.[149]

But, in fact, McClintock's earlier research raised problems for any model that could only allow for linear relationships. Her study of the chromosomal structure of maize suggested that genetic information was not strictly limited to the gene, and it raised problems for a framework accepted prior to the Watson and Crick model in which the gene was taken to be a bead on a string. McClintock's research indicated that the function of a gene might vary with position. Her findings were also problematic for Watson's and Crick's model in which genetic information is contained in the sequence of nucleotide bases. Like the earlier framework, Watson's and Crick's model could not account for positional dependency.[150]

Keller argues that the problems raised by McClintock's findings were ignored for some time by many other biologists because they were committed to a linear and hierarchical model of gene action.[151] According to Keller, that commitment precluded other researchers from seeing transposition, chromosomal changes revealed by McClintock's research. McClintock, she argues, was able to recognize transposition because she focused on relationships and processes, and ultimately, on the whole organism. In McClintock's model, DNA is "in delicate interaction with the cellular environment with control residing in the complex interactions of the entire system".[152] Thus, Keller argues, there is a fundamental difference between McClintock's methodological approach and an approach underwritten by a metaphysical commitment to linear and hierarchical causal relationships. The dominant research focused on finding a discrete and controlling factor, a factor eventually attributed to a "master molecule", but that view of gene action precluded recognition of the phenomenon of transposition.

Keller, Bleier, and Hubbard claim that when we study the models that have been prevalent in the biological sciences, issues emerge that warrant attention: first, the prevalence of the assumption that the range of relationships in human and nonhuman nature, including those within biological processes, are linear and hierarchical with discrete controlling entities determining discrete effects, a metaphysical and methodological commitment that they claim distorts the actual relationships in biological processes; and second, a relationship between our political experiences, including those of dominance, and our models of natural relationships.

The last issue incorporates two specific issues: the relationship between such models and biological determinist theories that legitimate current political arrangements; and the effect our political experiences have on our approaches to nature. Clearly, molecules are anthropomorphized in ways related to political experience when they are posited as "masters" or "executives" of organisms. And, as I noted earlier, Keller also maintains that even the commitment in science to "laws of nature" is political in origin.

> The very concept of "laws of nature" is, in contemporary usage, both a product and an expression of the absence of reflectivity. It introduces into the study of nature a metaphor indelibly marked by its political origins. The philosophical distinction between descriptive and prescriptive laws is invoked to underline the neutrality of scientific description. But nonetheless, laws of nature, the laws of the state, are historically imposed from above and obeyed from below. Laws of nature are (at least in principle) ordinances to which matter is forever subservient.[153]

Bleier also relates the centrality of dominance in scientific models, and in our understandings of the relationship of science to nature, to western political experience.[154]

> Hierarchies, relations of domination, subordination, power, and control are not necessarily inherent in nature but are an integral part of the conceptual framework of persons bred in a civilization constructed on principles of stratification, domination, subordination, power, and control, all made to appear natural. The relationship of culture to nature is not necessarily oppositional; . . . To be in control of things, people, phenomena, information, and institutions, is an essence of our Western industrial class culture. To know, to be certain, is part of being in control. It is important to know *causes* for events and phenomena, for without that "knowledge" one cannot know how to intervene effectively in order to remain or be in control.[155]

A further indication of relationships between politics and science emerges in the alternatives feminists are proposing to linear and hierarchical models. An ability to recognize that "control" and hierarchical relationships are not necessarily universal in nature, relies, in part, on an ability to envision alternative approaches to natural relationships. McClintock's work provides one example of such an alternative, but it is by no means the only contemporary example. It is to a general approach that is emerging in feminist criticism to which we will now turn.

ORDER, COMPLEXITIES, AND PROCESS

Like the issues involving androcentrism that we have considered, the debate between those who advocate an openness to nonlinear relationships and to complexity in biological organisms and processes and those who advocate linear and hierarchical models and simplicity involves metaphysical commitments. These commitments, and their analogues in methodologies, are being exposed, articulated, criticized, and proposed, at least by the feminist scientists whose arguments I have outlined. The commitments are not emerging through studies of the psychology of scientists or, at least for the most part, through interviews in which scientists report their most general understandings of nature.[156] Rather, the commitments are incorporated *within* scientific theories, models, methodologies, and practices.

The debate involves large metaphysical and methodological issues, including the appropriateness of linear and hierarchical causal models in the biological sciences, the universality of such relationships throughout the natural and social world, and the related issue of biological determinism. The debate also involves more specific issues: the status of "genes" as dominant entities that determine discrete "effects" and the appropriateness of assuming there are "masters" or single causes of complex behaviors and traits.

The most interesting issue raised by this aspect of feminist criticism is not that science incorporates metaphysical commitments. Nor is it that political experience is inherently distorting of scientific theorizing. The alternatives feminists are proposing to linear and hierarchical models also incorporate metaphysical commitments and these, too, are clearly related to political experience. In general terms, feminist critics are emphasizing organisms, whether biological or sociological, as whole and complex entities and criticizing the assumption that there must be "controllers" within or of these. They argue that models that encompass complexity and process are more appropriate to the description and study of biological organisms, evolutionary processes, and animal and human social organization. Finally, feminist criticism of models in the biological sciences involves criticism of the larger metaphysical commitment to the universality of dominance relations, a commitment they claim is incorporated in animal sociology, Sociobiology, anthropology, biology, our positing of laws of nature, and our view of science (and humanity) as needing to dominate nature.

The debate I have outlined is, in fact, part of a larger debate that has been surfacing for more than a decade, and it clearly involves metaphysical commitments. The issues include what human and nonhuman nature is like, and how our sciences and our conceptions of the scientific project bear the mark of modern western political experiences and categories. There has been a reemergence of questions concerning the status of biology as an "autonomous" science, critiques of various forms of reductionism, and at least part of the debate involves whether physics (at least, classical physics) can serve as a model for biology and other sciences.[157]

Part of the debate concerning the status of biology as an autonomous science involves the general metaphysical commitment to nature's being characterized by linear and hierarchical relationships. Keller maintains that not only does the commitment to "laws of nature" limit our approaches to nature, but it also leads to specific views of what a "mature science" is.

> Our understanding of what constitutes a law (in nature as in society) is of course subject to change, and not all laws necessarily imply coercion. Certainly not all scientific laws are either causal or deterministic; they may, for example, be statistical, phenomenological, or, more simply, just the "rules of the game". . . . But in many, perhaps most scientific disciplines, the finality of a theory continues to be measured by its resemblance to the classical laws of physics, which are both causal and deterministic. . . . The extreme case of the desire to turn observed regularity into law is of course the search for the one "unified" law of nature that embodies all other laws, and that hence will be immune to revision.[158]

In a discussion whose general concerns about the emphasis on dominance in western science are reflected in the writings of other feminist critics, Keller denies that the descriptive/prescriptive distinction supposedly distinguishing the law of nature metaphor from the coercive connotations of "law" is usually appropriate, and she suggests an alternative view of the scientific project. The alternative is based on a different approach to natural relationships.[159] Biology, rather than physics, has a central place in the alternative conceptions of science and nature that begin with a move from the search for "laws" to a more encompassing search for "order". It is an approach that values complexity rather than simplicity.

Order, Keller notes, can include linear and hierarchical causal relationships, but it can also encompass other kinds of relationship, including the nonhierarchical and nonlinear relationships that feminist and other science critics claim obtain within biological processes and organisms, and may also characterize other aspects of human and nonhuman nature.

> So deeply entrenched is the belief in the laws (or law) of nature as the primary object of scientific inquiry that it is difficult at first glance (especially in the physical sciences) to imagine any other. Yet reflection uncovers just such an alternative. The concept of order, wider than law and free from its coercive, hierarchical, and centralizing implications, has the potential to expand our conception of science. Order is a category comprising patterns of organization that can be spontaneous, self-generated, *or* externally imposed; it is a larger category than law precisely to the extent that law implies external constraint. Conversely,

the kinds of order generated or generable by law comprise only a subset of a larger category of observable or apprehensible regularities, rhythms, and patterns.[160]

Finally, Bleier argues that models in which dominance is a central feature, including linear and hierarchical models of gene action, underwrite biological determinist theories that justify current divisions in power in western societies by race, class, and gender. Thus, she explicitly relates the models and theories she and other feminists criticize and the alternatives they propose to political experiences and to the political consequences of the models adopted in science.

> Underlying the methodological problems in biological determinist theories of human behavior, the fundamental scientific issue is the role of genes and biology in determining characteristics and behaviors.[161]

> My hope and intent is the discarding of the [genes/environment] controversy and dichotomy between nature and nurture or biology and learning because the dichotomy is impossible, unresolvable, and scientifically meaningless. *It is a controversy that serves to obscure social and political origins of inequality and to undermine change* and, furthermore cannot lead to an understanding of human behaviors.[162]

In her analysis of the role primatology has been granted as a "source of insight" into human nature and the centrality of notions of dominance within that field, historian of science Donna Haraway articulates a view of a complex relationship between politics and science, a relationship becoming clearer as feminist criticism develops. She advocates, for example, that feminists study animal sociology and develop alternative models in the biosocial sciences. And she specifically relates such alternatives to politics, urging that feminists "reappropriate the biosocial sciences for new practices and theories".[163]

Thus, as I suggested earlier, the relationship between science and political experience being uncovered by feminist criticism is complex. For one thing, as Haraway notes, it is not linear, but dialectical. Haraway describes the relationship between the biosocial sciences and politics, for example, as mutually reinforcing, as constructing and reconstructing each other.

> One area of the biobehavioral sciences has been unusually important in the construction of oppressive theories of the body political: animal sociology, or the science of animal groups. . . . The biosocial sciences have not simply been sexist mirrors of our own social world. *They have also been tools in the reproduction of that world,* both in supplying legitimating ideologies and in enhancing material power.[164]

So, there are clear connections between the metaphysical commitments incorporated in the alternatives feminists propose and feminist politics. Feminists are specifically advocating that a recognition of the important and centrality of process that may, but need not necessarily, involve hierarchical causal processes might put an end to the long-standing nature/nurture controversy about human and other animal characteristics, behaviors, and social dynamics, which has resurfaced time and again in the history of science. The adoption of models that focus on whole organisms and on processes would allow for the recognition of the complexity of relationships and processes, still evolving and not complete—which neither the assumption of a simple biological determinism nor that of a simple environmentalism permits.[165] And the move away from models in which dominance relations are central could lead to different scientific and social practices.

Although feminists claim that the models and metaphysical commitments they advocate are more warranted than those they criticize—that these will enable us to recognize and encompass many more kinds of relationship that nature includes and could—they are also explicit in relating their ability to envision these alternatives, and the consequences of such alternatives, to feminist politics.

Consequently, a parallel conclusion to that of the preceding section is warranted here. We cannot construe the implications of feminist criticism to be that politics is inherently distorting of scientific theories and methodologies. There is no separating feminists' political concerns with dominance, hierarchies, and biological determinist theories from the criticisms of linear and hierarchical models of gene action and natural relationships that we have considered here. To try to separate these would be as unauthentic as separating the prevalence of notions of dominance in science's approaches to nature from western political experience and practice. We need to give up the myth that our theorizing in science communities is separable from our political experiences and to begin to develop an account of science that encompasses and self-consciously attends to those relationships.

Empiricism and Sex/Gender, Politics, and Science

The criticism we have considered in this chapter clearly warrants attention, but things become difficult when we try to characterize the current state of science and science criticism using the categories available in current empiricist accounts of science.

We have considered a range of issues, and certainly not all of the models and theories feminists criticize are able to be written off as straightforward examples of "bad science"—again, at least as that charge would currently be understood. These models and theories are well connected to other current research and theories, and we have not found evidence to suggest the conscious manipulation of theories or research. Nor, if we find some or all of the criticism sound, are we warranted in concluding that feminists are better scientists than others in the standard sense of more talented observers, more creative theoreticians, more *detached* from their research or its implications, or *less* politically motivated.

We also cannot say that there is no difference of consequence between the theories feminists criticize and those they advocate. If feminists are correct, the "man, the hunter" theory of human evolution provides an account of that process that in its male-centeredness is not warranted; a theory of evolution that recognizes women's activities as well as men's is more warranted given current evidence. Feminists also claim that research into the biological bases of alleged sex differences in cognitive abilities is unwarranted, although I have argued that recognizing this requires a broader perspective than that of individual research questions and programs or even of a substantial body of scientific theorizing. And feminists claim that natural and social relationships are more complex than those that linear, hierarchical models encompass. How do we characterize what is being uncovered in feminist criticism? And how will we seek to explain it and to explain feminists' abilities to recognize it?

We will certainly not *explain* these things here. Those explanations, for reasons that will become clear, will encompass current and historical social and political relations and practices, including feminist politics and sex/gender arrangements and the current state of science, narrowly construed. What I propose to do here is to characterize some of what sociologists, gender theorists, and historians of science will eventually explain—and primarily to clear obstacles to our recognizing that sex/gender and politics are neither separable from science nor inherently distorting. It is, I will argue, our denial that they are factors that has led to distortions and inaccuracies that have not been subjected to evaluation.

THEORIES AND OBSERVATION, METAPHYSICS AND SCIENCE

It might seem that the "theory-ladenness" of observation is the underlying issue in the cases we have considered. But this is not the most basic or important issue raised by feminist criticism. The issue of the relationship between observation and theories was settled thirty years ago: observation *is* theory laden, and as we came to see that there could be no observation unshaped by theory, foundationalism and Archimedean standpoints went by the board hand in hand.[166] In earlier consideration of three influential accounts of science, we found that what remains controversial is how to construe the *consequences* of the demise of foundationalism and the theory/observation dichotomy. Specifically, what do demises indicate about the nature and strength of the evidence scientific theories, and any of our theories, can enjoy?

More to the point, feminist science critics are not attempting to *establish* that observations are theory laden, and if they were, they would not be raising new or interesting issues. Nor, of course, can feminists (or anyone else) assume or argue for an "Archimedean standpoint" for their own critiques. But we do need to provide an account of the *nature* of the difference in the perspectives, theories, and assumptions at issue in feminist criticism and a way to characterize the *grounds* that support these.

Now, it may be that the conflicting theories offered by feminists and others—the conflicting accounts of human evolution and the conflicting approaches to biological processes—can be viewed as "competing paradigms" and, as Kuhn would have it, as incommensurable. But to assume the theories and models feminists and nonfeminists disagree about are "incommensurable", based on the theory-ladenness of observation and/or others of Kuhn's positions—including the autonomy he grants to science communities,[167] is tantamount to abandoning all hope of explaining how these alternatives are possible. Moreover, there are reasons to doubt that the frameworks at issue (or any others cited as alleged examples of incommensurability) are, in fact, incommensurable, as I will later argue in the context of discussing science's alleged autonomy.

Although feminist critics are not establishing, or trying to establish, *that* observations are theory laden, their criticism does reveal factors relevant to scientific theorizing and theories that current empiricist accounts of science and Kuhn's account preclude or fail to recognize.[168] One is a relationship between observers and the directions and content of scientific knowledge. The connection is not just revealed in androcentric assumptions, methodologies, and theories, or in models that reflect western political experiences and categories.

Currently, it makes a difference to one's observations, appraisals of theories, and one's own theorizing, if one *recognizes* androcentric and sexist assumptions, categories, or questions and if one questions the inevitability of male dominance and/or the universality of hierarchical dominance relationships. In short, it makes a difference if one is working from a feminist perspective, relating experiences of sex/gender and politics to, and bringing the category of sex/gender to bear on, models, assumptions, and theoretical frameworks that have previously been accepted as having no connection to gendered or political experience. Given the pervasiveness of the assumptions feminists criticize, their reinforcement in science and other practices, no simple explanation will do.

But before we can explore the connections between observers and the content of science, we will need to consider the relationships feminist criticism exposes between the directions and content of scientific knowledge, and the larger social and political contexts within which science is practiced. It is in such relationships that we will find the source of the relationships between observers and theories, or at least so I will later argue. And we will do well to begin that consideration against the background of some well-known issues and problems related to the theory/observation relationship. This will enable us to see what is unique about the issues raised in and by feminist science criticism, and it will prevent some decidedly unhelpful construals of these issues.

In considering feminist criticism of "man, the hunter" theory, we were faced, in part, with examples of what are well-known problems attendant to historical explanation. In reconstructing human evolution, we are, of course, terribly limited. In part, this is due to the relative lack of evidence for early hominid and human behavior, activities, and social organization. But it is also because the evidence is uneven. Stone artifacts, for example, will survive when other tools such as baskets and sticks will not—and this is directly relevant to ascertaining the activities that contributed to and were enabled by the evolution of our brain, language, and social organization. The differences in the survival rates of kinds of tool are also relevant to questions about the relative contributions made to that evolution by the activities of our female and male ancestors—so long as we *also assume* that some division of labor by sex/gender characterized these groups and differentiated tool use.[169]

But the lack and the unevenness of the evidence available for early hominid and human behavior and activities are not the only problems facing us when we attempt to reconstruct human evolution. We have long been aware that historical explanations are complicated and shaped by the demands and conceptual frameworks of present context; our expectations and assumptions shape our approaches to and our understandings of historical evidence and its implications. Having an abundance of evidence in the way of artifacts would not provide us with a goddess's eye view of that process. We can think of the role current context plays in shaping historical explanation as a special case of the theory/observation relationship.

So far, the issues facing us are not new lessons. We can also discuss the complexities that I have outlined in a more precise way using some of Quine's positions. Two are particularly relevant here: the first, holism, maintains that our theories are fundamentally connected and interdependent, so that it is as a whole that science (in the narrow and broader senses) explains and faces experience; the second, a coherence account of evidence, maintains that theories and claims are constrained both by experience *and* by their coherence with other going theories.

Given these positions, those theories that we find relevant to a reconstruction of human evolution (another decision that we will make on the *basis* of going theories) will shape our reconstruction of that story, including our appraisal and interpretation of the available evidence. A substantial body of going theory will shape the questions we ask, the other theories and research we will regard as relevant, and will be part of what we use to answer those questions.

Now, the issues feminist critics are raising about the "man, the hunter" theory—and the point holds as well for the research into sex differences—are evidence that Quine is correct in stressing the fundamental connections and interdependence of going theories. Feminist criticism of that theory revealed that a rather substantial body of theory is incorporated in its explanation of human evolution. The account draws on what have been generally accepted models and theories in primatology and anthropology, including observations of and theories about alleged differences in female and male behavior and activities, in its reconstruction of early human activities and social organization. Although we did not focus on these, the theory also draws, of course, on current theories in neurobiology, genetics, primate anatomy, geology, paleontology, archeology, and evolutionary biology to support its claim that tool use was a fundamental factor in the evolution of our brain and so on. And theories and research in these fields, in turn, draw on *other theories* and each other, and of course, even the assumption that primatology and hunter/gatherer societies are *relevant* to a reconstruction of human evolution is based on other going theories. What we can see is that the current state of science and, in very obvious ways, a substantial amount of the knowledge gained in a number of specific fields are part of what constitutes the explanation offered by "man, the hunter" theory.

Moreover, feminists who propose alternative accounts of human evolution and/or criticize "man, the hunter" theory are by no means working in a vacuum—and certainly not a "scientific" vacuum. Part of what they are using (as "man, the hunter" theorists are, in part, using) are current scientific theories. Feminists are drawing on recent research in primatology and anthropology that is not shaped by androcentric assumptions, on feminist criticism of the consequences of androcentrism in each of these fields, and on the growing evidence that sciences concerned with human and animal behavior have historically and currently ignored or misdescribed women's (and female's) activities and behavior. Thus, feminist criticism of "man, the hunter" theory and the alternatives being developed are also interdependent with other scientific theorizing.

Now, whether we regard the connections and interdependence between theories and theorizing that Quine insists on, and feminist criticism provides evidence for, as problems is another issue and I will address it later. But *that* such connections and interdependence characterize scientific theories should no longer surprise us. Indeed, the directions and the scope of feminist science criticism—a body of criticism leveled at sociology, primatology, anthropology, psychology, neuroendocrinology, evolutionary theory, molecular biology, and the most general metaphysical commitments incorporated in our approaches to nature—would be difficult, if not impossible, to explain if scientific theories and theorizing were not so connected and interdependent.

But there are new results. Our experiences of and views about sex/gender are clearly factors in historical explanation. Anthropologists and evolutionary theorists attribute divisions of labor by sex/gender that characterize the upper classes in modern western industrial societies to our ancestors of 250,000 years ago. They also attribute what they allege (some, we have seen, simply assume) are universal sex differences in behaviors and activities to those earliest humans. And, as one would expect if one insists on the interdependence of going theories and a coherence theory of evidence, the various assumptions about sex differences and divisions of labor by sex are shared by a number of sciences and research programs. I have also argued that experiences of and views about sex/gender are inseparable from *feminist criticism* of the "man, the hunter" theory and others, and from the development of alternatives that give women's activities a central role in human evolution and a central role in hunter/gatherer societies, and so on.

There are other new issues concerning historical explanation raised by feminist criticism. Feminist critics have made us far more aware that scientific theories, including historical reconstructions, have consequences for our current views and practices. The "man, the hunter" theory and others that incorporate the basic organizing principle linking males with social dynamics and females with biology and reproduction are used by scientists and laypersons as evidence that current divisions by sex/gender of labor and power in western societies are *natural and inevitable* because they have "always been so".[170] In problematizing the cognitive authority scientists enjoy and exercise in our larger community, and exploring the specific uses to which historical explanations are put, feminists have exposed the fact that historical explanations can be, and some clearly have been and are, *political.* As Haraway claimed of animal sociology, historical explanations not only reflect but reinforce current views and practices.

Feminists are also criticizing observations and descriptions of animal behavior and social organization. That there are problems attendant to our descriptions of animal behavior is also not a new insight. We may eventually replace our current approach to describing animal behavior and sociology so that it does not sound like animals are people in fur coats, developing ways of describing these that are more in keeping with what it is reasonable to say about species whose neural capacities could not support many of the things we now say. Granted, we do not have such an apparatus now or even a commitment to develop it. Hence, our descriptions and explanations of animal behavior and social organization are bound to be deeply anthropomorphic.

But feminist criticism exposes factors at work in our observations of and theorizing about other species of which we were unaware, brings others into sharper relief, and raises serious questions about whether that anthropomorphizing needs to be problematized. First, it reveals deep connections between social and political context, including our expectations and experiences of sex/gender, and our approaches to animal behavior and social organization. Behaviors and objects such as "bluebird adultery",[171] the "rampant machismo" of male insects,[172] "chimpanzee prostitution",[173] "coy" females, bees "raping" flowers,[174] and "primate harems"[175] that have figured in descriptions and explanations in primatology, animal sociology, and Sociobiology are obviously shaped by contemporary western experiences of sex/gender and of dominance relations.

Feminist criticism also reveals that there are pressing problems raised by the anthropomorphism evident here. The problem is not simply that the level of it in the above list seems unnecessary, if not outright ridiculous. One more far-reaching problem, as we saw in our consideration of Sociobiology, is that the connection between these alleged behaviors and the ways in which we characterize human behavior, including those shaped by androcentric and sexist assumptions, creates the impression that we *know* what these animal behaviors and characteristics are—that we have clear identity criteria for them. These connections, precisely because they are not acknowledged or attended to self-consciously, permit sloppy ontologies and unwarranted generalizations.[176]

Moreover, feminist criticism exposes the fact that behaviors and characteristics attributed to other species for which identity criteria are at best fuzzy, and whose sense for us (if there is any) relies on their relation to current social and political context, have far-reaching consequences precisely because there *are* fundamental connections between our going theories. As with historical explanations such as "man, the hunter" theory, the behaviors, characteristics, and forms of social organization scientists are attributing to insects, bluebirds, nonhuman primates, and other species are being used as *evidence* of genetically-determined human sex differences, for clues into the evolutionary "purposes" and causes of contemporary western behaviors, practices, expectations, and social organization, and for the "universality" of things such as rape, dominance hierarchies, aggression, male dominance, racial discrimination, and divisions of labor and power by sex/gender.[177] So, in addition to weakening any theory in which they are important features, such descriptions of and claims about animal behavior and social organization can be, and some clearly are, *political*.

Now, feminists are not arguing, nor is it an implication of the issues I am raising, that we should decide a priori that the behavior of other species is not relevant to the study of human behavior. Feminists are, in fact, *using* nonandrocentric and nonsexist descriptions of animal behavior to expose problems with the descriptions other scientists give of these, to undermine the alleged "universals" of Sociobiology, as well as to develop the "woman, the gatherer" theory of evolution. What feminist criticism suggests about animal sociology is much more straightforward: First, the *unself-conscious* anthropomorphizing that many scientists engage in prevents them from doing their homework: explicitly stating the grounds for assuming that similar behaviors across different species have similar causes (genetic, for example), so that the assumption can be critically evaluated,[178] and cleaning up their ontologies (clearly stating, for example, the behavioral criteria for "female coyness" or "male fickleness" that allegedly characterize all species, including the human species) so that the similarities can be evaluated. Doing that homework would make it far more likely that claims alleging similarities and/or universality of specific behaviors across species would be debated and critically evaluated and not simply smuggled in, as is now the case.

Second, feminist criticism indicates that observations and theories in animal sociology will not only be shaped by our sex/gendered and political experiences but they have had, and will have, political implications. So, the other change that feminist criticism indicates is warranted is that these consequences must be acknowledged by animal sociologists and by others who use their descriptions and theories, and that connections with our views and experiences of sex/gender and politics, need to be *self-consciously* attended to.[179] This means acknowledging in theory and practice that there are relationships between science and politics. In the end, feminist criticism indicates, they can be mutually reinforcing.

Another issue raised by the feminist criticism we have considered in this and the preceding chapter is also familiar to many of us. We have been aware that scientific research *begins* with metaphysical and methodological commitments, and that such commitments guide the general directions of research, the models and methodologies adopted, and what, in general terms, will count as an explanation.[180]

Research into human behavior, for example, begins with assumptions about the appropriateness of explaining human behavior using biology or sociology, with assumptions about whether the biological and sociological aspects of human behaviors can be teased apart and explained separately (and/or hierarchically), and with assumptions about whether the behaviors and characteristics to be discerned or explained are determined by discrete controllers such as genes or hormones. Research into biological processes begins with assumptions about the kinds of relationship to be looked for, and whether the whole organism or an executive "controller" of it is the appropriate focus in explaining biological processes. Organisms will themselves be regarded in specific and consequential ways: as, for example, miniature cities or production plants whose processes are thought of in terms of "flow charts",[181] as information systems,[182] or as complex wholes that respond constantly to the environment and are each unique—a view like that which underwrote McClintock's work and feminists and other biologists currently advocate.[183]

Now, unlike the Hempel/Nagel tradition and Kuhnian views, feminist criticism does not indicate that such metaphysical and methodological commitments and presuppositions are arbitrary or the mark of flawed or corrupted science. The implications of this aspect of feminist criticism are very similar to Quine's positions.

As we noted in the conclusion of Chapter Four, if we acknowledge that metaphysical commitments are incorporated in theories, methodologies, questions, and ontologies, and the discussion of this chapter further indicates that we must, then it is not surprising that feminist critics have found such assumptions in the biological and social sciences. It has also become clear that such metaphysical and methodological commitments are neither random nor arbitrary, nor the result of personal quirks or idiosyncrasies.

The cases we have considered indicate that it is, in fact, a substantial body of scientific theory or research that lends credence to some metaphysical commitments and denies it to others, and that individual research programs and theories neither develop nor "face the evidence" in isolation from others. Our consideration of research into sex differences and the "man, the hunter" theory revealed connections in metaphysical assumptions across theories and sciences. The linear and hierarchical models in molecular biology that feminists and other scientists are currently criticizing are also fundamentally connected to other aspects of science.

The metaphysical assumptions and methodological approaches that came to dominate genetics from the 1930s to the 1950s were shaped by the success of classical physics and a conscious attempt to make biology more like it—both of which led to great advances in molecular biology during the period and underwrote the adoption of linear and hierarchical models of gene action.[184] As Evelyn Fox Keller chronicles, the assumption that physics could or should serve as a model for a "serious biology", and specifically as a model for genetics, was a conscious one, coming in one of its most influential forms from Max Delbruck, a theoretical physicist who came to the United States in 1937 and invited biologists to view the gene as a "molecular object". As a physicist, Keller argues, Delbruck came from a tradition that "revered simplicity rather than complexity", and a commitment to simplicity and discrete entities came to dominate genetics under his influence and that of others who shared his views about the kinds of model that were appropriate in genetics.[185]

Keller's account of the revolution in genetics indicates that the commitment to linear and hierarchical models of gene action, and the ascendancy of this approach over the organicist approach, was due then, in great part, to the current state of science—specifically, the success of such commitments and models in classical physics and the prestige of physics—and, as Keller describes the period, "above all there was the fact that the principal characters [of the revolution in molecular biology] came from disciplines far removed from classical genetics . . . from biochemistry, microbiology, x-ray crystallography, and perhaps especially, from physics".[186] What the revolution indicates is that the metaphysical and methodological commitments to linear and hierarchical models we considered in the preceding section were connected not only to political experience but to a substantial body of scientific theory and consciously adopted in genetics. Keller also notes that some biologists remained committed to a more holistic approach. But because of the influx of a new generation of geneticists, many trained in fields in which simplicity and hierarchical models were emphasized, the approach advocated by Delbruck came to dominate molecular biology.

The revolution also suggests that Addelson is correct in holding that not all of the approaches that are at work in science will, in fact, have "equal time" and that prestige (in this case, the prestige of physics) will be a factor in which understandings come to dominate the field. But, this case indicates that other theories, models, and methodologies currently accepted will also play a role in deciding which approaches are pursued. So, in addition to studying the social arrangements within which scientific knowledge develops and the prestige hierarchies that divide scientists and sciences, we would want to adopt a holistic approach and an account of evidence that can encompass the fact that other theories are factors in shaping the commitments with which research begins. They are part of the *evidence* that warrants such assumptions.

There are other lessons. The presence and the role of such metaphysical commitments is not in itself a mark of bad science; nor, as long as we *acknowledge* them, are such commitments pernicious. The feminist criticism we have considered supports Quine's contention that such commitments can be discerned, criticized, and proposed—no matter how abstract or widely embedded in our going theories. Feminists are also clearly advocating different metaphysical and methodological commitments.

However, other issues feminists raise about metaphysical commitments are new, and they parallel issues we noted in discussing their criticism of "man, the hunter" theory and animal sociology. The commitments feminists have uncovered in science bear marks that most empiricists did not expect to find—at least that they did not expect to find in good science: experiences of and views about sex/gender are among the factors that shape these commitments—albeit, they are factors in a more substantial body of theory than a focus on individual theories or research might allow us to recognize. The long-standing and deeply embedded androcentrism of western societies does not disappear at the threshold of science, anymore than it did at the thresholds of philosophy and theology. It is reflected in the historical interest in establishing sex differences in cognitive abilities and the relationship between such interest and political movements, in the descriptions of animal behavior and social organization that feminist criticism exposes as not only anthropomorphic but deeply androcentric, in the use of these descriptions by scientists to justify current divisions in power by sex/gender, and in the assumption that the important activities that contributed to our evolution would have been those in which men engaged, and so on.

In addition, the categories, objects, and models we use to describe, organize, and justify political experiences and practices are also factors in our approaches to human and nonhuman nature. Our experiences of dominance and of hierarchies are reflected in and reinforced by our approaches to natural relationships. We have sought and posited "masters" and "executives" of biological processes, dominance hierarchies throughout the animal and human world, and laws to govern all that happens. And we have found that different political perspectives and practices can lead to alternative approaches to natural and human relationships.

In the end, then, we have found that science is detached neither from sex/gender nor politics—and that the consequences are not limited to individual or isolated theories. A large body of theory supports each of the research programs and theories we have considered and reflects and reinforces gendered and political experiences and practices.

And, as we have noted in several contexts, we cannot take the lesson of feminist criticism to be that given different or neutral assumptions about sex/gender, we could return to "science as usual"—or that what is needed are stricter methodological controls to filter out all of our experiences of politics and sex/gender. The reason we cannot so construe the lesson is that relationships between politics and experiences of and views about sex/gender, and approaches to human and nonhuman nature, are *neither overcome nor absent* in feminist criticism or in the alternatives feminists are developing. There are clear and obvious relationships between feminist political perspectives and experiences, and the criticisms and alternatives feminists propose to current theories and assumptions about male dominance, linear and hierarchical relationships, social dynamics in primate groups and other cultures, and so on.

Although feminist scientists and science critics claim that the alternatives they propose are more warranted than those they criticize, their ability to recognize androcentric assumptions and their consequences, to propose alternatives, and the specific alternatives they are developing are fundamentally connected to their political experiences and perspectives. In short, there is no avoiding the historical relativity of feminist science criticism, its sources in social and political changes in contemporary western societies, and the fundamental relationships between politics and science revealed in and through that criticism.

Nor can we block these conclusions or their implications for the epistemology of science by focusing on particular scientists as if they are the "owners" of androcentric bias or the "discoverers" of that bias. If we turn our attention to scientists to characterize or explain the current state of science and science criticism, then within current empiricist accounts of science, we would have to limit ourselves to considering individual scientists—both those who began with assumptions or offered theories that feminists claim are androcentric and those who challenge such frameworks, and those who advocate linear, hierarchical models and those who advocate a receptivity to nonlinear, nonhierarchical relationships.

But obviously it would be unenlightening to attribute androcentric or feminist assumptions to individual scientists in seeking or offering explanations for what we are now experiencing. No individual (not even Aristotle) invented the assumption that male dominance hierarchies characterize all animal and human social organization, or that linear hierarchical relationships characterize all of nature; nor can we credit any individual with the insight that social and natural relationships are *not* all hierarchical or that male dominance is neither universal nor inevitable. Relationships between other going theories *and* the social and political context of our larger society are being revealed by feminist criticism—and are *no less* a part of that criticism. Scientists, feminists and nonfeminists, work within an inclusive body of theory they inherit and, in their small ways, alter—again, on the basis of their experiences, including their social and political experiences, and other theories. And *they could do nothing else.*[187]

We are left with the question of how to accommodate these insights and, more specifically, how to accommodate the fact that a substantial body of going scientific theories reflects, reinforces, and serves to reproduce our experiences and views of sex/gender and politics. Obviously, we need to reconsider the view advocated by the postlogical positivist tradition and Kuhn that science is a self-regulating and autonomous enterprise.

THE AUTONOMY OF SCIENCE

We can begin to see how fundamentally the autonomy of science is challenged by feminist criticism by considering the problems that the Hempel/Nagel tradition would have in accommodating the issues we have considered. As we saw in earlier discussion, those working with a view of science shaped by the emphases of the tradition either argue explicitly that the context of discovery is irrelevant to the epistemology of science or ignore it completely and focus exclusively on issues and problems relevant to the justification of hypotheses and theories.[188] Either practice avoids attention to questions about how ontologies are generated, why the research undertaken is chosen, and how theories are generated and adopted. The "epistemology of science" is assumed to be exhausted by questions about the justification of individual theories. And although Kuhn to some extent, and Quine to a far greater extent, have successfully challenged aspects of that view of science, how theories are generated and which questions are pursued are still regarded by many scientists, laypersons, and philosophers as irrelevant to accounting for the development of scientific knowledge.

In what turns out to be a related position, the Hempel/Nagel tradition maintains that science—or, more correctly, the body of knowledge that it regards as science—is an autonomous entity: remote or detached from common-sense beliefs and, as Nagel puts it, "from things men [*sic*] value". The view decisively precludes the possibility that the factors feminist criticism links to science *could* be so linked, at least in good science.

Finally, the tradition's account of the empirical constraints on theories, of the theory/evidence relationship—an account in which individual theories are tested and linked to experience by observation sentences—precludes serious attention to other theories and assumptions related to and underlying ontologies and theories, and it requires that individual sentences and individual theories have empirical content in isolation from a going body of theory. Both Hempel and Nagel recognize that what they call "tacit and higher level" assumptions complicate their model of confirmation, but they maintain that individual theories can be and are tested on the basis of observation sentences.

Any one of these positions, and surely their conjunction, makes it impossible to consider the issues outlined in this chapter in anything like a reasonable manner. At the very least, the issues feminists raise would not be considered relevant to the epistemology of science. The theories feminists criticize and feminist criticism itself show fundamental relationships to other scientific theories *and* to social and political context.

Two aspects of the Hempel/Nagel view, its emphasis on the context of justification and the ruling out of social and political context as relevant to science, have been explored and criticized by feminist critics.[189] Unfortunately, these positions are frequently identified as necessary to or dogmas of empiricism. Using Quine's positions, I have argued that empiricism is a theory of evidence, and that many of the dogmas attributed to empiricism—including those of an autonomous science and the alleged distinction between contexts of discovery and justification—are not necessary consequences of that theory of evidence.

I want to focus on the third set of positions outlined above that would make it difficult, if not impossible, to say reasonable things about the issues raised by feminist criticism: the view that individual theories "face experience" in isolation from other going theories and the related view that individual sentences have specifiable empirical content in isolation from a body of theory. We will explore the understanding of evidence, of the empirical constraints imposed on theories, that are incorporated in these views using the feminist criticism we have considered. Although I have outlined two views, one about sentences and the other about individual theories, these are really one view—for the possibility of judging individual theories relies on the notion that individual sentences have empirical content in isolation from a going body of theory. And, ultimately, the view that individual scientific theories "face" experience requires that science, either as a set of practices or a body of knowledge generated by those practices, is self-regulating and insulated.

I will explore the feasibility of these last views by focusing on Kuhn's account of scientific revolutions. The implications for the Hempel/Nagel view will also emerge, for, as we saw earlier, Kuhn's account of science and scientific revolutions shares with the Hempel/Nagel view the assumptions that science is autonomous and that it is in isolation that individual theories (or paradigms) face experience and are judged. Focusing on Kuhn's view will also permit us to consider the possibility of the kind of "epistemological chasms" his thesis of incommensurability requires.

On one level, as we saw earlier, Kuhn's account of scientific revolutions seems to represent a fundamental break with the Hempel/Nagel account of science and to expose the most basic flaws in that account. It appears to draw the inevitable consequences of the theory/observation relationship, of the presence of metaphysical commitments in science, and of the actual activities, rather than rationalized reconstruction of these, in which scientists engage. But I argued earlier that the significance of the dissimilarities has been exaggerated. Kuhn's account would also require that we focus on individual science communities in giving accounts of the present state of science and science criticism[190] and of revolutions in science. Kuhn insists that science communities are fundamentally self-contained—and this, it turns out, is crucial to his account of revolutions and to the epistemology of science that emerges in that account.[191]

I also noted in Chapter Two that Kuhn discusses scientific revolutions (as well as normal science) in three ways: in terms of the psychology of individual scientists, the sociology of science communities, and artifacts that he calls "paradigms".[192] He also uses two notions of paradigms. In normal science, a paradigm is a concrete achievement that underwrites the formation and the activities of a science community; in revolutionary science, a paradigm is a disciplinary matrix, including theories, metaphysical commitments, and methodological principles. It is in the sense of disciplinary matrices that we will here consider paradigms.

We focused earlier on the role Kuhn attributes to the sociology of science communities in determining the outcomes of revolutions. Here I want to focus on revolutions in the content of science.[193] I will use the term 'theory' to discuss the artifact or content at issue, but I use it in a

Quinean sense that, in important ways, is well in keeping with Kuhn's use of 'paradigm' as a "disciplinary matrix". Theories, on this view, incorporate metaphysical commitments, methodological principles, and standards of evidence, as well as generalizations about what happens and how.

In his account of revolutions in science, Kuhn rejects the possibility that a choice between competing theories or paradigms is (or could be) determined or constrained by "observation". He also insists that logic will not decide between competing theories. And because he takes these things to mean that *evidence* cannot be used to decide matters, he views a revolution in science as akin to a religious conversion.

The insistence that either observation or logic must provide a clear decision between two individual theories (in ways I will shortly elaborate) or the resulting decision is not based on evidence is, I suggest, another legacy of positivism and can be avoided. The theory-ladenness of observation does not mean that we cannot decide between competing theories. And the view that logic alone will not tell us what the world is like is something often insisted on in introductory logic courses (although given the demise of the analytic/synthetic distinction, the view so stated is also strange[194]).

If we insist that the theory-ladenness of observation rules out "the world"—at least, an *untheorized* world—as a constraining and decisive factor, and if the theories at issue are not related in a way such that one encompasses or clearly contradicts the other (a further consequence, on Kuhn's view, of the theory/observation relationship), we are still not in the position Kuhn describes—that is, lacking a "higher authority" to which to appeal for a rational decision when deciding between two theories, however broad. For scientific revolutions to be something other than conversions, Kuhn's account would require an extratheoretic piece of evidence or some set of these to decide matters—*because* Kuhn claims that each theory (or disciplinary matrix) is a *closed world system.*[195]

Now, it is certainly true that when faced with two competing theories, we may be in a position that does not permit anything remotely resembling a crucial experiment—which, it would seem, Kuhn is demanding and despairing of. But Kuhn's account of this situation, and in particular his notion that such theories are incommensurable, requires that we are comparing two theories (however broad and complex) in isolation from *all others*—that the theories at issue are unconnected to any other going theories so that no other theories can be brought to bear on the decision. An alternative construal of his analysis of the decision facing scientists (although it is not clear that Kuhn could propose it given his commitment to science communities being fundamentally isolated entities) is that in revolutionary science we are comparing two theories that claim to explain *everything*.

The point I am making is that Kuhn's thesis of incommensurability requires that the whole world is up for grabs and this must be for one of two reasons: it is either because we are assuming (as Hempel and Nagel did) that *individual theories* face experience and that this is all we consider when deciding between two theories (or test theories, etc.); or because we are assuming that two groups within a science community disagree about *everything*—again, because we assume that this community is fundamentally isolated. Given one or the other of these assumptions, and the ruling out of decisive observations or logical relationships that can settle things, it would appear there is *nothing* to bring to bear on the situation to enable a rational decision. So, when one theory does eventually supersede another, it is, on Kuhn's view, social pressure (including the fear of being banished to a philosophy department) that causes scientists to adopt the new theory and abandon the old.

Recently, in considering feminist criticism of "man, the hunter" theory and the alternative, "woman, the gatherer" theory, feminist science critics Helen Longino and Ruth Doell seem to share some of Kuhn's skepticism about the possibility of deciding between the two competing accounts of evolution on the basis of *evidence*.[196] After outlining the data available, the problems facing historical explanation, as well as the androcentrism incorporated in the "man, the hunter theory" and the gynocentrism incorporated in its rival, Longino and Doell point out that only some of the issues about which the theories disagree could be settled by future evidence. Although they acknowledge that we might expect a third theory to eventually supersede these current theories, they also point out that the gap between our accounts of human evolution and the evidence available is a permanent one. And, on their view, that gap can and will be filled in by what they call "culturally determined ideas"— and, for now at least, these are gynocentric and androcentric ideas.

One of the specific issues that Longino and Doell maintain could not be settled by future evidence is the significance of chipped stones found near fossil remains of *Australopithecus* and *Homo erectus*. Are they evidence of male tool making for hunting, as "man, the hunter" theorists maintain? Or, if we assume, as advocates of "woman, the gatherer" theory do, that female gathering was the important behavioral adaptation, evidence that women began to develop stone tools as well as the tools they were already using for gathering? According to Longino and Doell, there is no *evidence* that can be brought to bear on settling that question, and because the same holds of other questions, the decision to adopt one or the other theory is not based on evidence.

> The two approaches to human evolution differ in their assessment of the relative contributions of males and females to the evolution of the species. . . .
> The issue here . . . is whether there is direct evidence for either of the interpretive frameworks within which the data, in this case chipped stones, acquire status as evidential support for hypotheses regarding the dietary and social behavior of early hominids. *Not only do we not now have such evidence; we cannot have it.* What the study of contemporary hunting and gathering societies should teach us is that, short of stepping into a time machine, any speculation regarding the behavior and social organization of early humans remains just that. *This leaves framework choice subject to influences such as the speculator's preconceived and culturally determined ideas of what human beings are.* The distance between evidence and hypothesis cannot be closed by anatomical and physiological knowledge, by principles from the theory of evolution, *or by common-sensical assumptions.* It remains an invitation to further theorizing, or as some would have it, *storytelling.*[197]

Longino and Doell do, of course, disagree fundamentally with Kuhn's contention that scientific theorizing is insulated from social and political context. But they imply that beliefs shaped by that context (beliefs they refer to as "preconceived and culturally determined ideas") are not subject to critical evaluation or constrained by evidence. Thus, they grant to science a status that is indistinguishable from that granted to it by those who insist science is insulated from social context, and for precisely the same reasons: namely, on the grounds that "common-sense beliefs", including androcentric and gynocentric beliefs, are not subject to evidential constraint. So their account of the disagreement between the two theories of human evolution has consequences like those entailed by Kuhn's incommensurability: because culturally determined ideas are all that can fill in "the gaps in evidence", the disagreement between "man, the hunter" theorists and "woman, the gatherer" theorists cannot be settled by evidence. One or the other theory will be chosen on the basis of "preconceived ideas".

I want to use some of Quine's positions to explore some assumptions at work in Kuhn's account of revolutions and in aspects of Longino's and Doell's account of the nature of the decision that can or would be made between the two competing theories of human evolution. I begin with the consequences of the theory/observation relationship because a specific understanding of those consequences and an insistence on the autonomy of science are what underwrite Kuhn's analysis and lead to his conclusions. Quine's positions suggest an alternative view of our current situation and of the evidence that will be used to decide between competing theories.

Quine, we have seen, also insists that observation is theory laden. Indeed, he maintains that it is possible only within a going body of theory. In our current largest conceptual framework, for example, observation and coherent experience are possible only after the mechanics of object ontology and individuation have been mastered.[198] So, Quine maintains, there can be no extrascientific grounding for science in observation or sense data. But he also argues that observation is *both* connected to sensory stimulation *and* constrained by experience. For a relevant *community*, observation sentences are on the "periphery" of our conceptual network and do, more than other sentences within the network, face experience. The community-bound status of observation sentences is both a consequence of their theory-ladenness and an indication that such sentences need not be "low level" theoretical sentences. As we noted earlier, the relevant community for which a sentence can serve as an observation sentence may be one of specialists.[199]

The general point is that such sentences can serve as observation sentences for the community *and* have the specific empirical content they do because of a *going body of theory* the community shares. Quine's understanding of the *dual constraint* of experience and other going theories is evident in this account of observation sentences, and they are the basis for his claim that it is as a whole that theories explain, and as a whole that they are constrained by experience.[200] These positions suggest that Kuhn's conclusions about the consequences of the theory-ladenness of observation for our ability to bring evidence to bear on a theory are unwarranted.

Given holism, whatever the theories (or disciplinary matrices) we are comparing—for Kuhn, geocentric and heliocentric views, for example; currently, "man, the hunter" and "woman, the gatherers" theories; and the "master molecule" theory of gene action and the alternative models feminists and others are developing—these theories will bear various relationships to a number of other going theories and, ultimately, to all the theories that make up our most inclusive view of the world. Much of this view, most of our community (our larger social community, our particular scientific community, our world community) will share—some of it, and perhaps some important and rather large portion, we may disagree about, and perhaps more than Quine himself ever considered, and obviously some of it (high-energy physics, for example), will not be of interest to many of us. The point is that we certainly cannot—and, as we have seen, we certainly *do not*—judge between or develop specific theories considered in isolation from a larger theory of nature. Nor are the observations that are *part* of the evidence for any theory separable from a going body of theory. We judge neither individual observations nor individual theories only by references to experience; these are also judged on the basis of their coherence with other going theories.

But it is just as clear that the "whole world" is not at issue when scientists disagree about theories or when science is in a period of crisis. No individual theory, or even a substantial body of theory, exhausts *all* the views we hold about what goes on. Nor, given the interdependence between standards of evidence and a going body of theory, can we disagree about all standards of evidence. As we noted earlier, Galileo and his inquisitors could discuss torture instruments and Aristotelian physics while disagreeing about the plan of the solar system. Advocates of "woman, the gatherer" theory and of the "man, the hunter" theory can discuss "chipped stones" without our having to think they are not discussing the same objects, and Hubbard and Bleier can discuss genes and disagree with other biologists about genetic determination of traits and behavior, and protein synthesis development. Indeed, it is only because these disagreements can and do occur that feminists can understand and criticize the "master molecule" theory and its commitment to a linear and hierarchical model of gene action, and that feminists and "man, the hunter" theorists can disagree about the significance of chipped stones. So, although feminist scientists and science critics disagree with nonfeminist scientists about specific theories—even, perhaps now, a very large number of theories, including some standards of evidence and even, currently, what science incorporates and is—these communities, subcommunities of our larger community, do not disagree about *everything*. They share theories about molecules, macroscopic objects, continents, societies, gravity, and so on.

Relatedly, the autonomy, the insulation, of science communities that Kuhn's thesis of incommensurability requires is untenable. The feminist criticism we have considered indicates that our "common-sense" beliefs and experiences, including those of sex/gender and politics, are inextricably related to our theorizing in science communities—and this is the case not only in terms of the androcentrism and experiences of dominance that are reflected in scientific theories, but also in feminist theorizing. And, clearly, many common-sense beliefs (although certainly not all) are shared by feminists and their nonfeminist colleagues.

In the end, then, there is nothing like the "epistemological chasm" that Kuhn's thesis of incommensurability would require. It is not the case that two groups share nothing that can be brought to bear as evidence on those things about which they disagree or that there is nothing else that *is* relevant. He is certainly correct that we cannot decide between competing theories without references to the current state of science in the broadest sense. He is wrong in thinking that the state of science *itself* is on the line—no matter how broad the disagreement might be. Even in a situation like our current one, there remains a containing network of theories, a large number of beliefs and theories not in question, that constitute the higher authority that Kuhn claims does not exist. But there may not be, of course, anything like a crucial experiment possible; nor may things be decided in a "moment".

An additional indication that the isolation of the theories in question that Kuhn's account requires is not real becomes clear when we consider the current state of science. We find nothing like the picture Kuhn draws of how new theories come into existence and provoke a period of crisis and revolutionary science. On Kuhn's account, alternatives to accepted theories present themselves to "deeply troubled" scientists "in the middle of the night". He does not explore how new theories might be related to other things going on in the specific science, to other sciences, or to common-sense practices and thinking. But it is clear that to begin to understand the current state of science and science criticism would not only involve analyzing the problems any individual theory is facing. We can clearly see that we would need to study what else is going on both in science communities and in our larger community—in terms of changes in common-sense and scientific theory and social and political arrangements and context.

So we have to give up several views incorporated in Kuhn's analysis of scientific revolutions, and these are all related to the alleged autonomy of science. One is the notion that we can or do take individual theories and consider them in isolation from all others, comparing them to alternatives (also taken in isolation) *or* to an "untheorized world". Evidence is not self-announcing or uniquely determined by the logical implications of a hypothesis. It is tied, firmly, to the current state of science in the broadest sense, including common-sense experiences, practices, and beliefs. But recognizing that all of our theories are connected, and that there are no "standpoints" outside some going body of theory, suggests that comparing and weighing theories is a fundamentally different kind of activity than Kuhn described.

Most importantly, feminists (and their nonfeminist colleagues) are neither adopting nor criticizing theories in isolation—or without reasons. And many of their reasons are being articulated clearly. Obviously, if frameworks or theories in the sciences have been androcentric, there are *reasons* for this, and obviously feminists have reasons for proposing alternative theories. We should prefer the "woman, the gatherer theory" if it is more in keeping with the evidence—and *there is evidence* that renders the assumptions underlying the "man, the hunter theory" unwarranted and implausible. It can be found in common-sense experiences of women's activities, *as well as* in current research in primatology, history, and anthropology. Similarly, we should prefer the alternatives being explored to "master molecule" theories of gene action if these models distort the actual relationships in cellular development. And we have considered various beliefs and theories, including other scientific theories, that served as evidential support for the theories, research, and models feminists are criticizing. These things are evidence that holism and a coherence account of evidence are sound approaches to understanding the current state of science.

We can also see that Longino and Doell's conclusions are warranted only if we assume that *no* other scientific theories can be brought to bear on the reconstruction of our evolution, theories that might lend more credence to one interpretation of the chipped stones over another, and/or that we assume that "culturally determined" beliefs, or common-sense beliefs including those about sex/gender, are not subject to empirical control and cannot be considered as evidence. Since we have found that feminists and "man, the hunter" theorists are using primatology and anthropology, it is obvious that other scientific theories are part of the evidence for both theories. But since these also show connections to experiences of sex/gender and politics, there is still the issue of "culturally determined" ideas.

So, the next question we need to consider is this: given that science is not autonomous of social and political contexts, what conclusions follow about the relationship between scientific theories and *evidence?* In other words, what is the status, in terms of their connection to *evidence*, of the views and experiences of sex/gender and politics that feminist criticism reveals as factors in scientific theorizing? We have found that focusing on individual theories and/or assuming that science is autonomous are not reasonable assumptions. At least part of the evidence supporting any scientific theory will be other scientific theories. But part of it will also be common-sense views and experiences. So, we will need to consider whether Longino's and Dowell's skepticism about "predetermined and culturally determined beliefs" is warranted—a skepticism that has long underwritten a commitment to maintaining science's autonomy. For if such beliefs are part of our evidence for scientific theories, then the status of the latter, insofar as they depend on or incorporate such beliefs, is, as Longino and Doell perceive, an issue.

COMMON SENSE, A COHERENCE THEORY OF EVIDENCE, AND THE UNDERDETERMINATION OF SCIENCE

We have two general reasons to doubt that "culturally determined" beliefs are not subject to empirical control, and, thus, to doubt that if science has anything to do with "common sense", the connection between science and evidence is fundamentally compromised. One is the existence of feminist science criticism, a body of criticism that indicates that common-sense beliefs, including those about sex/gender and politics, can be critically evaluated and are part of the evidence that needs to be brought to bear on scientific theories. The other is Quine's contention that common sense and science are fundamentally interdependent and his specific arguments for that claim. His arguments indicate that common-sense theorizing is itself subject to evidential constraint and that it is part of the evidence for science. I will begin by using Quine's positions to further support the view that emerged in our consideration of feminist criticism that common-sense theories are part of the evidence for scientific theories and that this relationship is the source (although not the explanation) of feminist science criticism. I will then turn to the question of whether the specific aspects of common-sense belief that are emerging as relevant to science, those involving sex/gender and politics, are subject to empirical control.

Quine, we saw in earlier discussion, maintains that "everything we say about the world" is fundamentally connected and included in the network of going theories that includes scientific theories. He also maintains that scientific theorizing is fundamentally dependent upon common-sense theorizing for it systematizes common-sense theorizing and, moreover, it relies on that theorizing for its most general standards of evidence.[201] (Indeed, we have seen that Quine argues that our more esoteric theories are "gibberish" in isolation from common-sense theory.) It is the whole of science, including common-sense theorizing, that organizes and explains what we experience, and that, along with experience, constitutes the *evidence* we have for any claim or theory.

Although these positions seem clearly relevant to issues we have considered and supported by the issues raised by feminist criticism, several specific issues raised by that criticism are not addressed by Quine. These include whether changes in something like our common-sense theories or beliefs could (or should) affect scientific theorizing—an obvious source of feminist science criticism. I begin with this issue: whether, given a holistic account of empirical content and a coherence account of evidence, it follows that changes in beliefs and theories outside science communities can affect scientific theory—whether they can (at least for those whose beliefs have changed) lead to differences in the evaluation of scientific theories and have a bearing on scientific theorizing. This would indicate that common-sense theorizing and theories are part of the evidential support for scientific theories.

We can begin by noting that although Quine does not maintain that changes in common-sense theorizing could result in changes in scientific theorizing (and we will shortly consider why he does not), the possibility is an obvious consequence of holism and his view that common-sense and scientific theories and theorizing are fundamentally interdependent. Granting more systematization and self-conscious attention to evidence to scientific theorizing does not make scientific theories independent of common-sense theorizing.

Second, Quine's view of the "slack" between theories and evidence, a slack that Longino's and Doell's analysis of the current disagreement between those advocating the "man, the hunter" and "woman, the gatherer" theories also appeals to, commits us to the view that there is room for changes in all our theories—both those of common sense and science. The "slack" is not a feature only of historical explanation or special situations; it is a fundamental feature of all our theorizing. Everything we say about how things are, Quine argues, is fundamentally underdetermined by the evidence we have—and could ever have—for saying it. We can imagine alternative theories commensurate with most of our experiences, and incompatible with a going theory, for each of the theories we now maintain—including our most esoteric theories in subatomic physics and our common-sense theory about physical objects. His view is now also supported by a contention among many scientists that the average half-life for theories is currently ten years.[202]

Moreover, not only will science never be complete, Quine argues that there is no unique story to organize, explain, and enable us to predict experience; alternatives, commensurate with most of our experiences, are possible. In short, the "fit" between all of the evidence we have and all of science and common sense leaves room for scientific and common-sense theories to evolve with experience. What feminist criticism indicates is that at least part of what will propel the evolution in scientific theories can be changes in common-sense beliefs and theories.

But others of Quine's positions are also relevant to the issue of the evidential relationship between common-sense theorizing and scientific theorizing. As Quine puts things, the network of our going theories has a structure that, although rendering no theory about revision, insulates some more so than others. The special position of such theories (our larger ontological commitments, logic, and mathematics, for example) is due to the fact that they do not face sensory experience directly, but do so indirectly "via" more "low-level theories". Their insulation is also due to their deep connections with the bulk of our other going theories. And, in general, scientific theories are more well insulated than common-sense theories because they represent higher theoretical ground—that is, they systematize common-sense theorizing.[203]

But these things do not preclude the possibility that changes in more well-insulated theories will not (or could not) be prompted by changes in those that are less well insulated. In the case of the "man, the hunter theory", for example, we saw that some members of our science communities and our larger community have come to question the assumption, and all of the models and theories that incorporated it, that males' activities are central and of fundamental importance in social groups and would have been in human evolution, and that females' activities are natural and exhausted by reproductive activities. Feminist criticism of "man, the hunter" theory evolved apiece with feminist criticism of other theories in anthropology, sociology, and primatology, and, in general terms, with feminist politics and scholarship about women. This is evidence, as are the theories feminists are criticizing, that part of the evidence for scientific theories are common-sense beliefs and theories and that changes in common-sense beliefs will prompt changes in scientific theorizing.

There are other aspects of Quine's account of the relationship between common sense and science that are relevant here. First, as I noted in the conclusion of the preceding chapter, most of what Quine has to say about "common-sense theory" is couched in terms of theorizing about physical objects. It can be objected that views about sex/gender and politics are not among the theories between which the kinds of connection I am positing can hold—or at least, that Quine does not think so. Quine emphasizes physical-object ontology, method, and theory, and their connections to scientific ontologies, methods, and theories. In addition, of course, Quine does not discuss sex/gender and science (but then most nonfeminists have not, at least not in a reasonable way), and he specifically maintains that values, including politics, have nothing to do with science when things are proceeding as they should.

So, we will need to contend with Quine's account of "common-sense theory". The first thing to note is that his account of physical-object theory is, as so far explicated, ahistorical. Although he insists that the positing of and theorizing about macroscopic material objects was an historical occurrence and that science constantly evolves in response to questions posed by our going theories and experiences, Quine leaves the work of explaining "physical-object theorizing" to empirical psychologists and an evolutionary epistemology—in particular, to an evolutionary theory of perception.[204] This, together with what he does say about physical-object theory, suggests that our theorizing about physical objects is static (for some historical period) and that it is able to be abstracted from the practices and activities in which we propound ontologies and theories about the physical objects we interact with and create.

When we consider our theorizing about physical objects in terms of our practices, what some have called the "default-drive status" granted by Quine to "physical-object theorizing" is not plausible.[205] But for the purpose of illuminating connections between our common-sense theories and beliefs and those we develop in science communities, the ultimate adequacy of Quine's account of physical-object theory is not the basic issue. The basic issue is whether common-sense theory, that theorizing we do outside science communities and on which, Quine maintains, scientific theorizing is fundamentally dependent, is exhausted by our theorizing about physical objects and is itself fundamentally separate (as science is supposed to be) from our political experiences and views.

The issues we have considered in this and the preceding chapter indicate that the organizing of experiences in which we engage outside of science communities that is relevant to science is not exhausted by the theorizing we do about physical objects. If Quine does not recognize that the network of our connected and interdependent theories contains beliefs and theories beyond those concerned with physical objects and that common-sense theory is not static, then feminist criticism indicates that we must expand on his views—and only later worry about the consequences for the constraints experience can impose on our theories. We do not *have* the option of declaring that such views have nothing to do with science. Both the theories feminists criticize and their criticism are related to experiences of sex/gender and politics.

Even without the insights into science currently afforded by feminist critics and the very existence of that body of criticism, the exclusion of social and political theories and beliefs, including those involving sex/gender, from relevance to science is unbearably strained once we recognize, as Quine does, that common-sense theorizing and science are interdependent. We have common-sense beliefs about interpersonal relationships including political relationships, about the nature of the relationships that exist between individuals and societies, about sex/gender differences, and so on. In our common-sense dealings with the world and each other, we describe and explain these relationships. Such theories are among the bridges we build to systematize, explain, and predict what we experience. There are no grounds for deciding that social and political beliefs and theories are not within the network of going theories that includes evolutionary theory, biology, and physics—and, on the basis of feminist criticism, an abundance of evidence to make any such move indefensible.

So, provided we do not insist on what are rather arbitrary boundaries, holism and a coherence account of evidence allow us to view some of the issues we have considered in this chapter in terms of relationships between common-sense beliefs and theories, including social and political theory, and scientific theories.

More specifically, we can see that common-sense theorizing is part of the evidence for scientific theorizing. I am appealing to Quine's denial that science in the narrow sense is autonomous and that individual theories or sentences "face experience" alone. But that is not all I am appealing to. The criticisms feminists have offered, the alternatives they propose, and the very existence of feminist science criticism are impossible to explain if science is autonomous and without fundamental connection to our common-sense experiences. They would be impossible to explain if views about sex/gender and politics are not fundamentally related to scientific theorizing. So, I am also explicitly challenging the boundary Quine insists separates science and values—for it is impossible to argue that that boundary is real in light of feminist science criticism.

Finally, I am drawing the consequences of the underdetermination of our theories. There is "room" for alternatives to our going theories—alternative ways of describing the order we have found in nature, including our current laws of nature—and our adoption of such alternatives in one area of science or in our common-sense dealings with the world will eventually reverberate through others of our theories.

The remaining issue underlying Longino's and Doell's contention that evidence cannot be brought to bear on our deciding between "man, the hunter" theory and alternatives currently being developed is the issue of whether views about sex/gender and political practices and beliefs are themselves subject to empirical control. Their skepticism is mirrored of course in Quine's and that of other empiricists.

I suggest that we are now particularly well situated to recognize such skepticism as unwarranted. Feminist scholarship, including science criticism, indicates that "culturally determined beliefs", including political views and views about sex/gender, can be and should be subjected to empirical controls. Feminist science critics have been able to evaluate the assumptions about sex/gender and politics involved in scientific theories and to do so on the basis of evidence. There is evidence that indicates that women's activities are central to the dynamics of human social groups, and that androcentrism has distorted cross-cultural studies, animal sociology, and evolutionary theory. There is evidence that indicates that male dominance is neither natural nor universal, that research into sex differences is wrongheaded, and that current divisions in power by sex/gender are not based on, or justifiable on the basis of, biology. Moreover, the evidence that calls the various theories into question that incorporated these things has as its most basic source common-sense experience and theorizing, including political experience and theorizing. So, common-sense theory is itself not static or unable to be subjected to empirical control. It is currently changing in dramatic ways within subcommunities in our larger community.

What these things indicate is that it is time to give up the view that science is autonomous or different in kind from other attempts to explain and systematize our experiences. Feminist criticism fundamentally undermines this view, and adopting a holism that does not stop at the line of "culturally determined" beliefs or "values" but encompasses these and explores the empirical constraints our common-sense views face, including our values and politics, is precisely what feminist criticism indicates can be done and needs to be done.

THE "PHYSICS QUESTION", THE QUESTION OF "BAD SCIENCE" (AGAIN), AND THE STATUS OF FEMINIST CRITICISM

I have argued that feminist critics are not just exposing that politics and sex/gender are relevant to bad science, a point that seems incontrovertible when we consider feminist criticism itself. But some may remain tempted by the view that this body of criticism does not really challenge what we thought we knew about science. Feminist criticism, after all, has been largely directed at the social sciences and biology, and these, some may argue (and have), are fundamentally unlike (not as good or as serious as) the "hard sciences" of physics, chemistry, mathematics, or whatever. As one philosopher assured me, feminist criticism just shows what he had suspected all along: the social sciences and much of biology "are a mess".[206]

According to this line of reasoning, feminist criticism is properly directed only at bad science. This line of reasoning must also either maintain that feminist criticism is not itself part of science or disassociate that body of criticism from feminism. The second option is clearly impossible and the first view is shared by traditional scientists and some of their feminist critics whose discussions sometimes imply that science is something fundamentally different from feminist criticism of it. Thus, ironically, those defending something like "science per se" and those criticizing "science per se" share a model of science that the existence of feminist criticism undermines: the view that science is a closely circumscribed activity, clearly distinct from other forms of critical inquiry—an activity that adds truths, incrementally, to a great "book of truths" and never revises or erases those entries.

I begin considering the plausibility of these positions by briefly addressing the first move to "save science itself", a cluster of questions involved in what, paraphrasing Sandra Harding, I will call "the physics question in feminist science criticism".[207] What, one may ask (and, as feminists know, many have), has feminism to say about—what *could* feminism have to say about—physics (or chemistry, mathematics, or logic)? Physics, after all, seems pure of any content that would (or could) be affected by sex/gender and politics.

There are two short answers to the question. The most obvious is *we simply don't know yet*. And because a priori reasoning has no place in science, and we have no reason to think that science (or physics or chemistry or . . .) is or could ever be complete, declaring that physics simply *could not* have anything to do with sex/gender or politics, or that it does not because feminists have not in fifteen years fundamentally challenged, for example, high-energy physics, is surely at most an act of faith.

What we can say is that as of now we do not know if interesting relationships exist between politics, sex/gender, and physics (or mathematics, and so on)—and if we think it is important to do so, we can add, based on our current understandings of how things are, why we think (or hope) it is likely or unlikely that such connections will emerge. In any event, we need to guard against the unwarranted inference from "we don't know yet" to "sex/gender and politics have nothing to do with physics".

The second "short answer" is best posed as a question: would it be *good news* if it turned out that only physics, mathematics, logic, chemistry, or whatever, show no evidence of our experiences of politics and sex gender? Are we willing to say "if physics is all right, so is science"? Even if we do not think that this would be a strange outcome—that it would be strange if the rest of science is subject to such influences but not the theory that is alleged to underlie or systematize it—is it something to be pleased about? Does it save "science"?

This also suggests a longer answer to the "physics question", one that

I will use Quine's views to sketch. Recently, Harding argued that the alleged "purity" of physics (if, in fact, it is pure in the way that is at issue) should not be taken as an indication that feminist science critics are not raising fundamental questions about western science. Rather, she argues, the special status of physics should be recast; specifically, physics should be recognized as limited[208]—an isolatable and fundamentally different endeavor from biology and social science.[209] Outlining a number of differences between physics and these, Harding argues that there "are reasons for reevaluating the assumption that physics should be the paradigm of scientific knowledge-seeking".[210] Physics may, on the view, be pure, but it is also much less interesting (at least as a key to understanding science generally) than we thought.

An alternative to Harding's approach can be had by using the implications of Quine's argument against the analytic/synthetic distinction, as well as other of his views that I have used—views that feminist criticism strongly supports. A fundamental part of Quine's argument against the analytic/synthetic distinction is that the *meanings* of mathematical and logical sentences, and the point holds no less for those of theoretical physics, are *related to* and *shaped by* the other sentences to which these bear a relationship—and, ultimately, to and by all the other things we say about the world.[211] Saying this is just another way of making the point that all of the sentences to which we agree, all of the theories we hold, will reflect and be dependent on others of our projects and theories.

> Pure mathematics . . . partly because of its additional utility in natural sciences other than physics, is segregated in name; so we do not see it as just a further part of a broader systematic enterprise, still connecting ultimately with the observations of experimental physics and other natural sciences.
>
> Boundaries between disciplines are useful for deans and librarians, but let us not overestimate them—the boundaries. When we abstract from them, we see all of science—physics, biology, economics, mathematics, logic, and the rest—as a single sprawling system, loosely connected in some portions but disconnected nowhere. Parts of it—logic, arithmetic, game theory, theoretical parts of physics—are farther from the observational or experimental edge than other parts. But the overall system, with all its parts, derives its aggregate empirical content from that edge; and the theoretical parts are only as good as they contribute in their varying degrees of indirectness to the systematizing of that content.[212]

Given this view of empirical content, no sentence or body of theory has the kind of purity or independence from other theories that Harding suggests we grant to physics. There is no separating physics, or pure mathematics, or logic, *or any other theory* from the rest of our going theories. The sentences of each are not "pure" of empirical content or without connections—a sharing of supports and a sharing of meaning—with other theories.

Thus, it is possible, however unlikely it seems now, that changes in others of our theories will reverberate with sufficient resonance through the network of our going theories, to carry with them a need for a different logic, a different mathematics, or a different physics. Of course we cannot *predict* this prior to its happening; but neither can we know now that it will not happen. Science is underdetermined. If such changes in other theories occur, mathematics and logic not only *could* be revised, they *would* be. The need, given the relationships that exist between various theories, would become apparent; it would be met concomitantly (although probably not simultaneously) with the occurrence of the relevant changes in other aspects of our largest theory of nature, the whole of our theories. Nor do we need to think that this means we will eventually decide that some mathematical truths are false. We are granting the possibility that we will come to organize things differently.[213]

So an alternative approach to the "physics question in feminism" (and the related "mathematics and logic question") emerges from a holistic view and a coherence account of evidence: it is to stress the relationships that exist between physics, mathematics, and logic, and our other going theories, rather than granting to physics the autonomy (isolation) Harding has suggested. No theory and no level of theorizing have that kind of autonomy—either from other theories, or from empirical content. Feminist criticism and various of Quine's positions illuminate the connections and interdependence of our theories. So, the answer to the physics question, if it matters (and certainly it does not count as an answer as to what science *is*), will emerge concomitantly with the doing of science, by feminists and nonfeminists alike.

Finally, a note about the view that only physics (or mathematics or logic . . .) is really science and, consequently, that neither biology nor the social sciences nor feminist science criticism *is* science. And, specifically, why might we be tempted to think feminists have been doing something "other than" science, or that feminist criticism is not itself science?

One reason is, of course, that feminists are motivated by political concerns, including concerns about sex/gender arrangements. But this will *not* serve as a way of separating that criticism from science—for feminists have uncovered politics and sex/gender (consciously as in Sociobiology and unconsciously elsewhere) at work in what certainly is science "as usual".

The moral, feminist criticism suggests, is that we need to enlarge and become more self-conscious of the views and beliefs that are relevant to science, not continue to try to isolate science from nonscience. Although we have not previously recognized the relationships between politics, sex/ gender, and science in "science as usual", they have been there—no less than they are so obviously present in feminist approaches. And unless we are willing to claim that feminists have been doing something *other than* constructing theories and naming objects, organizing and relating interactions with nature, discovering relationships between the bridges we have built to organize experience, subjecting beliefs, ontologies, and claims to critical evaluation—including, and perhaps especially, those that have taken on the guise of dogmas—and paying attention to evidence, we must conclude that their work is *within* science. Science has led us to recognize the need to reconsider scientific practices, including our understandings of what science is—albeit, not science as usual, for feminist critics are self-consciously political, and they deny science's autonomy from things we value.

The reasonable view is that feminist science critics have been and are doing science with a deepened and broader understanding of how much is relevant to science, and far more sensitivity to the consequences of science—understandings that, if they prove sound, will be traceable, ultimately, to our experiences and that will, with consequences it may not be possible for us to now envision, illuminate and change our practices.

Those of us interested in undertaking the study of science communities and the epistemology of science that feminist criticism indicates needs to be undertaken, and doing so within an empiricist framework, still face two problems. In some respects, my analysis of the current crisis remains influenced by Quine's insights, although I want to fundamentally recast these. For some, the question may remain as to whether politics and views about sex/gender really can be subjected to empirical constraint—or whether, if they are involved, as Keller puts it, "ideology has a field day".[214] I will not return to this issue until Chapter Seven, but the discussion so far and the existence of feminist criticism suggest that politics and views and practices concerned with sex/gender can be subjected to empirical control. Feminists are, and have been, so subjecting them so for some time.

A second problem will occupy us in the next chapter. In keeping with the holistic approach I have suggested we adopt on the basis of feminist criticism and Quine's positions, I have emphasized the fundamentally social nature of androcentric and feminist perspectives. This is in keeping with some aspects of Quine's philosophy of science, but it departs from others. Quine and other empiricists assume that the appropriate epistemological focus is the individual. So, I will use the next chapter to begin to consider several problematic issues that I have so far delayed pursuing in considering the insights provided by the interplay of Quine's positions and feminist science criticism. These problems need to be overcome if we are to be able to accurately characterize the current state of science and science criticism, and one day, using gender theory, sociology, psychology, and so on, explain it. They also need to be overcome if a feminist empiricism is to be a real possibility.

In particular, I will argue that although Quine is wrong in thinking that it does not matter *who* is theorizing, he is right in not emphasizing individual scientists. It is not individual scientists to whom feminist criticism draws our attention. Nor is it individuals, except in a derivative sense, who know.

CHAPTER SIX

Who Knows

Everything should be made as simple as possible, but not simpler.

—Albert Einstein

A CCEPTABLE ANSWERS to the question "Who knows?" include "Everyone", "All of *us*", "Lots of people", "Many of us", but only very problematically "Only me". What I know depends inextricably on what *we* know, for some we. My claims to know are subject to community criteria, public notions of what constitutes evidence, so that, in an important sense, I *can* know only what *we* know, for some we.

In those rare cases when I claim exclusive knowledge, my claim is usually either uninteresting (others could know if they looked) or false. In those even rarer cases when I claim to know something revolutionary, something that does not meet public and community standards of evidence, *and* my claim is eventually accepted, it will have taken a concomitant change in our standards of evidence before I really know. And then, of course, *we* will know, for some we.

These are not, as I intend or understand them, musings on the "meaning" of 'knowledge' or definitions of what is to count as knowledge. We can begin to illuminate how "my knowing" requires "our knowing" by considering beliefs.

Beliefs appear to be more like the "private property" of individuals. But for much the same reasons, this "private ownership" is mostly illusory.[1] Beliefs, like knowledge, require public conceptual schemes for their formulation. The allegedly "unvarnished news" of sense data[2] is not only never heard, it was never there to begin with.

And though beliefs are not as closely tied to evidence as claims to know, we do not really understand someone's claim to believe what is inconsistent with obvious evidence. Nor can we succeed in believing what we also recognize is unreasonable, given the evidence. The most we will tolerate is belief in the absence of convincing counterevidence. As Quine notes, the White Queen who engages in the "activity of believing" for at least half an hour a day, sometimes managing to believe as many as six impossible things before breakfast, is at least "atypical", on both counts.[3] Beliefs are constrained by evidence.

These considerations argue for the view that it is communities or groups that acquire and possess knowledge, and that focusing on individuals in epistemology is inappropriate. Individuals "have" beliefs and they know,[4] but only in a derivative sense. Their beliefs and their "knowing" depend on public language and the conceptual scheme it embodies, and what they know and believe is constrained by public standards of evidence. The primary epistemological agents are groups—or more accurately, epistemological communities.

An empiricist account of science that took communities rather than individuals to be knowers would not, of course, be like any current empiricist account of science. Although many of the considerations about knowing and belief that I have outlined are central features of Quine's empiricism, Quine's specific proposal for naturalizing epistemology suggests a commitment to the view that when "we know", 'we' really means "me and you and you . . . and you", and we will discuss it below.

The interesting questions, then, are these: When "we know", is this because "me and you and you and . . . you" each independently knows, or is the activity more communal than this? Is the 'we' of "we know" more like the 'we' of "we (each) bought a cup of coffee" or the 'we' of "we (collectively) bought a sail boat"? If the 'we' of "we know" is a collective 'we', is there life for empiricism as a theory of evidence without or post individualism?

Individualism

One of the most basic and far-reaching assumptions of the modern intellectual tradition is its view of persons. On the modern view, persons are basically independent of others and social context.[5] As Alison Jagger describes the view, persons—complete with projects, characteristics, beliefs, values, capacities, and interests—are, at least in principle, separable from society. That is, persons have such characteristics without essential need of social context or others.

> The assumption . . . is that human individuals are ontologically prior to society; in other words, human individuals are the basic constituents out of which social groups are composed. Logically if not empirically, human individuals could exist outside a social context; their essential characteristics, their needs and interests, their capacities and desires, are given independently of their social context and are not created or even fundamentally altered by that context.[6]

Feminists argue that modern political and ethical theories—Locke's political theory, social contract theory, the work of Kant, Rawls, and Nozick, for example—incorporate this view of persons, and many feminists have serious doubts about its soundness.[7]

Problems with the modern view are not new topics in contemporary philosophy,[8] and Marxist theorists have long questioned what Jaggar calls the "self/society dichotomy" that is the core of the modern view of persons.[9] In analytic philosophy Parfit has raised doubts about an individualistic metaphysics of persons and about the notion of responsibility that builds from it. Parfit's doubts are prompted by problems he finds in specifying the identity conditions of "persons",[10] and it is an open question whether these challenge the coherency of "individualism".[11]

The problems with the modern view that currently concern many feminist theorists are more fundamental, for feminists have come to doubt the possibility and the coherency of a "self" separable from a social context.[12] Jaggar, for example, considers the implications of the dependency of human young for the modern view of autonomous and basically independent "selves" and argues that viewing persons as fundamentally independent and self-sufficient is plausible only if one ignores the physical realities of human existence.

> As soon as one takes into account the facts of human biology, especially reproductive biology, it becomes obvious that the assumption of individual self-sufficiency [which is the core of modern liberal theory] is impossible. Human infants resemble the young of many species in being born helpless, but they differ from all other species in requiring a uniquely long period of dependence on adult care. . . . *Human interdependence is thus necessitated by human biology,* and *the assumption of individual self-sufficiency is plausible only if one ignores human biology.*[13]

Many feminist theorists also argue that persons are fundamentally shaped, psychologically and physically, by the societies within which they live. Jaggar, who advocates a Socialist feminism, offers such a view.

> If we reject [the modern assumption of individualism] and suppose
> instead that human desires and interests are socially constituted, then we
> can expect that the members of any society are likely to learn to want
> just those things that the society provides.[14]

> Socialist feminism is committed to the basic Marxist conception of
> human nature as created historically through the dialectical interrelation
> between human biology, human society and the physical environment.
> . . . The specific form of praxis dominant within a given society creates
> the distinctive physical and psychological human types characteristic of
> that society.[15]

Feminists' doubts about the modern focus on individuals are not
limited to the coherency of what Jaggar calls the "self/society dichotomy"
assumed in modern political and ethical theories. For some time, feminists'
discussions of epistemology and science have included criticism of a focus
on individuals in epistemology. According to some theorists, a focus on
individuals has led empiricists to accounts of how we know, of "objectivity", and of science that preclude a reasonable explanation—or, on some
accounts, justification—of feminist claims.[16]

With few exceptions,[17] feminist theorists have approached the issue
of the coherency of the self/society dichotomy and the empiricist focus on
individuals as separate issues. I will begin by outlining the specific criticisms feminists have offered of empiricism, but it will become clear that
treating these issues separately precludes our asking a more fundamental
question about a focus in epistemology on individuals: whether the portrait of the knower as an isolatable individual is even *coherent*. When
this questions is not addressed, two responses to feminist criticisms of
empiricism seem all too plausible.

The first is that the current state of science and of science criticism is
a "special" situation that does not really reflect on the empiricist view of
"knowers" or on other empiricist positions that build from that view;
feminist science criticism just requires (if empiricists are interested in
pursuing the project) a more complicated explanation than usual. The
second, and alternative, response is that if feminists are correct that their
claims cannot be accommodated with an empiricist account, so much the
worse for the soundness of feminist claims.

Neither response is adequate, and we can preclude them by asking the
more fundamental question outlined above, and then considering the
implications for empiricism if the portrait of a knower as an isolatable
individual is untenable.

Feminist Critiques of Empiricism

According to Jaggar, the account empiricists give of "knowledge acquisition" describes a solitary enterprise and achievement of a solitary individual.

> Because it conceives humans as essentially separate individuals, [the modern epistemological tradition that begins with Descartes] views the attainment of knowledge as a project for each individual on her or his own. The task of epistemology, then, is to formulate rules to enable individuals to undertake this project with success.
>
> . . . the empiricist tendency [of the modern epistemological tradition] views knowledge as achieved by inference from basic individual sense experiences . . . the attainment of knowledge is conceived as essentially a solitary occupation that has no necessary social preconditions.[18]

It should by now be clear that what Jaggar describes as "the empiricist account of knowing" is not Quine's account of the latter, the view I have been advocating. On that account, "social preconditions" are necessary for anyone to know, and "basic . . . sense experiences" are coherent *only because* they are shaped by public language and a conceptual scheme, a body of theories embodied in that language. Theorizing is a necessarily social activity. Nor, of course, does Quine construe the "task of epistemology" as Jaggar outlines the empiricist account of that task. We will consider the details of his view below, but I noted earlier that Quine views epistemology as finding out, from within science, how we go about theorizing. In short, he has abandoned many of the positivist tenets Jaggar ascribes to empiricism.[19]

But we will also find that, despite his insistence that social preconditions are necessary for knowing and that theorizing is public, Quine's specific proposal for naturalizing epistemology does presume that the appropriate epistemological focus is individuals. In addition, Quine holds two views that are similar to those Jaggar attributes to empiricists in the following passage. These views, Jaggar argues, underlie "the positivist conception of objectivity", a view she also attributes to empiricists generally. Given the views about knowers and knowing outlined, empiricists take

> the adequacy of a scientific theory is . . . to be guaranteed by its objectivity or lack or bias. . . . objectively produced claims are capable, in principle at least, of being verified by anyone. . . . A second aspect of the positivist conception of objectivity is that it excludes any evaluative element. . . . [a "scientific" enquiry is objective if it utilizes]

methodological controls to eliminate the influence of social interests, values, and emotions. . . . [for] intersubjective agreement is thought to be impossible unless these values, interests and emotions are prevented from directing the scientific enterprise.[20]

We have noted in several contexts that Quine and other empiricists have been concerned to exclude values, including political interests, from the content of scientific theories and from their accounts of the way we go about constructing theories—at least good theories. And the connection between "objectivity" and the exclusion of values is advocated by Quine on the basis of a quite specific reason.

On Quine's account, science's objectivity (with science understood in both the narrow and broader senses) is specifically a function of the empirical controls its claims are subject to,[21] and he maintains that values are not subject to such controls. It is the latter that prompts his exclusion of values from science, and we will return to that view in Chapter Seven.

Quine may also hold something akin to the other view Jaggar takes to contribute to "the positivist conception of objectivity", a conception she attributes to all empiricists: namely, that "objectively produced claims" can be verified by anyone. As we have noted in several contexts, Quine does seem to assume that at a given stage of inquiry "we" would "agree" in our judgment of a given claim, although the 'we' would be understood to sometimes encompass our largest community; at others, in the case, for example, of more highly theoretical claims, the relevant community would be a smaller one of specialists. And, of course, given Quine's account of evidence, claims are also historically relative, for they depend on the current state of science. But, in the end, Quine does not take the possibility into account that experiences within our larger social community might be fundamentally and extensively divided. Thus, concerns about divisions in cognitive labor, or other issues that involve the social arrangements within which scientific knowledge is produced, are not addressed in his work.

Thus, as Jaggar and others note,[22] a fundamental problem facing feminists interested in reconciling feminism and empiricism involves a view of objectivity that incorporates (or insists on) an exclusion of values, and political interests, from the content of science or as relevant to good theorizing, and that assumes under the qualifications noted above, community-wide agreement for objective claims. This understanding of objectivity would clearly render feminist claims "unobjective". The latter are politically motivated, and they certainly include social concerns and values. Moreover, they do not command community-wide agreement.

Accordingly, Jaggar rejects empiricism as an appropriate framework within which to frame feminist claims and, more generally, as an adequate epistemology. She does so on the grounds that the empiricist conception of objectivity is itself flawed: the "neutrality" it posits as the criterion for adequate theories and beliefs is, on her view, impossible. Empiricism, she claims,

> does not offer appropriate criteria of theoretical adequacy. . . .
>
> [Most feminists] challenge precisely the conception of objectivity that [empiricists] take as a primary condition of theoretical adequacy. In particular . . . [most feminists] attack the claim that there is any such standpoint as that of a neutral observer.[23]

Sandra Harding also argues that feminists who attempt to use empiricism to explain or justify their claims face fundamental problems. Feminists, according to Harding, are in the "apparently paradoxical situation" of having to explain how their ability to be objective and to offer objective claims has been increased by their political advocacy.[24] They need to be able to argue that their own claims are more objective than those that are androcentric and sexist, and they need, Harding maintains, to develop or adopt an epistemology that will make it possible for their claims to be justified.[25]

Harding considers several solutions to the apparent paradox of reconciling objectivity and advocacy, and concludes that what she calls "the feminist empiricist solution" actually "subverts empiricism".[26] Harding's characterization of feminist empiricism is consistent with Jaggar's account. Feminist empiricists, Harding maintains, must argue that their own claims are *unbiased*, and that it is the claims they criticize (for instance, androcentric and sexist claims) that are biased.[27] In short, according to Jaggar and Harding, a feminist empiricism would commit us to the view that only "bad science" requires explanation.[28]

> *Feminist empiricism* argues that sexism and androcentrism are social biases correctable by stricter adherence to the existing methodological norms of scientific inquiry. Movements for social liberation "make it possible for people to see the world in an enlarged perspective because they remove the covers and blinders that obscure knowledge and observation". [Millman and Kanter (1975, vii)]. The women's movement produces not only the opportunity for such an enlarged perspective but more women scientists, and they are more likely than men to notice androcentric bias.[29]

In claiming that this apparent "solution" actually subverts empiricism, Harding seems to mean several things. First, she notes that empiricists maintain that "who" is theorizing will not have a bearing on the content of that theorizing (at least, it will not when we are doing things right). But, according to Harding, feminist empiricists must claim, at least implicitly, that whether one is a feminist (or, on some accounts, a woman) does, at this time, make a difference. By "apparently" appealing to empiricism, feminists, Harding argues, are actually exposing a problem with the empiricist view that the particular identity of an observer does not matter—thus, she maintains, subverting empiricism.

> The social identity of the inquirer is supposed to be irrelevant to the "goodness" of the results of research. Scientific method is supposed to be capable of eliminating any biases due to the fact that individual researchers are white or black, Chinese or French, men or women. But feminist empiricism argues that women (or feminists, whether men or women) *as a group* are more likely to produce unbiased and objective results than are men (or nonfeminists) as a group.[30]

As Harding's reference to a group suggests, the issue involving "who" is theorizing incorporates more than a claim that the individual identity of a researcher matters. It involves the claim that, currently, being a member of a group (feminists or women) carries an epistemological advantage. Unless we chalk up to coincidence the fact that people who are feminists also happen to be people who recognize androcentric bias, or more generally, just happen to be more careful or more capable scientists who more strictly adhere to methodological norms, the claim that feminists have such an advantage seems to undermine the empiricist view that social identity is not a factor in the acquisition of good beliefs or in the construction of good theories. In addition, the claim that feminists have such an advantage suggests that focusing on individuals would not allow for an adequate explanation of how feminists know what they do.

Harding argues that a second problem with the "feminist empiricist solution" (on my count, a third) is that feminist empiricists (at least Millman and Kanter) claim that "movements for social liberation", like feminism, "promote objectivity". But, Harding maintains, empiricism rules out the necessity, and more importantly, the *appropriateness* of causal explanations for arriving at good scientific theories and beliefs.

Harding refers to this position as one of empiricism's "dogmas": specifically, the "sacred science dogma".

> We are told [by empiricists] that human understanding is decreased rather then increased by attempting to account for the nature and structure of scientific activity in the ways science recommends accounting for all other social activity. This belief makes science sacred. Perhaps it even removes scientists from the realm of the completely human—at least in their own view and the view of science enthusiasts.[31]

Although it is true that many empiricists have resisted—and many (perhaps most) scientists continue to resist—causal accounts of science, it should be clear that Quine does not, and that he does not hold, nor am I advocating, anything like the "sacred science" dogma Harding attributes to empiricists. Indeed, the "task" of epistemology, as Quine construes it, is precisely to look for causal explanations for science, narrowly and broadly construed. The reason for the difference between his view and those the postpositivists held and which Harding attributes to empiricists in general is also clear. We do not, on Quine's view, "passively" take in, via our senses, unvarnished news about how things are. We actively construct the bridges between our experiences, subject to the constraints those experiences and others of our theories impose. Given the demise of the empiricist hope of grounding science in observation unshaped by theory (either through induction or through the testing of theories by pretheoretic observation), it becomes obvious that *good* beliefs and theories (those that enable us to make sense of things and to predict), are as much in need of *explanation* as bad ones.

Quine also denies a more basic aspect of the "sacred science" dogma as Harding describes it and attributes it to empiricists: the view that science "is a fundamentally unique kind of social activity".[32] Science, in the narrow sense, is not different in kind from common sense, on Quine's view, and it shares a fundamental interdependence with it. So the "sacred science dogma" is not a problem for a "feminist empiricism" that is based on the understanding of empiricism and science I am advocating. The closest thing in Quine's work to viewing science as somehow "sacred" is his insistence that science "stands aloof from values". That, I have indicated, is a problem, and one that needs to be addressed. Feminist criticism indicates that the view is untenable.

A last problem Harding cites with the "feminist empiricist solution" is also not a problem if one's view of science and epistemology has evolved along the lines we have explored. Harding argues that feminist criticism raises issues that "the empiricist" focus on the alleged "context of justification" will not even permit as "issues".

A key origin of androcentric bias can be found in the selection of problems for inquiry, and in the definition of what is problematic about these phenomena. But empiricism insists that its methodological norms are meant to apply only to the "context of justification"—to the testing of hypotheses and interpretation of evidence—not to the "context of discovery" where problems are identified and defined. Thus a powerful source of social bias appears completely to escape the controls of science's methodological norms.[33]

Hempel, Nagel, and the postlogical positivist empiricist tradition did indeed attempt to distinguish between two "contexts" of science, and we have seen that they did so because of the failure of the inductivist program and in an attempt to salvage what inductivism was to accomplish. And Harding is certainly correct in holding that they, and other scientists and philosophers of science, have thought a focus on the justification of theories is sufficient to insure the soundness of scientific theories. Thus, Harding's criticism is appropriate to a view of science that many scientists and laypersons were taught and continue to maintain—with, we have seen, far-reaching consequences. The view has underwritten the institution of science's cognitive authority and the myth of its autonomy on which that authority is partly based.

But Quine breaks, decisively, with positivists and their immediate heirs on the issues of the "autonomy" of science, on there being distinctions between "contexts" of science, and on the related issue of whether single sentences or individual theories have empirical content in isolation from the whole body of our theories. The positions Quine rejects are precisely those that underwrite Hempel's faith in the logic of justification as an adequate account of the epistemology of science. So, the positions Harding rightly criticizes are widely held but not necessary to *empiricism*.

Moreover, feminist criticism makes the abandonment of these positions compelling—on both empirical and moral grounds. A coherence account of evidence and the recognition, deeply related to that account, that there is no unique story to be told about how things are preclude any such distinction between alleged "contexts" of science. They force the recasting of epistemology in ways that make a focus on *how* beliefs are acquired and theories constructed—including, we can now see, the social arrangements that divide experience and cognitive labor and authority—of central importance. If there are no self-announcing questions, no extra-theoretic standards of evidence, no extra scientific foundations for science, and no unique story to be discovered, then we cannot write off questions about how we go about acquiring beliefs and constructing theories—or the consequences of those we construct.

Finally, it is a consequence of these views, and the arguments offered in Chapter Five to the effect that feminist criticism is *within* science, that *bad science* is not the important issue facing us or in need of explanation.

So, many of the objections to empiricism that Harding and Jaggar raise are not obstacles to developing a feminist empiricism if we move beyond the account of science developed in the postlogical positivist tradition.

But there are views held by Quine and other empiricists that still present serious obstacles to a feminist empiricism that could encompass the issues discussed in the preceding two chapters, and they are related to some of the concerns raised by Harding and Jaggar. Several of these are, at bottom, variations on one problem: namely, how the social identity of an observer could make a difference—at least, how it could make a difference if we are doing things correctly.

One problem is that a focus on individuals, on what they believe and why, precludes our looking to feminists or nonfeminists as members of groups. But it is clear that in the current state of science and science criticism, group membership is an epistemological variable. A second problem is that Quine and other empiricists do not allow for the relevance of, for instance, political advocacy, social interests, and values, to common-sense or scientific theorizing about how things are. At the very least, empiricists do not acknowledge that these could *increase* our abilities to arrive at warranted beliefs. Yet all of these factors are currently playing a role in science and science criticism. And finally, Quine does not seem to take into account that *we* (even if we only take into account those in our own society) are not homogeneous in our beliefs and theories. He uses the first-person plural consistently, underscoring the public nature of theorizing but also implying that at a given stage of inquiry, questions, evidence, and going theories will be uncontroversial (unless some of us are making mistakes or out of the room) within our largest community.

To get beyond the commitment to focusing on individuals and beyond the idea that social identity is not a variable in scientific theorizing, I want next to explore some of what contributes to the plausibility of the apparently paradoxical view outlined at the conclusion of Chapter Five. Although feminist science criticism indicates, both in its findings and by its very existence, that who is theorizing matters, Quine's general inattention to individuals, his use of "we", is appropriate. It is not individuals to whom feminist science criticism draws our attention. Nor, I will suggest, is the current state of science and science criticism special in this regard. It is forcing us to reconsider the focus on individuals, but that is a project long overdue.

Epistemological Communities

We have found that one of the implications of feminist science criticism is that who is theorizing has a bearing on the content of science. From the point of view of traditional, positivist, and Quinean empiricism, this is perhaps the most radical implication of that criticism. The connection between who is theorizing and the content of that theorizing is revealed in several ways.

In uncovering androcentrism in the assumptions, methodologies, and theories developed in the biological and social sciences, feminist critics have exposed relationships between the so-called extrascientific experiences of scientists and the directions and findings of scientific research. They have revealed that these experiences have had consequences for the content of science. The connection between "who" is theorizing and the content of science becomes clear as evidence mounts that sex/gender has been, and currently is, a factor in scientific theorizing.

One does not need to claim or argue that women and men use different methods in acquiring knowledge to recognize sex/gender as a factor. The claim is that sex/gender is a factor in the questions asked and the theories offered and adopted, a claim for which we have found there to be substantial evidence, and our standard conceptions of "good" scientific method will neither illuminate nor "factor out" that factor.[34]

In exploring the use and consequences of models that reflect western political categories and principles in physics, the biological sciences, cross-cultural studies, animal sociology, and our general understandings of science and natural relationships, feminists are also linking the identity of the knower to what is known. Specifically, they are linking the western identity and western political experiences of dominance and hierarchies to our approaches to human and nonhuman nature.[35]

In what is perhaps the most obvious work to link the knower to what is known, feminist critics have explored the social organization of science communities and urged that divisions of cognitive labor and authority in these communities,[36] and the positions of women at the lower end of the hierarchies,[37] be studied for their epistemological consequences.

Feminist critics who address the connections between divisions in cognitive authority and the directions and findings of research are explicitly relating the identity of scientists to the directions and content of scientific understanding. As we explored earlier, they are not arguing that "more heads" would be better than "fewer". These critics are explicitly linking divisions in social and political experience, including experiences of sex/gender, to the questions pursued and the theories that seem reasonable. Were science more broadly based, if the populations of scientific communities represented a cross-section of the larger population rather than one or a few groups of that population, then, these critics argue, the content of science would reflect the difference in the makeup of the scientific community: the questions addressed, the assumptions underlying research, the theories that seemed reasonable, and what Levins calls the "distributions of knowledge and ignorance" would be different.

Finally, we have considered the work of many scientists who are bringing feminist perspectives to bear on their disciplines, on the scientific enterprise as it is currently understood and practiced, and on their own research. Ruth Bleier, Evelyn Keller, and other scientists self-consciously use feminist perspectives in their evaluation of metaphysical commitments and research, including their own approaches to nature.[38]

There are some obvious reasons why it is unrealistic and unuseful to focus on individual scientists in trying to characterize, explain, or evaluate the perspectives that have become apparent, and, in some cases, possible, because of feminist inquiry and politics.

Assuming that at the outset we can think of feminist and androcentric perspectives as incorporating some relevant beliefs and theories (with the understanding that we are not *explaining* these perspectives by illuminating the latter), the perspectives at issue in feminist criticism could exist only within some social context. A solipsist could be neither a feminist nor androcentric.

In addition, the feminist and androcentric perspectives that we have considered reflect, and, it seems clear, they require, experiences in a political and social context of a specific sort. A host of categories, social relations, practices, experiences, and assumptions are necessary for these perspectives to be possible, and these factors would need to be incorporated in any purported explanation of such perspectives.

Even "ascribing" these perspectives to individuals abstracted from social and political context is at best artificial, if, indeed, we could make sense of "selves" so abstracted.[39] In any event, the ascription would be unhelpful. We cannot reasonably credit any individual with the assumptions, research questions, or methodologies we have been considering—feminist or androcentric. Androcentric assumptions, no less than feminist assumptions, incorporate and build from social experiences, from public ways of conceptualizing sex/gender, from experiences of sex/gender and other political experiences, and from the practices from which such conceptualization cannot be separated. Nor am I suggesting that there is "a" feminist or "an" androcentric perspective at issue; each kind of perspective can be discerned in a variety of assumptions and views.

A second factor that weighs against focusing on individuals in the current situation is that the acceptability of feminist and androcentric perspectives is currently relative to subcommunities within our larger community. The social and political context of a community with divisions like ours have made these perspectives possible, but the acceptability of each is limited and relative to subcommunities. In characterizing these perspectives and ascertaining their differences, we would need to refer to standards of evidence, and their dependence on recognized categories, going theories, and experiences that are relative to two different "epistemological" communities, subcommunities of our larger community.

These reflections indicate that the perspectives that have become visible in feminist criticism have been acquired by communities. Their existence, their content, and their acceptability are inextricably dependent on a number of factors that are, themselves, community dependent. Similar issues would preclude our looking to individuals for explanations of those perspectives and models at issue in the biological sciences, for these reflect modern western political experience. A commitment to "the existence and prevalence of laws" of nature, and to the prevalence of linear, hierarchical relationships throughout nature, presupposes a history of inquiry, of political experience, an expectation of what nature is like—in short, a historically relative state of science in the broadest sense. So, too, the commitment among feminists to rethink these approaches in the biological and social sciences is fundamentally dependent on a history of inquiry and social and political experience.

In suggesting that theories and standards of evidence are relative to communities and only derivatively to individuals, I have so far considered only the perspectives that have become visible through feminist criticism. The dependence of such "perspectives" on community-bound experiences, theories, practices, and standards of evidence can be established straightforwardly.

We could acknowledge that the perspectives at issue are not appropriately ascribed to individuals but deny that this is the case generally. If we were interested in saving the view that individuals are the acquirers of knowledge, that individuals are the appropriate epistemological focus, we could say that in the cases in which feminists have uncovered androcentric perspectives, the "capacities" of the individual scientist were "compromised". We could add that the compromising was a result of "its" membership in a community of a certain sort. We would, in short, accept the "feminist empiricist solution" as Harding outlines it, and some feminists have used it. Bad science would be the problem.

But, as Harding points out—and this is a crucial "but"—we could not say, within such a framework, why feminists came to recognize androcentric perspectives and others did not.[40] Clearly, focusing on feminists as individuals would not provide a reasonable explanation of their ability.

The empiricist-derived epistemology which has directed most social and natural scientific inquiry for the last three centuries explicitly holds that historical social relations can only distort our "natural", transhistorical abilities to arrive at reliable beliefs. Historically specific social relations cannot "improve" these abilities to provide progressively more complete and undistorted belief. . . .

All that requires [causal, scientific] analysis is the social causes which produce . . . errors in thought.[41]

If we share the general understandings of epistemology and evidence that I am advocating, we would of course look for causal explanations for beliefs and for *historically specific* explanations—not just for bad beliefs, but we would be more interested in explaining *good* ones.

However, if we acknowledge the soundness of feminist insights into androcentrism in science but are also committed to the view that it is individuals that acquire knowledge, then we find ourselves in the situation of having to say that feminists are better scientists than their nonfeminist colleagues.[42] In addition, if we think that, given a current stage of inquiry, evidence is something like self-announcing for a homogeneous "we" and feminists are simply more able to "see" the latter, we would not be able to relate the alleged "superiority" of feminist scientists and scholars to their political advocacy, and clearly these are deeply related.

The more adequate feminist accounts [given empiricist views] are simply the result of unspecifiable "natural human tendencies" which, evidently, feminists can actualize more effectively than can non-feminists. (Which tendencies? Why can feminists actualize them now but not in the past?) [Empiricism] would lead us to the conclusion that it is the *lack* of "social influences" on feminists which have allowed free play for our "faculties of perception" and "sensory motor apparatuses" to produce these accounts.[43]

I argued in Chapter Five that neither view of feminist criticism—that feminists are better scientists or that their political views and experiences are unrelated to their science criticism—is in any way plausible. Moreover, of course, each of these views would require that science is what feminist criticism indicates it is *not*: an activity fundamentally static and insulated from our experiences of, and views about, sex/gender and politics.

And, in any event, I am not proposing that a focus on communities and attention to these is appropriate only in certain kinds of theorizing or in special situations. I am suggesting that the focus is more appropriate for characterizing, studying, and explaining *all* of our theorizing—and for the very same reasons outlined as factors in terms of feminist and androcentric perspectives: the role that community membership, theories, and experiences play in shaping our views, and the role of community standards in determining what counts as "knowledge" and as "knowing". The current state of science and of science criticism is not a special situation. It is a situation forcing us to see that knowing and science are different than we thought.

I want to next consider what is considered by many feminists to be the most viable alternative to empiricism, feminist standpoint epistemologies. The latter are being developed by feminists on the assumption that an "antiempiricist" solution is necessary to the epistemological problem facing feminists, a problem I have argued is really one of relating the social identity of scientists to the content of science.

The discussion will further clarify the issues that need to be addressed by a feminist empiricism. What becomes clear when we consider this antiempiricist solution is that empiricism warrants abandonment only if one of the following turns out to be the case: that there is no life for empiricism without individualism; that there is no way, given an empiricist theory of evidence, to accommodate the fact that all our ways of organizing experience, including our values and politics, are a single fabric; or that feminist claims are true and *only* feminists can know it. Here I will raise questions about the plausibility of the last of these. In the following section, we will consider the first. We will return to the second in Chapter Seven.

An Antiempiricist Solution

A number of feminist theorists argue that the problems I have outlined, both those that are not relevant to the views of empiricism and science I am advocating and those that are, constitute insurmountable barriers to reconciling feminist claims with empiricism, for they indicate that empiricism is, in fact, too flawed to be fixed.[44] Harding calls the aspects of empiricism that she criticizes the "empirical inadequacies in empiricist epistemologies", and argues in several discussions that these inadequacies preclude empiricism from being able to explain, in a reasonable way, how feminist perspectives have become possible. "Conceptual problems", she maintains,

> damage the general efficacy of empiricist-derived epistemology, as well
> as the usefulness of this epistemology for providing explanations of why
> the sex/gender system has emerged into visibility only at this moment in
> history. This epistemology must argue either that feminists' "natural

talents and abilities" are superior to those of past inquirers; or that the sudden flourishing of feminist talents needs no causal explanation and that all that requires explanation is the unfortunate social influences blocking earlier inquirers' exercise of their natural talents and abilities.
. . . (So much for the role of the Women's Movement in guiding feminist inquiry.)[45]

To solve the problem, a number of feminists are developing feminist standpoint epistemologies with the understanding that these are "antiempiricist" epistemologies.

The notion of standpoint epistemology originates with Marx. Nancy Harstock, who began the work of developing a distinctly feminist standpoint epistemology, started from what she called "a meta-theoretical claim" and attributed to Marx.

> I set off from Marx's proposal that a correct vision of class society is available from only one of the two major class positions in capitalist society. On the basis of this meta-theoretical claim, he was able to develop a powerful critique of class domination. . . . I am implicitly suggesting that [Marxian meta-theory] . . . can be most helpful to feminists. . . . women's lives make available a particular and privileged vantage point on male supremacy.[46]

Although there are differences among the feminist standpoint epistemologies currently being developed, all share some general insights, the most central and important of which is a claim something like the "meta-theoretical" claim Harstock outlines. Feminist standpoint epistemologists claim that in societies in which experiences are fundamentally differentiated by sex/gender and politics resulting in an oppressed group (among other groups in western societies, women are such a group) and a privileged group (men), a sound perspective on social and political life is possible only for members of the oppressed group. It is as a member of a group (feminist standpoint epistemologists differ about whether that group is women, or feminists be they women or men) and through political advocacy that one achieves a standpoint—the epistemological vantage point Marx claimed was possible only from the perspective of one "class" in a society characterized by classes.[47]

Harding's description of feminist standpoint epistemologies incorporates all of these features.

> The feminist standpoint epistemologies ground a distinctive feminist science in a theory of gendered activity and social experience. They simultaneously privilege women or feminists (the accounts vary) epistemologically.[48]

> Briefly, [feminist standpoint epistemologists] argue that men's dominating
> position in social life results in partial and perverse understandings,
> whereas women's subjugated position provides the possibility of more
> complete and less perverse understandings. Feminism and the women's
> movement provide the theory and motivation for inquiry and political
> struggle that can transform the perspective of women into a
> "standpoint"—a morally and scientifically preferable grounding for our
> interpretations and explanations of nature and social life.[49]

The features these epistemologies incorporate that their advocates understand as "antiempiricist" are probably clear.

First, according to these epistemologies, social identity is an epistemological variable. Standpoint epistemologists deny that "objective" claims
can be verified by "anyone"; nonfeminists (or men) would not (and
maybe, *could* not) be in a position to verify the more objective claims that
are possible from the standpoint available to feminists. That they at least
"would not" (and I think the claim is "could not") is a consequence of
the metatheoretical claim.

Second, according to standpoint epistemologists, the standpoint, the
epistemologically privileged vantage point, can be achieved only through
a political movement and political advocacy. But the exclusion of politics
and values (and, for those empiricists who hold the view, the exclusion
of causal explanations for *good* theories and beliefs) would not allow for
the possibility of such a connection.

I noted earlier that I share a number of views that underlie and prompt
standpoint epistemologies. These epistemologies are being developed as
a means of explaining the epistemological gap that separates feminists
and nonfeminists (or, for some theorists, women and men) without allowing for relativism. The "meta-theoretical" claim that they incorporate
denies that the claims made by feminists and nonfeminists are equally
justifiable. Feminist claims are more sound, more warranted, than androcentric and sexist beliefs and theories. I have also argued that relativist
epistemologies are inadequate and that the feminist positions I have outlined are more warranted than others.

As I argued in the preceding section, it is also clear that "social
identity" is an epistemological factor and variable at this time.

In addition, at least implicit in standpoint epistemologies is the view
that focusing on individuals (whether feminists or nonfeminists) will not
permit a reasonable characterization or explanation of the current state
of science criticism. I have also argued to this effect.

Last, underlying these epistemologies is the general insight that differences in experiences—including those of sex/gender and politics—are the

source of the epistemological advantage feminists currently enjoy. The appeal to *experience* is empiricist through and through. It is also in keeping with a coherence account of evidence that our questions and standards of evidence will be historically specific, emerging and made possible at a given stage of inquiry and given specific experience.

What current empiricist accounts of science (including Quine's) do not allow for is the appeal to social identity (one's being a member of a particular group) and political experiences, including those of sex/gender, as factors that could increase one's ability to know.

Although these things raise problems for current empiricist accounts of science, I think there are problems incorporated in standpoint epistemologies that a coherence account of evidence avoids. For one thing, and despite the fact that they are being developed as a nonrelativist alternative to empiricism, these epistemologies propose (or begin with the assumption of) an epistemological chasm that appears, by hypothesis, to be unbridgeable. As I argued in the preceding chapter, feminists disagree with nonfeminists about a number of assumptions, theories, and beliefs, but they do not disagree with nonfeminists about *everything*. We all take gravity seriously, know what we are talking about when we talk about the moon, assume that bodies are mutually exclusive of one another, and so forth. Some of us at least can even agree that we disagree, as feminists and nonfeminists (or as women and men), about the claims feminists make about science and other aspects of social life, and we can know, to some degree at least, what it is about each other's claims that we find wrongheaded.

If the differences in beliefs, assumptions, and theories that currently separate feminists and nonfeminists are ultimately grounded in differences in *experiences* (and standpoint epistemologists are relating these things), and if the differences (however vast and consequential) are *not global* (they are not, but how would we know if they were?), then if we assume something like a coherence theory of evidence, there is no reason, at this time, to assume that the chasm is unbridgeable—unless we begin with a "meta-theoretical" claim that maintains (or of which it is a consequence) that it is unbridgeable. If it is not unbridgeable, *in principle*, and the differences are based on experience, then it is not clear that this claim is one an empiricist could not accept.

I confess to not being sure what a "meta-theoretical" claim is. Perhaps the view is that the general claim with which standpoint epistemologies begin is a "meta" claim to the specific epistemology, and that the claim is, itself, based on other going theories. Then, of course, we are appealing to the interdependence of epistemology and other going theories, and not to a claim that is "prior" to all others. In any event, the claim seems to be functioning in a funny way if it is to be understood as underwriting an "antiempiricist" epistemology or is itself a claim an empiricist could not agree to. I will begin with the latter.

It might very well turn out to be true that new and more sound theories, including understandings of social life, evolve from the experiences of those who are subordinate in societies that include divisions in power, that divisions in experience are deep in such societies, and that only those with a vested interest in knowing how things look from "above" and "below" go about learning how the other half lives and thinks. Thus, it might turn out that those who are in politically advantaged positions are, as a result of that advantage, epistemologically disadvantaged. And it might turn out that we will all come to think that feminists have the epistemological advantage they currently claim to have, and that they have that advantage precisely because of their political experiences and advocacy. If these things turn out to be true, they will be shown to be true empirically. It will be through studying how scientific revolutions and revolutions in political thinking come about and how they are related— including, eventually, the study of the revolution in which feminists are currently engaged.

My point is that if we understand the "meta-theoretical" claim as an empirical hypothesis, then it is not clear that what it claims is actually antiempiricist. As Harding notes, empiricists have been loath to acknowledge that social identity, politics, and sex/gender are relevant to scientific theorizing. If we can get beyond these exclusions and, as part of that, beyond the focus on individuals, then *unless* we are also claiming that what feminists (or women) currently know is *both correct—and unable to be known by anyone who does not currently know it* (by anyone who is not a feminist or a woman), we are not claiming something that empiricists cannot agree to. But we do not have the evidence, and I do not think we have the motivation, to make the claim that no one else can come to know what feminists do. (After all, those of us who are feminists were, at one time, nonfeminists.) And that lack of evidence, I am tempted to think, is the good news.

As long as we are relating the differences in what feminists know and what nonfeminists know to differences in experiences (or differences in what women and men know to differences in experience), then what is being called a "meta-theoretical" claim seems to be an explanation of how feminist claims have become possible. In its appeal to experience, it is not antiempiricist—even in its appeal to historically specific experience, so long as we subscribe to a view of evidence like that I am advocating and feminist criticism supports. If it is the appeal to political experiences or experiences of sex/gender that are regarded as antiempiricist, and/or the appeal to social identity, including membership in groups, then the issue is whether such appeals are irreconcilable with the empiricist account of evidence—not with any particular empiricist account of science. That issue, I have argued, is not settled yet.

Now it might be that the meta-theoretical claim is not being understood as an empirical hypothesis, but that it is understood as providing a *justification* of feminist claims, as several of Harding's discussions, for example, suggest.[50] But no epistemology or claim can justify those or any other claims. Both the meta-theoretical claim (if we view it as an empirical hypothesis) and other feminist claims will be justified, if they are, empirically—by their coherence with our experiences. So, I suggest that we do not need an antiempiricist explanation of feminist science criticism if we can find a way to accommodate the fact that who is theorizing has a bearing on the content of science. In large part, the issue of "social identity" is an issue for empiricism because of its focus on individuals. So we will first consider who knows.

Who Knows

The views I proposed at the outset of this chapter about knowing and belief, short of the proposal that communities are the appropriate focus in epistemology, are found in Quine's work. They are, in fact, central features of it. But it is also true that empiricists, including Quine, might initially find it difficult to take the alternative view of "knowers" that I propose seriously. Several objections present themselves immediately.

The first is that the empiricist account of knowers is tied to an important view we discussed earlier, the modern view of persons. The epistemological agent, the knower, of empiricism is the counterpart of the autonomous person of modern political theory, social theory, and moral theory.

But the interrelationship between empiricism and these theories is far less compelling than it was before feminism and Marxism began undermining the coherence of the self/society dichotomy that is the core of the modern view.[51] Moreover, the fact that empiricism shares a starting place with other theoretical frameworks does not preclude our rethinking that starting point and all of the frameworks that incorporate it. The history of philosophy attests to the rise of epistemologies in response to new situations and experiences, for example, in modern thought, in positivism, and in Marxism. Epistemologies have to be judged on their adequacy in accounting for how we know and theorize.

I am not suggesting, of course, that an epistemology is, or could be, developed and adopted without connection to our other going theories. When we gave up foundationalism, we gave up a "first science" in epistemology. As one of our going theories, an epistemology will be connected to, indeed interdependent with, other theories. Thus, it will evolve with them, not be set down prior to them. The shift to a "naturalized epistemology" that Quine advocates is one example of such change; it came about because of Quine's understanding of developments in science and philosophy in the past five decades. The attention feminists are currently paying to epistemology is another indication of the interdependence epistemology shares with other theories. This attention has evolved apiece with feminist scholarship, including feminist science criticism, and some of the implications of that body of criticism are the immediate impetus for my proposal that it is communities who know.

A second objection is fundamental. The impetus for the *empiricist* commitment to focusing on individuals in obvious and compelling. Within the empiricist framework, the need to tie our theories to the world is met by taking into account the way an individual accumulates information. This, according to our current understandings of things, is through the firings of an individual's sensory receptors.

But we now recognize that explicating the connection between theories and the world is far more complicated than traditional, positivist, and postlogical positivist empiricists had hoped. The lack of "extratheoretic" observation or experience indicates that the connection that can be explicated is not a direct one between theories and the world, but rather one between a *system* of going theories and our *experiences* of the world. And although Quine understands experience as the firings of our sensory receptors,[52] it is also clear that we do not, in fact, experience those firings.

We experience *the world*, including what others say and do, through the conceptual scheme, the theory of nature, we begin learning as we learn language, and continue to learn and refine—also within a language and going theory of nature.[53] These experiences, themselves made possible because we have sensory receptors and are able to learn public theory, together with our going theories, constitute the constraints on what it is reasonable to believe. This understanding of experience is also in keeping with Quine's.

> I assume no awareness of the firing [of sensory receptors] or any interim contemplation of sense data. I treat of stimulus and response. . . . the link between the stimulus and the response is forged in some cases by simple conditioning or ostension and in other cases by analogy or verbal explanation.[54]

In the end, then, it is the need to provide an account of how theories are constrained by experience and the central role that sensory experience plays in this task that provide respectable objections to my suggestion that we forgo focusing on individuals in pursuing epistemology. And it is the need of such an account, and the role sensory experience will play in it, that prompt Quine's specific proposal that epistemology be pursued in empirical psychology.

But it is not clear that we need to give up the notion that observation and theories are constrained by sensory stimulations in order to recognize that it is communities or groups that acquire knowledge. It is especially not clear if we recognize that the things others say and do are indispensable aspects of the information any individual is provided, that these go a long way in shaping what that individual experiences, and that they provide standards by which the individual and the rest of us will judge her or his beliefs and claims.

Indeed, a focus on individuals appears straight forwardly inconsistent with a number of Quine's views. Quine insists that our membership in a language community plays a necessary role in the theorizing in which we engage. It is a system of going theories, the questions these and experiences of the rest of the world pose, and work to answer these questions that constitute the state of science, in both the narrow and broadest senses, at a given time. The theories and questions are necessarily the product of social activity, and the experiences of individuals are made possible and shaped by these. On this view, it is not the unaided and uninhibited exercise of an individual's "faculties of perception" or "sensory-motor apparatus" that Harding, among others, describes as the "empiricist account of knowing", that leads to or produces true belief—or, for that matter, that leads to or produces *any* beliefs. Science is not a solipsistic enterprise.

We have also seen that a consequence of these positions is that evidence is a public standard. It is deeply dependent on public theorizing and, more specifically, on "common-sense" theorizing.[55] What constitutes evidence for a claim is not determined by individuals, but by the standards a community accepts concomitantly with constructing, adopting, and refining theories. Those standards constrain what it is possible for an individual to believe as well as the theorizing we engage in together.

Given these views, it is clearly *we* who know.

The question, again, is whether when we say "we know", the 'we' in question is a collective entity or merely a collection of individuals, me and you and you. . . , each of whom, individually knows. Alternatively put, the question is whether we know *because* each of us knows, or each of us knows derivatively because *we* know. I am advocating the latter; when we say "we know", 'we' is, in fact, a primitive term. The views of Quine's that I have just outlined, as well as the implications of feminist criticism that I explored in an earlier section of this chapter, indicate that this is how 'we' must be understood.

But Quine's specific proposal for how epistemology should be naturalized takes the other option; it assumes that, at bottom, 'we' really means "me and you and . . . you". In the project he visualizes, the explanation of how and what "we" know is the connection between neurophysiological states and stimuli. But the project exposes some fundamental problems with focusing on "me and you and . . . you" to provide an account of how we go about acquiring beliefs and theorizing.

Quine's proposal can be interpreted in two ways, but each suggests that the explanation to be sought of how we go about theorizing and of the relationship between that theorizing and evidence is the connection between neurophysiological states and stimuli. Quine's description of the model is very general. It is intended as an outline, in broad strokes, of the epistemological project, and not of any particular research program. But its generality is such that our consideration of it should reflect on any attempt to locate and pursue epistemology exclusively in the neurosciences and/or to continue to focus on individuals in epistemology.

In "Epistemology Naturalized" he outlines the experimental model this way:

> Epistemology, or something like it, simply falls into place as a chapter of psychology and hence of natural science. It studies a natural phenomenon, viz., a physical human subject. This human subject is accorded a certain experimentally controlled input—certain patterns of irradiation in assorted frequencies, for instance—and in the fullness of time the subject delivers as output a description of the three-dimensional external world and its history. The relation between the meager input and the torrential output is a relation that we are prompted to study for somewhat the same reasons that always prompted epistemology; namely, in order to see how evidence relates to theory, and in what ways one's theory of nature transcends any available evidence.[56]

Although Quine discusses correlating behaviors and "input" in this description, he also maintains, as I outlined in Chapter Three, that behaviors are not themselves mental states.[57] Mental states are physical states; behaviors are a way of individuating and identifying the latter. We underwrite our attention to the behavior of individuals (and, ultimately, our belief talk) with the understanding that mental states are physical states. In *Word and Object*, and other discussions we explored earlier, Quine argues that talk about "mental entities" can and should be given up for talk about physiological states.[58]

> If a certain organization of theory is achieved by . . . positing distinctive mental states and events behind physical behavior, surely as much organization could be achieved by positing merely certain correlative physiological states and events instead. . . . Lack of a detailed physiological explanation of the states is scarcely an objection to acknowledging them as states of human bodies, when we reflect that those who posit the mental states and events have no details or appropriate mechanisms to offer nor, what with their mind-body problem, prospects of any. The bodily states exist anyway; why add the others?[59]

Given these views, Quine's outline of the experimental model suggests that an explanation of my belief that x would involve correlating the physical state of the environment, the firings of my sensory receptors, and the neurophysiological changes brought about by these stimulations— although we would begin by correlating my behavior with stimuli.[60]

As I also noted earlier,[61] Quine is not committed to the view that each "mental state" correlates with a particular "brain state" (as, for example, J. C. Smart proposed some years ago). Although he has discussed the desirability of a "perceptual atomism" in which, as he describes it, "every neurologically possible human perception and perceptual distinction can be specified",[62] he also acknowledges that, by current lights, that kind of atomism is not at all plausible.[63]

Nevertheless, the project as so far explicated, including the recognition of the difficulties now apparent for anything like a one-to-one correlation between stimuli and neurophysiological states and events, presumes that epistemological questions are appropriately phrased and answered in terms of individuals. Given our current abilities, what we might explain are the behaviors of individuals, and perhaps in the future, their neuro-physiology. And, in any event, we have also noted that Quine is underwriting a focus on individuals and their behavior with the understanding that behaviors are indications of physical states.

> Causal explanations of psychology are to be sought in physiology, of physiology in biology, of biology in chemistry, and of chemistry in physics—in the elementary physical states.[64]

(That underwriting explanations at one level with explanations at an-other—and not reductionism—is what is involved here became clear in our earlier consideration of reductionism. Quine, we saw, maintains that it is the whole of science that explains; our more esoteric ontologies depend for their sense on common-sense theory.[65])

At this time we are not able, of course, to provide the list of correlations that would constitute an account of how we go about constructing theories and acquiring beliefs, as Quine has outlined that project. Nor are we close to providing the domino-like series of "causal explanations" he outlines in the above passage. But we could be satisfied with a promissory note if the prospects for answering our epistemological questions in empirical psychology were promising. We could, as Quine suggests, leave the pursuit of epistemology to empirical psychology and continue to pay attention to the behavior of *individuals* on the assumption that the project represents, in principle, the way beliefs and theorizing are to be explained.

The question I want to explore is whether the model is adequate for answering our epistemological questions—for providing an account of how we go about theorizing, and of the relationship between that theorizing and the evidence we have for it, that can further our understanding of science, in both the narrow and broadest senses.

I have said there are two ways of interpreting Quine's proposal, and I will consider each briefly to illuminate some basic problems presented by the focus on individuals. The difference between the two interpretations concerns what it is that empirical psychology is supposed to explain.

On one construal of the project, we would work, using the model, to explain specific beliefs. Using what Quine describes as "the meager input" accorded in an experimental situation and noting the slippage between how a subject behaves and the stimuli provided, we learn how a particular belief is acquired and the nature of the relationship between that belief and the evidence available. (Again, we are understanding the behavior of the individual as an indication of a physiological state—itself, the "having" of a belief.)

If this model represents the future of epistemology (at least, in principle), then we need to assume that it reflects what occurs in actual cases of belief acquisition, that it represents how we come to have beliefs. I want to consider what the model implies about that process by considering its application in an actual situation.

Suppose with research in empirical psychology well under way and successful in correlating environmental stimuli and behaviors (perhaps, eventually, even neurophysiological states) in experimental situations, that we find ourselves faced with something like the current state of science criticism. Suppose that there are two subcommunities of our larger community who disagree about some theories and standards of evidence (although certainly not all), and that we are interested in explaining the situation. Suppose, for example, that we are interested in explaining the presence of androcentric and feminist perspectives in the sciences.

Given the most ideal (but, by current lights, highly unlikely) situation—one in which all the relationships presumed in the model obtain and lend themselves to one-to-one correlations—would we obtain useful insights into the current state of science and of science criticism by focusing on how *individual scientists,* including feminist scientists, have come to have the beliefs they do? Would we learn something useful about the current state of science by studying the behavior—even the neurophysiological states—of scientists and elucidating the relationship between the firing of sensory receptors, discrete events in the environment, and the "beliefs" these scientists have?

I want to make the nature of the question I am asking clear and, in particular, that I am not being facetious about the project. If we adopt the general model of belief acquisition and explanation proposed here, *either* by actively pursuing the research or by continuing to focus on individuals, then whether we were ever interested or proficient enough to pursue such research, we must be assuming that such research is, in principle, how we would go about explaining something like our *current situation. Accepting the model would preclude other focuses.*

I am also not denying that we would find behavioral differences between those of us who can read x-ray films and those who cannot, and between those of us who "see" androcentric assumptions and those who do not. Nor am I denying that, in principle, we could find that there are neurophysiological differences between those who can read x-ray films and those who cannot and so forth. That we could recognize the relevant neurophysiological differences is, of course, a leap of faith, but it is not unreasonable. It is also, of course, a leap of faith—and perhaps less reasonable—to presume that all those who can read x-ray films, or recognize androcentric or sexist assumptions, share some identifiable neurophysiological "signature" that distinguishes them from those who cannot.

It is not, however, unreasonable, even allowing for our growing sense of the complexity of our brain and its functions, to assume that *my* neurophysiological makeup would change if I were to learn to read x-ray films. I am not advocating dualism or denying that there is a change in the physical state of an individual when a belief is acquired. I am also not denying that what the neurosciences can tell us is *relevant* to an epistemology of science.

What I am asking is whether the neurophysiological states and differences so presumed—those that underwrite our attention to the behaviors of individuals—even if they were found, are interesting differences from an *epistemological* standpoint. What sort of *explanation* of our present situation would we achieve if the project of relating behaviors and stimuli (or neurophysiological states and stimuli) turns out to be a feasible one? And what would we *do* with such an explanation, in and of itself? Specifically, what, in focusing exclusively on the behavior or physical states of individuals, would we have learned about how we go about generating theories and acquiring beliefs, how scientific understanding actually develops, and the relationship of each of these to the evidence available?

That there are problems with the model and with the assumptions underlying it actually emerges in the experimental situation Quine outlines. We have assumed from the outset, from the first description of the experiment, that the subject is accorded "meager" input. If we were going to be able to correlate stimuli and behavior, let alone stimuli and neurophysiological states, we would need to limit ourselves to quite specific stimuli. But we should ask if, in the normal course of things, beliefs can be linked to discrete and/or meager input; and we should ask if all of us who believe that *x* have come to have that belief through the same input (as well as whether we all were in the same neurophysiological state either before or after its acquisition).

However, there is a more fundamental problem with assuming that the meager input produces the output (whether that output is torrential or more modest). Even in the controlled environment of the experiment Quine outlines, it is certainly *not* the stimuli provided by the psychologist that prompts the *torrential output* or even a far more modest output. Our subject is not a solipsist.

The subject speaks a language (presumably, one the psychologist speaks) and has a lifetime (however short) of prior experience and a system (however unsystematized) of going beliefs and theory. It is on the basis of these that our subject is even *able to respond* to the now present stimuli and that she or he responds in certain ways. Neither the behavior nor the subject's current neurophysiological state—either of which, given the model, can count as the subject's "response", although only the physical state can be construed as the subject's belief—is caused by the present stimuli alone. An explanation of the subject's behavior or belief on this occasion would be inclusive of a lot of input, including, *necessarily*, prior interpersonal experiences and public theory. The behavior and thus the belief are not explained *without these factors*.

Now I just do not see any way to cut out this "noise". Interpersonal experiences and public theory are causal factors in the acquisition of any belief. Indeed, if our subject *is* a solipsist who has found her or his way to the laboratory (somehow managing to survive infancy and childhood without others), the ascription of beliefs to this subject would be very strange. The content of such alleged beliefs would be impossible for the psychologist to figure out and, if Quine is correct about the necessity of public theory for coherent experience, the content would be impossible for this *subject* to figure out or later recall.

Because we cannot assume that the subject is a solipsist, focusing on the relationship between present stimuli and the behavior or neurophysiological states will not provide an explanation of our subject's belief. This is not to deny that the belief is a neurophysiological state or that it would be discerned by behavior. (Frankly, I do not know of a way to ascertain beliefs, including my own, without attention to behavior.) It is to deny that an *explanation* of that belief is accomplished by correlating these things, even in the most ideal of situations.

Of course, Quine might have envisioned the experiment he outlines as the following of our subject through her or his entire development, from womb to maturity. This experiment would lead to including all the individual's interactions with the world; nothing would be left out. But neither does it, in advance, circumscribe a range of epistemologically relevant variables.

Now, it is possible that Quine's proposal is to be interpreted differently. Quine may not foresee that we will ever be involved in the project of correlating *specific* beliefs to specific neurophysiological states and correlating these states (or specific behaviors) to specific stimuli. He may envision the task of a naturalized epistemology as arriving at a general explanation of how beliefs, understood to be neurophysiological states, are caused by stimuli, and seeing what the "slippage" is between the "meager input" accorded the species as evidence for its theories, and the "torrential output" the species produces—but without concern to explain any specific belief. His assumption of "meager input" might reflect his view that what we say about how things are is underdetermined by all the evidence we have for saying it.

But so understood, the project still assumes that answers to these more general epistemological questions will or could be found in the relationship between the neurophysiological states of *individuals* and events in the environment. There are difficulties with the project even if we understand it as a project to provide a general explanation of belief acquisition and theorizing.

Some are technical problems that apply to either interpretation of Quine's proposal, and they have been implied somewhat in the discussion so far. They include the apparent complexity of our brains—a complexity that makes an atomism of correlations between neurophysiological states and specific beliefs unlikely, the possibility (some would call it more than a possibility) that the "mental states" so studied are not the same "physiological" states for different persons, and the possibility (also a consequence of current research in the neurosciences) that the same stimuli would not cause the same neurophysiological event in even *one* person at different times—perhaps only moments apart.[66]

In addition, if we limit ourselves to a model that focuses on individuals but cannot explain specific beliefs—and it is possible that replacing epistemology with neuroscience commits us to giving up the explanation of specific beliefs—then we are apparently assuming that situations like the one we currently find ourselves faced with will not occur or that we will not be interested in "explaining" them if they do. We seem to be assuming that at a given stage of inquiry, "we" do not and "we" will not disagree (again, except in terms of the possibility that some of us have made a straightforward mistake or in terms of differences in education). If "we" were all that homogeneous in our beliefs because there were no differences in our experiences—none, that is, of epistemological consequence—then perhaps we would never need more than a general explanation of belief acquisition and evidential connections. Perhaps nothing of consequence would be lost if we settled for giving a most general account of the relationship between discrete events in the environment and the physical states of individuals, and noting that there is a slippage between these— a meagerness of input in relation to output.

But would such an account help us to say, in a way that would be useful to us, that would further our understanding of science, how the current state of science and of science criticism have come about? Isn't it precisely the "slippage", on the one hand, and fundamental differences in experiences, on the other, that need our attention in explaining the current situation—an explanation we would hope would give us insight into how knowledge develops? Wouldn't we expect an epistemology to incorporate a model that could be used, at least in principle, to explain the current situation in a way that could further those understandings?

There are other difficulties that indicate that the specific project Quine has in mind cannot be the exclusive, or even the central, direction we take in seeking even the most general explanation for how, as a species, we have gone about theorizing. We can insist that the neurosciences are relevant to epistemology—to paraphrase Quine, we can recognize that neuroscience would be a "chapter" in a naturalized epistemology—while also recognizing that it could not be exhaustive of the latter.

One indication that psychology will not tell us all we want to know about our theorizing, and the most important, has already been discussed in terms of the first interpretation of Quine's model: namely, Quine's own recognition that what appears to be a "meager input" produces a "torrential output". Now, whether Quine is discussing the meager input accorded a particular subject in a particular situation, or the input that we, as a species, have relative to the theories we construct and the beliefs we have, that slippage is interesting and worthy of attention. As I implied earlier, it is *not enough* simply to note it. In developing an account of how we go about constructing theories, we need to include the factors that fill in the gap that Quine recognizes. What factors beyond the meager input provided the species are necessary for the torrential output we do produce? Indeed, why are we confident that recording the resulting belief of one subject can be generalized to others?

It would appear to be the *rest of us*, the communities within which individuals come to be capable of having beliefs at all, the communities that actually construct theories and arrive at standards of evidence, that fill in the gap for the species that is noted in the first question. And it is because individuals are members of epistemological communities that we feel confident in generalizing from the behavior of an individual in an experimental situation to talk about the rest of us. We are reminded of Quine's own arguments against foundationalism—in particular, his claim that pretheoretic experience will not of itself hold together—an argument I appealed to earlier in noting that the subject of our experiment was not a solipsist. Alternatively put, if Quine's notion of the physical environment (the stimuli) is meant to encompass the things others say and do, and if these play the role he grants them in his arguments against foundationalism, then the focus incorporated in his model for naturalizing epistemology is misplaced. We should be focusing on communities.

The necessity of community for individuals to have beliefs and to know is also indicated by current research in the neurosciences. Our current understandings of neurobiological development, for example, indicate that interpersonal experience is a necessary causal factor in the fetal and postnatal neurobiological development that permits language acquisition, conceptualization, and many perceptual experiences.

Although fetal and postnatal development of the brain results in the structural capacities for learning, the development of this structure—in particular, the major expansion in the dendritic and synaptic network— occurs only in complex interaction with the rest of the organism and external stimuli, including, *necessarily,* interpersonal experience.[67] Membership in a sociolinguistic community, as I noted above, is apparently necessary for the structures that support language acquisition.[68] It now appears that if a child is not exposed to language and has not learned to use it by puberty, the development necessary to language use will never occur. And experiments involving other species also indicate that sensory deprivation at early ages in species like ours in which much neuronal development occurs postnatally precludes the occurrence of the neuronal development that allows for the relevant perceptual experiences.[69]

So, in the process of developing the neurological features that an empirical psychologist might ultimately correlate with stimuli, and the neurobiological structure that allows an individual to respond to that stimuli in a way they could recall and the psychologists could understand, the relevant input has been by no means "meager" and interpersonal relationships have been necessary factors. Indeed, the "causal" relationships are apparently not even linear. Bleier and others studying neuronal development suggest there is "functional interaction" between the input afforded through interpersonal relationships and postnatal neuronal development.[70]

> Critical to any consideration of the environmental impact on the developing brain is the fact that in mammals a significant part of brain growth and development occurs after birth, even though no new neurons are formed (except for two known areas in the brain, cerebellum and olfactory bulbs). . . .
>
> The primate brain is relatively more immature at birth than most other mammals, and the human brain is the most immature. It more than doubles in size within a year after birth and almost doubles again by the age of four years. . . .
>
> Since the primate brain undergoes its major growth spurt following birth, this means that a significant amount of growth occurs under the influence of and in functional interaction with input from the external world. . . . it appears that [for language], adequate environmental stimulation is needed during a critical postnatal period for normal neuronal development to occur (Walker, 1981). Without exposure to a sociolinguistic environment, language does not develop, and the normal acquisition of language cannot occur, so far as is known, after puberty.[71]

The complexity of our neurobiological development indicates that an explanation of the neurobiological development of an individual would encompass factors that are not neurobiological factors, and that these will be as fundamental to that development as anything we might say about the individual's biology.[72] This complexity raises additional questions about the soundness of focusing on individuals, including their physical states, in epistemology.

Further, the histories of our individual neurobiological developments are unique, as are our histories of acquiring beliefs—even our histories in acquiring the *same* belief. There is no reason to think we could explain, in a general way, how individuals come to have any particular belief. Even were we to find the same neurophysiological state in everyone who held a particular belief, we would not have explained that belief using the model Quine proposes, since the relationship between the state and stimuli would be different for different people. There is no reason to think that the neurophysiological state just prior to anyone's coming to believe that *x* was the same as everyone else's.

Finally, we recognize that a "naturalized" epistemology would need to incorporate the fact that our brain has a history. Its evolution, along with our development of language and the history of our positing and theorizing about middle-sized objects, would need to be included in any account of how we theorize. This may, in fact, be one of the research programs Quine would be most interested in seeing develop and he might envision that empirical psychology, evolutionary biology, and anthropology would provide the pieces of the story.

But any theory that reconstructed our evolutionary history, including our epistemological and biological histories, would need to include interpersonal relationships and social activities as fundamental factors. These relationships and activities, biologists and anthropologists tell us, were causal factors in the evolution of our brain.[73] Thus, an evolutionary epistemology would need to incorporate, among its most basic organizing principles, that we are *fundamentally social*, that the acquisition of language and the positing of physical objects (or, more generally, the construction of theories) are *social feats*, that, as individuals, our acquisition of language and beliefs are possible only because we are members of sociolinguistic communities, and that among the causal factors that led to the evolution of a brain that facilitates and/or prompts physical-object theorizing are *human communities and their practices*. These things would need to be central features in any study of, or story about, how we have gone about the business of surviving—through, in part, together explaining, shaping, and predicting our experiences.

These preliminary considerations of two interpretations of Quine's proposal, of our current understandings of neurobiological development, and of the factors that were necessary to the evolution of our brain, indicate that a naturalized epistemology will need to include more than neuroscience. Its primary focus will be human social groups. Focusing on individuals, even in terms of their neurophysiological states, is not adequate. To be more than a "rational reconstruction", even to be a fruitful rational reconstruction, a naturalized epistemology will need to make use of all the knowledge that we find to be relevant to how we go about theorizing. And for now it is clear that, in addition to psychology, we would need sociology, biology, and evolutionary theory and that no one of these would be sufficient.

Our neurophysiology is, of course, relevant to the epistemology of science. But the nature of the complexity of something like our neurobiological development, our evolution, and the factors necessary to an individual's coming to have a belief—complexities that involve interpersonal experience—suggest some directions that we need to explore in developing an epistemological framework that is sufficiently rich.

To get at some of these directions, we can use Quine's own arguments against foundationalism. These underscore the central role of the very factor that emerged above as important and relevant to a "naturalized epistemology", namely, interpersonal relationships. The fundamental importance of these is directly relevant to the issue of whether an "individual knower" is even *coherent*. Thus, we can begin to pull various considerations together and bring them to bear on the question I posed earlier concerning the coherency of the view of knowers that the modern self/ society dichotomy leads to.

In arguing against foundationalism, Quine takes great pains to show that persons who theorize and have beliefs emerge and function only within social context, the context that affords public theory including standards of evidence.[74] A "solipsistic knower" is impossible if there is no coherent pretheoretical experience.

In Quine's account of childhood development, the child arrives, so to speak, in the middle of things and learns what we, in the middle of things, have learned.[75] But the child who is capable of having beliefs and of theorizing is not an autonomous "knower".[76] The child is dependent epistemologically, requiring the evolving public conceptual scheme that bridges her or his sensory experiences, categorizing and shaping them in ways that make intersubjective experience possible and give the notion of evidence content. And the child's contributions will be judged, by herself or himself no less than others, according to public standards of evidence.

Though Quine couched his account of childhood development in behaviorist terms and was primarily concerned to undermine foundationalism and the skepticism the traditional empiricist knower threatens, we can use the insights into the necessity of interpersonal relationships and a public conceptual scheme in other ways. It may also be that the behaviorism in Quine's account is due in part to a lingering commitment to epistemological individualism, to thinking that we need to characterize and explain what it means that an individual "has a belief". I am suggesting that we need to get beyond the constraints within which Quine is working.[77]

As we saw in Chapter Three, the learning of language is central to Quine's account of how a child learns to individuate objects. The learning, we can assume—and his account certainly implies this—is one the child's mother is facilitating. What is being learned, on Quine's view, as a child learns language and begins to have coherent experiences is physical-object theory.

> We in our maturity have come to look upon the child's mother as an
> integral body who, in an irregular closed orbit, revisits the child from
> time to time; and to look upon red in a radically different way, viz., as
> scattered about. Water, for us, is rather like red, but not quite; things
> can be red, but only stuff is water. But the mother, red, and water are
> for the infant all of a type: each is just a history of sporadic encounter,
> a scattered portion of what goes on. . . .
>
> Once the child has pulled through the individuate crisis, though, he
> [sic] is prepared to reassess prior terms. "Mama", in particular, gets set
> up retroactively as the name of a broad and recurrent but withal
> individual object, and thus as a single term *par excellence*. [78]

"Mama", as Quine describes things, is for the child the name of an object rather than a subject—she is one of many objects to be individuated.

Although Quine offers this as an account of the learning of physical-object theory, it is clear the child is *simultaneously* learning about persons and relationships, and about herself or himself. In the account offered of this period of development by object-relations theorists, the importance of learning about how to individuate objects is also stressed. But the significance of that learning is recast.

The important thing that a child is learning at the stage at which she or he is learning to individuate physical objects, according to Nancy Chodorow and other object-relations theorists,[79] is her or his own individuality and separateness from others—and, in particular, from her or his mother, still the primary caretaker for most young children. But, in Chodorow's account, while the child is learning about objects and, through this learning, coming to recognize itself as an individual subject, the most important factor in that recognition is coming to see the mother as a *subject*—of recognizing that she is not on a par with objects. Keller describes the significance of Chodorow's account as follows.

> What Chodorow adds [to our understanding] is an emphasis on the dual
> character of the separation-individuation process—a process leading not

only to the recognition of self as different from other, but also to the ultimate recognition of the other as subject like oneself. This duality is born out of the reciprocity of the mother-child interaction.[80]

In the light of object-relations theory, we would want to recast Quine's description of childhood development and the learning of common-sense theory about physical objects, so that mother is no longer a "mass" object to be individuated by the child; instead, she is coming to be understood as what in fact she is: another subject interacting with the child who is learning the knowledge that her or his species has attained to date: a body of knowledge not acquired by the discrete experiences of discrete knowledge acquirers, but by a community. We would also want to incorporate in this picture of language learning and public-theory learning Chodorow's insight that the child is learning about relationships apiece with learning to individuate objects.[81] For although Quine's account undermines the appropriateness of focusing on individuals in its emphasis on the role public theory plays in epistemological development, supplementing and/or recasting his account of this period of development with what else the child is simultaneously learning allows us to see that separating the learning of even something like physical-object theory from our relationships, and from our learning about relationships, is impossible. Both child and mother are *subjects*, something the child is learning concomitantly with learning how to individuate objects according to the scheme her or his community accepts. The child is learning far more than how to be a member of a *linguistic* community, but how to be a member of a human community—and that incorporates far more than language and appropriately individuating and identifying physical objects.

And it is a consequence of Quine's own arguments against foundationalism, including his account of how a child acquires language and public theory, that we do not develop epistemologically—we are not and could not be "knowers" or have beliefs—without intersubjective experience, and that we do not, individually or collectively, observe or experience the world from outside the theories our species and our particular communities have developed to date.[82]

Finally, in illuminating the problems with an epistemological focus on individuals, we can remind ourselves of the immediate impetus for Quine's general suggestion that epistemology be "naturalized". The proposal is precipitated by Quine's recognition that constructing a "sense data" language is impossible. Quine takes that impossibility to signal the demise of the empiricist dream that science would be grounded at the level of raw sense data,[83] and he claims that attempts to "rationally reconstruct" such a language are "make believe". He does so on the grounds that, outside theory, an individual's experiences would be a meaningless barrage of sensory stimulations.[84]

Now, the necessity of the bridges we together construct for an individual to have coherent experience signals the *demise* of the coherence of "epistemological individualism", of the coherence of an autonomous knower. If theories, standards of evidence, and theorizing are necessarily public, then an emphasis within epistemology on individuals is just inappropriate. The "solipsistic knower" that has allegedly haunted empiricism is impossible.

Science, knowing, believing, and standards of evidence are *social*—through and through. These are *our* activities and creations, not those of "me and you and you . . .".

Really Naturalizing Epistemology

In its general intent, Quine's insistence that epistemology needs to be naturalized is extremely important. It has several far-reaching implications.

One implication has to do with the role of an epistemology. Turning to the neurosciences—or to any science or current theory—to construct an account of how we know cannot be thought of as a way of *justifying* the theories we have constructed. When epistemology is recognized to be a part of science and not antecedent to it, it is not playing a justificatory role—at least not as that role is commonly construed.

A naturalized epistemology, and given the demise of foundationalism there can be no other kind, will explain how we have gone about constructing theories. If our theories prove successful—if they help us to make sense of and to predict experiences—then, if an epistemology provides a correct account of how we know, that epistemology provides the "how" of successful theorizing.

This understanding of the role of an epistemology may be different than that underlying the work Harding and Jaggar have undertaken in developing a feminist epistemology. Although Jaggar maintains that the relationship between an epistemology and other theories is always circular (she locates the circularity in the views of human nature the theories involved share), she also maintains that the purpose of an epistemology is to justify these other theories, although, again, in a circular way.[85] Harding, as I noted in the Introduction, argues that justificatory grounds always have to be provided by something other than the theory or theories in question,[86] and her construal of the "epistemological problem" facing feminists includes the assumption that an epistemology is needed that can "justify" feminist claims. So, for example, in a recent discussion of the epistemologies feminists are developing, Harding asked, "On what grounds should . . . feminist claims be justified?"[87]

I am denying that an epistemology can do the job of justifying any claim or theory. We *begin*, unlike Descartes or the White Queen, with the assumption that what we believe is *true*. It is the ability to make sense of what we experience and to predict our experiences that will, in the end, justify any theory or claim. What we are concerned to do in constructing an epistemology is to offer causal explanations for how theories, beliefs, and claims have been arrived at, explanations that are in keeping with what we experience. Because, for example, we have been successful at theorizing, an adequate epistemology will need to be able to explain why and how, and this is why I have insisted that epistemologies that do not (or cannot) provide an account of how theories are constrained by evidence are inadequate.

A second view underlying Quine's proposal is related to the issue of the role of an epistemology. A general implication of Quine's proposal is that in going about developing a theory of theorizing, we will make use of the knowledge we have that is relevant. For Quine, the neurosciences seemed the obvious place to pursue epistemological questions, and I have suggested that this is because he assumes that as one forges a connection between theories and experiences, individuals need to be the primary focus.

But a more general argument underlying his appeal to psychology is that the circularity involved in appealing to science to explain science is not vicious. His argument can be generalized to our use of any knowledge that is relevant to how we go about constructing theories and acquiring beliefs. The important insight is that developing an explanation of how we know is not *proving* what we know.

> A surrender of the epistemological burden to psychology is a move that was disallowed in earlier times as circular reasoning. If the epistemologist's goal is validation of the grounds of empirical science, he [sic] defeats his purpose by using psychology or other empirical science in the validation. However, such scruples against circularity have little point once we have stopped dreaming of deducing science from observations. If we are out simply to understand the link between observation and science, we are well advised to use any information, including that provided by the very science whose link with observation we are seeking to understand. . . . *We are after an understanding of*

science as an institution of process in the world and we do not intend
that understanding to be any better than the science which is its object.[88]

I accept our prevailing physical theory and therewith the physiology of
my receptors, and then proceed to speculate on how this sensory input
supports the very physical theory that I am accepting. *I do not claim*
thereby to be proving the physical theory, so there is no vicious circle.[89]

As I argued above, a feminist epistemology cannot "prove" or, in and of
itself, "justify" feminists' claims. Feminists believe to be true what they
claim is true. The justification of feminist claims will be on the basis of
their empirical adequacy.

So the immediate impetus for reconsidering the empiricist commitment
to individualism is that focusing on individuals will not allow for a
reasonable *explanation* of how feminists have come to know what they
do. But I have argued that the current state of science and science criticism
is not special in this regard. Rather, it is forcing us to rethink a commitment that has, in fact, been strained for some time. Indeed, and ironically
given the specific project Quine outlines, the strain is precisely what
prompts him to propose that epistemology be naturalized.

It is clear that a naturalized epistemology will have to encompass more
than empirical psychology, and that it will need to focus, centrally, on
communities rather than individuals. Although what it means, in terms
of neurophysiological states, for an individual to have a belief and what
kind of neurological processes are prompted by stimuli are interesting
and important questions, answers to them will not explain all we want
to know. Attention to the physical states of individuals does not hold the
promise of providing an adequate account of how we go about theorizing
and acquiring beliefs. The issues we considered in the previous section
indicate that a naturalized epistemology will require the insights that a
variety of sciences can offer, and that we should expect that sociology
will play a major role, for a central principle in any epistemology will
need to be the necessary and fundamental role that interpersonal experience and community membership plays in "knowing".

The current state of science and science criticism indicates some additional factors that would need to be incorporated in an adequate epistemology. Feminist science criticism exposes many social and political experiences and arrangements relevant to our most rigorous theorizing that
we have not recognized as such. It is now clear that we will need to draw
upon the insights that gender theory and political theory can offer to
arrive at explanations for how we theorize, and we should expect that

the insights these theories can offer will have a central role in any explanations we offer about how scientific theories have been constructed to date. Divisions in experience, and divisions in cognitive labor and authority, will need to be incorporated in an account of the epistemology of science, at least as currently and historically practiced.

But my suggestions that we focus on communities and encompass all the factors we find relevant to our theorizing, including social and political experience and divisions in cognitive labor, prompt three immediate concerns—each, at some level, is a concern about relativism.

The first is whether the suggestion that we forgo focusing on individuals can be reconciled with empiricism. Does recognizing communities as the primary epistemological agents sever the connection between our theories and the world? This would be a serious objection to my proposal on empiricist grounds—including, the way I see things, feminist grounds.

A related concern is whether the arguments offered in the last sections commit us to the view that sociology of knowledge is all there is to epistemology. The latter, at least in the eyes of those advocating the view that "the world" has little or no role in constraining belief and theories, is a relativist epistemology. It is, therefore, inadequate as epistemology as long as we are convinced that we can, and want to, distinguish between good theories and bad theories.[90] To be able to make such distinctions, and to be able to support them, is one of the important reasons I am suggesting that we begin to develop a feminist empiricism.

A third concern is whether a focus on communities as epistemological agents and the inclusion of political factors and values as relevant to *good* theorizing make it more likely that feminist criticism can be reconciled with empiricism—or will we find it reasonable, when we focus on communities, to posit epistemological chasms? The flip side of the question is one we have already begun to consider. Have we introduced, as central factors causing the "torrential output" we put forward, things that are not subject to empirical control, for example, political commitments, sex/gender, values?

In terms of the first concern, there seems no reason to think that the connection between our theories and "the world" would be severed by the proposed shift in focus. We can recognize that, the firings of our sensory receptors are how we, as individuals, accumulate knowledge but also recognize that the knowledge acquired by an individual has been, or is being, constructed by our species and our more specific communities (we may belong to more than one).

Indeed, when we look closely at Quine's work, we can even say that in the end, Quine *does not have individualism*—the "we" whom he talks about most of the time (when he is not discussing the project of pursuing epistemology in psychology) cannot be "me and you and you . . . "; it must be a primitive "we". Despite his proposal that we pursue epistemological questions in empirical psychology and relate behaviors (or neurophysiological states) to environmental stimuli, it is clear that on his own view, others—at least the things they say—are a necessary part of the stimuli that lead to any individual's coming to have a belief.

Yet, *without* individualism, and with his insistence that science is a bridge of our own making, Quine does not conclude that the connection between our theories and "the world" is severed. He has managed to carve out a theory of evidence, specifically, a coherence theory of the latter, that is commensurate with our current understandings of how we obtain information and that is able to account for theories being constrained by experience. That account of evidence, I have suggested in several contexts, undermines the "knowledge is passively discovered/ knowledge is socially constructed" dichotomy.

So we can continue to insist that evidence is sensory, while recognizing that our sensory experiences are made possible and shaped by our membership in communities, and focusing on the latter rather than on individuals. The impossibility, on both practical and logical grounds, of anything like a sense-data language already challenges the coherency of an "individual knower" who is theorizing about the world, and the connection to be forged is different in kind than that explicated in traditional and positivist empiricism. We are relating experience to a system of theories—not individual theories to a world untheorized.

Relatedly, the move from individuals to communities does not commit us to sociology of knowledge. Though I have argued that persons who theorize emerge only within social context and stressed the role that public theory plays in shaping that theorizing, I have not suggested that the *only* causes for beliefs are social causes. I am not advocating that sociology of knowledge is all there is, or could be, to epistemology. "Knowledge" is socially constructed through and through—but the construction is constrained by evidence.

We assume there is a world, including a social world, that constrains what it is reasonable for us to believe because that assumption makes the most sense of what we experience. To be sure, we construct theories rather than discover them, and these theories are underdetermined by all the evidence we have for them. But it is not up to us whether gravity is real or whether many research programs are androcentric and this has led to distorted accounts of how things are. Beliefs and theories are shaped and constrained by public theory and their consistency with each other, but they are also constrained by their consistency with our experiences of the world, including our social world.

So although feminist and androcentric perspectives are not fruitfully explained by paying attention to individuals, although they require historically and culturally specific experiences and community-bound theories and standards, these perspectives are not special in this regard. Nor are they (or other beliefs and theories) able to be explained by sociology of knowledge. There are social causes for feminist and androcentric beliefs, and these are necessary, but they are not the only causes.

The insistence that we pay attention to both experience and community membership suggests some things about the third issue, and the concern it prompts: whether a focus on communities can help to further the project of making empiricism available to feminists, but without leading us to posit unbridgeable epistemological chasms. Can we accommodate a relationship between the claims feminists make and their experiences, without abandoning empiricism in our characterization and explanation of that relationship?

For the most part, I have talked of communities and subcommunities in a somewhat Quinean sense, implying that epistemological communities can be discerned by a network of theories and beliefs, including standards of evidence, and that subcommunities can be discerned in terms of more local sets of theories, including standards of evidence.

Given the notion of an epistemological community, we can begin to characterize some aspects of the current state of science by saying that a community of feminist scientists and a community of their nonfeminist colleagues differ in terms of a number of theories. They do not, of course, differ in terms of all theories, so incommensurability is not the issue.

But if we are to go further to explain and evaluate these differences, the notion of an epistemological community will require a good deal more work. We will need to go beyond the initial focus on going theories as a way of identifying and distinguishing communities, and certainly we will need to go beyond Quine's focus on language communities—a focus that, along with his exclusion of politics and values as relevant to science, is probably responsible for his assumption of a "homogeneous" "we". We will need to look at the practices and experiences within the relevant subcommunities and our largest community to explain the differences separating subcommunities, and to evaluate these differences.

In relating experiences to going theories, we can use the work that feminist scholars have done to expose those aspects of our larger community and the feminist community that are relevant to the theories and standards of evidence in question, to give content to the notion of community, not only in terms of theories but in terms of practices and experiences. We will need to include the work that feminists have done in evaluating social and political theories to reconsider the assumption that political beliefs and theories, and values, are not subject to empirical control, that there is no way to judge between them.

Would a focus on communities help with explaining, as Harding and other feminists perceive an adequate epistemology would need to be able, how feminists have come to know what they do?[91]

On one level, the focus on communities is in keeping with a long-standing feminist insight into the "collective" nature of the feminist political experience and feminist "knowing",[92] an insight that is clearly reflected in standpoint epistemologies, but also in the claims made by some feminists who have opted for a feminist empiricism.[93] What I am suggesting is that the shift in focus to communities precludes the conclusion that feminist empiricism "subverts" empiricism. The shift I am advocating does not subvert empiricism, but it does fundamentally alter it. It is also not prompted by feminist criticism alone, but by a number of issues we have considered in this chapter.

But, again, though insisting on the role played by community membership in the ability of feminists to "know things others have not", I am not advocating a sociology of knowledge. I am advocating that we look for the relationship between what feminists know and their experiences within a real social order, and I am arguing that those experiences and a real social order constrain what it is *reasonable* to believe.

One fairly obvious objection to the alternative I am proposing should be addressed. I am not denying that it is possible for members of a community to differ in terms of some beliefs. Obviously, they do—even within what we may find it useful to recognize as epistemological subcommunities (for instance, the feminist community). But such a denial is not made necessary by recognizing that it is communities that acquire knowledge.

We can each contribute to the evolving corpus of our theories, so we do not need to deny that we can make sense of your having a belief that I do not have. The point is that we come to hold beliefs at all, and the specific beliefs we do, based on experiences that are, in a fundamental sense, shaped, and ultimately made possible, by our membership in communities and by the theories our community holds. The standards by which our contributions will be judged—including how we judge our own contributions—are public standards. These standards apply not only to our claims to know, but also to our beliefs. As I noted earlier, we really do not understand someone's claim to believe what is inconsistent with obvious evidence—nor can we will to believe things in the face of convincing counterevidence.

Some examples may help to further clarify these points.[94] At the outset of this chapter, I proposed that claims to *exclusive* knowledge were either false or uninteresting—that is, their *exclusiveness* is uninteresting. Suppose, as Gerald Massey asked, I am the only one who sees a rabbit on the porch this morning. There is a sense in which we want to say that only I know she paid us a visit. But the exclusivity of that knowledge is uninteresting, for my knowledge is dependent on a theory whose ontology includes rabbits, and standards for appropriately noting their presence, and so on—and these things are necessarily public. If I am correct about the rabbit, any member of my "epistemological community" who was present would have agreed. My knowing is fundamentally dependent on that. Indeed, my even having a belief about a rabbit visit is dependent on my knowledge of public theory and appropriate use of it.

Similarly, if I construct a proof for a theorem, a proof that has eluded all of my colleagues, my knowing there is such a proof will depend on their acceptance of the proof. They will accept it (assuming they are not perverse) provided it is in keeping with a going body of theory, including rules of inference, and correctly executed. It may be interesting that I was the first to construct the proof, but my knowing is still dependent on ours—for some group. If what I allege to be a proof is *not* commensurate with accepted theory, then I do *not* know, and I will not unless there is a change in my community's theories. In this case, unlike that involving the rabbit, the relevant community would probably be one of specialists.

What I am denying, then, is that an individual can know *what no one else could know*. A solitary mathematician who "discovers" a geometry incompatible with any accepted and/or incompatible with some substantial portion of other accepted theories does not "know" something that no one else knows. She or he will not know unless and until we do, for some we. Any alleged "discovery" will either be in keeping with going theories, in which case its discoverer can be said to know, or it will not, in which case, until our going theories change, its "discoverer" cannot be said to know.

What might the alternative be? To assume that an individual can know something that is not compatible with public theory (for some public) would require that there is a unique story that will organize and explain our experiences waiting to be discovered. If there is no such story, then the notions of "discovery" and knowledge are relative to the going state of science. Thus, I cannot know what no one else could. I know what we do or could, for some we.

One could object that my proposal is too one-sided, that it places too much emphasis on groups. Bill Lycan has suggested that if I am the president of an organization, it is certainly true that I could not be the president without the organization's existing. But that does not mean that, as an individual, I am not the president—even though my being so depends on the existence of the organization. There is something true of me that is true of no one else: namely, that I am the current president of that organization. Isn't there, he asked, a similar relationship between individual knowers and groups? Isn't there an interdependency, a sharing equally of the epistemological burden, between individuals and a community?

The first thing to note about the shift I am proposing is that it does not entail that we cannot attribute knowledge to individuals. I am insisting that when we do, it is on the basis of going theory, a theory *we* accept. Like being the only president of an organization, I can be the only one who saw the rabbit this morning, and, perhaps, no one else could have been there to see it, and so on. But, again, the exclusivity here is uninteresting. It does not indicate that my being in the vicinity of the rabbit (and having the right sensory apparatus and so on) is equally as important to my knowledge of its visit as my ability to recognize rabbits, something for which I am dependent on public theory. Unlike organizations, and presidencies of these, which individuals could, as individuals, create and of which they could declare themselves president, I *cannot be* a solitary knower. There is not an equal sharing of the epistemological burden. Individuals have beliefs and know, but both are possible because of and constrained by public theory, including standards of evidence.

Finally, in considering the shift I am proposing, we can use Quine's general vision of a "naturalized epistemology" as a reminder that it is not inexplicable that changes in our social and political theorizing should call for changes in our epistemology—provided, of course, that we are willing to recognize such beliefs and theories in the network of our going theories—a recognition made compelling by feminist science criticism.

The interesting questions involve the directions we should take in revising an epistemology, and how the changes have come about that have prompted us to reconsider the empiricist commitment to individualism. If we are doing things right, our answers to the latter should affect our answers to the former, indicating which of the directions we might explore are likely to be fertile.

For now it is clear that one of the directions we must take involves reappraising what Bill Wisdom calls Descartes' covenant: his promise, as Quine characterizes and advocates it, that science will "stand . . . aloof" from values.[95]

Science Communities

It does not seem unreasonable to expect that the development of
feminist scientific theory . . . will proceed hand-in-hand with the feminist
struggle to change the conditions of our lives and work and with the
development of feminist theory in general.

—Ruth Bleier

[My aim] is the reclamation, from within science, of science as a human
instead of a masculine project, and the renunciation of the division of
emotion and intellectual labor that maintains science as a male preserve.

—Evelyn Fox Keller

IT IS NOT UNCOMMON in feminist science criticism to discuss how
science might be different in a society that did not include the divisions
in power and experience by sex/gender, race, and class that western
societies currently incorporate, and if the values emerging in feminism
were generally accepted and reflected in practices.[1] The ability to consider
how science might be different, and to relate such differences to social
and political arrangements and values, suggests that feminists are working
with a fundamentally different view of science than traditionally and, to
a large extent, currently held. Many of us have been tempted by the view
that science is autonomous from social and political context. And many
have been tempted by the view that there is one unique true story about
how things are and that science is discovering that story.

The view of science I have been exploring and advocating enables us
to see that the content of science might have been different. There is, given
the views of Quine's we have considered, no unique set of theories that will
organize, and be coherent with, our experiences. The barrier remaining for

300

many empiricists is that feminists are considering how science, both as an activity and in terms of its content, might be different if values and politics were different, and they are relating their own critiques of science, and those aspects of science they criticize, to political and sex/gendered experiences.

The most basic insights underlying feminists' ability to envision a different or a changed science, not just as an intellectual possibility but as a science that might actually come about, and to do so with reference to social and political arrangements and values, involve what feminists are learning about science communities.

To pull together some of what their criticism indicates about these communities, I want to consider a proposal frequently offered in feminist discussions: that science will be better when critical self-reflection is recognized as necessary to achieving objectivity, and considered basic to scientific method.[2] I will, however, stay close to home, exploring the proposal in terms of what we have learned about science as it is, rather than as it might be in the future. It has been, after all, on the basis of what they have learned about science as it is that feminists have found it possible to consider how science might be different and that the need for critical self-reflection came to be recognized as acute.

Against the background of the issues raised by feminist science criticism, the relationship of self-reflection to objectivity can be construed in two ways, and these, it turns out, are deeply incompatible. One construal builds from a view of objectivity that is well developed and entrenched, tracing its roots to a constellation of views that emerged as modern science did, and specifically to the work to develop an epistemology that could explain and justify that endeavor. (The modern epistemological tradition was long interested in the project of "justifying" science, a project, following Quine, I have argued needs to be abandoned.)

If we begin with the traditional view of objectivity, including self-reflection in the canons of scientific method would be a way of cleansing science of the signatures of its practitioners, and achieving that would be a way of insuring science's objectivity.

It is important to explore the feasibility of the traditional ideal—the assumptions about knowing and science that underlie it and the requirements it incorporates—for relativism and skepticism of various stripes are lurking as traps should we settle for an ideal of objectivity that we could not possibly live up to. If, as feminist criticism suggests, we cannot help but fail to meet the requirements the traditional view sets forth, if the ideal builds on views about knowing and science that are themselves untenable, then we will need to develop an alternative understanding of objectivity—provided, of course, that we remain confident that striving for objectivity does not need to be and should not be abandoned.

It is also clear, given the issues we have considered, that critical self-reflection is necessary to objectivity. Experience indicates that it is not enough to assume that our social and political experiences and our social identities, including our experiences of sex/gender and our values, will not have a bearing on the theorizing we do in scientific communities. Declaring that they will not have a bearing, as scientists and philosophers are prone to do, or *defining* science as not incorporating these factors, certainly is not enough to insure that science as practice or knowledge will not or does not incorporate them.

The authentic question is what we should expect critical self-reflection to accomplish. To a great extent, our answer to that question will depend on what we think science is and science communities are like. Since the traditional ideal of objectivity begins from a view about the nature of knowledge rather than the nature of the communities in which it develops, we will begin by considering what scientific knowledge was supposed to be like and how it was to be acquired.

Descartes' Covenant

The first construal of the proposal, in which self-reflection is taken to be a means of cleansing science of the signatures of its practitioners, builds on ideas about knowing and science that can be traced to Descartes' "Meditations", a project, in Descartes' words (and despite the subtitle of the work)[3] to "establish [a] firm and permanent structure in the sciences".[4] One is the view that we can separate "the knower" and "what is known": that when we are doing things correctly, there is a clear and decisive distance between these. A second view, bolstering part of what the first incorporates, is that evidence is self-announcing. And a third view, deeply related to each of these, is that with the exception of those values that are constitutive of science (honesty in reporting results, and the like),[5] science should be as free of values as we can manage.

If these views are tenable, then the explanation for some of the problems feminists have uncovered (androcentrism, for example), is that we have not always done things well enough. We have allowed politics, experiences of and views about sex/gender, and other values and "subjective" interests to "contaminate" science. The proposal that critical self-reflection be incorporated in scientific method would be understood as a way of insuring that we consciously maintain the boundaries between science and these other commitments, interests, and experiences, by maintaining the boundaries between those who are theorizing and the content of science.

In considering the feasibility of this understanding of the proposal, we will need to see if we can, in fact, sustain the views we have inherited from Descartes.

The "firm and permanent structure" Descartes is seeking in the "Meditations" is not a certain truth, but a method for arriving at certain truth.[6] From the outset of the "methodological doubt" of the First Meditation, Descartes is concerned to evaluate the methods (the "principles") by which his beliefs have been acquired. Using the doubt to decisively undermine psychological certainty as a "mark" of truth,[7] Descartes opens the Third Meditation with an argument to the effect that there is a "mark" of true belief. We can, he argues, be certain that beliefs are true that have been arrived at by the use of a particular method—a method he calls (decidedly unhelpfully) "clear and distinct perception".[8]

The argument is a transcendental one. At the outset of the Second Meditation, Descartes has arrived at a belief which he is sure is (for him) a certain one: namely, the fact of his own existence. On the assumption that the only "tool" he has used to get this "piece of truth" is the "method of clear and distinct perception", Descartes concludes that having used the method is the mark of a true belief.[9] (His argument for the soundness of the method makes use of the reasoning Quine suggests we use when doing epistemology: we assume to be true what we believe to be true and then explain how we came to believe it.)

Embedded in Descartes' argument for the method is an assumption that evidence is self-announcing. The method he has used to arrive at the certain truth of his own existence is, in fact, a familiar one: he has put forth a hypothesis and then considered and replied to objections to it.[10] Beginning with the question "am I not at least something?"[11], Descartes has considered objections to the idea that he is, answered each, and run out of objections. To conclude that beliefs arrived at by the use of this method are certain, Descartes needs to assume that all of the evidence relevant to the hypothesis with which one begins, will, so to speak, declare itself. (He also needs to assume that the matter of where the hypothesis came from is unimportant. But, here, as we know, he is in good company.)

Descartes' knower is not, in the end, as passive a "receiver of evidence" as the argument might suggest. In the Fourth Meditation, faced with the problem of explaining how error is possible despite a method that insures certainty, Descartes argues that knowers play an active part in the acquisition of beliefs—and here separates, firmly and decisively, "the knower" from what is "known". To avoid error, Descartes argues, the knower has to "withhold assent" from what has not been "clearly and distinctly perceived".[12] The linchpin of the argument is that acquiring a belief involves an act of the will.[13]

Descartes' solution to the "problem of error" accomplishes a number of things.[14] It establishes that error is not an inherent by-product of the nature of the human intellect, or of the method used in the Second Meditation and discovered and justified in the Third. The solution reaffirms that evidence is self-announcing, and it establishes that evidence is independent of the knower. The knower has "only" to *not* "will to believe" until all of that evidence is in.[15] And, finally, though the knower has an active part to play in the acquisition of true beliefs, it is only in the alleged "willing". The *content* of true beliefs, of knowledge, will be determined solely by the evidence; the latter, given the chance (given, that is, that we do not "will to believe" precipitously), will announce itself unequivocally. Thus, without a failure of the will, what is known will be "uncontaminated" by the knower's personal signature.

Many of us have given up the views that prompted some of the issues Descartes has to contend with in the "Meditations"—in particular, the view that science aims at or could achieve "certain knowledge". Though Descartes' "method" is recognized as good scientific method, we are no longer convinced, at least we ought not to be, that it is possible to know that all the evidence is in. Some of us have also come to recognize that hypotheses are no more self-announcing than evidence, so that writing off the issue of where they come from in an account of how knowledge develops is not justifiable. Moreover, even if we have no objection to transcendental arguments, we can recognize that the "certain truth" that convinced Descartes that the method was foolproof was not one he understood or arrived at in isolation from other of his beliefs.[16]

But much else at work in these arguments continues to influence us. Descartes' view of "the knower" as a solitary receiver of the evidence provided by the world, and the related assumption that evidence announces itself, contribute substantially to the traditional ideal of objectivity we set out to explore. Given views about knowers and evidence that incorporate or build from Descartes' arguments, objectivity requires the separation of the particular identity or subjective interests of an individual knower from the process, given Descartes' description of it, best called "knowledge acquisition".[17] Such separation insures that "only the evidence" determines the direction in which knowledge develops or the fate of a particular hypothesis. And although we are no longer tempted to think that acquiring beliefs involves an act of will, we have retained the view that one can or will, if one is "too interested", force the evidence or a conclusion before it is warranted.

Eventually, the knower/known dichotomy and the view of "objectivity" it underwrites became fused with the third view noted above as underlying the traditional understanding of objectivity: the view that with the exception of those values taken to be constitutive of science, science should be free of values—or, as Quine describes things, science should be "divorced" from values.

The relationship between the ideal of a "value-free" science and the views of knowers and evidence we are considering is neither extraneous nor accidental. Descartes' compromise with the church—in effect, an agreement to cleave the world in two, separating values and facts in its severance of mind and body, the spiritual and material—is, at its core, a covenant to leave the business of values to something *other than* science. The covenant and the compromise it facilitated were made to enable science to go about the business of finding out "how things are" without interference, and at the time, it was a good bargain.

But in order to enter into this particular convenant to facilitate the compromise, Descartes had to issue a blank check: that knowledge of the material world is different in kind from knowledge of values, and that science would concern itself only with the former.

From its inception, the compromise has been a tense one. For some, Descartes' bifurcation of knowledge collapsed, and with it the covenant, as science got into the business of providing explanations for areas previously designated as the province of spiritual knowledge or moral theorists, as it began to offer explanations for human origins, psychology, sexuality, behaviors, and, in explaining these, human values. Darwin, Freud, the social sciences, and Sociobiologists and others, like Quine, who use natural selection to explain (and thus, justify) values, breach the chasm Descartes thought would separate science and values.[18]

But breaches of this kind are by no means the only important tension provoked by the covenant. Some of us are uneasy with the idea that moral and political values should be free floating, disengaged from science in the broadest sense, and unfettered by the standards and knowledge that evolve within science. We are uncomfortable with the view, advocated by some who hold moral theory and political views in high regard and also by those who do not, that values, including political values, are not subject to empirical controls.

Convinced that not all values or value systems, not all politics or political practices, are created equal, we are also tempted to think that the promotion, evaluation, and justification of values and political practices, without connection to science in the broadest sense, are propaganda—perhaps benign enough when limited to philosophy journals, but potentially of great consequence. The separation of values and politics from science, the granting to these their own, and allegedly "nonempirical" domains, contributes to the view that if values or politics are involved, objectivity is not—in short, that ideology has a field day. The latter worry builds, unequivocally, on the bifurcation of knowledge Descartes agreed to.

Equally troubling given the technological possibilities yielded by contemporary science, is a science unfettered and unconstrained by values other than "knowledge for its own sake". Even were we to think that the directions of scientific knowledge are determined solely by the logic of science and/or unmediated empirical evidence (and most of us presumably no longer do think this is so), it is not clear that the value of knowledge for its own sake should be expected, by itself, to successfully and safely guide scientific research. Currently, the stakes are far too high to grant "knowledge for its own sake" such status.

Increasingly, the concern to defend or to refute the special status of the value exposes the fact that an ideal of a science "distanced" from social, political,and ethical issues, concerns, and values is, as Sibyl Cohen notes, "an ideal we have chosen to the exclusion of others".[19] That such distance is not an inevitable feature of science is indicated by our ability to imagine sciences that concern themselves with whether proposed research should be undertaken, and we have recent examples of scientists asking precisely that question of proposed research, with some deciding not to engage in it.[20]

A third kind of tension has become pronounced in the past five decades. Descartes' compromise and the view of objectivity to which it contributes require that there are funds to cover his blank check: that we are able to separate ways of knowing into two distinct kinds, that the things to be known are also able to be so divided, and more fundamentally, that we are able to separate ourselves into "knowing beings" and "beings who value"—with only the first aspect of each bifurcation finding its way into science. Each of these divisions is necessary to achieving both a "value-free" science and a moral and political realm whose standards, bases, and justifications are different in kind and independent of those evolving in science.

Feminist science criticism and other recent science criticism[21] makes it clear that scientists do bring their social identities, their political and sex/gendered experiences, and their values into the laboratory and that we often fail to achieve sciences so envisioned. One way of construing the source of these failures is that neither we, nor the knowledge we seek and construct, can be so divided.

Having inherited Descartes' covenant, we continue to struggle with the tensions it provokes, and though it may not be clear how we will ultimately resolve them, it is clear that they require our concerted attention. In short, the blank check Descartes wrote is due, and the covenant, for a number of reasons, must be reappraised.

It may be that we will eventually find a way of covering the blank check and of living up to the covenant, but our past and our present give us little reason to think so. We might be tempted to try on the grounds that the only alternative to a value-free science is relativism. But that conclusion requires two additional assumptions: that there are no grounds for choosing between and evaluating values and political views, and that there is no alternative to the understanding of objectivity we have inherited. These assumptions, as we have seen, are deeply related, and to the extent that they are, they stand or fall together.

Alternatively, we might recognize that there are deep problems with the blank check or the covenant or both but be interested in keeping up at least a charade of upholding Descartes' covenant because we view the covenant as a "noble lie"—a mystification that makes it more difficult for science to be used to advance social and political oppression, or to bring about or be used to justify human suffering.

"Nazi science" indicates that these worries are warranted. A mix of science and politics can enable cruelty and suffering of unspeakable magnitude. Less dramatic examples of the harm that can result from a mix of the two also abound. Science has repeatedly been used to "prove" the inferiority of groups and to justify divisions in power, opportunity, and well-being. We have studied the "IQ", the shape of the brain, the size of the brain—and whatever else we could think of —of blacks, women, eastern Europeans, and other groups, in attempts to find explanations and claiming to find them, for the social, political, and economic inequities and oppression that might otherwise have been explained as the effects of institutional prejudice. In many cases we have furthered the prejudice and the inequities by "underwriting" them with "scientific evidence".

But while the dangers are real and warrant our most serious and collective attention, the "noble lie" is far more dangerous. It precludes scrutiny and evaluation of values and politics that are incorporated in research questions, methodologies, and theories, thus allowing all of these to go unchallenged. The need for an alternative approach can be seen to be compelling when we recognize that the lie underwrites science's cognitive authority at the same time that it removes from the bounds of critical discussion the values and politics that do find their way into and are reinforced by scientific research. Sociobiology serves as a tragic example of unsophisticated and unsupported politics posing as "apolitical truth".

It would seem that the only remaining justification for maintaining the lie is that we harbor a basic skepticism about values and politics (a skepticism that also underwrites the traditional ideal of objectivity) and, relatedly, a basic skepticism about us. If there were, in fact, no basis for deciding between values, or between political views and practices, and if we could not trust ourselves to arrive at values and political views that are at least harmless, then we cannot afford to let down our commitment to the barrier we have tried to construct, however unreal or unrealizable that barrier is.

I do not share the pessimism about values or politics, nor that about us, that would justify the mystification involved here. First, when we do subject vales and political views and practices to "empirical controls" as feminists and others do, it becomes clear that all values and politics are *not* equally defensible. Second, abandoning the covenant would allow the work of scrutinizing and evaluating the values incorporated in science to become recognized as part of the *doing* of science.

Finally, if we also recognize that science communities are not autonomous entities—that the knowledge developed in them shapes, and is shaped by, knowledge and practices in the larger community in which they are embedded—then the work of wrestling with the values and politics underlying or incorporated in scientific research can be recognized to be a matter for our larger community to undertake. Though there is no guarantee that our larger community will not make a mistake in evaluating the values or politics implied in or incorporated in scientific research, there is far less security in the current situation.

The mystification leaves the business of values and politics in science to a relative few—who are, by and large, steadfastly committed to the view that science has nothing to do with values or politics, a view, unlike almost any other, they are singularly unwilling to test by reference to evidence. There are no moral grounds for leaving the question of whether science incorporates these to that small a group of our larger community, particularly a group to whom we grant cognitive authority.

In beginning to build an alternative to Descartes' covenant, and thus to the traditional ideal of objectivity, I propose that we incorporate what we are learning about the nature of "knowing", the nature of "knowledge" including that of values and politics, and the nature of science communities. We will need to look to science without the artificial boundaries invoked in the covenant and underlying the ideal. And these will not be future sciences, but our own. These are in fact without the boundaries that underwrote the traditional view of objectivity and the covenant.

Knowledge, Knowing, and Science Communities

The larger discussion began with structural metaphors: with building blocks and signposts, and this was in keeping with the metaphor of science as a structure or building, a metaphor that Descartes used to describe science, and one that has lasted for as long as the search for the "foundations of science" has continued. For Descartes, the "edifice of science" was an inverted pyramid, secured by "certain truth" at its base, and growing, by cumulative and certain steps, themselves inexorably determined (without failures of our wills) by a logic inherent to inquiry, and evidence that announced itself.

We next considered the challenges to the view that the "structure" of science rests on an "extrascientific" foundation, and ultimately the demise of the view. For Hempel, Nagel, and Popper, science remains an "edifice" with a clear "empirical basis". Popper thinks the edifice of science will continue to grow cumulatively, determined by logic and evidence, but the presence of theory at the base leads him to conclude that the structure's "pilings . . . rise above a swamp".

Kuhn also uses a building metaphor to describe science, but in his analysis the structure of science begins to blur. Rather than a Cartesian inverted pyramid or a Popperian edifice, Kuhn finds science to be "a ramshackle structure with little coherence among its various parts",[22] and sociology, more so than either logic or evidence, determining the direction of its long periods of detailed refinements and, more so than either, the directions of its periodic and fitful razings and new construction. A connection between evidence and science is tenuously and subtly present in Kuhn's view that it is the detailed work of refining that characterizes normal science and the obstinacy of nature that provoke the fitful razing and rebuilding. But the rebuilding is without clear plan until philosophers and historians "rationally reconstruct" things long after the fact. The decision to build according to a new plan is, when it is made, literally a leap of faith forced by professional pressure.

Common to Descartes' and Popper's metaphors is the notion that science is a product, a body of knowledge, and that this body of knowledge has a "base". For Kuhn, science is an activity, and he finds much in the product and earlier building metaphors difficult, if not impossible, to maintain. Common to all three and to the post logical positivist tradition represented in the work of Hempel and Nabel, science, either as product or activity, is a structure or entity unto itself—an island that is self-constructed and reconstructed, and self-regulating. The seeds were sown for Hempel's and Nagel's account of science's objectivity, Popper's despair of science's foundations, and Kuhn's incommensurability.

As we considered Quine's view of science, building metaphors gave way to networks, fabrics, and arches. As a bridge of our own making, the network of science was neither simply product nor process. The soundness of the bridges we construct is determined solely by their coherence with our experiences, themselves shaped by theory but constrained by their coherence with our experiences of the world, and by their coherence with one another, and there could have been different bridges, commensurate with our experience.

Of most significance, science, Quine insists, is not an isolated network, As what had long been viewed as the "load-bearing" walls connecting theories and theorizing with an extrascientific foundation began to collapse, Quine was exposing necessary and fundamental connections between our common-sense efforts to organize our experience and those more self-conscious efforts viewed by the postpositivist and Kuhnian traditions as exhaustive of science.

The network metaphor reflects Quine's distrust of most (but not all) of the "boundaries" traditionally constructed between science and "other things", and many of the alleged divisions he challenges we found also fundamentally challenged in and by feminist criticism. In the two frameworks, several specific boundaries constructed to isolate science from other things collapse, in part of their own weight and in part as a result of the challenges Quine and feminists posed to them. We can now see that the network metaphor is the sounder of the metaphors for science. The connections Quine maintains are there, are there—but there are more besides, and these a notion of objectivity must encompass.

The alleged boundary separating metaphysics and science collapsed for several reasons. We have found that science cannot avoid metaphysics, and through a consideration of Quine's positions and issues raised by feminist science critics, we gained ways to undermine an alleged boundary constructed to insure that our role in organizing our experiences was largely a passive one—that a boundary could be drawn between our theorizing and the world about which we theorize, and that science as product could be extricated from the activity of theorizing.

Quine's view of the relationship also incorporated a way of locating the metaphysical commitments embodied in theorizing: of making explicit what a given theory, question, or methodology *commits us to*. In addition, his views, issues in feminist criticism,and a current debate in the biological sciences indicate that metaphysical commitments are not arbitrary—they will be related to the current state of science, including common-sense views—and that they can be evaluated and compared. This indicates that science can lead to better metaphysics, to metaphysics that helps to inform and guide science. So, it is now possible not only to envision sciences that incorporate metaphysical commitments different than those currently prevalent but to envision a canon of "scientific method" and ideal of objectivity that includes self-conscious attention to the metaphysical commitments embedded in research questions, methodologies, and theories. What we are never in a position to do, I have used Quine's positions to argue, is to accept a theory and reject the metaphysics inherent in it.

There is a further consequence of the relationship between metaphysics and science. And that is that feminist criticism of current metaphysical commitments must be *within* science, broadly construed. We do not first discover or decide what to talk about, and then what to say about it. Metaphysical commitments emerge and evolve in the process of theorizing. If our present metaphysical commitments give way to others or are giving way to others, it will be, or it is occurring within, not prior to, that process. So, we can also see that the project of evaluating the metaphysical commitments in research and of proposing alternatives can include and be prompted by political views and experiences, for these have prompted feminist attention to the metaphysical commitments incorporated in research programs, no less than such views and experiences were incorporated in the theories and methodologies feminists criticize.

We have known for some time that another boundary, that alleged to separate theory and observation, cannot be drawn—or at least not in the way, or to the ends, that scientists and philosophers traditionally attempted to draw it. But the relationship of theories to observations is recast by Quine's insight that few sentences have their own specificable empirical content, and by his recognition that even our most basic sentences are underdetermined by the evidence available for them.

Each of these things undermines the notion that there are pieces of evidence available to us in isolation from a larger network of theories that we are taking for granted. They underscore that evidence is not self-announcing, that science is a bridge of our own making, and that there is slippage between the bridge and the evidence for it. We should not be surprised that we find it necessary to refashion aspects of that bridge, however long-standing—albeit, a piece at a time.

Feminist science criticism has now expanded our understanding of the kinds of theories and beliefs that can shape "scientific" observation. Our experiences of sex/gender and politics are factors in our most systematic and rigorous theorizing. Because these are factors in feminist theorizing no less than they are in the theories feminist criticize, we cannot reasonably maintain the view that politics and sex/gender have nothing to do with science—either good science or bad. Quine's insistence that "everything we say about the world" is connected just needs to be taken more literally than he or many of us thought.

We would expect to find such relationships, without the alleged boundaries between common sense and science, political experience and science, or sex/gendered experience and science, and we would not be tempted to assume that feminists must be doing something "other than" science when they criticize aspects of science. And without the artificial boundaries, it is also possible to see that conscious and critical attention to the ways our social and political experiences, including those of sex/gender, shape our theorizing in scientific communities is necessary to "good science" and objectivity.

The importance of conscious attention to the relationships between our experiences outside scientific communities and our theorizing within them is also a consequence of the collapse of another alleged boundary. Our sense of the lack of a distinction between the "context" in which a theory is offered and that within which it is evaluated deepened as it became clear that theories can not only survive but thrive when failing to meet even the most narrow construals of "scientific method", and when there is no apparent and pressing gap in our knowledge to warrant their development. Sociobiology stands out in this regard, for its acceptance is clearly related to factors other than the alleged poverty of the social sciences or a lack of alternative theories of human cultural evolution. But historic and current research in the biological sciences into "sex differences" and other issues we have considered also indicate that what has been separated into "contexts" of discovery and justification is one and the same context, and that the context of science encompasses more than the context of a scientific community (as Kuhn maintains) or current "scientific" theories (as the postlogical positivists would have it). Given science's cognitive authority, recognizing the context of science to be inclusive of theories, beliefs, and practices in the larger community, including political beliefs and practices, makes the need for conscious attention to the role of these in shaping scientific theorizing compelling.

I have urged that Quine is correct in his contention that one of the more important of the boundaries traditionally invoked to explain and insure the separation of the knower and what is known, the alleged boundary between epistemology and science, is not real. We explored his arguments against the possibility of "extrascientific" foundations for science, and those to the effect that epistemology is always deeply related to and interdependent with our other theories. Quine's arguments indicate that we do not complete an epistemology, a theory of theorizing, first and then do substantive science. These proceed apiece, each influencing the other.

These views are borne out by feminist rethinking of some of the basic assumptions of empiricism. It is because epistemology and other theories are interrelated that we currently find ourselves asking how sex/gender and political experience could be factors in scientific theorizing, how either could have a bearing on the content of science. These questions have become possible because of feminist insights into science, and the latter have become possible because there are clear relationships between the theories we construct in scientific communities and our experiences, practices, and beliefs in the larger community.

We have also found there to be no hard-and-fast boundaries between standards of evidence and going theories. Standards of evidence are not "pretheoretical"; they are adopted as theories are adopted and they evolve as theories evolve. Quine's positions and feminist science criticism also indicate that standards of evidence and theories are community bound. The development of feminist scholarship indicates that we can come to disagree in terms of some standards of evidence—though, I have argued, not in all. Because there are no global chasms in standards of evidence or theories, discussion of both can proceed. So, self-conscious attention to epistemology, to standards of evidence, and to the differences between communities are also part of the doing of science—not antecedent, or irrelevant, to it.

The interdependence of epistemology and science, and of evidence and going theories, along with our deepening sense of the necessity of interpersonal relationships for "knowing", have led us to reconsider the possibility of a solipsistic knower—an individual who could "know" independently of social context and practices, and "know" independently of the theories that emerge from and shape these. When we pay attention to the dependence of the young and to the lack of pretheoretical experience, it is clear that an autonomous, solipsistic knower is impossible. Communities know, individuals only derivately so.

The collapse of "boundaries" between solitary knowers is one of the most important consequences of feminist science criticism. The collapse undermines the traditional skeptical worries that focusing on individuals provoked or encouraged, and it permits us to characterize our current situation in a way that can inform and guide us.

The problem of how sex/gender or political experience can be a factor in our scientific theorizing, and currently a variable in that theorizing, becomes less acute when we recognize that our appropriate focus is communities rather than individuals. We are not discovering relationships between the sex of an individual, or, in any interesting sense, an *individual*'s views about sex/gender, to the content of her or his theorizing—and, therefore, to the content of science. We are relating experiences of sex/gender and politics, themselves *inherently social*, and views about sex/gender and politics, also *inherently social*, to the theorizing we do in scientific communities—itself a social endeavor in every sense. The relationships that make it possible for an individual to have beliefs and to know, and those that obtain between the various aspects of our experiences, are not features of a special situation.

The critical self-reflection warranted by the collapse of these traditional boundaries is not, then, a matter of working to erase an individual's signature from the content of science. There's a problem, first of all, with the "individual" part of the construal. When such reflection is undertaken by an individual, it involves reflecting on one's *social identity*—on the social, sex/gendered, racial, class, and political experiences and beliefs that one has as a member of a community. And in a society like ours in which experiences are divided by such things, it involves conscious attention to the special experiences one has as a member of one or several subcommunities within the larger community, in addition to those we share with our larger community and, ultimately, our world community.

Moreover, if we recognize that individuals are knowers only in a derivative sense, then "self"-reflection can be seen to be, at bottom, something a community needs to undertake, a matter in which those of us who are members of a scientific community critically reflect on the practices, assumptions, metaphysical commitments, and so on of our community.

And, in fact, the community for whom critical self-reflection is appropriate cannot even be limited to those special communities we recognize as science communities. The alleged boundary between those communities and our larger community, deeply related to other boundaries that have collapsed, is also a false boundary.

As an "epistemological community", a community in which knowledge is constructed and shared, and experiences are possible and shaped, our largest community is, in every sense, a science community. The relationships between scientific communities and our larger community include the communicating of the knowledge developed within scientific communities to our larger community and the consequences of this for our common-sense beliefs, experiences, and practices. And the "epistemological relationship" is not a one-way relationship.

Science is not autonomous from common-sense dealings with the world, or from social and political interests, and values. The beliefs, practices, and experiences of scientists as members of our larger community both permit and shape the theorizing done in these special communities. The relationships between these communities are multilayered and deep.

In considering the implications of the collapse of these boundaries for our developing an alternative understanding of objectivity, I want to return to one of Quine's metaphors for science.

> Neurath has likened science to a boat which, if we are to rebuild it, we must rebuild plank by plank while staying afloat in it. . . .
> Our boat stays afloat because at each alteration we keep the bulk of it intact as a going concern.[23]

The good news is that once we stop erecting and promoting boundaries between our ways of organizing things, and between our various practices, and we stop searching for (or despairing of) extrascientific foundations for science, we are in a position to recognize that the impetus for the changes feminist criticism calls for in our views about science has come from *within* science.

As I argued earlier, unless feminists have been doing something other than constructing theories and naming objects, organizing experiences, discovering relationships between our ways of organizing and explaining experience, subjecting beliefs and claims to critical evaluation, and paying attention to evidence, then we must conclude that feminist criticism is within science. To do these things requires going theories and standards of evidence. Thus it is from within science that the need to reconsider things, including our understandings of who knows, how they know, and what they know, has emerged.

But although I have stressed the continuities between feminist arguments and what we recognize as science, the science in which feminists are engaged does differ in two fundamental respects from how science, by and large, is currently practiced. The differences of consequence are that feminists are self-conscious in their inclusion of values and they insist on subjecting values to empirical controls. If there is more distinguishing what feminists are doing from what we recognize as science, we will ultimately, of course, need to name it, and if feminist claims are justified, these new methods will be incorporated in our understandings of what doing science is. But I suspect feminists have been doing precisely these things—albeit with a deepened and broader understanding of how much is relevant to science, and that understanding, if it proves sound, we will find to be related to experience.

What this suggests is that we should not lament the lapsing of the traditional boundaries between metaphysics, epistemology, science, methodology, values, and politics. Rather, accepting science as being value laden allows us to make sense out of both scientific practice and values, including political values. Scrutinizing and evaluating the values, political and otherwise, incorporated in our approaches to human and nonhuman nature, and taking responsibility for their consequences, must, without the assumption of false boundaries, become part and parcel of good scientific practice. And because not anything goes in science, insofar as values, politics, and science are interfused, the same holds of values and politics. When we subject values and political practices and views to scrutiny, we are in a position to see that not all values or value systems, not all politics and political views, are created equal.

The most fundamental thing feminist criticism indicates about scientific communities is that these are far more in the thick of social and political currents than many of us had thought; they are really subcommunities of a larger science community. Science will always reflect the society within which it is embedded. But if society is to change in ways feminists envision, science will need to be changing apace. Alternatively put, the relationships we have explored indicate that a different science and a different society will come about together, if at all. A different science will not be *the result* or by-product of a different kind of society, but part and parcel of any such society coming to be.

Whence Now?

If feminist science criticism is part of science broadly construed, if the views about knowing that underwrite the traditional ideal of objectivity are untenable, and if our largest community is, in fact, our largest science community, then clearly it is time to reject Descartes' covenant.

It is premature to say what the future of science will be like in the absence of that covenant. Clearly, we will need to use the insights outlined to develop a new notion of objectivity, but not one that is unrecognizable. In large part what has sustained the covenant has been a basic skepticism about values and politics, that they cannot be subjected to evaluation, and the view that science is an autonomous undertaking. Feminist criticism indicates we must reject both views. The suggestion that values and politics can be objective is not new. An enormous amount of ink has been spilled in the past attempting to show that one or another set of a priori values embodies the objective truth about morality or politics. Many of us have found these uniformly unconvincing perhaps because, with a few notable exceptions, we have not taken seriously the view that knowledge is of a piece, that how things are in part determines how things ought to be, and that how things ought to be in part determines how we take things to be. It is time we did so.

I am not here imagining a simple intermingling of present values and politics and present science. Once we abandon the view that science, values, and politics are forever disparate, we can expect our science, our values, and our politics to evolve, and each to inform the others and, perhaps, ultimately to become indistinguishable. But what direction the evolution will take, and what the form of future science inclusive of values and politics will be, we cannot now say. That is something that will unfold through our collective and reflective endeavors.

Notes

1. See, e.g., Jaggar [1983], esp. chap. 11, and Harding [1983A, 1983B, 1986].

2. See, e.g., Harding [1983A, 1983B, 1986] and Jaggar [1983], esp. chap. 11. Discussions that also imply that nonfeminists (or men) cannot know what feminists (or women) know include Flax [1983], Harstock [1983], and Rose [1983].

3. Feminist standpoint epistemologies, for example, are concerned to explain the epistemologically advantaged standpoint feminists enjoy (although some, including Harstock [1983] imply that it is women who have such an advantage and that this is grounded in their labor). As will emerge in this and subsequent chapters, I am concerned that the work to date to develop these epistemologies suggests that there are things nonfeminists (or men) *could* not know. See, for example, Flax [1983], Harding [1983B, 1986], Harstock [1983], Jaggar [1983], esp. chap. 11, and Rose [1983]. The issue of "epistemological chasms" is addressed in several contexts in my larger discussion, and feminist standpoint epistemologies are discussed in the conclusion of Chapter One and at some length in Chapter Six.

4. Bartky [1977], p. 25.

5. See, e.g., Harding [1983B, 1986], Jaggar [1983], esp. chap. 11, and Rose [1983].

6. See, e.g., the epistemology ascribed to Liberal feminists in Jaggar [1983], pp. 355–58, which Jaggar characterizes as "[the] neo-positivist development of ... the empiricist strand of Cartesian epistemology", and the account of feminist empiricism Harding gives in [1986], pp. 24–26 and 161–62. See also Harding [1983B].

7. See, e.g., Fee [1981], Harding [1983A, 1983B, 1986], and Jaggar [1983], esp. chap. 11.

8. Harding [1986], p. 25.

9. I am paraphrasing Harding's title "The Science Question in Feminism" [1986].

10. Feminists are not alone, of course, in identifying empiricism as positivism. Sociologists of knowledge Barnes and Bloor also do so. See Barnes [1977], p. 49, and Bloor [1977].

11. A number of feminist theorists use the term 'sex/gender' rather than 'sex' or 'gender', and I will do so in this discussion. Current research in anthropology, sociology, psychology, neurobiology, reproductive biology, and history indicates a dynamic interaction between the biological, sociological, and psychological aspects of sex/gender. This indicates that "women" and "men" are not simply biological or simply sociological categories. Some of this research will be discussed in later chapters, and an overview of feminist research is provided by *Signs: Journal of Women in Culture and Society* (1975–present). See also Bleier [1984, 1988A, 1988B], Harding [1986], Hubbard, Henifin, and Freid [1982], and Jaggar [1983, 1984]. When I am discussing research that claims or attempts to find biological bases for what feminists and others argue are actually socially determined differences between women and men, I use the phrase 'sex difference' because the research is committed to there being sex differences. When I discuss the attribution of gender (femininity or masculinity) to nonhuman objects—like science and nature—I use the term 'gender'.

12. Kuhn's notion of the incommensurability of competing paradigms is discussed in Chapters Two and Five. Such "epistemological chasms" are also discussed in Chapters Five and Six.

13. Harding [1986], p. 49. I believe it might also distinguish my approach from that taken by Harstock [1983], in which what Harstock calls "a metatheoretical claim" appears to serve the role of "circle breaker". Jaggar [1983] maintains that the justificatory status of an epistemology is always circular (see, esp., the introduction to chap. 11). She locates the connection in the views of human nature shared by a political theory and its epistemology. My arguments for the radical interdependence of science and epistemology build on Quine's and are different.

14. This includes the "dogmas" Harding discusses [1986], pp. 36–52. Although many (if not most) empiricist philosophers and scientists have certainly maintained positions very much like those she outlines (e.g. "that science is a fundamentally unique kind of social activity", p. 38), none of these "dogmas" is a logical consequence of the empiricist account of evidence (nor does Harding claim that any is). As will become clear in later discussion, one of the most influential of contemporary empiricists, Quine, does not hold most of the positions she discusses. This indicates that the views Harding appropriately ascribes to many scientists and empiricists are not necessary to *empiricism*.

15. The literature is extensive. My way of outlining issues here follows Harding [1983A]. See, also, Addelson [1983], Bleier [1984, 1988A, 1988B], Gould [1977, 1981], Harding [1986], Harding and O'Barr [1987], Hubbard, Henifin, and Fried [1982], Keller [1982, 1983A, 1983B, 1985A, 1985B], Levins [1977], and Sayers [1982]. See also *Signs* (1975–present).

16. Again, the literature is extensive, but I have found the clearest and most inclusive discussion to be Addelson [1983]. My views about science communities are very much influenced by that paper, as will be clear in the discussion of Chapter Four. See also Bleier [1984, 1988A], Haraway [1978A, 1978B, 1988], and Harding [1986].

17. See, for further discussion of the "embeddedness" of science communities in the larger social and political context, the works cited in nn. 15 and 16, and the discussion and notes of Chapters Four and Five.

18. The notion of "cognitive authority" is introduced and developed in Addelson [1983]. We will consider her analysis of that authority and its consequences in Chapter Four.

19. In responding to a question about Quine, Sandra Harding once described his work as representing "the bankruptcy of empiricism" (remarks following "The Science Question in Feminism", delivered at Villanova University [1983A]). I think we agree that his work represents one way of working out key empiricist ideas, and this is also Harding's approach in [1986], pp. 36–37.

20. Quoted in Shebar [1987], p. 47. Several feminist theorists have recently discussed specific aspects of Quine's work. See Harding [1986], pp. 36–37 and Addelson [1990].

21. Not everyone would agree that Kuhn's work should be characterized as being within the *empiricist* tradition in philosophy of science. I think it can be so characterized for reasons that will become clear in Chapters Two and Five. In particular, I argue that his account represents something like "the flip side" of views held by Hempel and Nagel.

22. See, e.g., Harding [1983A, 1986]. The issues will be discussed in Chapters Two, Five, and Six.

23. Quine, "On the Nature of Moral Values" in [1981].

24. Arguments against the modern commitment to individualism are being developed in a number of areas. See, e.g., Parfit [1984] (esp. Pt. III), for arguments against an individualist metaphysics of persons. See Scheman [1983] and Addelson and Potter [1989] for arguments against what Addelson calls "epistemological individualism" that are somewhat different from mine. MacKinnon [1981], Harstock [1983], and Harding [1983A, 1986] imply that focusing on individuals is at least inappropriate in explaining how feminists have come to know what they do, and Jaggar [1983] uses Scheman's arguments in Scheman [1983] to challenge the self/society dichotomy that forms the basis of Liberal political theory. In [1983A] Harding cites a commitment to individualism as the most basic reason why empiricism cannot accommodate feminist claims and in [1986] she claims that feminist empiricists "subvert" empiricism because they claim that women (or feminists) as a group have an epistemological advantage. Problems with individualism in social and political theory have, of course, been exposed by Marxists, socialists, and feminists. See, for an overview of this literature and of arguments against the self/society dichotomy, Jaggar [1983].

25. My use of the term 'acquire' here reflects the view, argued for in the course of the larger discussion, that standards of evidence and knowledge are public and

relative to the current state of science, broadly construed, and that beliefs are constrained by these and by experience. I will argue that knowledge, to the core, is socially constructed, not passively acquired—but that it is not constructed by individuals but by groups.

26. As I noted in n. 24, Harding [1983A, 1986] cites individualism as the major obstacle to reconciling empiricism and feminist science criticism. See also Jaggar [1983], chap. 11.

27. This echoes a very important discussion, Addelson [1983]. It will be clear in Chapters Four and Seven that her discussion has greatly influenced my views about science communities. I am also indebted to Sibyl Cohen for helping me to clarify my views in this section and in Chapter Seven.

28. The expressions, and the insight, are Harding's in [1986].

29. Dyke [1988], p. ix.

30. Ibid.

31. Keller [1985A], p. 73.

32. Quine [1960], p. 4. Thus, my view of the relationship of feminist science criticism to what is recognized as science is different from that implied in some feminist science criticism. Not only do I think feminist criticism has evolved within science, both narrowly and broadly construed, I think there is a need for a critique from within a broadened empiricism of views held by some empiricists. Such criticism, although only one of the approaches that should be taken, furthers dialogue between feminists and other scientists. See also n. 68 of Chapter One.

CHAPTER ONE

1. See, e.g., Collins [1981].

2. That empiricism is a theory of evidence, and neither a theory of truth nor a particular account of science, will emerge in this chapter and Chapter Three. See also Quine's argument that empiricism is a theory of evidence in his "On the Very Idea of a Third Dogma" in [1981].

3. Quine [1960], pp. 1–3.

4. Ibid., p. 3.

5. I am not assuming or endorsing a language/ontology distinction here. I will later support Quine's contention that we cannot separate the objects we talk about from our ways of talking about them.

6. See, e.g., Jaggar [1983], pp. 355–57. Jaggar's description of the empiricist account of "knowing" is an accurate description of traditional and positivist accounts, but it does not reflect the changes in empiricism that have occurred in the last five decades, in large part because of Quine's challenges to logical positivist and "post logical" positivist positions. I will discuss Jaggar's account in Chapter Six.

7. See, e.g., Scheman [1983], Harding [1983B, 1986], and Jaggar [1983] whose accounts of empiricists' views of epistemology are fundamentally different from Quine's views.

8. Quine, "On Mental Entities" in [1966], p. 212.

9. Quine, "Posits and Reality" in [1966], p. 239. For those who are not familiar

with Quine's work, this paper and "Two Dogmas of Empiricism" in [1963] touch on some of the most central themes in his work.

10. Quine, "Posits and Reality" in [1966], p. 240.

11. Stimulation of our sensory receptors is, of course, triggered by verbal as well as nonverbal stimuli.

12. Harding [1983B] rejects sociology of knowledge as an adequate epistemology on the grounds that it is unable to make such distinctions.

13. See Barnes [1977], p. 21, who explicitly denies that sociology of knowledge should offer criteria for judging beliefs and theories.

14. These traditions will be discussed in Chapter Two.

15. The view of correspondence I am referring to here is the notion that sentences and theories "correspond" to nonlinguistic reality, a relation much explored and debated in the philosophy of science and language over the last decades. See, e.g., Quine's "On the Very Idea of a Third Dogma" in [1981], "Speaking of Objects" and "Ontological Relativity" in [1969], and "Posits and Reality" in [1966].

16. I have found that a number of philosophers view Tarski's theory of truth as a correspondence theory of truth, and attribute that view of Tarski's theory to Quine and, therefore, a correspondence theory of truth to Quine. Bob Barnes and Norm Melchert do, for example (private conversation). For reasons that will begin to emerge in this chapter and become clearer in Chapter Three, Quine does not—indeed, Quine *could not*—hold a correspondence theory of truth, because he denies that there is any sense to be made of a distinction between that which we talk about and the way we talk about it. So, there is no notion of "correspondence" as the latter relies on a dualist scheme of "organizing scheme" and "that to be organized", that can be made out in his work. Moreover, attributing anything other than a redundancy, or disappearance, "theory of truth" to Quine (with the exception of the use of the predicate 'true' in the special context noted below) including attributing a "pragmatic theory of truth" to him, misconstrues many of his positions and his most basic view of science. (For those unconvinced, Quine's "On the Very Idea of a Third Dogma" in [1981] should settle matters—at least in terms of what Quine considers himself committed to.) The reasons underlying Quine's denial of the dualism presupposed in correspondence theories will be discussed at length in Chapter Three.

17. I am grateful to Jack Nelson for this, and other insights, into Quine's work. For those who take the pragmatism in Quine's views as representing the general view that "the most we can ask of our theories is that they work *and not* that they be true", I draw attention to Quine's "Things and Their Place in Theories" in [1981]. The nature of Quine's pragmatism is also discussed in Chapter Three.

18. See, e.g., Quine "Two Dogmas of Empiricism" in [1963], especially the last section; Quine, "On the Very Idea of a Third Dogma" in [1981], pp. 38–42; and chap. 1 and 2 of [1960].

19. Again, see Quine, "On the Very Idea of a Third Dogma" in [1981], and Quine, "Two Dogmas of Empiricism" in [1963].

20. See n. 16, above.

21. The most fundamental reason why Quine's positions force the abandonment of "correspondence" is discussed above in n. 16.

22. Quine's denial of a dualism of a "world theorized about" and "our theorizing about the world" will not, because of its complexity, receive direct attention until Chapter Three.

23. I am grateful to Joe Volpe for the conversations we have had about the coherence of a radical skepticism. See also Chapter Three.

24. We are not, however, in discussing the grounds for "warranted belief", smuggling in a notion of "correspondence" by presupposing a distinction between a world we theorize about and our theorizing about it. We are relating *experiences* to warranted belief. It is via experience, itself shaped by theory, that the world constrains warranted belief. The notions of "experience" and "the world" involved in my claim will emerge in the discussion of Chapter Three.

25. Quine, "Things and Their Place in Theories" in [1981], p. 21.

26. The "strong program" in sociology of knowledge has been accused of this. See Barnes [1977], Bloor [1977], and Harding [1983B].

27. The literature is extensive and we will be considering some of it in Chapters Four and Five. See, e.g., Addelson [1983], Bleier [1984, 1988A, 1988B], Fee [1981, 1982, 1988], Haraway [1978A, 1978B, 1988], Harding [1983A, 1983B, 1986], Harding and O'Barr [1987], Keller [1983A, 1983B, 1985A, 1985B], Longino and Doell [1983], Reiter [1975], Rose [1983], and Sayers [1982]. An overview of the past decade of feminist research is provided by the last fifteen years of *Signs: Journal of Women in Culture and Society.*

28. Clearly many traditional thinkers thought sex/gender was a variable in terms of the abilities necessary to being a scientist, and many scientists (including some currently engaged in science) have discussed sex/gender and science. Some have maintained that science is "masculine"; others, that "women can't do science", as the discussion and notes of Chapter Four chronicle. But these positions have not found their way into discussions in contemporary empiricist philosophy of science, and their implications for the epistemology and content of science have not been considered. Nor are there categories available in contemporary empiricist accounts of science that would permit or prompt a discussion of issues having to do with sex/gender and science, as will become clear in the larger discussion. Indeed, current empiricist accounts of science rule out factors like sex/gender and politics in scientific theorizing—at least when things are going correctly. Other frameworks, Marxist science criticism, for example, do incorporate some of the categories that would make such discussions possible, and some Marxist science critics have discussed androcentrism and sexism in the sciences. See, for example, Dyke [1988], Gould [1977, 1981] and Lewontin, Rose, and Kamin [1984].

Good discussions of the historical associations of science with "masculinity" and men, and of nature with "femininity" and women, and the consequences of these associations for views about science and nature, for metaphysical assumptions, and for methodology are provided in Merchant [1980] and Keller [1983A, 1983B, 1985A].

29. I will be focusing on feminist scholarship concerned with contemporary

western societies including western science. See n. 11 of the Introduction for discussion of the term 'sex/gender'.

30. The literature in feminist scholarship is extensive. There is an extensive body of literature in which feminist scholars have explored relationships between views about women (or femininity), and men (or masculinity), and many aspects of traditional and contemporary thought. See, e.g., the collection of papers in Harding and Hintikka [1983], and Held [1985], Mahowald [1978], Ortner [1974], Spelman [1982], Bishop and Weinzweig [1979], and Spender [1981]. See, also, Bleier [1984, 1988A, 1988B], Merchant [1980], Grimshaw [1986], and Keller [1983A, 1983B, 1985A, 1985B].

Recent feminist scholarship is often more "reconstructive" in nature. See, for example, Addelson [1983], Arditti, Brennan, and Cavrak [1980], Bleier [1988A, 1988B], Dahlberg [1981], Gould [1984], Harding [1986], Harding and O'Barr [1987], Keller [1985A], Kittay and Meyers [1986], MacCormack and Strathern [1980], and Sherman and Beck [1979]. See also *Signs* [1975–present]. Anthologies whose contributors come from a number of fields include Eisenstein and Jardine [1980] and Spender [1981]. The Bibliography contains more references.

31. The last two decades have produced a substantial body of literature exploring women's activities and experiences. For overviews and bibliographies, see Jaggar [1983] and *Signs* [1975–present]. I have also included many references in the Bibliography. A significant amount of feminist research is focusing on the alternatives that women's perspectives and practices suggest to the dichotomous, dualist, oppositional, and hierarchical ways of organizing and thinking about the human experience and other aspects of nature that inform western thought. Some of the research has been prompted by, or has enabled, the illumination of problems with the modern commitment to "individualism" in social and political theory, epistemology, and moral theory. See, for example Whitbeck [1984] for a discussion of individualism and, specifically, the self/other dichotomy; Jaggar [1983] on the self/society and public/private dichotomies of Liberal political theory; and Scheman [1983], Harding [1986], and Addelson and Potter [1989] on what Addelson calls "epistemological individualism" (private conversation). In Chapter Six I argue that epistemological individualism is untenable.

32. The introduction to Harding and Hintikka [1983] clearly states that distortion and not "incompleteness" is at issue, and the view is increasingly evident in feminist discussions.

33. The discussion will be limited to the social organization of science communities in western societies. See the works cited in n. 27.

34. Addelson [1983].

35. See Addelson [1983], Bleier [1984], Harding [1983A, 1986], Keller [1983B, 1985A, 1985B] and Levins [1977].

36. See Harding [1986] for a clear overview of these questions.

37. However, as the discussions of Chapters Four and Five indicate, this has not precluded many male scientists from having doubts about whether women can "do science".

38. Some feminists are exploring a different question: namely, whether women "know" *differently*. See, e.g., Jaggar [1983] for an overview of the literature.

39. This section echoes Addelson [1983], although I think the "rationality" of science is only partly insured by its openness to criticism, as will become clear in the larger discussion.

40. See, e.g., Harding [1983A, 1986] and Jaggar [1983].

41. See Harding [1983A, 1983B, 1986] and Harstock [1983]. I will be considering the views empiricists in the Hempel/Nagel tradition hold in terms of this and Kuhn's views in Chapter Two and Quine's views in Chapter Three.

42. The issue and issues related to it are discussed in Addelson [1983], Bleier [1984], Fee [1982], Harding [1983A, 1983B, 1986], Harstock [1983], Jaggar [1983], and Keller [1983B, 1985A, 1985B].

43. Marx [1844]. Feminist theorist Nancy Harstock [1983] makes use of what she calls Marx's "meta-theoretical claim" that in societies in which there are "dominant" and "subordinate" groups, only members of the latter are in a position to see how things "really are". Harstock uses Marx's claim to begin to develop a "feminist standpoint epistemology." Harstock's claim, like Marx's, is that political advocacy and engagement result in an epistemologically advantaged standpoint. See, also, Harding [1983B, 1986], Jaggar [1983], esp. chap. 11, Rose [1983], and Smith [1981].

44. Popper and Lakatos apparently hold this, although perhaps for different reasons. See, for discussion, Bloor [1977] and Harding [1983B].

45. Bloor [1977] and Barnes [1977] and others in developing this "strong program" in the sociology of knowledge do maintain this. The strong program has resulted in something of a debate. See, e.g., Harding [1983B].

46. See, e.g., Harding [1983B].

47. See, for an argument to this affect, Harding [1983B].

48. There are exceptions. Sarah Ruddick, for example, seems to advocate relativism. At least, this was a position she advocated in a panel discussion with Sandra Harding at the Society for Women in Philosophy conference at Bryn Mawr in the fall of 1986.

49. See Ravetz [1984] for discussion and bibliography. Harding [1986] explores the parallels between science's "origins myth" and other origin myths, and there are interesting parallels between the political tone of the positivist manifestos and the later positivist insistence that science has nothing to do with politics, a consequence of the "verification theory of meaning".

50. This is not, of course, true of many Marxist scientists and science critics. I will be discussing some of the issues raised by Levins [1977] in Chapter Four. See also Dyke [1988], Gould [1977, 1981], and Lewontin, Rose, and Kamin [1984], among others listed in the Bibliography.

51. See Quine, "Epistemology Naturalized" in [1969], and the first chapter of Quine [1960].

52. The classic paper in "evolutionary epistemology" is Campbell [1974]. See, also, Hull [1982] and Wuketits [1986].

53. Again, I am not endorsing a gender/politics dichotomy here. Sex/gender

arrangements *are* political, but the experiences of sex/gender and of politics that feminists are relating to science are not everywhere coextensive. On the other hand, given what Kathryn Addelson describes as science's cognitive authority, the relationship between practices and views concerning sex/gender and science *is* political*, as we will see when we use her analysis in Chapter Four to consider Sociobiology. In Chapter Five, we will find other theories and assumptions to be political as well.

54. See, e.g., Harding [1983A, 1983B, 1986], Jaggar [1983], and Scheman [1983]. Quine does not hold that individuals know autonomously (in fact, he denies they could), although his proposal for naturalizing epistemology would commit us to focusing on individuals, a problem I address in Chapter Six. I explore a number of his positions and arguments in Chapter Three and use these in Chapter Six to show that taking individuals to be the primary epistemological agents is unbearably strained in the light of many of Quine's own positions and in light of feminist science criticism.

55. See, e.g., for science criticism that is shaped by Marxist approaches, Dyke [1988], Gould [1977, 1981], Levins [1977], Lewontin, Rose, and Kamin [1984]. Recent social studies of science include the collection in Knorr-Cetina and Mulkay [1983], and Latour [1986] and Latour and Woolgar [1986].

56. See Dyke [1988], and Levins [1977], and n. 55.

57. There are exceptions. See Dyke [1988], Gould [1981], and Lewontin, Rose, and Kamin [1984].

58. See, also, Addelson and Potter [1989], Harding [1983A, 1983B, 1986], and Jaggar [1983].

59. Harding poses the question this way in [1983A]. She also raises it in her discussion of feminist empiricism in [1986]. Implicit in Harding's point and mine is the view that the sex/gender of an observer cannot be understood in terms of an ahistorical and socially unmediated biology. For those who remain unconvinced, we can at least agree that there is no evidence to suggest that sex/gender is a variable in terms of *sense organs*.

60. See, e.g., Dyke [1988] and nn. 27, 30, and 55.

61. See, e.g., Addelson [1983], Harding [1983A, 1983B, 1986], Fee [1981], and Jaggar [1983], chap. 11.

62. That sex/gender arrangements *are* political is, of course, supported by feminist scholarship.

63. I am not endorsing a politics/epistemology dichotomy here. Relationships between these will emerge strongly in the course of the larger discussion.

64. See Harding [1986], Harstock [1983], Jaggar [1983], and Rose [1983].

65. The classic paper introducing and exploring "feminist standpoint epistemology" is Harstock [1983]. See also Harding [1985B, 1986], Jaggar [1983], esp. chap. 11, Rose [1983], and Smith [1981].

66. Harstock [1983].

67. Harding [1986], p. 26.

68. The argument here echoes, but with a different conclusion, Harding's argument in [1986], and those offered in Eisenstein [1981B] and Jaggar [1983],

about liberal feminism, and specifically about the radical consequences of "work-ing from within" established frameworks. Harding maintains that feminist empiri-cists "subvert empiricism", as I noted earlier and will discuss in some detail in Chapter Six. I am convinced there is a distinction to be drawn between empiricism as a theory of evidence and the accounts empiricists have offered of science. The latter, I agree, *are* subverted by the kind of analysis I am engaging in, but not the former. But I am also convinced that illuminating the relationships between feminist theorizing and science allows us to see that science is other than we thought. In short, I am not willing to grant science an autonomous status. I believe feminist science criticism is properly construed as being within science. Thus, it is from within science that challenges are being made to the views many of us have had about what science is. So as Eisenstein and Jaggar claim of liberal feminism, and Harding claims of the positions she describes as "feminist empiri-cism", the consequences of working within established frameworks from a femi-nist perspective can be quite radical. And, of course, we are *always* working within some aspects of established theory—or at least so I will later argue. Feminists disagree with nonfeminists about many things, and many of them are among the most important issues currently facing us—but they certainly do not disagree with nonfeminists about everything. We are members of a larger social community and, ultimately of course, a world community.

CHAPTER TWO
    1. Although I will, in fact, focus on aspects of Hempel's and Nagel's work, the tradition is badly named. Carnap's work is central in the tradition, and Quine, who is the heir apparent of this "postlogical" positivist tradition, is more directly influenced by him than either Hempel or Nagel. Moreover, some aspects of the cluster of views that have come to be called the "Hempel/Nagel view" of science are probably not correctly ascribed to Nagel. However, I am interested in laying out specific positions that Hempel and Nagel do share, and discussing the view of science underlying these positions and commonly associated with "empiricism". These positions continue to influence current views about science and to shape criticism of empiricism. For example, feminist critics Jaggar [1983] and Harding [1986] direct much of their criticism of "empiricism" to this tradition, and specifi-cally to positions that Quine abandons, as the discussions of Chapters Three, Four, Five, and Six indicate. Their criticism is important (if not aptly directed at empiricism per se) because the "postlogical" positivist tradition of Hempel and Nagel had a deep influence on many currently engaged in and teaching science and, more generally, on common-sense views of science.
    2. See, e.g., Ayer [1950, 1955, 1959], the collection in Schilpp [1963], and Carnap [1962].
    3. See, e.g., Carnap [1967], Ayer [1950], and Wittgenstein [1968].
    4. Hempel [1965], pp. 101–102. Emphasis added.
    5. Ibid., pp. 4–6.
    6. See, e.g., Quine's "Epistemology Naturalized" in [1969].
    7. Hempel [1965], p. 245.

8. Ibid., p. 247. Emphasis added.

9. Nagel [1961], pp. 3–5.

10. See, e.g., Hempel [1965]. In chap. 10 he explores the "logic" of explanation; in a section entitled "Aspects of Scientific Explanation" he outlines the now standard "Deductive-Nomonological" model of explanation; in section 2.3 of the latter he outlines the conditions that need to be met if a sentence is to be considered "law-like" and function in an explanation (a topic also explored in chap. 10); and in chap. 8, pp. 182–85, he outlines the conditions under which a set of sentences constitutes a theory. In all of these discussions the logical relationships between kinds of sentences are the central focus.

11. See, e.g., Hempel's discussion of theories in [1965], pp. 182–85.

12. Ibid., pp. 182–83.

13. Nagel [1961], p. 91.

14. Hempel [1966], p. 17.

15. Hempel [1965], pp. 4–6.

16. Hempel [1966], pp. 19–20. Emphasis in original.

17. See, e.g., Popper [1959], p. 31.

18. See, e.g., chaps. 1, 2, and 5 of Popper [1959].

19. See, e.g., ibid., chaps. 1 and 2.

20. Ibid., p. 86. Emphasis in original.

21. Ibid., p. 31.

22. Hempel [1965], p. 21. Emphasis added.

23. Ibid., p. 22. Emphasis added.

24. Ibid., pp. 23–25.

25. Ibid.

26. Ibid.

27. Ibid.

28. See, e.g., Hanson [1958], Kuhn [1962], and Popper [1959], esp. chap. 5.

29. See, e.g., Popper [1972], chap. 1.

30. Popper [1959], p. 103.

31. Ibid., p. 106.

32. Hempel [1966], p. 33.

33. Popper [1959], pp. 110–111. Emphasis added.

34. Hempel [1966], pp. 14–15. Emphasis in original.

35. Hempel [1965], p. 5.

36. Nagel [1961], p. 12.

37. Ibid., p. 12–13.

38. Ibid.

39. Ibid.

40. Ibid., pp. 10–11. Emphasis added.

41. In ibid., e.g., one chapter, "Explanation and Understanding in the Social Sciences", is devoted to the feasibility of generalizing the ideas of scientific explanation developed in the first thirteen chapters to the social sciences. In Hempel [1965], the social sciences are discussed in a chapter concerned with functional analysis, in discussions concerned with taxonomy and "typological methods",

and in a discussion of inductive-statistical models of explanation. Hempel does maintain, however, that his characterization of explanation, though developed using cases from the "physical sciences", is applicable to "various types of behavior in laboratory animals and in human subjects" (p. 251). But much of Hempel's and Nagel's analyses are framed by reference to what they call the "natural sciences".

42. Hempel [1965], p. 141. Emphasis in original.

43. Ibid., pp. 95–96.

44. Ibid., p. 35. Hempel goes on in this work to provide a formal analysis of the relation of confirmation.

45. Hempel [1966], p. 16.

46. See, e.g., Hempel [1965], in particular chap. 10, pp. 245–95.

47. See ibid., pp. 14–20 and 47–48, and Nagel [1961].

48. Tarski, "The Concept of Truth in Formalized Languages" in [1956].

49. See, e.g., Kripke [1982].

50. The classic works associated with what I am here referring to as a "tradition" are Kuhn [1962], which was reprinted and enlarged [1970], Hanson [1958], and Lakatos [1970]. See also the collection in Lakatos and Musgrave [1970]. Focusing on the activities that actually engage scientists, Kuhn, Hanson, and Lakatos explore problems with aspects of the positivist and postlogical positivist traditions in philosophy of science. There are a number of more recent social studies of science. See n. 51.

51. See, e.g., Latour [1986], Latour and Woolgar [1979], Lynch [1985], and Woolgar [1982]. Some of the more influential work in sociology of knowledge include Barnes [1977, 1983], Bloor [1977, 1983], and Collins [1981]. See, also, the collection in Knorr-Cetina and Mulkay [1983].

52. Hanson [1958].

53. See, e.g., Lakatos and Musgrave [1970] and Quine, "Epistemology Naturalized" in [1969].

54. See, for some of the controversy that has arisen because of the things Kuhn has said about "paradigms" and about other notions that are central to his analysis, the collection of papers in Lakatos and Musgrave [1970]. See, in particular, Masterman's "The Nature of a Paradigm" in that collection, in which she outlines the multiple senses Kuhn gives the notion. See, also "Postscript—1969" in Kuhn [1970] and Kuhn [1972].

55. See, e.g., Kuhn's postscript to [1970], his "Reflections on My Critics" in Lakatos and Musgrave [1970] and Kuhn [1972].

56. See, for an excellent overview of these multiple focuses, the discussion in Chalmers [1978], pp. 101–104, and Masterman [1970]. See, also, Kuhn's postscript to [1970].

57. See, for discussion of the issue, Chalmers [1978] and Lakatos and Musgrave [1970]. See, also, Kuhn's "Postscript" in [1970].

58. Kuhn [1970], p. 10.

59. Ibid., p. 23.

60. Ibid., p. 24.

61. Ibid., pp. 35–36.
62. Ibid., p. 23.
63. Ibid., pp. 181–87.
64. Ibid., p. 37.
65. Popper's likening of the decision involved in determining which sentences are to count as "basic statements" to "judicial decisions" incorporates the notion that some larger theoretical system is in place and involved in the decision, as we discussed above.
66. Kuhn [1970], p. 39.
67. Ibid., pp. 40–42. Emphasis added.
68. Ibid., p. 43.
69. See ibid., esp. sections 4 and 5, and pp. 46–47.
70. Ibid., pp. 46–47. Emphasis added.
71. Ibid., p. 46.
72. Ibid., p. 47.
73. I am grateful to Jack Nelson for suggesting that Kuhn's account of normal science is not different in terms of this from his account of scientific revolutions.
74. Kuhn [1970], p. 49.
75. Ibid., p. 42. As I noted earlier, it is not clear that the way "paradigm" is used in Kuhn's account of normal science is the way it is used in his account of scientific revolutions, and I will discuss that briefly below and more extensively in Chapter Five. It is also not clear that the "paradigm" that Kuhn is careful to distinguish from all those commitments and/or rules of the sort outlined above is the "paradigm" commonly associated with Kuhn and now common in discussions about science. In common parlance about Kuhn's view of science (at least about "Kuhn's") a paradigm is something much more like a network of commitments or rules of the sort he initially distinguishes from paradigms in his discussion of normal science—including theory, methodology, and (quasi) metaphysical commitments. (In his analysis of revolutionary science, of course, paradigms do include these things—at least the "old" one does.)
76. See, e.g., ibid., pp. 46–48.
77. Ibid., pp. 46–47. Emphasis added.
78. Ibid., p. 37.
79. Ibid., section 6 and p. 68. Kuhn maintains "to be admirably successful is never, for a scientific theory, to be completely successful" and "there is no such thing as research without counter instances" (p. 79).
80. This raises, of course, an interesting issue of how anomalies could be *recognized* if, in fact, the fit between theory (paradigm) and observation is as tight as Kuhn's account of revolutions requires—that is, if one were able to see only what the paradigm prepared one to see—and there "was", in effect, nothing else to see. And if this is *not* so, as his account of the anomalies that eventually prompt crisis would suggest, then it is not clear that his notion that competing paradigms are incommensurable can stand.
81. Kuhn [1970], pp. 89–90.
82. That "conversion" is involved in clearly argued for in sections 9 and 12

in ibid. Kuhn uses the term in several places, e.g., pp. 148 and 152. More to the point, the discussion of his section 12 clearly indicates that the term is appropriate to his analysis.

83. Ibid., pp. 93–94. Emphasis added.

84. See Harding [1986], p. 199, for an outline of the sequence of events and an alternative account of the implications of Kuhn's claims.

85. Kuhn [1970], p. 103.

86. Ibid., p. 111.

87. Ibid., p. 114.

88. See section 12 of ibid.

89. See ibid., section 11 and esp. pp. 145–48.

90. Ibid., section 9, esp. p. 103.

91. Ibid., p. 97. Emphasis added.

92. Ibid., p. 135.

93. Ibid., p. 93.

94. Ibid., section 11.

95. Ibid., p. 94.

96. Of course, the work to fit nature into the boxes supplied by the paradigm can be claimed to represent something like a test of the paradigm. Kuhn's point is that scientists are not working to test the paradigm, and failures of a match between paradigm and world are, for the most part, perceived as failures of the scientist, not of the paradigm. The only time paradigms are tested, according to Kuhn, is during crisis (ibid., p. 144.). The contrast with Popper's view is clear, but Kuhn also denies that normal science attempts to "confirm" paradigms as Hempel and Nagel had maintained. The paradigm is never in question in normal science.

97. See Hanson [1958] and section 10 of Kuhn [1970] in which Kuhn draws on Hanson's arguments that observations are theory laden to argue that scientific revolutions are changes in world view.

98. Kuhn [1970], p. 111.

99. Ibid., p. 116.

100. See, e.g., ibid., esp. section 10.

101. Ibid., section 9 and pp. 97 and 107.

102. See, e.g., the collection of essays in Lakatos and Musgrave [1970], and Kuhn's responses to criticism in the postscript to Kuhn [1970], his "Reflections on my Critics" in Lakatos and Musgrave [1970], and Kuhn [1972].

103. Kuhn [1970], p. 94.

104. Popper [1972], chap. 3.

105. Davies [1968], p. 8.

106. Hempel [1965], p. 141. Emphasis in original.

107. See Addelson [1983] for discussion of the sources, nature, and consequences of what she calls the institution of science's "cognitive authority". I use her analysis of that authority in Chapter Four. See, also, Harding [1986], esp. pp. 38–41, for an argument similar to that made by Addelson, that science's "absolute" cognitive authority to give an account of itself (the granting to science of a

status Harding calls "sacred", p. 38) is unwarranted. Both Harding and Addelson are discussing science in the narrow sense.

108. Anthony [1948], p. 145. Cited in Chalmers [1978].

109. Popper [1959], pp. 279–81. Emphasis in original.

110. Collins [1981], p. 3. See also the collection of papers in Knorr-Cetina and Mulkay [1983], Barnes [1977, 1983], and Bloor [1977].

CHAPTER THREE

1. Schuldenfrei [1972], p. 1.

2. Quine [1960], p. 4.

3. Quine, "The Limits of Knowledge" in [1976], p. 64.

4. Quine, "Things and Their Place in Theories" in [1981], pp. 1–2.

5. Quine, "The Scope and Language of Science" in [1966], p. 221.

6. Quine, "On Mental Entities" in ibid., pp. 212–13. Emphasis added.

7. Quine, "Things and Their Place in Theories" in [1981], p. 21.

8. Quine [1960], p. 2.

9. Quine, "Epistemology Naturalized" in [1969], p. 83.

10. Indeed, I will suggest in a later section of this chapter that Quine's positions raise problems for a distinction between "metaphorical language" and "nonmetaphorical" language.

11. Quine, "Postscript on Metaphor" in [1981], pp. 188–89.

12. See Whitbeck [1984] for a similar view of the use of metaphor.

13. Quine [1960], p. 3.

14. Ibid., p. 4.

15. Quine, "Epistemology Naturalized" in [1969], p. 75.

16. See, e.g., Harding [1986], pp. 36–52.

17. Quine, "Five Milestones of Empiricism" in [1981].

18. Ibid., p. 68.

19. See, for a discussion of the skepticism and solipsism that has traditionally haunted empiricism, Jaggar [1983], esp. her discussion of liberal political theory and its epistemology. I address the issue of the "knower" of empiricism in Chapter Six. As will become clear in that chapter, Jaggar's discussion aptly describes traditional and positivist empiricism, including some aspects of the Hempel/Nagel tradition. It is not, however, an apt description of Quine's empiricism, or empiricism "post-Quine".

20. Quine, "Five Milestones of Empiricism" in [1981].

21. Ibid., p. 69.

22. Hempel does recognize that in judging a theory, one can make adjustments to save it should the observation sentence implied turn out to be false, e.g., we can add ad hoc hypotheses. He also maintains that, given recalcitrant experience, it will not be clear which sentence of a theory or higher level assumption is falsified. See, e.g., Hempel [1966], chap. 3. But as we have seen, his account of "confirmation" and of the logic of justification does presume that observation sentences have their "own" empirical content.

23. Quine, "Epistemology Naturalized" in [1969], p. 79.

24. Quine, "Posits and Reality" in [1966], p. 241.

25. Quine [1960], pp. 11–13.

26. Quine, "Two Dogmas of Empiricism" in [1963], p. 41.

27. Quine, "Five Milestones of Empiricism" in [1981], p. 71.

28. Quine [1960], p. 13.

29. Quine, "Five Milestones of Empiricism" in [1981], p. 71.

30. Ibid.

31. Quine, "Two Dogmas of Empiricism" in [1963], p. 42. Emphasis added.

32. Indeed, Quine maintains in ibid. (p. 41), where both the third and fourth "shifts" are recommended (as two "dogmas of empiricism" are given up), that they are at bottom one "dogma".

33. Quine's argument against the distinction, as it is explicated in his classic paper "Two Dogmas of Empiricism", does conclude that the problem is one of making sense of "analyticity", but establishing the latter involves a lot of work to show that the ways that notion might be worked out (and there are more than one) are each problematic and, on his view, ultimately unworkable. In addition, as I note below, the view that the distinction cannot be made out is what Quine calls "the flip side" of the demise of the verification theory of meaning, which requires that individual sentences have empirical content in isolation from a body of theories, the "second dogma" (Quine says is at root the same as the first) that he argues empiricists must abandon. My discussion of these arguments is limited, in that I focus on only some of the consequences of the demise of the analytic/synthetic distinction. There is an extensive literature addressing his arguments in "Two Dogmas of Empiricism". A good if somewhat dated anthology is Davidson and Hintikka [1969]. See, for recent feminist discussions of Quine's argument, Harding [1986], pp. 36–37 and 48–52, and Addelson [1990].

34. Quine, "Two Dogmas of Empiricism" in [1963], p. 32.

35. In "Epistemology Naturalized" in [1969] Quine considers the idea that the traditional notion of "analyticity" might be "dispensed with . . . in favor of . . . a straightforward attribute of community-wide acceptance" but notes that since the community would probably agree to "there have been black dogs", this is not an explication of "analyticity" in terms of "meanings" (p. 86).

36. See also Harding [1986] and Addelson [1990] for somewhat different accounts of the consequences of Quine's argument against the analytic/synthetic distinction.

37. Quine, "Two Dogmas of Empiricism" in [1963], p. 43.

38. See, e.g., the discussion in Harding [1986], pp. 48–52, in which she uses Quine to argue against the "dogma" that mathematics is "pure" (a dogma that she attributes to scientists who see it as the "conversation stopper" when feminists argue that science bears the marks of politics and sex/gender—and my own experience bears this out). I understand and use Quine's argument against the analytic/synthetic distinction somewhat differently, as my discussion in Chapter Five will indicate.

39. Although this last feature of some sentences is one aspect of Quine's account of "observation sentences", his account is very different from the account

of observation sentences given by Hempel. This will become clear in a section of this chapter in which I discuss the theory/observation relationship.

40. Quine, "Two Dogmas of Empiricism" in [1963], p. 44.

41. Harding [1986].

42. Harding (ibid.) discussed Quine's argument and uses it to support the view that mathematics "looks at aspects of the world that are less distorted by formal description than does anthropology and history—less distorted, but not entirely free of distortion" (p. 52).

43. Harding [1986], p. 52.

44. See esp. the conclusion of Quine, "Two Dogmas of Empiricism" in [1963]. See also Quine, "Identity, Ostension, and Hypostasis" in ibid., p. 79, where "pragmatism" is advocated in contrast to a correspondence theory.

45. Those who view Quine's position as a skeptical or conventionalist view about mathematics and logic should read Quine, "Truth by Convention" [1966].

46. Quine, "Things and Their Place in Theories" in [1981], p. 22.

47. For a recent discussion see Quine, "On the Very Idea of a Third Dogma" in ibid. See also the discussion in Chapter One.

48. Quine, "Things and Their Place in Theories" in ibid., pp. 21–22. Emphasis added.

49. Quine, "Two Dogmas of Empiricism" in [1963], p. 41.

50. Addelson [1983].

51. Quine, "Epistemology Naturalized" in [1969].

52. Ibid., p. 90.

53. This is manifest, for example, in Quine's elimination of singular terms from standard logical grammar. Names, Quine claims, either are redundant or fail to denote, and, in any event, they do not commit us ontologically (as in the case of Pegasus). In addition, substitutional semantics limit us, Quine argues, to denumerable ontologies, thus preventing us, for example, from including the real numbers in our overall ontology. For these reasons, Quine rejects substitutional quantification. His rejection of a distinction between epistemology and metaphysics is also clear in his treatment of ontic commitment in terms of values of variables and the satisfaction of open sentences. See Quine, "Existence and Quantification" in [1969], pp. 91–113.

54. In Quine [1963].

55. Quine, "Ontological Relativity" in [1969], p. 53.

56. See, in addition to "On What There Is" in [1963], "Ontological Relativity" and "Speaking of Objects" in [1969], "Posits and Reality" in [1966], Quine [1960], and Quine, "Things and Their Place in Theories" in [1981]. I will not be able to discuss the issue of ontological relativity or Quine's position on the "inscrutability" of reference. I hope that these omissions will not convey any misunderstanding about Quine's views on ontology.

57. Quine, "Existence and Quantification" in [1969], p. 105.

58. Quine makes use of Russell's account of singular descriptions in Quine, "On What There Is" in [1963]. See Russell [1905].

59. The importance of the "there is" idiom, and a slippage between names

and objects, causes Quine to omit the former from standard logical grammar. Names, Quine claims, are either redundant or fail to denote; in any event, they do not commit us ontologically. Thus, he rejects substitutional quantification. See n. 53 and Quine, "Existence and Quantification" in [1969].

60. Quine, "On What There Is" in [1963], pp. 13–14.

61. Ibid., p. 8.

62. Quine, "Existence and Quantification" in [1969], pp. 93–94.

63. Quine, "On What There Is" in [1963], p. 15. Emphasis in original.

64. Quine, "Existence and Quantification" in [1969], p. 100.

65. Ibid., p. 97.

66. Quine [1960], p. 4.

67. I will be collapsing somewhat Quine's arguments for ontological relativity, the relativity of all ontological decisions to a "home theory" we take at "face value", and the primacy of physical-object ontology. See Quine, "Ontological Relativity" and "Speaking of Objects" in [1969].

68. Quine [1960], p. 2.

69. Quine, "Speaking of Objects" in [1969], pp. 7–10.

70. Ibid., pp. 8–10. Emphasis added.

71. Quine [1960], p. 16.

72. Quine, "Posits and Reality" in [1966], pp. 233–35.

73. Ibid., pp. 236–37.

74. Ibid., p. 239. Emphasis added.

75. Quine, "Facts of the Matter" [1978], p. 160.

76. See, in particular, Quine, "Posits and Reality" in [1966], and Quine [1960], esp. the first two chapters.

77. Quine, "Posits and Reality" in [1966], p. 238. Emphasis added.

78. Quine [1960], pp. 2–3.

79. Quine, "Two Dogmas of Empiricism" in [1963], p. 44.

80. Quine [1960], p. 22. See also Quine, "Posits and Reality" in [1966].

81. Quine, "Posits and Reality" in [1966], p. 239.

82. As later discussion indicates, Quine claims that in two situations, the learning of language (in the initial use of "words" learned in response to stimulation) and radical translation (the translation of an entire alien language to our own), "reference" is not involved because ontology is not involved. See Quine, "Ontological Relativity" and "Speaking of Objects" in [1969].

83. Quine [1978], pp. 64–65.

84. See also Quine, "Empirical Content" in [1981].

85. Quine, "Empirical Content" in [1981], p. 24.

86. It is also clear, as I explore in Chapter Six, that Quine envisions this investigation of "ideas" as taking place in the neurosciences. See, e.g., his "Responding to Schuldenfrei" in [1981], p. 184, "Things and Their Place in Theories" in ibid., p. 2, and "Epistemology Naturalized" in [1969].

87. Quine [1960], pp. 3–4.

88. See, e.g., Quine, "Things and Their Place in Theories" in [1981].

89. Quine [1960], pp. 9–13.

90. Quine, "Empirical Content" in [1981], p. 24.

91. Quine [1960], p. 12.

92. Actually Quine seems to classify two kinds of sentence as observation sentences, and we will be concerned with only one of these, those that are obviously theoretical. But in his account of a child's learning of language Quine calls one-word sentences first learned with reference to stimulations "observation sentences". However, at first these sentences do not (for the child) involve reference (or denotation) and so they are not theoretical.

93. "Standing sentences" are sentences that speakers would repeatedly assent to or dissent from without being prompted by current stimulation, e.g., "Spring has arrived". See Quine [1960], pp. 35–40.

94. Ibid., p. 42. Emphasis in original.

95. Ibid., pp. 43–44.

96. Quine's account of "stimulus meaning" is detailed. See ibid., pp. 31–35, and Quine, "Epistemology Naturalized" in [1969], p. 85.

97. See Quine, "Epistemology Naturalized" in [1969], pp. 85–87.

98. Quine, "Empirical Content" in [1981], p. 28.

99. Ibid., pp. 25–26.

100. Quine, "On the Very Idea of a Third Dogma" in [1981].

101. Quine [1960], p. 22.

102. Quine's "indeterminacy of translation" thesis is not the same view as underdetermination, and the former is not the issue here.

103. Quine, "Posits and Reality" in [1966], p. 241.

104. Quine [1960], p. 23.

105. Harding [1986], p. 43.

106. See also Volpe [1989].

107. Quine, "Things and Their Place in Theories" in [1981], p. 22. Emphasis added.

108. For discussions of reductionism, see Dyke [1988], Lewontin [1983], Mayr [1988], Rose [1982], and Wartofsky [1968].

109. Harding [1986], p. 37.

110. Quine, "Two Dogmas of Empiricism" in [1963], pp. 40–41.

111. Quine calls this view "reductionism" in ibid. See, also, "Five Milestones of Empiricism" in [1981].

112. See, in addition to Harding's discussion in Harding [1986], Scheman [1983], Addelson [1990], and Rorty [1979].

113. Schuldenfrei [1972], p. 1.

114. Quine, "Facts of the Matter" [1978], p. 160.

115. Ibid., pp. 165–66. Quine uses "place-time" rather than "space-time" in a more recent discussion, "Things and Their Place in Theories" in [1981], and he also suggests that these "regions" might be replaced in favor of "corresponding classes of quadruples of numbers" (p. 17). The details in the discussions are not necessary for the general understanding of physicalism that he has in mind and I am exploring here.

116. Wartofsky [1968], p. 347.

117. I am grateful to Jack Nelson for the example and his help in clarifying issues in this section.

118. See, e.g., Dyke [1988], pp. 8–9 and Rose [1982].

119. Quine [1960], p. 228.

120. See, e.g., Quine, "Things and Their Place in Theories" in [1981], pp. 1–23.

121. Ibid., p. 232.

122. Quine, "Ontological Relativity" and "Existence and Quantification" in [1969].

123. At least I think this is the position Quine has come to about "events" in "Things and Their Place in Theories" in [1981], pp. 1–23.

124. See, e.g., Dyke [1988], Keller [1983A, 1985], Lewontin [1983], Mayr [1988], and Rose [1982].

125. Schuldenfrei [1972], p. 1.

126. Schuldenfrei does acknowledge that Quine denies alleged differences in knowledge that are based on the analytic/synthetic distinction, assumed in conventionalist accounts, and assumed by those who distinguish some knowledge as a priori, but he does not note (and the passage implies the opposite) that Quine denies there are distinctions between the methods or goals of common-sense knowing and science in the narrow sense. Schuldenfrei [1972], p. 6.

127. Schuldenfrei, quoted in Quine, "Responding to Richard Schuldenfrei" in [1981], p. 184.

128. Schuldenfrei [1972], pp. 5–6.

129. Ibid.

130. See, e.g., Quine, "Facts of the Matter" [1978], pp. 166–67. Quine also says this in a number of other discussions.

131. See, e.g., the collection of papers in Quine [1966], chap. 6 of Quine [1960], and "Responding to Schuldenfrei" in [1981].

132. See, e.g., Scheman [1983], who attributes such a position to Quine.

133. Quine, "Response to Schuldenfrei" in [1981], p. 184.

134. Ibid.

135. Quine, "Facts of the Matter" [1978], p. 167.

136. Quine, "On Mental Entities" in [1966], p. 213.

137. See, e.g., Scheman [1983], who denies such ascription is appropriate.

138. See Dyke [1988], pp. 7–9, for an alternative view of the implications of what he calls "physical reductionism".

139. I am not here begging the issue of whether there are ultimate constituents of the universe. If there are not, then when Burns creates the stuff out of which he makes fish, he ipso facto must create all the constituents of that stuff even if each such constituent itself has constituents.

140. Quine [1985].

141. Ibid., p. 477.

142. Quine, "Has Philosophy Lost Contact with People?" in Quine [1981], p. 193.

143. Quine [1974], p. 49.

144. Ibid., pp. 51–52. Emphasis added.

145. Quine, "On the Nature of Moral Values" in [1981], p. 64.

146. Ibid., p. 63. Emphasis added.

147. Ibid., p. 64.

148. See, ibid., Quine [1974], pp. 49–52, and Quine and Ullian [1978], p. 137.

149. In "On the Nature of Moral Values" Quine refers to the morality of a society as a "derivative concept. . . , as distinct from that of an individual" (p. 63).

150. Ibid.

151. Quine [1974], p. 51.

152. Quine, "On the Nature of Moral Values" in [1981], p. 60.

153. Quine and Ullian [1978], p. 137.

154. Quine, "On the Nature of Moral Values" in [1981], p. 62.

155. Kuhn [1970], p. 89.

156. Quine, "Posits and Reality" in [1966], p. 239.

CHAPTER FOUR

1. The notion of "cognitive authority" is introduced and developed in Addelson [1983], and I will be using her analysis throughout most of this chapter. Addelson's notion of cognitive authority is similar to the notion of "pedagogic authority" developed in Bourdieu and Passeron [1977].

2. See Addelson [1983], Cole and Cole [1973], Harding [1986], Hubbard, Henifin, and Fried [1982], Keller [1983A, 1983B, 1985A], Reskin [1978], and others listed in the Bibliography.

3. The literature is extensive, and some of it will be discussed here. See also Bleier [1984], Harding [1986], Hornig [1979, 1982, and 1984], Hubbard, Henifin, and Fried [1982], Keller [1983B, 1985A], Mattfeld and Van Aken [1965], National Academy of Sciences, Committee on the Education and Employment of Women in Science and Engineering [1983], and National Science Foundation [1982–present, biennial].

4. Addelson [1983].

5. See n. 1.

6. Addelson [1983], p. 165.

7. Ibid., p. 167.

8. Ibid.

9. Ibid.

10. Ibid.

11. Ibid.

12. Ibid., p. 171.

13. Addelson is drawing here on Haraway [1978A, 1978B], and she notes that Haraway does not use the notion of "metaphysical commitments" as she herself uses it. Haraway [1979] chronicles a shift in the biological sciences from functionalist models to models that take organisms to be "automated technological devices, understood in terms of cybernetic systems" (p. 207). Cited in Addelson [1983].

14. Merton's commitment to the methodological framework is further clarified

in Addelson [1983]. I am outlining only those features of her discussion relevant to the issue of whether methodologies incorporate metaphysical commitments, and the consequences of such commitments' being communicated to the larger community.

15. Addelson [1983], p. 173. Addelson is citing Haraway [1978-A-B].

16. Addelson [1983], pp. 173–75.

17. Ibid., pp. 176–77.

18. My most recent experience with the way what scientists "prove" gets communicated to the general public was in teaching an introductory course in philosophy. Several students claimed that mind/body dualism was false because researchers had "just proven that women and men think differently because their brains are different"—a reference, it turned out, to research into sex differences in hemispheric lateralization, which I discuss in the next chapter. Their information about this research (or, more accurately, about the things "proven" in this research), came from the media.

19. Addelson [1983], pp. 176–77. Emphasis added.

20. Ibid. and Haraway [1978A, 1978B].

21. Addelson [1983], p. 176.

22. The pioneer work of Sociobiology is Wilson [1975A]. See also Barash [1977, 1979], Dawkins [1976], Hamilton [1964, 1975], Lumsden and Wilson [1981], and Wilson [1975B, 1978A]. Dyke [1988] distinguishes between what he calls the "Hamiltonian" and the "Wilsonian" versions of Sociobiology. Two of the clearest analyses of the flaws in Sociobiology's methodology are Bleier [1984] and Lewontin, Rose, and Kamin [1984]. For criticisms of the program, see also Gould [1977, 1978, 1981] and the collection of papers in Caplan [1978]. See Dyke [1986, 1988] for insights into the controversy in the biological science concerning the underlying model of evolutionary processes used in Sociobiology, and an alternative approach to the evolution of complex systems, including social systems.

23. See, e.g., Howell [1979].

24. See, e.g., Bleier [1984, 1988A], Brown [1975], Dyke [1986, 1988], Lewontin, Rose, and Kamin [1984], and Washburn [1978]. See also Beach [1974A], in which Beach, who is a comparative psychologist, denies that hormones can cause particular behaviors. Later, however, in Beach [1974B], he does talk about how "male genotypes" contributed to the "hunter role" that promoted human survival and suggests there is a hormonal basis for "sex differences." Beach apparently became angry over a dismissal by Wilson of comparative psychology, as one of many fields that, according to Wilson, will be "cannibalized" by Sociobiology. In Beach [1978] the interdisciplinary battles are reflected in Beach's description of Wilson as "the high priest of Sociobiology". Segerstrale [1986] chronicles the battles that have split the Harvard colleagues, Wilson and Lewontin, and Wilson and Gould.

25. See Barash [1979], pp. 21–22, and Wilson [1975A], p. 1, and [1978A] for outlines of these theses.

26. See the collection of papers in Caplan [1978] for an overview of the debate and bibliography.

27. See Wilson [1975A], chap. 27, for a clear statement of the methodology. See also Barash [1977, 1979]. In Gould [1977, 1978], Bleier [1984], and Lewontin, Rose, and Kamin [1984] problems with the methodology are explored.

28. See, e.g., Barash [1977], p. 160.

29. See Barash [1977, 1979] and Wilson [1978A]. I will be discussing some of Barash's views in this section. Ironically, Wilson claims to be alarmed by the uses to which the research program has been put (Wilson to C. Dyke, in private conversation), but other Sociobiologists are not. Nor is Wilson's "alarm" understandable in the light of some of his own claims. See, e.g., Wilson [1978A].

30. See, e.g., Alper et al. [1978], Bleier [1984], Burian [1978], Dyke [1986], Gould [1977, 1981], Lewontin [1976, 1977A, 1977B, 1981], Waddington [1975], the collection in Caplan [1978], and Lewontin, Rose, and Kamin [1984]. The Bibliography contains additional references.

31. See, e.g., Bleier [1984], Caplan [1978], Dyke [1988], and Gould [1977]. See, also, nn. 26 and 30.

32. Barash [1979], pp. 9–10.

33. Ibid., p. 10.

34. Ibid., pp. 28–29. "Fitness", as I have noted, is understood in terms of the ability of genes to replicate themselves and/or the ability of individuals to reproduce (or to enable their relatives, with whom they share genes, to reproduce).

35. Dawkins [1976] and Wilson [1978A].

36. Barash [1977], p. 283.

37. Ibid., Wilson's remarks on back cover.

38. Ibid., p. 160.

39. Barash [1979], chap. 3. Chap. 4 is entitled "Parenting: Murderous Monkeys, Paternal Marmots and Sexism (Continued)".

40. Ibid., p. 90.

41. Ibid., p. 3.

42. I am not being facetious here. Sociobiologists do assume that they can (indeed, have) "looked" at all human societies and *understood* the practices, behaviors, and arrangements within them. See n. 43.

43. Wilson in an interview with Ullica Segerstrale, cited in Segerstrale [1986], p. 84, n. 48.

44. Barash [1979], p. 2.

45. Wilson [1975A], p. 4.

46. Ibid.

47. See Wilson [1978A].

48. See Barash [1979], p. 11, and Wilson [1978A], chap. 4. Despite the many caveats, the universals—and particularly in terms of male dominance—are explained as "natural" and fitness promoting in these works by Barash and Wilson.

49. See, e.g., Barash [1977, 1979], Dawkins [1976], van den Berghe and Barash [1977], and Wilson [1978A].

50. See, e.g., Barash [1977, 1979], van den Berghe and Barash [1977], and Wilson [1975B, 1978].

51. Wilson [1978A], p. 129. See also Barash [1977, 1979] and Dawkins [1976].

52. See Barash [1977]. His view that "rape" is a reproductive strategy that maximizes fitness is discussed below.

53. Wilson [1975A].

54. Barash [1977, 1979].

55. See Bleier [1984], Caplan [1978], Dyke [1988], Gould [1977, 1978, 1981], Howell [1979], Hubbard [1978], Lewontin [1976], and Midgley [1978A, 1978B].

56. Gould [1977, 1978, 1981].

57. See Bleier [1984], Lancaster [1975], Ortner and Whitehead [1981], Rowell [1972, 1974], and Sacks [1979], among others listed in the Bibliography.

58. An overview of this literature is provided by Bleier [1984], Caplan [1978], and Montagu [1980].

59. See Dyke [1988]. See also Dyke [1986], Gould [1977, 1981], Hubbard [1978], Lewontin [1976], and Sober and Lewontin [1982].

60. See, e.g., Dyke [1986, 1988], Gould and Lewontin [1979], Lewontin [1976], and Sober and Lewontin [1982].

61. See, e.g., Bleier [1984] and Gould [1978].

62. Bleier [1984], Gould [1977], Hubbard [1983], and Midgley [1980A, 1980B].

63. For an excellent discussion of the "ontology" of Sociobiology, see Bleier [1984].

64. The metaphor of "parental investment" that Barash uses here originates in Trivers [1972], and the differences in female and male investment Trivers outlines are embraced by Sociobiologists as the explanation of "harems", polygamy, "male fickleness", "female coyness", what Barash calls "the double standard", and male domination of females and culture. See Barash [1977, 1979], Dawkins [1976], and Wilson [1978A].

65. Barash [1979], pp. 114–15. Emphasis added.

66. Wilson [1975A], chap. 27.

67. Ibid.

68. Ibid.

69. Wilson claims to view Sociobiology as a "promising and incomplete research program" but not "confirmed" (Wilson to Dyke in private conversation), and it is possible to see that attitude in Wilson [1975A], although it is not compatible with the tone of everything said in chaps. 1 and 27. However, the way the program is publicized and promoted by other of its advocates, including Wilson [1978A], implies that it is successful, and some advocates do put it forth as if confirmed. See, e.g., Barash [1977, 1979], and Dawkins [1976].

70. See Wilson [1975B, 1978B] and the collection of papers in Caplan [1978].

71. Wilson [1978B], p. 292.

72. Ibid., p. 298.

73. This is especially clear in the case of Levins, Lewontin, S. J. Gould, Hubbard, and Bleier, whose political views are stated clearly in works cited in this chapter and listed in the Bibliography.

74. Wilson [1978A], p. 129.

75. See Wilson [1975A, 1978B].

76. See Midgley [1980B].

77. Dawkins [1976], p. 158, quoted in Bleier [1984].

78. Bleier [1984], p. 9.

79. See ibid.

80. It has been argued that this is an inappropriate way of describing mating in other species, and that rape only occurs in the human species. See Brownmiller [1976] and Bleier [1984]. Barash [1979] is apparently well read in feminist literature (indeed, he frequently notes that what he says will be "infuriating" to feminists and seems to enjoy this—as his catchy chapter titles using the term 'sexism' suggest. In [1979] he dismisses Brownmiller's extensive study and analysis of rape without addressing them specifically and—as he does with most claims he attributes to feminists—he does so from the lofty stance of science and without ado.

81. Barash [1979], p. 30.

82. Bleier [1984], p. 32.

83. Barash [1977], p. 269.

84. Barash [1979], pp. 30–31. Emphasis added.

85. Ibid., p. 55. Emphasis added.

86. Ibid.

87. Trivers, in DeVore and Trivers [1976].

88. See Barash [1977, 1979], Dawkins [1976], Hamilton [1964], Trivers [1972], and Wilson [1978A].

89. The National Front in Britain has embraced Wilson's Sociobiology as showing there is a biological basis and justification for racial and sexual oppression. See, e.g., Verrall [1979].

90. See, e.g., Bleier [1984] and the collection in Caplan [1978].

91. Barash [1979], p. 72.

92. See, e.g., Bleier [1984], Leacock [1977, 1978], Quinn [1977], Rogers [1978], and other work listed in the Bibliography. An excellent bibliography is provided in Hubbard, Henifin and Fried [1982], pp. 302–306.

93. See Bleier [1984], pp. 22–34.

94. For criticisms of this sort, see Bleier [1984], Eaton [1974], Haraway [1978A, 1978B, 1988], Hrdy [1988], Lancaster [1975], Leibowitz [1975, 1978], and Rowell [1972, 1974].

95. Barash [1977, 1979] consistently uses such terminology.

96. Barash [1979], p. 47.

97. Ibid.

98. Bleier [1984], p. 8.

99. See Kuhn's analysis of this revolution [1962].

100. See, e.g., Dyke [1988], Gould [1977, 1978, 1981], Lewontin [1976, 1977A, 1977B, 1979, 1981, 1982, 1983], and Lewontin, Rose, and Kamin [1984].

101. See n. 100.

102. See chaps. 1 and 2 of Quine [1960], "On What There Is" in [1963], "Posits and Reality" in [1976], and "Speaking of Objects" in [1969].

103. Addelson [1983], pp. 168–69.

104. Ibid., pp. 177–78.

105. In Levins [1977], on which I will draw later in this section, it is argued that many of these features (e.g., funding practices) are contingent, determined by factors in the larger social and political context, and consequential for the directions of research.

106. Addelson [1983], p. 178.

107. Levins [1977].

108. Ibid.

109. Ibid.

110. Ibid.

111. Ibid.

112. Ibid.

113. Ibid.

114. Ibid.

115. Ibid.

116. Ibid. Levins cites cases in which the directions of research were determined by the practice of funding a small group of what he calls "hotshots" to solve problems and by the assumption among funders and "hotshots" that the larger population was "unscientific".

117. There is an extensive literature. See, e.g., Aldrich [1978], Haas and Perrucci [1984], Harding [1986], Hornig [1979, 1982, 1984], Rossiter [1982A, 1982B], Tuchman [1980], National Academy of Sciences, Committee on the Education and Employment of Women in Science and Engineering [1983], and National Science Foundation [1982–present, biennial].

118. See n. 117. Harding [1986] tells several stories about the sort of "adjustments" that were made when formal barriers to women were lifted.

119. See, e.g., Gornick [1982], Hubbard, Henifin, and Fried [1982], Hornig [1984], Keller [1983A, 1983B], Rossiter [1982A, 1982B], and Tuchman [1980]. See also n. 117.

120. Christine Gray attributes the phrase to Judith Scholman.

121. Weisstein [1982], pp. 265–67.

122. Ibid., p. 272.

123. Ibid., p. 267.

124. The literature is extensive. See, e.g., several articles in Hubbard, Henifin and Fried [1982], and an issue of MIT's *Technology Review* largely devoted to studies dealing with women's positions and experiences in science and engineering [1984]. See also Dziech and Weiner [1984] for statistics on sexual harassment and other problems that women in graduate education in the sciences report. Again, some of what women scientists report is difficult to characterize. Male scientists in some fields are apparently conscious of, and attempting to preserve, the "masculine" image their fields enjoy. See, e.g., Traweek [1984, 1987]. In other cases, apparently the fact that the field originally had an all-male population led

to practices, methods, and expectations of appropriate behavior that many women find difficult (adversarial behavior in graduate courses, for example) and strained. See, e.g., Hynes [1984].

125. National Academy of Sciences, Committee on the Education and Employment of Women in Science and Engineering [1983]. Summarized in Hornig [1984]. See also Harding [1986].

126. Hornig [1984].

127. Ibid.

128. Some of the restrictions reflect long-standing views about women. At Carlton, for instance, while the number of women increased in other science programs, it did not in geology. A faculty member thought the explanation might be that women were not allowed on field trips, because of what he called "the chaperoning problem". An experimental psychologist notes that educators and male scientists frequently express the view that "women in science are trouble" (Weisstein [1982]).

129. In computer science, for instance, studies suggest that a high incidence of sexual harassment and discrimination, and a direct relationship between that harassment and the large numbers of women who have left specific programs. See Hynes [1984].

Women in the computer science program at MIT found the problem so pervasive, in terms of things like the use of the computers to harass them with obscene mail or printouts of nude women, that they organized a committee and drafted a report that is now distributed to incoming faculty and students each fall. See Hynes [1984].

130. Hornig [1984], p. 41.

131. Harding [1983A, 1986], esp. pp. 58–64. Harding's notion of "reinvestment potential" is similar to the notion of "cultural capital" developed in Bourdieu and Passeron [1977]. Like the statistics I will cite here, Bourdieu and others working in the Marxist tradition have amassed a significant amount of quantitative data on the socioeconomic differentiation in "cultural capital". See, on the differences in such "reinvestment" for women and men, Rossiter [1982A], Tuchman [1980], Harding [1986], and other works cited in n. 117.

132. National Science Foundation, [1982].

133. Hornig [1984], p. 35.

134. National Science Foundation, [1982].

135. Ibid.

136. Hornig [1984], p. 36.

137. Ibid.

138. Ibid. p. 40.

139. See, for discussion, Dziech and Weiner [1984], Gornick [1983], Harding [1986], Hornig [1984], Hynes [1984], Hubbard, Henifin and Fried [1982], Keller [1983A, 1983B, 1985A, 1985B], Mattfeld and Aken [1965], and Traweek [1984].

140. Keller [1985A], pp. 75–76.

141. See Harding [1986], Keller [1983A, 1983B], Merchant [1980], and the works cited in n. 117.

142. See Harding [1986] for an analysis of "gender" as an analytic category that has many "layers". For discussions in which the perceived "masculinity" of science is argued to influence scientific practice and the views of male scientists about female scientists, see, e.g., Griffin [1978, 1981], Harding [1986], Hornig [1984], Hubbard, Henifin, and Fried [1982], Hynes [1984], Keller [1983A, 1983B, 1985A, 1985B], Merchant [1980], and Traweek [1984].

143. The literature in which relationships between views about masculinity and views about science are explored is extensive. See, e.g., Griffin [1978, 1981], Harding [1986], Hornig [1984], Hubbard, Henifin, and Fried [1982], Hynes [1984], Keller [1983A, 1983B, 1985], Merchant [1980], and Traweek [1984]. Traweek, for example, was told by those in a high-energy physics department she studied (a field in which women are more underrepresented than in others in physics, but they are significantly underrepresented in physics generally) that "only bright blunt bastards can make it in this field". Traweek studied the relationship between the traits required for "success" in the field with those associated with masculinity and concluded that "high energy physics remains a male preserve because the traits associated with success are . . . those associated with extreme masculinity . . . social eccentricity, disdain for others, and careful insubordination. . . . Such a practice excludes those women and men who are unwilling to pursue that ethos" (Traweek [1984]).

144. Pollard [1964], quoted in Rossi [1964], p. 117.

145. See, for example, Harding [1986], Keller [1983A, 1985A, 1985B], and Traweek [1984].

146. See, e.g., Griffin [1978, 1981], Harding [1986], Hornig [1984], Hubbard, Henifin, and Fried [1982], Hynes [1984], Keller [1983A, 1983B, 1985A, 1985B], Merchant [1980], and Traweek [1984].

147. Addelson [1983], p. 166.

148. Ibid., p. 182.

149. Ibid.

150. Kuhn [1970]. See the discussion of Chapter Two.

151. Levins [1977].

CHAPTER FIVE

1. See, also, Harding [1986] for an overview of feminist science criticism, the last fifteen years of *Signs*, and other works listed in the Bibliography.

2. The literature is extensive. Some works will be cited here, and many others are listed in the Bibliography.

3. See, for example, Bleier [1984], esp. chap. 8, Fee [1981], Harding [1983B, 1986], and Jaggar [1983], esp. chap. 11.

4. The literature documenting cross-cultural and historical variations in views about sex/gender and sex/gender arrangements is extensive. Important collections include Ortner and Whitehead [1981], Reiter [1975], Rosaldo and Lamphere [1974], Scott [1988], and Smith-Rosenberg [1985]. See also Bleier [1984], esp. chap. 6, Leacock [1977, 1978, 1981], Quinn [1977], Sacks [1976, 1979], and *Signs* [1975–present].

5. See n. 4.

6. See Birke [1982], Bleier [1984, 1988A, 1988B], Harding [1986], Hubbard [1982], Hubbard, Henifin, and Fried [1982], Hubbard and Lowe [1979], Jaggar [1983, 1984], Lerner [1986], Lowe [1982], Rose [1982], and Sayers [1982]. Other work is cited in the Bibliography.

7. See, also, Bleier [1984, 1988A, 1988B], Collier and Rosaldo [1981], Etienne and Leacock [1980], Harding [1986], Leacock [1977, 1978], Lee [1979, 1982], Leibowitz [1978], Lowe [1982], Ortner and Whitehead [1981], Palmeri [1980], Reiter [1975], Rogers [1978], Rosaldo and Lamphere [1974], and Sacks [1976, 1979].

8. See, for discussions of the multi-layeredness of gender as a category and the complexity of the feedbacks among the layers, Bleier [1984], esp. chap. 6, Harding [1986] esp. chaps. 2 and 5, Jaggar [1983, 1984], Lerner [1986], Scott [1988], and Smith-Rosenberg [1985]. See also the collections in Ortner and Whitehead [1981], Reiter [1975], Rosaldo and Lamphere [1974], and *Signs* [1975–present].

9. Longino and Doell [1983], p. 182, n. 29.

10. See n. 7 and n. 8, Hochschild [1975], Millman and Kanter [1975], Reiter [1975], and *Signs* [1975–present].

11. See, e.g., the collections in Millman and Kanter [1975], Ortner and Whitehead [1981], Reiter [1975], and Rosaldo and Lamphere [1974]. See also Anderson [1983], Bernard [1981], Gilligan [1982], Gould [1984], Harding and Hintikka [1983], Harding [1986], Hartmann [1981], Jaggar [1983], Kelly-Gadol [1976], Leacock [1981], Lloyd [1984], Scott [1988], Smith [1977, 1979, 1981], and Smith-Rosenberg [1985]. See also *Hypatia* [1983–present].

12. Erikson [1950, 1968], Freud [1905, 1925], Kohlberg [1958, 1981], and Gilligan [1982], esp. chap. 1.

13. See Freud [1905, 1925, 1930].

14. See Edwards [1975], Gilligan [1982], and Simpson [1974].

15. See Erikson [1968] and Gilligan [1982].

16. See, e.g., Chodorow [1974, 1978], Gilligan [1982], Miller [1976], and "Works in Progress", The Stone Center, Wellesley College.

17. Gilligan [1982].

18. See, e.g., Broverman, Vogel, Broverman, Clarkson, and Rosenkrantz [1972], Chodorow [1974, 1978], Edwards [1975], Erikson [1968], Freud [1925, 1930], Gilligan [1982], Harding [1986], Holstein [1976], Horner [1972], Lever [1976, 1978], Miller [1976], Piaget [1932], Sassen [1980], Simpson [1974], and "Works in Progress", The Stone Center, Wellesley College. Ironically, since the publication of Gilligan's work, some psychologists are now quick to deny that women's and men's developments are different.

19. Gilligan [1982].

20. See, e.g., Chodorow [1974, 1978], Gilligan [1982], Harding [1986], Keller [1985A], Kittay and Meyers [1986], Miller [1976], Ruddick [1980], and Trebilcot [1984].

21. See, e.g., Chodorow [1974, 1978], Gilligan [1982], Keller [1984], Miller

[1976], and "Work in Progress", The Stone Center, Wellesley College, 1982–present.

22. See Chodorow [1974, 1978], Gilligan [1982], and Miller [1976].

23. The literature is extensive. See, e.g., Bridenthal and Koonz [1977], Kelly-Gadol [1976], Kessler-Harris [1982], Lerner [1979, 1986], Lewis [1981], Scott [1988], Scott and Tilly [1978], Sicherman, Monter, Scott, and Sklar [1980], Smith-Rosenberg [1975, 1985], Vicinus [1972, 1977], and *Women and History*.

24. See, e.g., Caufield [1977], David [1971], Etienne and Leacock [1980], Friedl [1975], Jacobs [1976], Lamphere [1977], Leacock [1981], MacCormack [1977, 1981], MacCormack and Strathern [1980], Martin [1987], Ortner and Whitehead [1981], Parker and Parker [1981], Reiter [1975], Rohrlich-Leavitt et al. [1975], Rosaldo [1980], Rosaldo and Lamphere [1974], Sacks [1976, 1979], Sanday [1981], Stack et al. [1975], Steady [1981], Strathern [1972, 1981], and *Signs* [1975–present].

25. The literature is extensive. See, e.g., Ann Arbor Science for the People Collective [1977], Bleier [1984, 1988A, 1988B]; Brighton Women and Science Group [1980], Fausto-Sterling [1981, 1985], Goddard and Henifin [1984], Gould [1978, 1981], Haraway [1978A, 1978B, 1981, 1988], Harding [1986], Harding and O'Barr [1987], Hubbard [1981, 1982], Hubbard, Henifin, and Fried [1982], Hubbard and Lowe [1979], Longino [1981], Longino and Doell [1983], Keller [1982, 1983, 1985A], Lowe [1983], Midgley [1980A, 1980B], and Sayers [1982].

26. See, e.g., Ferber and Teiman [1981], Smith [1977, 1979, 1981].

27. See, e.g., Lovenduski [1981] for an overview.

28. See, e.g., Ann Arbor Science for the People Collective [1977], Bleier [1984], Dagg [1983], Dahlberg [1981], Haraway [1979, 1983], Harding [1986], Harding and O'Barr [1987], Hrdy [1981, 1988], Hubbard [1982], Hubbard, Henifin, and Fried [1982], Lancaster [1975], Leacock [1977, 1981], Leibowitz [1975, 1978], Lerner [1986], Lewontin [1976, 1979], Longino and Doell [1983], Shields [1975], Tanner [1981], Tanner and Zihlman [1976], Zihlman [1978, 1981, 1985], the bibliographies in Hubbard, Henifin, and Fried [1982], and in Bleier [1988], and *Signs* [1975–present].

29. See, e.g., Anderson [1983], Bernard [1971, 1981], Daniels [1975], Gornick and Moran [1971], Hartmann [1981], Kelly-Gadol [1976], Kuhn and Wolpe [1978], Millman and Kanter [1975], Oakley [1974, 1979, 1980], Roberts [1983], Smart and Smart [1978], Smith [1974, 1977, 1979, 1981], Standish [1982], Wolpe [1978], *Signs* [1975–present].

30. See, e.g., Carlson [1972], Chodorow [1978], Dinnerstein [1977], Flax [1978, 1983, 1986], Gilligan [1982], Horney [1967], Miller [1973, 1976], Mitchell [1973, 1974], Parlee [1979], Smith and David [1975], Walker [1981], and "Works in Progress", the Stone Center, Wellesley College.

31. The literature is extensive. See, e.g., Addelson [1983], Bishop and Weinzweig [1979], Fee [1981, 1988], Gould [1984], Gould and Wartofsky [1976], Grimshaw [1986], Harding [1980, 1982, 1983A, 1983B, 1986], Harding and Hintikka [1983], Harding and O'Barr [1987], *Hypatia: A Journal of Feminist Philosophy* [1983–present], Jaggar [1983], Jaggar and Struhl [1978], Keller and

Grontkowski [1983], Kittay and Meyers [1986], Lange [1983], Lloyd [1984], MacGuigan [1973], McMillan [1982], Moulton [1977, 1983], Ruddick [1984], Ruth [1981], Scheman [1983], Spelman [1983], Trebilcot [1984], Vetterling-Braggin, Elliston, and English [1977], and Whitbeck [1983, 1984].

32. See, e.g., Abel and Abel [1983], Gilbert and Gubar [1979], Jacobus [1979], Moi [1985], and Showalter [1977].

33. In outlining this research, I will use the phrase "sex differences" rather than "sex/gender differences" because the studies and research programs involved are committed to explaining and/or establishing a biological basis for what they assume or claim are differences between women and men in cognitive abilities and behavior.

34. I have relied on Bleier [1984, 1988A, 1988B], Hubbard, Henifin, and Fried [1982], Sayers [1982], and Star [1979] for my description of this research.

35. Bleier [1984], p. 83.

36. Ibid., p. 85.

37. Ibid., pp. 94–101.

38. Ibid., p. 81 and Bleier [1988B]. See also Hubbard [1982] and Star [1979].

39. Bleier [1984], p. 81. Emphasis mine.

40. See Bleier [1984, 1988B], Star [1979], and Hubbard, Henifin and Fried [1982].

41. See Bleier [1984, 1988B].

42. Bleier [1984], p. 81.

43. Ibid., p. 86.

44. Ibid., p. 90.

45. Ibid., p. 87.

46. Ibid.

47. Ibid., p. 86.

48. Ibid., p. 82.

49. Ibid., p. 84 and Bleier [1988B].

50. See Bleier [1984], Gould [1977, 1981], Hubbard [1982], and Lewontin, Rose and Kamin [1984] for detailed discussions of the relationships between hormones, neural events, and behaviors.

51. See, e.g., Beckwith and Durkin [1980], Bleier [1984, 1988B], Harding [1986], Harding and O'Barr [1987], Haven [1972], Hubbard, Henifin, and Fried [1982], and Shafer and Gray [1981].

52. Bleier [1984, 1988B], Gorski [1979], and Gorski, Gordon, Shryne, and Southam [1978]. Gorski [1979] set out to find "a clear signature of sexual differentiation in the brain", cited in Bleier [1984].

53. Bleier [1984, 1988B].

54. Bleier [1984, 1988B] chronicle the borrowing of hypotheses and research findings among research programs.

55. See Bleier [1988B] and Diamond, Dowling, and Johnson [1981]. See, for the extrapolation to human brains, Geschwind and Behan [1982], who appeal to a study by Chi, Dooling, and Gilles [1977] that did indicate a one to two week difference between the development of two convolutions in the right hemisphere and the

left during gestation in human fetal brains. But Chi, Dooling, and Gilles [1977] also maintained that there were no significant sex differences in measurements of ten to forty-four weeks gestational age [Bleier 1988B]. Bleier claims that the fact that these were not sex differences was not noted in Geschwind and Behan [1982].

56. Bleier [1988B], pp. 156–58.

57. Bleier [1984, 1985, 1988B]. See also Hubbard, Henifin, and Fried [1982], Sayers [1982], and Star [1979].

58. Bleier [1988B], pp. 156–57.

59. Chi, Dooling, and Gilles [1977].

60. See Bleier [1984, 1988B] for overviews of the studies involved and the borrowing of results and hypotheses.

61. Bleier [1988B]

62. Ibid., p. 154.

63. Bleier [1984], esp. chap. 4, and [1988B] document the "borrowing" of unconfirmed hypotheses among fields and specialists in this research.

64. See, in addition to Kinsbourne [1980], Bleier [1988B], Fairweather [1976], and Star [1979].

65. Kinsbourne [1980] is a review of McGlone [1980].

66. Kinsbourne [1980] cited in Bleier [1988B], pp. 153–54.

67. See, e.g., Benbow and Stanley [1980, 1983], Bleier [1984, 1985, 1988B], Brophy and Good [1970], Ehrhardt and Money [1967], Fennema and Sherman [1977, 1978], Gould [1977, 1981], Harding and O'Barr [1987], Haven [1972], Hubbard, Henifin, and Fried [1982], Maccoby and Jacklin [1974], and Sayers [1982]. See Nelson [1989] on "sex" as an isolatable variable.

68. See, e.g., Bleier [1984], esp. chap. 3, and [1988B], Gould [1981], Harding [1986], Harding and O'Barr [1987], Hirsch and Leventhal [1978], Hubbard, Henifin, and Fried [1982], Jacobsen [1978], Lewontin, Rose, and Kamin [1984], Rose [1982], and Walter [1981].

69. Levy-Agresti and Sperry [1968].

70. Buffery and Gray [1972].

71. See also Bleier [1984, 1988B] and Star [1979] for critiques of hemispheric lateralization research and findings.

72. See Bleier [1984] and [1988B]

73. Gorski [1979], cited in Bleier [1984], p. 91.

74. Bleier [1984], pp. 91–92, and [1988B].

75. See Alper [1985], Caplan, MacPherson, Tobin [1985], Kimball [1981], and McGlone [1980].

76. See n. 51.

77. See, e.g., Alper [1985], Caplan, MacPherson, and Tobin [1985], Kimball [1981], Kinsbourne [1980], and McGlone [1980].

78. See Bleier [1985, 1988B], and Diamond, Dowling, and Johnson [1981].

79. See Barash [1977, 1979], and Wilson [1978A].

80. Goldberg [1973].

81. Harris and Levine [1965].

82. The literature is extensive. See, e.g., Bleier [1984, 1988B], Gould [1977,

1981], Harding [1986], Harding and O'Barr [1987], Hubbard [1982], Hubbard, Henifin, and Fried [1982], Lewontin, Rose, and Kamin [1984], Rose [1982], Sayers [1982], Smith-Rosenberg and Rosenberg [1973], and the last fifteen years of *Signs: Journal of Women in Culture and Society.*

83. See Barash [1977, 1979], Dawkins [1976], Goldberg [1973], Verrall [1979], and Wilson [1978A].

84. See n. 83, Chapter Four, and other works by Sociobiologists listed in the Bibliography.

85. See Walsh [1982].

86. See, e.g., Bleier [1984, 1988B], Gould [1981], and Sayers [1982].

87. See, e.g., Bleier [1984], Gould [1981], Hubbard, Henifin, and Fried [1982], Lewontin, Rose, and Kamin [1984], and Sayers [1982].

88. Clarke [1973]. See also Sayers [1982].

89. See nn. 66 and 67.

90. See Gould [1981], Sayers [1982], and n. 67.

91. See nn. 66 and 67.

92. See, e.g., Sayers [1982].

93. Ibid.

94. See Bleier [1984, 1988B], Gould [1977, 1981], Harding [1986], Hubbard, Henifin, and Fried [1982], Lewontin, Rose, and Kamin [1984], Star [1979], and Walsh [1982].

95. See, e.g., Bleier [1984], esp. chaps. 3 and 4, and [1988B], and Nelson [1989].

96. Bleier [1984], p. 2.

97. Hubbard [1982], p. 3.

98. See Sayers [1982], and Shields [1975].

99. See Gould [1978] and Sayers [1982], esp. chap. 6.

100. Sayers [1982].

101. Quoted in ibid., p. 92.

102. Bleier [1988B], pp. 148–49.

103. The literature concerned with the theory, and other frameworks and theories on whose insights it built, is extensive. The criticism also encompasses more than the organizing principle on which I will focus here. See, e.g., Bleier [1984, 1988A], Crompton [1980], Dahlberg [1981], Draper [1975], Haraway [1978A, 1978B, 1981, 1983, 1988], Harding [1986], Harding and O'Barr [1987], Hubbard [1982], Hubbard, Henifin, and Fried [1982], Leibowitz [1975], Longino and Doell [1983], Martin and Voorhies [1975], Reed [1978], Reiter [1975], Sayers [1982], Slocum [1975], Tanner [1981], Tanner and Zihlman [1976], Zihlman [1978, 1981, 1985], and the last fifteen years of *Signs: Journal of Women in Culture and Society*, including the special issue "Women, Science, and Society", vol. 4, no. 1. (Autumn, 1978).

104. See, e.g., the collections in Bleier [1988A], Harding and O'Barr [1987], Ortner and Whitehead [1981], Reiter [1975], and Rosaldo and Lamphere [1974].

105. My account of "Man, the hunter theory" is influenced in part by the discussions in Bleier [1984], Hubbard [1982], and Gross and Averill [1983].

106. Herschberger [1948], Lancaster [1975], Leavitt, Sykes, and Weatherford [1975], and Rowell [1972, 1974], among others.

107. See, e.g., Hubbard [1982], Reiter [1975], Rogers [1978], Slocum [1975], Tanner [1981], and Tanner and Zihlman [1976]. See also n. 103.

108. See, e.g., Leacock [1978], Lee [1982], Ortner and Whitehead [1981], and Rosaldo and Lamphere [1974].

109. See, e.g., Dagg [1983] and Haraway [1978A, 1978B, 1983, 1988].

110. Hubbard [1982], p. 37.

111. Washburn and Lancaster [1976], pp. 293–303. Emphasis added.

112. Fox [1967], cited in Bleier [1984]. Emphasis added.

113. Oakely [1972], p. 81, cited in Hubbard [1982].

114. Hubbard [1982], p. 37.

115. Emphasis mine. Wilson [1975A], pp. 567–69.

116. See, e.g., the collections in Reiter [1975], Ortner and Whitehead [1981], and Rosaldo and Lamphere [1974]. See also nn. 102 and 103.

117. See, e.g. Bleier [1978, 1984, 1988A], Dagg [1983], Haraway [1978A, 1978B, 1983, 1988], Harding and O'Barr [1987], Lancaster [1975], and Reed [1971, 1978]. See also nn. 102 and 103.

118. See Bleier [1978, 1984, 1988A], Haraway [1978A, 1978B, 1988], Lancaster [1975], and Reed [1971].

119. Feminists also point out that neither the study of contemporary primates nor of hunter/gatherers permits us to travel in a "time machine"; neither contemporary primates nor hunter/gatherer societies are our *ancestors*. See, e.g., Longino and Doell [1983].

120. See nn. 102 and 103.

121. The literature is enormous. See nn. 102 and 103. See, also, in anthropology, the collections in Bleier [1988A], Dahlberg [1981], Harding and O'Barr [1987], Hubbard, Henifin, and Fried [1982], Hubbard and Lowe [1979], Martin and Voorhies [1975], Ortner and Whitehead [1981], Reiter [1975], Rosaldo and Lamphere [1974], Tobach and Rosoff [1978], and *Signs: Journal of Women in Culture and Society* [1975–present], especially the special issue "Women, Science, and Society, vol. 4, no. 1 (Autumn 1978). See, in primatology and animal sociology, the collections in Bleier [1978, 1988A], Harding and O'Barr [1987], and Reiter [1975] collections, and Haraway [1978A, 1978B, 1988]. See, in history, Scott [1988] and Smith-Rosenberg [1985].

122. See nn. 101, 102, and 103.

123. See, e.g., Bleier [1978, 1984, 1988A], and Haraway [1978A, 1978B, 1988].

124. See, e.g., Bleier [1978, 1984] and Haraway [1988].

125. See Dahlberg [1981], Ortner and Whitehead [1981], Reiter [1975], Rosaldo and Lamphere [1974], Tanner [1981], Tanner and Zihlman [1976], and Zihlman [1978, 1981, 1985].

126. See the collections in Bleier [1988A], Harding and O'Barr [1987], Hubbard, Henifin, and Fried [1982], Hubbard and Lowe [1979], Martin and Voorhies [1975], Ortner and Whitehead [1981], Reiter [1975], Rosaldo and

Lamphere [1974], and *Signs: Journal of Women in Culture and Society* [1975–present].

127. See, e.g., Dahlberg [1981], Longino and Doell [1987], Slocum [1975], Tanner [1981], Tanner and Zihlman [1981], and Zihlman [1978, 1981, 1985].

128. Slocum [1975], p. 43. Emphasis in original.

129. Hubbard [1982], p. 41.

130. See, e.g., Bleier [1984], Fee [1982], Griffin [1978, 1981], Haraway [1978A, 1978B, 1983, 1988], Harding [1986], Hubbard [1982], Keller [1983B, 1985A], and Merchant [1980].

131. Keller [1983B, 1985A]. See also Dyke [1986], and n. 130.

132. See, e.g., Dyke [1988], Gould [1978, 1981], Lewontin [1974, 1976], Lewontin, Rose, and Kamin [1984], and *Biology and Philosophy* [1986–present].

133. See, e.g., Bleier [1984], Griffin [1978, 1981], Haraway [1978A, 1978B], Hubbard [1986], and Keller [1985A].

134. Feminists are often more specific, however, in relating men's experiences in western societies to the models they criticize. It is beyond the scope of my discussion to consider their arguments that the centrality of dominance is specifically related to men's experiences. See, e.g., Bleier [1984], Haraway [1978A, 1978B, 1988], Hubbard [1982], and Keller [1985A].

135. "Selfish gene" was apparently coined by the Sociobiologist Dawkins in (1976).

136. Bacon's metaphors, but they are also to be found in contemporary thought. See Griffin [1978, 1981], Harding [1986], Keller [1985A], and Merchant [1980].

137. There have been several studies of the use of these metaphors to describe the scientific project. See, e.g., Keller [1985A] and Merchant [1980]. Francis Bacon's recommendation that experimental method should characterize the new science was couched in terms of the method James I had successfully used to "expose" witches; nature, for Bacon, was a "she", more specifically, a "common harlot", and the secrets of her "womb" were to be exposed and penetrated by a male science and scientist. See Merchant [1980] and Keller [1985A].

138. See Keller [1985A], pp. 129–31 for a different argument as to why scientists, at least, do not separate the language they use from something like "the relationships" incorporated in their models.

139. Keller [1983B, 1985A] calls theories that incorporate linear and hierarchical models of gene action "master molecule theories".

140. See Bleier [1984], Dyke [1988], Gould [1981], Hubbard [1982], Keller [1983B, 1985A], and Rose [1982].

141. Hubbard [1982].

142. Ibid., p. 65. Emphasis in original.

143. Ibid., p. 85.

144. See also Lewin [1981], p. 43.

145. Hubbard [1982], p. 71.

146. Bleier [1984], p. 43.

147. Ibid.

148. See also Dyke [1988], Gould [1978, 1981], and Lewontin, Rose, and Kamin [1984] for other discussions of the problems that linear, sequential causal models run into in biology.

149. Crick [1957], quoted in Keller [1983B], p. 168.

150. Keller [1983B], p. 170.

151. Ibid.

152. Ibid., p. 185.

153. Keller [1985A], pp. 131–32.

154. In fact, Bleier [1984] relates it specifically to *men's* experiences within western societies, which are, of course, patriarchal. Keller [1985A] also implies that the development of gender identity in western societies results, among other things, in a difference in girl's and boy's approaches to objects (including a more pronounced interest in individuating and dominating them among boys). Thus, both (and other feminists) would construe the prevalence of dominance in scientific models and our understandings of nature as reflecting men's experiences and their domination of science, and not only reflective of western political experience. It is beyond the scope of my discussion to discuss the relationship between dominance and men's experiences. I will focus on the relationship with western political experience, itself dominated by men.

155. Bleier [1984], pp. 200–202.

156. There are exceptions. See Keller [1985A], esp. Pts. 2 and 3, and Traweek [1984].

157. See, e.g., Ayala and Dobzhansky [1974], Dyke [1988], Keller [1985A], Lewontin [1983], Mayr [1982, 1985, 1988], Ruse [1973], and *Biology and Philosophy* [1986–present].

158. Keller [1985A], pp. 131–33.

159. Similar theses can be found in the writings of Bleier [1984], Haraway [1978A, 1978B, 1988], Hubbard [1982], and in the interviews McClintock gave to Keller in Keller [1983B]. Discussions of nonlinear models in the sciences, and of a reconceptualization of the metaphysical commitment to a deterministic and mechanistic universe are found in many writers including those cited above. See also Dyke [1988], Griffin [1978, 1981], Harding [1986], and Merchant [1980].

160. Keller [1985A], p. 132. Emphasis in original.

161. Bleier [1984], pp. 40–41.

162. Ibid., p. 76. Emphasis added.

163. Haraway [1978A], p. 25.

164. Ibid.

165. Bleier [1984] argues that this may be one of the more important consequences of the work being done by feminists in the sciences. The view is also advocated in Gould [1977, 1978, 1981] and Lewontin, Rose, and Kamin [1984], and these authors are also explicit in relating political experience to science, including their own positions.

166. Although we saw earlier that Quine does carve out a notion of "observation sentences" in which such sentences are connected directly to sensory evidence, the status of such sentences as observation sentences is relative to a community

of speakers and fundamentally connected to a going body of theory the community accepts. See the discussion in Chapter Three.

167. See my preliminary discussion in Chapter Two of the relationship between Kuhn's assumption that science communities are insulated and self-regulating, and his incommensurability thesis. I will continue to explore that relationship below.

168. I was once asked by Joseph Margolis if feminist perspectives on science were really necessary. After all, he maintained, "most" of what feminists were claiming about science has already been claimed by others (private conversation). Even if the latter were true (and, of course, neither feminist criticism nor any other framework is or ever could be *complete*), as long as activities, experiences, and power are divided by sex/gender, there will be a need for feminist perspectives.

169. See, e.g., Bleier [1984], Dahlberg [1981], Harding [1986], Leacock [1978, 1981], Longino and Doell [1983], Reiter [1975], Tanner [1981], Tanner and Zihlman [1976], and Zihlman [1978, 1981, 1985].

170. See, e.g., Barash [1977, 1979], Goldberg [1973], and Wilson [1978A]—all of which were written for the general public and argue or imply that current sex/gender arrangements are "natural". See also the discussion of Sociobiology in Chapter Four.

171. Barash [1979].

172. Wilson [1975A].

173. Yerkes [1943].

174. Barash [1979].

175. See the discussion of primatology in Bleier [1984] and Haraway [1978A, 1978B, 1988].

176. See, e.g., Bleier [1984], Haraway [1978A, 1978B, 1983, 1988], and Hrdy [1988].

177. The most obvious current examples are Sociobiology, as the discussion in Chapter Four documents. But I recently gave a paper at the University of Minnesota-Duluth on which occasion a member of the Philosophy Department seemed convinced that because male rats do "better" than female rats in negotiating mazes, this was evidence that human brains are probably sex-differentiated. The fact that we currently lack any theoretical framework for making sense of such connections, or that our current understandings of fetal and postnatal neurobiological development strongly suggest that environmental influences are integral to that development, or that girls have been closing the gap even on standardized tests as education policies have changed, did not seem to him to represent counterevidence for such generalizations.

178. See for good discussions of this issue Bleier [1984] and Gould [1978].

179. See for excellent discussions of these issues Haraway [1978A, 1978B, 1988].

180. My way of presenting the general issue owes a good deal to Jaggar [1983] and Bleier [1984].

181. See Martin [1987].

182. See Addelson [1983], and Haraway [1979].

183. See Keller [1983B] and [1985A], esp. chap. 9.

184. I am grateful to Barbara Brownstein for much of this background (private conversation), and I am also using the discussion in Keller [1985A], esp. chap. 10.

185. Keller [1985A], pp. 159–61.

186. Ibid., p. 159.

187. See ibid., esp. Pt. 3 and the Epilogue, for an argument that I think suggests that a feminist science will evolve, if at all, from within science and that does so on the basis of views that are similar to those I am advocating here.

188. See the discussion of Chapter Two.

189. See, e.g., Harding [1983B, 1988] and Jaggar [1983], esp. chap. 11.

190. See the discussion in Chapter Two.

191. Kuhn [1970], pp. 163–64.

192. As I noted in Chapter Two, Chalmers [1978] also claims this.

193. As I argue in Chapter Two, Kuhn's attention to the behavior of scientists, and his claim that it is only in retrospect that historians and philosophers do and can abstract, or rationally reconstruct, the theories at issue in revolutionary science, do not vitiate the point that part of what determines the behavior of scientists must be explicable in terms of the content of theories, assumptions, methodological principles, and the like. Kuhn's denial of this is simply not credible. If we ask scientists which of some set of sentences they agree is true and which are false, they would be able to answer us, however "tacit" their knowledge until questioned.

194. See the discussion in Chapter Three and Quine's "Two Dogmas of Empiricism" in [1963].

195. See the discussion of Chapter Two as to whether Kuhn is claiming (as he says at one point) that scientist's "world of research engagement" is a closed system—or that the whole world is up for grabs. Incommensurability requires the second *or* that other theories are not part of the evidence we have for individual theories. If Kuhn does not think scientists who disagree about competing paradigms disagree about everything, then—in order for competing paradigms to be incommensurable—it must also be the case that it is as discrete entities that individual theories (paradigms) face "the world".

196. Longino and Doell [1983].

197. Ibid., pp. 171–75. Emphasis added.

198. See the discussion of this in Chapter Three.

199. Quine's positions, and his arguments for them, are outlined and explored in some detail in Chapter Three.

200. As he notes in "Two Dogmas of Empiricism" in [1963], the analytic/synthetic distinction and the view that individual sentences have their own specifiable empirical content in isolation from a going body of theory are at bottom one view.

201. See the discussion of Chapter Three.

202. Nelson [1989].

203. Quine [1960] esp. chap. 1, and "The Limits of Knowledge" in [1976].

204. See, e.g., Campbell [1974], Paller and Campbell [1985], Hull [1982], Wuketits [1986], and Quine's "Epistemology Naturalized" in [1969].

205. C. Dyke holds both of these views (private conversation).

206. This was the reaction to a paper I gave to the Philosophy Department at Lafayette College several years ago.

207. I am paraphrasing the title of Harding [1986].

208. Harding [1986], pp. 44–47.

209. Ibid., pp. 43–48.

210. Ibid., pp. 43–47.

211. See, e.g., Quine, "Two Dogmas of Empiricism" in [1963] and "Posits and Reality" in [1966]. The issue was also discussed in Chapter Three in the section entitled "Rubbing Out Boundaries".

212. Quine, "Necessary Truth" in [1966], p. 56.

213. We should add that feminist scientists and science critics have begun to explore physics. Keller and others have criticized a commitment to unidirectional and hierarchical relationships, and the assumptions underlying the Copenhagen interpretation of quantum physics. See, e.g., Keller [1985A] and Traweek [1984, 1987]. Feminist critics are also using object-relations theory to explore the connections between boy's development of gender identity as they learn about objects, on the one hand, and the ontologies and models incorporating linear and hierarchical relationships that have dominated many sciences, on the other. See, e.g., Keller [1985A]. We could also add, hoping that someone will pay attention to the claim, that some quantum physicists are relating nature, reality, and the quantum realm to *gender*. An introduction for the layperson to quantum physics, for example, begins with the claim that we had thought the relationship between science and nature was *masculine*, but now see that it is *feminine* (Zakav [1979]). But, in the end, the evidence to date suggests that the appropriate answer to the physics question is "we just don't know yet"—by no means the same answer as "sex/gender and politics have nothing to do with physics".

214. Keller [1985A].

CHAPTER SIX

1. See also Scheman [1983] for arguments against the "private ownership" of beliefs. Scheman's arguments are different from those I will offer here.

2. Quine [1960], p. 2.

3. Quine [1987], p. 19.

4. Scheman [1983] also argues against "epistemological individualism", but she denies that "beliefs", and psychological states in general, are appropriately ascribed to individuals. I do not.

5. By the "modern intellectual tradition," I am referring to the cluster of political, metaphysical, and epistemological assumptions that we have inherited from sixteenth-, seventeenth-, and eighteenth-century Europe. In the analytic tradition in philosophy, and in a variety of ways in liberal political societies, we have continued to assume and elaborate many of these assumptions. I include

among the theorists who presume the modern view of persons as basically autonomous entities Descartes, Locke, Hume, Rawls, and Nozick, among many others.

6. Jaggar [1983], pp. 28–29.

7. See n. 17.

8. See, e.g., Parfit [1984], esp. Pt. III, in which he discusses personal identity.

9. See Jaggar [1983] for an overview of feminist attention to individualism.

10. Parfit [1984].

11. See, e.g., Quine [1987], pp. 89–92.

12. For an overview of feminist literature on the self/society dichotomy and
discussion of Marxist and socialist doubts about the latter, see Jaggar [1983].

13. Ibid., pp. 40–41. Emphasis added.

14. Ibid., p. 43.

15. Ibid., p. 125.

16. See, e.g., Harding [1983A, 1983B, 1986], Jaggar [1983], and Scheman
[1983].

17. Scheman [1983] is one such exception. Using Wittgenstein's arguments,
Scheman argues that "psychological individualism" is incoherent because "mental
states", beliefs and the like, are not appropriately ascribed to individual persons.
Jaggar [1983] uses Scheman's argument to argue against the self/society dichotomy
of Liberal theory, and she then relates Liberal feminism to empiricism. The core
of any political theory, Jaggar argues, is its view of human nature; and that view
will also underwrite the epistemology used, on her views, to justify the claims
made by those ascribing to the political theory. Empiricism, on her view, is the
epistemology that liberal theorists use to justify their theory. As will become
clear, my arguments for a relationship between the coherency of the self/society
dichotomy and "epistemological individualism" (the phrase originates in Addelson and Potter [1989]) share assumptions with each of these theorists, and disagree
with each.

18. Jaggar [1983], p. 355.

19. Ibid., chap. 11.

20. Ibid., p. 356.

21. For his comparison of values and science, see Quine, "On the Nature of
Moral Values" in [1981] and Chapter Three.

22. See Fee [1981] and Harding [1983A, 1983B, 1986].

23. Jaggar [1983], pp. 377–78.

24. Harding [1986], pp. 24–25.

25. Ibid., p. 24.

26. Ibid., p. 25.

27. As examples of the kind of "justificatory strategies" Harding and Jaggar
discuss as "feminist empiricism", see the introduction to Millman and Kanter
[1975].

28. Harding [1986], p. 25, and Jaggar [1983], chap. 11.

29. Harding [1986], p. 25.

30. Ibid. Emphasis in original.

31. Ibid., p. 38.

32. Ibid.

33. Ibid., pp. 25–26.

34. I am assuming that what I refer to here as "androcentric perspectives", and others refer to as "androcentric bias", will ultimately be understood in terms of the historically and culturally specific *social* identity of observers, rather than in terms of the biology of observers—at least not a biology that is viewed as a "given" and ahistorical. I have argued in Chapter Five that the positing of biologically based "male" and/or "female" ways of knowing is deeply suspect, given the cross-cultural and historical variations in human biology and social organization, including sex/gender arrangements and expectations.

35. See the discussion in Chapter Five.

36. See Chapter Four, and Addelson [1983] and Harding [1986].

37. See Chapter Four and Harding [1983A, 1986].

38. See Chapters Four and Five.

39. See, e.g., Jaggar [1983] for arguments against the plausibility of what she calls "the self/society dichotomy".

40. Harding [1983B, 1986].

41. Harding [1983B], pp. 314–15.

42. John Hare, for example, believes that this is an obvious implication of feminist science criticism. (private conversation).

43. Harding [1983B], p. 316.

44. See Jaggar [1984], chap. 11, Harding [1983B, 1986], and the work to develop alternative epistemologies in Harstock [1983], Flax [1983], Smith [1981], and Rose [1983].

45. Harding [1983B], pp. 316–37.

46. Harstock [1983], p. 284.

47. As Harding [1986] points out, Marx builds from Hegel's arguments about the difference in vantage points available to a slave and a master (p. 26).

48. Ibid., pp. 141–42.

49. Ibid., p. 26.

50. Ibid., p. 24, and [1983B].

51. For an overview and extensive bibliography of the challenges Marxism and feminism have made to the self/society dichotomy of liberal theory, see Jaggar [1983].

52. See the discussion in Chapter Three, and Quine, "On the Very Idea of a Third Dogma" in [1981].

53. Quine, "Empirical Content" in ibid.

54. Quine, "On the Very Idea of a Third Dogma" in ibid., pp. 40–41.

55. See the discussion in Chapter Three, Quine, "The Scope and Language of Science" and "Posits and Reality" in [1966], and Quine [1960], esp. chaps. 1 and 2.

56. Quine, "Epistemology Naturalized" in [1969], pp. 82–83.

57. See the discussion of "mental objects" in Chapter Three.

58. See "Reductionism" in Chapter Three.

59. Quine [1960], p. 264.

60. See the discussion of "mental objects" in Chapter Three.

61. See the section "Reductionism" in Chapter Three.

62. Quine [1987], pp. 14–16.

63. Ibid., pp. 12–16.

64. Quine [1978], p. 167.

65. See "Reductionism" in Chapter Three.

66. See, e.g., Quine [1987], pp. 12–16.

67. See, e.g., Bleier [1984].

68. Bleier [1984] and Hubbard [1982].

69. See Bleier [1984].

70. Ibid. See also Jaggar [1983].

71. Bleier [1984], pp. 64–65.

72. See Bleier [1984], Dyke [1988], and Jaggar [1983, 1984] for discussions of the difficulty involved in demarcating a "given" biology, including neurobiology, from environment, including sociology.

73. Bleier [1984] and Hubbard [1982].

74. See, e.g., Quine [1960], esp. chap. 1. and Chapter Three.

75. Quine [1960], pp. 4–5. See also "Speaking of Objects" in [1969].

76. Quine [1960], chaps. 1 and 2, and Quine, "Speaking of Objects" in [1969].

77. Quine was working within several. Perhaps the most important are his discomfort with the assumption of "mental objects" as if such an assumption were unproblematic (he thinks the former are an appropriate subject of study, but not yet clarified enough to be assumed), and his belief that psychology would ultimately be understood in terms of physical states, via physiology, biology and chemistry. Both constraints are spelled out in Quine, "Facts of the Matter" [1978]. See also my outline of his views on "mental objects" in Chapter Three.

78. Quine, "Speaking of Objects" in [1969], pp. 7–10.

79. Chodorow [1978]. See also Keller [1985A].

80. Keller [1985A], p. 106.

81. Quine's account of childhood development is intriguingly similar to Chodorow's account [1978] of the developing male infant's sense of objects and relations.

82. Quine [1960], chaps. 1 and 2. See also Quine, "Speaking of Objects" in [1969].

83. Quine, "Epistemology Naturalized" in [1969].

84. Ibid.

85. Jaggar [1983], chap. 11.

86. Harding [1986], p. 49.

87. Ibid., pp. 24–29.

88. Quine, "Epistemology Naturalized" in [1969], pp. 75–76. Emphasis added.

89. Quine, "Empirical Content" in [1981], p. 24.

90. See also Harding [1983B, 1986].

91. Ibid., and Jaggar [1983].

92. See, e.g., MacKinnon [1981].

93. As noted above, Millman and Kanter [1975] suggest this in their introduction.

94. Most of these examples (at least something very like them) were suggested by members of the Center for Philosophy of Science, University of Pittsburgh. I am grateful for them and especially to Peter Machamer and Gerald Massey, whose comments helped to clarify parts of this chapter. They may, however, disagree with my conclusions.

95. Quine [1974], p. 49.

CHAPTER SEVEN

1. See, e.g., "Partriarchal Science, Feminist Visions" in Bleier [1984], Keller [1985A, 1985B], Haraway [1978A, 1978B], Harding [1986], and Rose [1983].

2. Keller [1982], p. 594, and Bleier [1984], pp. 203–205.

3. The full title of the work is "Meditations On The First Philosophy In Which The Existence of God and the Distinction Between Mind and Body Are Demonstrated".

4. *The Philosophical Works of Descartes*, trans. Haldane and Ross [1911], p. 144. Subsequent quotations from the "Meditations" are from this edition.

5. See Longino [1983] for a discussion of values that are recognized to be intrinsic to science.

6. I am drawing here on an unpublished paper by H. P. Grice in which he argued that finding such a method was the project Descartes undertakes in the "Meditations". Grice argued, as I will below, that the "method of clear and distinct perception" is really that of hypothesis, objection, and reply—the method Descartes actually uses to arrive at the "certain truth" of his own existence in the Second Meditation. I do not know the title of Grice's paper.

7. The dream argument, the arguments to cast doubt on the certainty of the knowledge acquired through the senses, and the evil genius hypothesis are all geared to supporting a view Descartes states quite clearly in the First Meditation, namely, "I sometimes imagine that others deceive themselves in the things which they think they know best" (p. 147). The point is, that psychological certainty cannot guarantee truth.

8. *Works*, p. 158. The argument is "Certainly in this first knowledge [that I am a thing which thinks] there is nothing that assures me of its truth, excepting the clear and distinct perception of that which I state, which would not indeed suffice to assure me that what I say is true, if it could ever happen that a thing I conceived so clearly and distinctly could be false; and accordingly it seems to me that already I can establish as a general rule that all things which I perceive very clearly and very distinctly are true".

9. Ibid., p. 158.

10. As I note above (in n. 6), this argument was made by H. P. Grice in an unpublished paper.

11. *Works*, p. 150.

12. Ibid., pp. 174–76. "Whence . . . come my errors? They come from the sole fact that since the will is much wider in its range and compass than the

understanding, I do not restrain it within the same bounds, but extend it also to things which I do not understand" (pp. 175–76).

13. Ibid., p. 176.

14. It does not, in fact, take god off the hook, for Descartes goes on *after* this argument to offer possible explanations for why god allows evil—in this case, error.

15. This is stated clearly. "But if I abstain from giving my judgment on any thing when I do not perceive it with sufficient clearness and distinctness, it is plain that I act rightly and am not deceived. . . . the light of nature teaches us that the knowledge of the understanding should always precede the determination of the will". *Works*, p. 176.

16. The matter of the nature of that "truth" has been the subject of considerable debate in philosophy.

17. I have argued that groups "acquire" knowledge, but the views I have advocated suggest that they construct knowledge, not passively take it in.

18. See the conclusion of Chapter Three.

19. Private conversation. I am grateful to Sibyl Cohen for helping me to clarify my ideas in this chapter. There is work being done by feminist theorists that links the ideal of "distance" and "disengagement" to ideas about masculinity, and also to childrearing practices—specifically, the fact that mothers are the primary caretakers of young children and the consequences of this for the different senses of "self", and of one's relation to others and objects, that female and male infants develop as they separate from a female in societies in which anything that can be associated with "femininity" is prohibited for the male. See, for example, Keller [1985A] and Chodorow [1978].

20. See, e.g., Wade [1977] for discussion of the recent debates over whether, in Wade's words, the "key" (of gene splicing) should be "thrown away". See also Holtzman [1989].

21. A number of scientists and science critics who describe themselves as Marxists have linked social identity and values to the content of science. See, e.g., Gould [1979, 1981]; Lewontin, Rose, and Kamin [1984], Dyke [1988], and other works listed in the Bibliography and notes for Chapters Four and Five.

22. Kuhn [1970], p. 49.

23. Quine [1960], pp. 3–4.

Bibliography

Abel, E., and E. Abel, eds. 1983. *The "Signs" Reader: Women, Gender, and Scholarship*. Chicago: University of Chicago Press.

Addelson, K. P. 1983. "The Man of Professional Wisdom". *Discovering Reality*. Edited by S. Harding and M. Hintikka. Dordrecht: D. Reidel.

——. 1990. "Why Philosophers Should Become Sociologists (and vice versa)". *Symbolic Interactionism and Cultural Studies*. Edited by H. Becker and M. McCall. Chicago: University of Chicago Press.

Addelson, K. P., and E. Potter. 1989. "Making Knowledge". *Gender and Knowledge*. Edited by E. Messer-Davidow and J. Hartmann. Forthcoming.

Aldrich, M. L. 1978. "Women in Science". *Signs: Journal of Women in Culture and Society* 4, no. 1.

Alper, J., et al. 1976. "The Implications of Sociobiology". *Science*, April 30, pp. 424 – 27. Reprinted in *The Sociobiology Debate*. Edited by A. Caplan. New York: Harper & Row, 1978.

Alper, J., J. Beckwith, and L. G. Miller. 1978. "Sociobiology Is a Political Issue". *The Sociobiology Debate*. Edited by A. Caplan. New York: Harper & Row.

Alper, J. S. 1985. "Sex Differences in Brain Asymmetry: A Critical Analysis". *Feminist Studies* 11.

Anderson M. 1983. *Thinking about Women*. New York: Macmillan.

Ann Arbor Science for the People Collective, eds. 1977. *Biology as a Social Weapon*. Minneapolis: Burgess.

Anthony, H. D. 1948. *Science and Its Background*. London: Macmillan.

Arditti, R., P. Brennan, and S. Cavrak, eds. 1980. *Science and Liberation*. Boston: South End Press.

Ayala, F. J. 1987. "The Biological Roots of Morality". *Biology and Philosophy* 2, no. 3: 235 – 52.

Ayala, F. J., and T. Dobzhansky, eds. 1974. *Studies in the Philosophy of*

Biology: Reduction and Related Problems. Berkeley: University of California Press.

Ayer, A. J. 1950. *Language, Truth, and Logic*. New York: Dover.

———. 1955. *The Foundations of Empirical Knowledge*. London: Macmillan.

———, ed. 1959. *Logical Positivism*. Glencoe: Free Press.

Barash, D. 1977. *Sociobiology and Behavior*. New York: Elsevier.

———. 1979. *The Whisperings Within*. New York: Harper & Row.

Barnes, B. 1977. *Interests and the Growth of Knowledge*. Boston: Routledge & Kegan Paul.

———. 1983. "On the Conventional Character of Knowledge and Cognition." *Science Observed*. Edited by K. D. Knorr-Cetina and M. Mulkay. London: Sage.

Barry, K. 1979. *Female Sexual Slavery*. Englewood Cliffs, N.J.: Prentice-Hall.

Bart, P. B. 1977. "Biological Determinism and Sexism: Is It All in the Ovaries?" *Biology as a Social Weapon*. Edited by Ann Arbor Science for the People Collective. Minneapolis: Burgess.

Bartky, S. 1977. "Toward a Phenomenology of Feminist Consciousness". *Feminism and Philosophy*. Edited by M. Vetterling-Braggin, F. Elliston, and J. English. Totowa, N.J.: Littlefield, Adams.

———. 1979. "On Psychological Oppression". *Philosophy and Women*. Edited by S. Bishop and S. Weinzweig. Belmont, Calif.: Wadsworth.

———. 1982. "Narcissim, Femininity and Alienation". *Social Theory and Practice* 8, no. 2.

Bayer, A. E., and H. S. Astin, 1968. "Sex Differences in Academic Rank and Salary Among Science Doctorates in Teaching". *Journal of Human Resources* 3.

Bayer, A. E., and J. Austic. 1975. "Sex Differentials in the Academic Reward System". *Science* 188.

Beach, F. 1974A. "Behavioral Endocrinology and the Study of Reproduction". Fifth Annual Carl G. Hartman Lecture, cited in R. Bleier (1984).

———. 1974B. "Human Sexuality and Evolution". *Reproductive Behavior*. Edited by W. Montagna and W. Sadler. New York: Plenum.

———. 1978. "Sociobiology and Interspecific Comparisons of Behavior". *Sociobiology and Human Nature*. Edited by M. S. Gregory, A. Silvers, and D. Sutch. San Francisco: Jossey-Bass.

Beckwith, J., and J. Durkin. 1980. "Girls, Boys and Math". *Science for the People*. Edited by Ann Arbor Science for the People Collective. Minneapolis: Burgess.

Benbow, C., and J. Stanley. 1980. "Sex Differences in Mathematical Ability: Fact or Artifact?" *Science* 210.

———. 1983. "Sex Differences in Mathematical Reasoning Ability: More Facts". *Science* 222.

Bergmann, B. R. 1974. "Occupational Segregation: Wages and Profits When Employers Discriminate by Race or Sex". *Eastern Economic Journal* 1, April/July.

Bernard, J. 1971. "The Myth of the Happy Marriage". *Woman in Sexist Society: Studies in Power and Powerlessness*. Edited by V. Gornick and B. Moran. New York: Basic Books.

————. 1981. *The Female World*. New York: Macmillan.

Bethel, L., and B. Smith. 1979. *Conditions: Five, The Black Women's Issue* (pamphlet). N.p.

Biology and Philosophy. 1986 – present. Dordrecht: D. Reidel.

Birke, L. 1982. "From Sin to Sickness: Hormonal Theories of Lesbianism". *Biological Woman—The Convenient Myth*. Edited by R. Hubbard, M. S. Henifin, and B. Fried. Cambridge: Schenkman.

Bishop, S., and M. Weinzweig, eds. 1979. *Philosophy and Women*. Belmont, Calif.: Wadsworth.

Blau, F. D. 1977. *Equal Pay in the Office*. Lexington, Mass.: Lexington Books.

————. 1979. "Women in the Labor Force". *Women: A Feminist Perspective*. Edited by J. Freeman. New York: Mayfield.

Bleier, R. 1976. "Myths of the Biological Inferiority of Women: An Exploration of the Sociology of Biological Research". *University of Michigan Papers in Women's Studies* 2.

————. 1978. "Social and Political Bias in Science: An Examination of Animal Studies and Their Generalizations to Human Behavior and Evolution". *Genes and Gender I: First in a Series on Hereditarianism and Women*. Edited by E. Tobach and B. Rosoff. New York: Gordian Press.

————. 1979. "Social and Political Bias in Science". *Genes and Gender II*. Edited by R. Hubbard and M. Lowe. New York: Gordian Press.

————. 1984. *Science and Gender: A Critique of Biology and Its Theories on Women*. New York: Pergamon Press.

————. 1985. "Gender and Science", paper delivered at Princeton University.

————, ed. 1988A. *Feminist Approaches to Science*. New York: Pergamon Press.

————. 1988B. "Sex Differences Research: Science or Belief?" *Feminist Approaches to Science*. Edited by R. Bleier. New York: Pergamon Press.

Bloor, D. 1977. *Knowledge and Social Imagery*. London: Routledge & Kegan Paul.

————. 1983. *Wittgenstein: A Social Theory of Knowledge*. London: Macmillan.

Boalt, G., H. Lantz, and H. Herlin. 1973. *The Academic Pattern: A Comparison Between Researchers and Non-Researchers, Men and Women*. Stockholm: Almquist and Wiksell.

Boston Nurses Group. 1978. "The False Promise: Professionalism in Nursing" (pamphlet). Somerville, Mass.: New England Free Press.

Bourdieu, P., and J. Passeron. 1977. *Reproduction in Education, Society and Culture*. Translated by Richard Nice. London: Sage.

Bourdieu, Pierre. 1977. *Outline of a Theory of Practice*. Cambridge: Cambridge University Press.

Braverman, H. 1974. *Labor and Monopoly Capital: The Degradation of Work in the Twentieth Century*. New York: Monthly Press.

Bridenthal, R., and C. Koonz. 1977. *Becoming Visible: Women in European History*. Boston: Houghton Mifflin.

Brighton Women and Science Group. 1980. *Alice Through the Microscope.* London: Virago Press.

Brophy, J. E., and T. L. Good. 1970. "Teacher's Communication of Differential Expectations for Children's Classroom Performance". *Journal of Educational Psychology* 6.

Broverman, I., S. Vogel, D. Broverman, F. Clarkson, and P. Rosenkrantz. 1972. "Sex-role Stereotypes: A Current Appraisal". *Journal of Social Sciences* 28.

Brown, J. K. 1975. "Iroquois Women: An Ethnohistoric Note". *Toward an Anthropology of Women.* Edited by R. Reiter. New York: Monthly Review Press.

Brownmiller, S. 1976. *Against Our Will: Men, Women and Rape.* New York: Bantam Press.

Buffery, W., and J. Gray. 1972. "Sex Differences in the Development of Spatial and Linguistic Skills". *Gender Differences: Their Ontogeny and Significance.* Edited by C. Ounsted and D. C. Taylor. Edinburgh: Churchill Livingstone.

Burian, R. M. 1978. "A Methodological Critique of Sociobiology". *The Sociobiology Debate.* Edited by A. Caplan. New York: Harper & Row.

———. 1981. "Human Sociobiology and Genetic Determinism". *Philosophical Forum* 13.

———. 1983. "Adaptation". *Dimensions of Darwinism.* Edited by M. Grene. Cambridge: Cambridge University Press.

Campbell, D. T. 1974. "Evolutionary Epistemology". *The Philosophy of Karl Popper.* Edited by P. A. Schilpp. La Salle, Ill.: Open Court.

Caplan, A. L., ed. 1978. *The Sociobiology Debate.* New York: Harper & Row.

Caplan, P. J., G. M. MacPherson, and P. Tobin. 1985. "Do Sex-Related Differences in Spatial Abilities Exist?" *American Psychologist* 40.

Carlson, R. 1972. "Understanding Women: Implications for Personality Theory and Research". *Journal of Social Issues* 28, no. 2.

Carmichael, L., ed. 1954. *Manual of Child Psychology.* New York: John Wiley and Sons.

Carnap, R. 1962. *Logical Foundations of Probability.* Chicago: University of Chicago Press.

———. 1967. "Empiricism, Semantics, and Ontology". *The Linguistic Turn.* Edited by R. Rorty. Chicago: University of Chicago Press.

Caufield, M. 1977. "Universal Sex Oppression? A Critique from Marxist Anthropology". *Catalyst,* Summer.

———. 1985. "Sexuality in Human Evolution: What is 'Natural' in Sex?" *Feminist Studies* 11, no. 2.

Chalmers, A. F. 1978. *What Is This Thing Called Science?* Queensland: University of Queensland Press.

Chi, J. G., E. C. Dooling, and F. H. Gilles. 1977. "Gyral Development of the Human Brain". *Annals of Neurology* 1.

Chodorow, N. 1974. "Family Structure and Feminine Personality". *Woman, Culture and Society.* Edited by M. Z. Rosaldo and L. Lamphere. Stanford: Stanford University Press.

————. 1978. *The Reproduction of Mothering*. Berkeley: University of California Press.

Christian, B. 1983. "Alternate Versions of the Gendered Past: African Women Writers vs. Illich". *Feminist Issues* 3.

Clarke, E. H. 1873. *Sex in Education: or, A Fair Chance for Girls*. Boston: J. R. Osgood.

Clarke, L. and L. Lange, eds. 1979. *The Sexism of Social and Political Theory: Women and Reproduction from Plato to Nietzsche*. Toronto: University of Toronto Press.

Cole, J. 1977. *Woman's Place in the Scientific Community*. New York: John Wiley.

Cole, J., and S. Cole. 1973. *Social Stratification in Science*. Chicago: University of Chicago Press.

Collier, J. F., and M. Z. Rosaldo. 1981. "Politics and Gender in Simple Societies". *Sexual Meanings: The Cultural Construction of Gender and Sexuality*. Edited by S. B. Ortner and H. Whitehead. Cambridge: Cambridge University Press.

Collins, H. 1981. "Stages in the Empirical Programme of Relativism". *Social Studies in Science* 11.

Crick, F. 1957. "On Protein Synthesis". *Symposium of the Society of Experimental Biology* 12.

Crompton, R. 1980. "Old Bones Shatter Hunter Myths". *Science for the People* 12.

Dagg, A. I. 1983. *Harem and Other Horrors: Sexual Bias in Behavioural Biology*. Waterloo, Ont.: Otter Press.

Dahlberg, F., ed. 1981. *Woman the Gatherer*. New Haven: Yale University Press.

Daly, M. 1978. *Gyn/Ecology: The Metaethics of Radical Feminism*. Boston: Beacon Press.

————. 1984. *Pure Lust: Elemental Feminist Philosophy*. Boston: Beacon Press.

Daniels, A. 1975. "Feminist Perspectives on Sociological Research". *Another Voice*. Edited by M. Millman and R. M. Kanter. New York: Anchor.

Davidson, D., and J. Hintikka. 1969. *Words and Objections: Essays on the Work of W. V. Quine*. Boston: D. Reidel.

Davies, J. J. 1968. *On the Scientific Method*. London: Collins.

Dawkins, R. 1976. *The Selfish Gene*. New York: Oxford University Press.

Delefes, P., and B. Jackson. 1972. "Teacher-Pupil Interaction as a Function of Location in the Classroom". *Psychology in the Schools* 9.

DeVore, I., and R. Trivers. 1976. *Sociobiology: Doing What Comes Naturally* (film). Produced and distributed by Document Associates, Inc., 880 Third Avenue, New York, N.Y.

Diamond, J. T. 1978. "The Dialectical Relationship of Medicine and Nursing". Unpublished manuscript.

Diamond, M. C., G. A. Dowling, and R. E. Johnson. 1981. "Morphologic

Cerebral Cortical Asymmetry in Male and Female Rats". *Experimental Neurology* 71.

Dinnerstein, D. 1977. *The Mermaid and the Minotaur: Sexual Arrangements and the Human Malaise*. New York: Harper & Row.

Draper, P. 1975. "!Kung Women: Contrasts in Sexual Egalitarianism in Foraging and Sedentary Contexts". *Toward an Anthropology of Women*. Edited by R. Reiter. New York: Monthly Review Press.

Dyke, C. 1986. "The Evolutionary Window and the Ultimate Sieve". Paper delivered at San Diego State, Feb. 26.

———. 1988. *The Evolutionary Dynamics of Complex Systems*. New York: Oxford University Press.

Dziech, B. W., and L. Weiner. 1984. *The Lecherous Professor: Sexual Harassment on Campus*. Boston: Beacon Press.

Eaton, G. G. 1974. "Male Dominance and Aggression in Japanese Macaque Reproduction". *Reproductive Behavior*. Edited by W. Montagna and W. Sadler. New York: Harper & Row.

Edwards, C. 1975. "Societal Complexity and Moral Development: A Kenyan Study". *Ethos* 3.

Ehrenreich, B., and D. English. 1979. *For Her Own Good: 150 Years of the Expert's Advice to Women*. Garden City, N.Y.: Anchor Books.

Ehrhardt, A., and J. Money. 1967. "Progestin-induced Hermaphroditism: IQ and Psychosexual Identity in a Study of Ten Girls". *Journal of Sex Research* 3.

Ehrhardt, A., R. Epstein, and J. Money. 1968. "Fetal Androgens and Female Gender Identity in the Early-treated Adrenogenital Syndrome". *Johns Hopkins Medical Journal* 122.

Eisenstein, H. 1983. *Contemporary Feminist Thought*. Boston: G. K. Hall.

Eisenstein, H., and A. Jardine, eds. 1980. *The Future of Difference*. Boston: G. K. Hall.

Eisenstein, Z. 1978. "Some Notes on the Relations of Capitalist Patriarchy". *Capitalist Patriarchy and the Case for Socialist Feminism*. Edited by Z. Eisenstein. New York: Monthly Review Press.

———, ed. 1978. *Capitalist Patriarchy and the Case for Socialist Feminism*. New York: Monthly Review Press.

———. 1981A. "The Sexual Politics of the New Right: Understanding the 'Crisis for Liberalism' for the 1980s". *Feminist Theory: A Critique of Ideology*. Edited by N. Keohane, M. Rosaldo, and B. Gelpi. Chicago: University of Chicago Press.

———. 1981B. *The Radical Future of Liberal Feminism*. New York: Longman.

Erikson, E. H. 1950. *Childhood and Society*. New York: W. W. Norton.

———. 1968. *Identity: Youth and Crisis*. New York: W. W. Norton.

Etienne, M., and E. Leacock, eds. 1980. *Women and Colonization: Anthropological Perspectives*. New York: Praeger.

Fairweather, H. 1976. "Sex Differences in Cognition". *Cognition* 4.

Farley, L. 1978. *Sexual Shakedown: The Sexual Harassment of Women on the Job*. New York: Warner Press.

Fausto-Sterling, A. 1981. "Women and Science". *Women's Studies International Quarterly* 4.

———. 1985. *Myths of Gender: Biological Theories about Women and Men.* New York: Basic Books.

Fee, E. 1981. "Women's Nature and Scientific Objectivity." *Woman's Nature: Rationalizations of Inequality.* Edited by M. Lowe and R. Hubbard. New York: Pergamon Press. First published in 1980 as "Is Feminism a Threat to Scientific Objectivity?" *International Journal of Women's Studies* 4.

———. 1982. "A Feminist Critique of Scientific Objectivity". *Science for the People* 14.

———. 1988. "Critiques of Modern Science: The Relationship of Feminism to Other Radical Epistemologies". *Feminist Approaches to Science.* Edited by R. Bleier. New York: Pergamon Press.

Fennema, E., and J. Sherman. 1977. "Sex-related Differences in Mathematics Achievement, Spatial Visualization, and Affective Factors". *American Educational Research Journal* 14.

———. 1978. "Sex-related Differences in Mathematics Achievement and Related Factors: A Further Study". *Journal for Research in Mathematics Education* 9.

Ferber, M., and M. L. Teiman. 1981. "The Impact of Feminism on Economics". *Men's Studies Modified.* Edited by D. Spender. New York: Pergamon Press.

Ferguson, A. 1979. "Women as a New Revolutionary Class." *Between Labor and Capital.* Edited by P. Walker. Boston: South End Press.

———. 1980. "Patriarchy, Sexual Identity and the Sexual Revolution". *Signs: Journal of Women in Culture and Society* 7, no. 1.

Ferguson, A., and N. Folbre. 1981. "The Unhappy Marriage of Patriarchy and Capitalism". *Women and Revolution: A Discussion of the Unhappy Marriage of Marxism and Feminism.* Edited by L. Sargent. Boston: Southend Press.

Feyerabend, P. 1970. "Against Method". *Minnesota Studies in the Philosophy of Science* 4.

Flax, J. 1978. "The Conflict Between Nurturance and Autonomy in Mother-Daughter Relationships and Within Feminism". *Feminist Studies* 4, no. 2.

———. 1983. "Political Philosophy and the Patriarchal Unconscious". *Discovering Reality.* Edited by S. Harding and M. Hintikka. Dordrecht: D. Reidel.

———. 1986. "Gender as a Social Problem: In and For Feminist Theory". *American Studies/Aermika Studien.*

Fox, R. 1967. *Kinship and Marriage.* New York: Penguin Books.

Freeman, J., ed. 1979. *Women: A Feminist Perspective,* 2nd ed. New York: Mayfield.

Freud, S. 1905. "Three Essays on the Theory of Sexuality". *The Standard Edition of the Complete Psychological Works of Sigmund Freud.* Translated and edited by J. Strachey. London: Hogarth Press, 1961.

———. 1925. "Some Psychical Consequences of the Anatomical Distinction Between the Sexes." *The Standard Edition of the Complete Psychological Works of Sigmund Freud.* Translated and edited by J. Strachey. London: Hogarth Press.

———. 1930. "Civilization and its Discontents". *The Standard Edition of the*

Complete Psychological Works of Sigmund Freud. Translated and edited by J. Strachey. London: Hogarth Press.

Fried, B. 1982. "Boys Will Be Boys: The Language of Sex and Gender". *Biological Woman—The Convenient Myth.* Edited by R. Hubbard, M. Henifin, and B. Fried. Boston: G. K. Hall.

Friedl, E. 1975. *Women and Men: An Anthropologist's View.* New York: Holt, Rinehart, Winston.

Frolov, I. T. 1986. "Genes or Culture? A Marxist Perspective on Humankind". *Biology and Philosophy* 1, no. 1.

Gamarnikow, E. 1978. "Sexual Division of Labour: The Case of Nursing". *Feminism and Materialism.* Edited by A. Kuhn and A. Wolpe. Boston: Routledge & Kegan Paul.

Garside, C. 1971. "Can a Woman Be Good in the Same Way as a Man?" *Dialogue* 10, no. 3.

Geschwind, N., and P. Behan. 1982. "Left-Handedness: Association with Immune Disease, Migraine, and Developmental Learning Disorder". *Proceedings of National Academy of Sciences* 79.

Gilbert, S. M., and S. Gubar. 1979. *The Madwoman in the Attic: The Woman Writer and the Nineteenth-Century Literary Imagination.* New Haven: Yale University Press.

Gilder, G. 1981. *Wealth and Poverty.* New York: Basic Books.

Gilligan, C. 1977. "In a Different Voice: Women's Conceptions of Self and Morality". *Harvard Educational Review* 47, no. 4.

———. 1979. "Woman's Place in Man's Life Cycle". *Harvard Educational Review* 49, no. 4.

———. 1982. *In a Different Voice: Psychological Theory and Women's Development.* Cambridge: Harvard University.

Gilligan, C., and J. Murphy. 1977. "Development from Adolescence to Adulthood: The Philosopher and the 'Dilemma of the Fact' ". *Intellectual Development Beyond Childhood* 5.

Glazer, N., and H. Waehrer, eds., 1977. *Women in a Man-Made World.* Chicago: Rand McNally.

Glenn, E., and R. Feldberg. 1979. "Clerical Work: The Female Occupation". *Women: A Feminist Perspective,* 2nd ed. Edited by J. Freeman. New York: Mayfield.

Glennon, L. 1979. *Women and Dualism.* White Plains, N.Y.: Longman Press.

Goddard, N., and M. S. Henifin. 1984. "A Feminist Approach to the Biology of Women". *Women's Studies Quarterly* 12.

Goldberg, S. 1973. *The Inevitability of Patriarchy.* New York: Morrow.

Goldfoot, D. 1983. "On Measuring Behavioral Sex Differences in Social Contexts". *Neurobiology of Reproduction.* Edited by N. Adler and D. Pfaff. New York: Plenum Press.

Gordon, L. 1982. *Woman's Body, Woman's Right.* New York: Penguin Books.

Gornick, V. 1983. *Women in Science: Portraits of a World in Transition.* New York: Simon and Schuster.

Gornick, V., and B. Moran, eds. 1971. *Woman in Sexist Society*. New York: New American Library.

Gorski, R. 1979. "The Neuroendocrinology of Reproduction: An Overview". *Biology of Reproduction* 20.

Gorski, R., J. H. Gordon, J. E. Shryne, and A. M. Southam. 1978. "Evidence for a Morphological Sex Difference Within the Meidal Preoptic Area of the Rat Brain." *Brain Research* 148.

Gorski, R., R. E. Harlan, C. D. Jacobsen, J. E. Shryne, and E. M. Southam, eds. 1980. "Evidence for the Existence of a Sexually Dimorphic Nucleus in the Preoptic Area of the Rat". *Journal of Comparative Neurology* 193.

Gould, C., ed. 1984. *Beyond Domination: New Perspectives on Women and Philosophy*. Totowa, N.J.: Rowman & Allenheld.

Gould, C. and M. Wartofsky, eds. 1976. *Women and Philosophy: Towards a Philosophy of Liberation*. New York: Putnam.

Gould, S. J. 1977. *Ever Since Darwin*. New York: W. W. Norton.

———. 1978. "Biological Potential vs Biological Determinism". *The Sociobiology Debate*. Edited by A. L. Caplan. New York: Harper & Row.

———. 1981. *The Mismeasure of Man*. New York: W. W. Norton.

Gould, S. J., and R. C. Lewontin, 1979. "The Spandrels of San Marco and the Panglossian Paradigm: A Critique of the Adaptationist Programme". *Proceedings of the Royal Society of London* B 205.

Gregory, M. S., A. Silvers, and D. Sutch, eds. 1978. *Sociobiology and Human Nature*. San Francisco: Jossey-Bass.

Grene, M., ed. 1983. *Dimensions of Darwinism*. Cambridge: Cambridge University Press.

Griffin, S. 1978. *Woman and Nature: The Roaring Inside Her*. New York: Harper Colophon.

———. 1979. "Rape: The All-American Crime". *Feminism and Philosophy*. Edited by M. Vetterling-Braggin, F. Elliston, and J. English. Totowa, N.J.: Littlefield, Adams.

———. 1980. "The Way of All Ideology". *Feminist Theory: A Critique of Ideology*. Edited by N. Keohane, M. Rosaldo, and B. Gelphi. Chicago: University of Chicago Press.

———. 1981. *Pornography and Silence: Culture's Revenge Against Nature*. New York: Harper Colophon.

Grimshaw, J. 1986. *Philosophy and Feminist Thinking*. Minneapolis: University of Minnesota Press.

Gross, M., and M. B. Averill. 1983. "Evolution and Patriarchal Myths of Scarcity and Competition". *Discovering Reality*. Edited by S. Harding and M. Hintikka. Dordrecht: D. Reidel.

Haas, V., and C. Perrucci, eds. 1984. *Women in Scientific and Engineering Professions*. Ann Arbor: University of Michigan Press.

Hacking, I., ed. 1982. *Scientific Revolutions*. Oxford: Oxford University Press.

Hamilton, W. D. 1964. "The Genetical Theory of Social Behavior". *Journal of Theoretical Biology* 7.

————. 1975. "Innate Social Aptitudes of Man: An Approach from Evolutionary Genetics". *Biosocial Anthropology.* Edited by R. Fox. New York: Wiley.

Hampshire, S. 1978. "The Illusion of Sociobiology". *New York Review of Books,* October 12.

Hanson, N. R. 1958. *Patterns of Discovery.* Cambridge: Cambridge University Press.

Haraway, D. 1978A, B. "Animal Sociology and a Natural Economy of the Body Politic," Parts I and II. *Signs: Journal of Women in Culture and Society* 4. Reprinted in 1987 in *Sex and Scientific Inquiry.* Edited by Sandra Harding and Jean O'Barr. Chicago: University of Chicago Press.

————. 1979. "The Biological Enterprise: Sex, Mind, and Profit from Human Engineering to Sociobiology". *Radical History Review* 20.

————. 1981. "In the Beginning Was the Word: The Genesis of Biological Theory". *Signs: Journal of Women in Culture and Society* 6, no. 3.

————. 1983. "The Contest for Primate Nature: Daughters of Man the Hunter in the Field, 1960 – 1980". *The Future of American Democracy.* Edited by Mark Kann. Philadelphia: Temple University Press.

————. 1988. "Primatology is Politics by Other Means". in *Feminist Approaches to Science.* Edited by R. Bleier. New York: Pergamon Press.

Harding, S., ed. 1976. *Can Theories Be Refuted? Essays on the Quine-Duhem Thesis.* Dordrecht: Reidel.

————. 1980. "The Norms of Social Inquiry and Masculine Experience". *PSA* 2.

————. 1981. "The Gender Politics of Infancy." *Quest: A Feminist Quarterly* 5, no. 3.

————. 1983A. "The Science Question in Feminism". Paper delivered at Temple University and Villanova University.

————. 1983B. "Why Has The Sex/Gender System Become Visible Only Now?" *Discovering Reality: Feminist Perspectives in Epistemology, Metaphysics, Methodology, and Philosophy of Science.* Edited by S. Harding and M. Hintikka. Dordrecht: D. Reidel.

————. 1984. "Is Gender a Variable in Conceptions of Rationality?" *Beyond Domination: New Perspectives on Women and Philosophy.* Edited by C. Gould. Totowa, N.J.: Rowman & Allenheld.

————. 1986. *The Science Question in Feminism.* Ithaca, N.Y.: Cornell University Press.

Harding, S., and M. Hintikka, eds. 1983. *Discovering Reality: Feminist Perspectives on Epistemology, Metaphysics, Methodology, and Philosophy of Science.* Dordrecht: D. Reidel.

Harding, S., and J. F. O'Barr, eds. 1987. *Sex and Scientific Inquiry.* Chicago: University of Chicago Press.

Hardyck, C., O. Tzeng, and W. Wang. 1978. "Cerebral Lateralization of Function and Bilingual Decision Processes: Is Thinking Lateralized?" *Brain and Language* 5.

Harris, G., and S. Levine. 1965. "Sexual Differentiation of the Brain and its Experimental Control". *Journal of Physiology* 181.

Harstock, N. 1979. "Feminist Theory and the Development of Revolutionary Strategy". *Capitalist Patriarchy and the Case for Socialist Feminism.* Edited by Z. Eisenstein. New York: Monthly Review Press.

———. 1983. "The Feminist Standpoint: Developing the Grounds for a Specifically Feminist Historical Materialism". *Discovering Reality: Feminist Perspectives on Epistemology, Metaphysics, Methodology, and Philosophy of Science.* Edited by S. Harding and M. Hintikka. Dordrecht: D. Reidel.

Hartmann, H. 1981. "The Unhappy Marriage of Marxism and Feminism: Towards a More Progressive Union". *Women and Revolution.* Edited by L. Sargent. Boston: South End Press.

Haven, E. W. 1972. "Factors Associated with the Selection of Advanced Academic Mathematical Courses by Girls in High School". *Research Bulletin* 72 – 12, Princeton Educational Testing Service.

Held, V. 1985. "Feminism and Epistemology: Recent Work on the Connection Between Gender and Knowledge". *Philosophy and Public Affairs* 14, no. 3.

Hempel, C. 1965. *Aspects of Scientific Explanation and Other Essays in the Philosophy of Science.* New York: Free Press.

———. 1966. *Philosophy of Natural Science.* Englewood Cliffs, N.J.: Prentice Hall.

Herschberger, R. 1948. *Adam's Rib.* Reprinted in 1970 in New York: Harper & Row.

Hirsch, H. V. B., and A. G. Leventhal. 1978. "Functional Modification of the Developing Visual System". Handbook of Sensory Physiology 9.

Hochschild, A. 1975. "The Sociology of Feeling and Emotion: Selected Possibilities". *Another Voice: Feminist Perspectives on Social Life and Social Science.* Edited by M. Millman and R. M. Kanter. New York: Anchor Books.

Holcomb, H. R. 1987. "Criticism, Commitment, and the Growth of Human Sociobiology". *Biology and Philosophy* 2, no. 1.

Hole, J., and E. Levine. 1971. *Rebirth of Feminism.* New York: Quadrangle.

Holloway, R. 1975. *The Role of Human Social Behavior on the Evolution of the Brain.* New York: American Museum of Natural History.

Holstein, C. 1976. "Development of Moral Judgment: A Longitudinal Study of Males and Females". *Child Development,* 47.

Holtzman, N. A. 1989. *Proceed with Caution: Predicting Genetic Risks in the Recombinant DNA Era.* Baltimore: The Johns Hopkins University Press.

Horner, M. S. 1972. "Toward an Understanding of Achievement-related Conflicts in Women". *Journal of Social Issues* 28.

Horney, K. 1967. *Feminine Psychology.* London: Routledge & Kegan Paul.

Hornig, L. S. 1979. *Climbing the Academic Ladder: Doctoral Women Scientists in Academe.* Washington, D.C.: National Academy of Sciences.

———. 1982. "National Academy of Science's Committee Report on the Education and Employment of Women in Science and Engineering". Summarized in *Technology Review* (MIT), November/December 1984.

————. 1984. "Women in Science and Engineering: Why So Few?" *Technology Review* (MIT), November/December.

Howell, N. 1979. "Sociobiological Hypotheses Explored". *Science* 206.

Howell, W. 1973. *Evolution of the Genus Homo*. Reading, Mass.: Addison-Wesley.

Hrdy, S. B. 1981. *The Woman That Never Evolved*. Cambridge: Harvard University Press, 1981.

————. 1988. "Empathy, Polyandry, and the Myth of the Coy Female". *Feminist Approaches to Science*. Edited by R. Bleier. New York: Pergamon Press.

Hubbard, R. 1978. "From Termite to Human Behavior". *Psychology Today* 12.

————. 1981. "The Emperor Doesn't Wear Any Clothes: The Impact of Feminism on Biology". *Men's Studies Modified*. Edited by D. Spender. New York: Pergamon Press.

————. 1982. "Have Only Men Evolved?" *Biological Woman—The Convenient Myth*. Edited by R. Hubbard, M. Henifin, and B. Fried. Cambridge: Schenkman.

Hubbard, R., M. Henifin, and B. Fried, eds. 1982. *Biological Woman—The Convenient Myth*. Cambridge: Schenkman.

Hubbard, R., and M. Lowe, eds. 1979. *Genes and Gender II: Pitfalls in Research on Sex and Gender*. New York: Gordian Press.

Hull, D. 1982. "The Naked Meme". *Learning, Development, and Culture: Essays in Evolutionary Epistemology*. Edited by H. C. Plotkin. Chichester, N.Y.: Wiley.

Hyde, J. S., and B. G. Rosenberg. 1976. *Half the Human Experience: The Psychology of Women*. Lexington, Mass.: D. C. Health.

Hynes, H. P. 1984. "Women Working: A Field Report". *Technology Review* (MIT), November/December.

Hypatia: Journal of Feminist Philosophy. 1982 – present. Bloomington: Indiana University Press.

Isaac, G. 1976. "Stages of Cutlural Elaboration in the Pleistocene". *Annals of the New York Academy of Sciences* 280.

Isaac, G., and R. Leakey, eds. 1979. *Human Ancestors*. San Francisco: W. H. Freeman.

Jacobs, S. 1976. "Women in Perspective: A Guide for Cross-Cultural Studies". Urbana, Ill.: University of Illinois Press.

Jacobsen, M. 1978. *Developmental Neurobiology*. New York: Plenum.

Jacobus, M., ed. 1979. *Women Writing and Writing about Women*. London: Croom Helm.

Jaggar, A. 1983. *Feminist Politics and Human Nature*. Totowa, N.J.: Rowman & Allenheld.

————. 1984. "Human Biology in Feminist Theory: Sexual Equality Reconsidered". *Beyond Domination: New Perspectives on Women and Philosophy*. Edited by C. Gould. Totowa, N.J.: Rowman & Allenheld.

————. 1985. "Feminism, Liberal Theory, and Marxism". Paper delivered at Villanova University.

Jaggar, A., and P. R. Struhl. 1978. *Feminist Frameworks: Alternate Theoretical Accounts of the Relations between Women and Men.* New York: McGraw-Hill.

Jordan, J., M. Surrey, and J. Kaplan. 1982. "Women and Empathy". Work in progress, The Stone Center Colloquium on Women, Wellesley College.

Keller, E. F. 1974. "Women in Science: A Social Analysis". *Harvard Magazine,* October.

———. 1982. "Feminism and Science". *Signs: Journal of Women in Culture and Society* 7, no. 3.

———. 1983A. "Gender and Science". *Discovering Reality: Feminist Perspectives on Epistemology, Metaphysics, Methodology, and Philosophy of Science.* Edited by S. Harding and M. Hintikka. Dordrecht: D. Reidel.

———. 1983B. *A Feeling for the Organism: The Life and Work of Barbara McClintock.* New York: W. H. Freeman.

———. 1985A. *Reflections on Gender and Science.* New Haven: Yale University Press.

———. 1985B. "Women and Basic Research: Respecting the Unexpected". *Technology Review* (MIT), November/December.

Keller, E. F., and C. Grontkowski. 1983. "The Mind's Eye". *Discovering Reality: Feminist Perspectives on Epistemology, Metaphysics, Methodology, and Philosophy of Science.* Edited by S. Harding and M. Hintikka. Dordrecht: D. Reidel.

Kelly, J. 1979. "The Doubled Vision of Feminist Theory: A Postscript to the 'Women and Power' Conference". *Feminist Studies* 5, no. 1.

Kelly-Gadol, J. 1976. "The Social Relation of the Sexes: Methodological Implications of Women's History". *Signs: Journal of Women in Culture and Society* 1, no. 4.

———. 1977. "Did Women Have a Renaissance?" *Becoming Visible.* Edited by R. Bridenthal and C. Koonz. Boston: Houghton Mifflin.

Keohane, N., M. Rosaldo, and B. Gelpi, eds. 1981. *Feminist Theory: A Critique of Ideology.* Chicago: University of Chicago Press.

Kessler-Harris, A. 1982. *Out to Work: A History of Wage-Earning Women in the United States.* New York: Oxford University Press.

Kimball, M. M. 1981. "Women and Science: A Critique of Biological Theories". *International Journal of Women's Studies* 4.

Kinsbourne, M. 1980. "If Sex Differences in Brain Lateralization Exist, They Have Yet to be Discovered". *The Behavioral and Brain Sciences* 3.

Kittay, E., and D. Meyers, eds. 1986. *Women and Morality.* Totowa, N.J.: Rowman & Allenheld.

Klein, V., and A. Myrdal. 1956. *Women's Two Roles.* London: Routledge & Kegan Paul.

Knorr-Cetina, K., and M. Mulkay, eds. 1983. *Science Observed: Perspectives on the Social Study of Science.* London: Sage.

Koedt, A., E. Levine, and A. Rapone, eds. 1973. *Radical Feminism.* New York: Quadrangle Press.

Kohlberg, L. 1958. "The Development of Modes of Thinking and Choices in Years 10 to 16". Ph.D. diss., University of Chicago.

———. 1981. *The Philosophy of Moral Development*. San Francisco: Harper & Row.

Kohlberg, L., and Kramer, R. 1969. "Continuities and Discontinuities in Child and Adult Moral Development". *Human Development* 12.

Kripke, S. A. 1982. *Wittgenstein on Rules and Private Language*. Cambridge: Harvard University Press.

Kuhn, A., and A. Wolpe, eds. 1978. *Feminism and Materialism*. Boston: Routledge & Kegan Paul.

Kuhn, T. S. 1962. *The Structure of Scientific Revolutions*. Chicago: University of Chicago Press.

———. 1970. *The Structure of Scientific Revolutions*, 2nd ed. Chicago: University of Chicago Press.

———. 1972. "Second Thoughts on Paradigms". *The Structure of Scientific Theories*. Edited by F. Suppe. Urbana: University of Illinois Press.

Lakatos, I. 1970. "Falsification and the Methodology of Scientific Research Programs". *Criticism and the Growth of Knowledge*. Edited by I. Lakatos and A. Musgrave. Cambridge: Cambridge University Press.

———. 1976. *Proofs and Refutations: The Logic of Mathematical Discovery*. Edited by J. Worrall and E. Zahar. Cambridge: Cambridge University Press.

Lakatos, I., and A. Musgrave, eds. 1970. *Criticism and the Growth of Knowledge*. Cambridge: Cambridge University Press.

Lamphere, L. 1977. "Review Essay on Anthropology". *Signs* 2.

Lancaster, J. B. 1975. *Primate Behavior and the Emergence of Human Culture*. New York: Holt, Rinehart & Winston.

Lange, L. 1983. "Woman Is Not a Rational Animal". *Discovering Reality: Feminist Perspectives on Epistemology, Metaphysics, Methodology, and Philosophy of Science*. Edited by S. Harding and M. Hintikka. Dordrecht: D. Reidel.

Latour, B. 1986. *Science in Action: How to Follow Scientists and Engineers through Society*. Milton Keynes: Open University Press.

Latour, B., and S. Woolgar. 1979. *Laboratory Life: The Social Construction of Scientific Facts*. Beverly Hills: Sage. Reissued, 1986. Princeton: Princeton University Press.

Leacock, E. 1977. "Ideologies of Sex: Archetypes and Stereotypes". *Annals of the New York Academy of Science* 285.

———. 1978. "Women's Status in Egalitarian Society: Implications for Social Evolution". *Current Anthropology* 19.

———. 1981. *Myths of Male Dominance*. New York: Monthly Review Press.

Leacock, E., and R. Lee, eds. 1982. *Politics and History in Band Societies*. Cambridge: Cambridge University Press.

Leakey, R., and R. Lewin. 1977. *Origins*. New York: Dutton.

Leavitt, B., B. Sykes, and E. Weatherford. 1975. "Aboriginal Women: Male and Female Anthropological Perspectives". *Toward an Anthropology of Women*. Edited by R. R. Reiter. New York: Monthly Review Press.

Lederer, L., ed. 1980. *Take Back the Night: Women on Pornography*. New York: Bantam.

Lee, R., 1979. *The !Kung San. Men, Women, and Work in a Foraging Society*. New York: Cambridge University Press.

———. 1982. "Politics, Sexual and Non-sexual, in an Egalitarian Society". *Politics and History in Band Societies*. Edited by E. Leacock and R. Lee. Cambridge: Cambridge University Press.

Lee, R. B., and I. DeVore, eds. 1976. *Kalahari Hunter-Gatherers*. Cambridge: Harvard University Press.

Leibowitz, L. 1975. "Perspectives in the Anthropology of Women". *Toward an Anthropology of Women*. Edited by R. R. Reiter. New York: Monthly Review Press.

———. 1978. *Females, Males, Families: A Biosocial Approach*. North Scituate, Mass.: Monthly Review Press.

Lerner, G. 1979. *The Majority Finds Its Past*. New York: Oxford University Press.

———. 1986. *The Creation of Patriarchy*. New York: Oxford University Press.

Lever, J. 1976. "Sex Differences in the Games Children Play." *Social Problems* 23.

———. 1978. "Sex Differences in the Complexity of Children's Play and Games". *American Sociological Review* 43.

Levine, E. 1971. *Rebirth of Feminism*. New York: Quadrangle Press.

Levins, R. 1977. "Marxism and Science." Unpublished manuscript.

Levy-Agresti, J., and R. W. Sperry. 1968. "Differential Perceptual Capacities in Major and Minor Hemispheres". *Proceedings of National Academy of Sciences* 61.

Lewin, R. 1981. "Seeds of Change in Embryonic Development". *Science* 214.

Lewis, J. 1981. "Women, Lost and Found: The Impact of Feminism on History". *Men's Studies Modified*. Edited by D. Spender. New York: Pergamon Press.

Lewontin, R. C. 1976. "Sociobiology—A Caricature of Darwinism." *Journal of Philosophy of Science* 2.

———. 1977A. "Caricature of Darwinism". *Nature* 266.

———. 1977B. "Biological Determinism as a Social Weapon". *Biology as a Social Weapon*. Edited by Ann Arbor Science for the People Editorial Collective. Minneapolis: Burgess.

———. 1979. "Sociobiology as an Adaptationist Program." *Behavioral Science* 24.

———. 1981. "Sleight of Hand". *The Sciences*, July/August.

———. 1982. "Keeping It Clean". *Nature* 300.

———. 1983. "The Organism as the Subject and Object of Evolution". *Scientia* 118.

Lewontin, R. C., S. Rose, and L. Kamin. 1984. *Not in Our Genes: Biology, Ideology and Human Nature*. New York: Pantheon.

Lloyd, G. 1984. *The Man of Reason: "Male" and "Female" in Western Philosophy*. Minneapolis: University of Minnesota.

Longino, H. 1981. "Scientific Objectivity and Feminist Theorizing". *Liberal Education* 67.

———. 1983. "Beyond "Bad Science": Skeptical Reflections on the Value-Freedom of Scientific Inquiry". *Science, Technology, and Human Values* 8, no. 1.

Longino, H., and R. Doell. 1983. "Body, Bias, and Behavior: A Comparative Analysis of Reasoning in Two Areas of Biological Science". *Signs: Journal of Women in Culture and Society* 9. Reprinted in *Sex and Scientific Inquiry*. Edited by Sandra Harding and Jean O'Barr. Chicago: University of Chicago Press, 1987.

Lovenduski, J. 1981. "Toward the Emasculation of Political Science: The Impact of Feminism". *Men's Studies Modified*. Edited by D. Spender. New York: Pergamon Press.

Lowe, M. 1978. "Sociobiology and Sex Differences". *Signs: Journal of Women in Culture and Society* 4.

———. 1980. "The Biology of Exploitation and the Exploitation of Biology" National Womens Studies Association conference.

———. 1982. "Social Bodies: The Interaction of Culture and Women's Biology". *Biological Woman—The Convenient Myth*. Edited by R. Hubbard, M. S. Henifin, and B. Fried. Cambridge, Mass.: Schenkman.

———. 1983. "The Dialectic of Biology and Culture". *Woman's Nature: Rationalizations of Inequality*. Edited by M. Lowe and R. Hubbard. New York: Pergamon Press.

Lowe, M., and R. Hubbard, eds. 1981. *Woman's Nature: Rationalizations of Inequality*. New York: Pergamon Press.

Lugones, M., and E. Spelman. 1982. "Have We Got a Theory For You! Feminist Theory, Cultural Imperialism and the Woman's Voice". *Women's Studies International*, Fall.

Lumsden, C. J., and E. O. Wilson. 1981. *Genes, Mind, and Culture: The Coevolutionary Process*. Cambridge: Harvard University Press.

Lynch, M. 1985. *Art and Artifact in Laboratory Science*. London: Routledge & Kegan Paul.

Lyons, N. 1983. "Two Perspectives: On Self, Relationships and Morality". *Harvard Educational Review* 53, no. 2.

Maccoby, E., and C. Jacklin. 1974. *The Psychology of Sex Differences*. Stanford: Stanford University Press.

MacCormack, C. P. 1977. *Biological Events and Cultural Control*. Chicago: University of Chicago Press.

———. 1981. "Anthropology—A Discipline with a Legacy". *Men's Studies Modified*. Edited by Dale Spender. New York: Pergamon Press.

MacCormack, C., and M. Strathern, eds. 1980. *Nature, Culture and Gender*. Cambridge: Cambridge University Press.

McGlone, J. 1980. "Sex Differences in Human Brain Asymmetry: A Critical Survey". *The Behavioral and Brain Sciences* 3.

MacGuigan, M. 1973. "Is Woman a Question?" *International Philosophical Quarterly* 13, no. 4.

Mackinnon, C. 1981. "Feminism, Marxism, Method and the State: An Agenda for Theory". *Feminist Theory: A Critique of Ideology*. Edited by N. Keohane, M. Rosaldo, and B. Gelpi. Chicago: University of Chicago Press.

———. 1987. *Feminism Unmodified: Discourses on Life and Law*. Cambridge: Harvard University Press.

McMillan, C. 1982. *Women, Reason and Nature*. Princeton, N.J.: Princeton University Press.

Mahowald, M. 1978. *Philosophy of Women: Classical to Current Concepts*. Indianapolis: Hackett.

Martin, E. 1987. *The Woman in the Body: A Cultural Analysis of Reproduction*. Boston: Beacon Press.

Martin, M. K., and B. Voorhies. 1975. *Female of the Species*. New York: Columbia University Press.

Marx, Karl. 1844. *Economic and Philosophic Manuscripts of 1844*. Edited by D. Struik. New York: International Publishers.

Masterman, M. 1970. "The Nature of a Paradigm". *Criticism and the Growth of Knowledge*. Edited by I. Lakatos and A. Musgrave. Cambridge: Cambridge University Press.

Mattfeld, J. A., and C. G. van Aken. 1965. *Women and the Scientific Professions: The MIT Symposium on American Women in Science*. Cambridge, Mass.: MIT Press.

Maynard Smith, J. 1976. "Group Selection". *Quarterly Review of Biology* 51.

———. 1978. "Constraints on Human Behavior". *Nature* 276.

Maynard Smith, J., and N. Warren. 1982. "Models of Cultural and Genetic Change". *Evolution* 36.

Mayr, E., 1982. *The Growth of Biological Thought*. Cambridge: Harvard University Press.

———. 1985. "How Biology Differs from the Physical Sciences". *Evolution at a Crossroads: The New Biology and the New Philosophy of Science*. Edited by D. J. Depew and B. H. Weber. Cambridge, Mass.: MIT Press.

———. 1988. *Toward a New Philosophy of Biology: Observations of an Evolutionist*. Cambridge: Belknap Press of Harvard University Press.

Merchant, C. 1980. *The Death of Nature: Women, Ecology and the Scientific Revolution*. San Francisco: Harper & Row.

Midgley, M. 1980A. "Gene-juggling". *Sociobiology Examined*. Edited by A. Montagu. Oxford: Oxford University Press.

———. 1980B. "Rival Fatalism: The Hollowness of the Sociobiology Debate". *Sociobiology Examined*. Edited by A. Montagu. Oxford: Oxford University Press.

Miller, J. B., ed. 1973. *Psychoanalysis and Women*. Harmondsworth, England: Penguin.

———. 1976. *Toward a New Psychology of Women*. Boston: Beacon Press.

———. 1983. "Women and Power". Work in Progress, The Stone Center, Wellesley College.

Millman, M., and R. M. Kanter, eds. 1975. *Another Voice: Feminist Perspectives on Social Life and Social Science*. New York: Anchor.

Mitchell, J. 1973. *Women's Estate*. New York: Pantheon.

———. 1974. *Psychoanalysis and Feminism*. New York: Vintage.

Moi, Toril. 1985. *Sexual/Textual Politics*. New York: Routledge.

Money, J., and A. Ehrhardt. 1972. *Man and Woman, Boy and Girl*. Baltimore: Johns Hopkins University Press.

Montagna, W., and W. Sadler, eds., 1974. *Reproductive Behavior*. New York: Plenum.

Montagu, A., ed. 1980. *Sociobiology Examined*. Oxford: Oxford University Press.

Moulton, J. 1977. "The Myth of the Neutral 'Man' ". *Feminism and Philosophy*. Edited by M. Vetterling-Braggin, F. Elliston, and J. English. Totowa, N.J.: Littlefield, Adams.

———. 1983. "The Adversary Method." *Discovering Reality: Feminist Perspectives on Epistemology, Metaphysics, Methodology, and Philosophy of Science*. Edited by S. Harding and M. Hintikka. Dordrecht: D. Reidel.

Nagel, E. 1961. *The Structure of Science: Problems in the Logic of Scientific Explanation*. New York: Harcourt, Brace & World.

National Academy of Science. Committee on the Education and Employment of Women in Science and Engineering (Office of Scientific and Engineering Personnel, National Research Council). 1983. *Climbing the Ladder: An Update on the Status of Doctoral Women Scientists and Engineers*. Washington, D.C.: National Academy Press.

National Science Foundation. 1982 – present, biennial. *Women and Minorities in Science and Engineering*. Washington, D.C.: National Science Foundation.

Nelson, C. 1989. "Fostering More Powerful Voices". Paper presented at Glassboro State College, May.

Nicholson, L. 1984. "Feminist Theory: The Private and the Public". *Beyond Domination*. Edited by C. Gould. Totowa, N.J.: Rowman & Allenheld.

Noddings, N. 1984. *Caring: A Feminine Approach to Ethics and Moral Education*. Berkeley: University of California Press.

Oakely, A. 1974. *The Sociology of Housework*. London: Martin Robertson.

———. 1979. *Becoming a Mother*. London: Martin Robertson.

———. 1980. *Women Confined: Towards a Sociology of Childbirth*. London: Martin Robertson.

Oakley, K. 1972. *Man the Toolmaker*. London: British Museum.

Okin, S. 1979. *Women in Western Political Thought*. Princeton, N.J.: Princeton University Press.

Ortner, S. 1974. "Is Female to Male as Nature Is to Culture?" *Woman, Culture and Society*. Edited by M. Rosaldo and L. Lamphere. Stanford: Stanford University Press.

Ortner, S., and H. Whitehead, eds. 1981. *Sexual Meanings: The Cultural Construction of Gender and Sexuality*. Cambridge: Cambridge University Press.

Paller, B. T., and D. T. Campbell. 1985. "Reconciling Maxwell and Van

Frassen through Consideration of Sense-Organ Evolution, the Ostensive Basis of the Term 'Observe', and Optima Justificatory Practice in Science". Mimeographed.

Palmeri, A. 1980. "Feminist-Materialism: On the Possibility and the Power of the Nature/Culture Distinction". Mimeographed.

Parfit, D. 1984. *Reasons and Persons*. Oxford: Clarendon Press.

Parker, S., and H. Parker. 1981. "The Myth of Male Superiority: Rise and Demise". *American Anthropologist* 2.

Parlee, M. B. 1979. "Psychology and Women". *Signs: Journal of Women in Culture and Society* 5.

Piaget, J. 1932. *The Moral Judgment of the Child*. New York: Free Press.

———. 1968. *Six Psychological Studies*. New York: Viking.

Pomeroy, S. 1974. *Goddesses, Whores, Wives and Slaves: Women in Classical Antiquity*. New York: Schocken.

Popper, K. 1959. *The Logic of Scientific Discovery*. New York: Harper & Row.

———. 1972. *Objective Knowledge*. Oxford: Oxford University Press.

———. 1982. "The Rationality of Scientific Revolutions". *Scientific Revolutions*. Edited by I. Hacking. New York: Oxford University Press.

Quadagno, D., R. Briscoe, and J. Quadagno. 1977. "Effect of Perinatal Gonadal Hormones on Selected Nonsexual Behavior Patterns". *Psychological Bulletin* 84.

Quine, W. V. 1960. *Word and Object*. Cambridge, Mass.: MIT Press.

———. 1963. *From a Logical Point of View*. Revised ed. New York: Harper & Row. First printing, 1953.

———. 1966. *The Ways of Paradox and Other Essays*. New York: Random House.

———. 1969. *Ontological Relativity and Other Essays*. New York: Columbia University Press.

———. 1970A. *Philosophy of Logic*. Englewood Cliffs, N.J.: Prentice Hall.

———. 1970B. "Grades of Theoreticity". *Experience and Theory*. Edited by L. Foster and J. W. Swanson. Amherst: University of Massachusetts Press.

———. 1974. *The Roots of Reference*. LaSalle, Ill,: Open Court Press.

———. 1976. *The Ways of Paradox and Other Essays*. 2nd ed. Cambridge: Harvard University Press.

———. 1978. "Facts of the Matter". *Essays on the Philosophy of W. V. Quine*. Edited by R. W. Shahan and C. Swoyer. Norman: University of Oklahoma Press.

———. 1981. *Theories and Things*. Cambridge: Harvard University Press.

———. 1985. *The Time of My Life: An Autobiography*. Cambridge, Mass.: MIT Press.

———. 1987. *Quiddities: An Intermittently Philosophical Dictionary*. Cambridge: Harvard University Press.

Quine, W. V. O., and J. S. Ullian. 1978. *The Web of Belief*. 2nd ed. New York: Random House.

Quinn. N. 1977. "Anthropological Studies on Women's Status". *Annals of Anthropology* 6.

Ravetz, J. 1984. "Ideology in the Philosophy of Science". *Journal of Radical Philosophy*, Summer.

Rawls, J. 1971. *A Theory of Justice*. Cambridge: Harvard University Press.

Reed, E. 1971. *An Answer to the Naked Ape and Other Books on Aggression*. New York: Pathfinder Press.

———. 1978. *Sexism and Science*. New York: Pathfinder Press.

Reiter, R. R., ed. 1975. *Toward an Anthropology of Women*. New York: Monthly Review Press.

Reskin, B. F. 1978. "Sex Differentiation and the Social Organization of Science". *Sociological Inquiry* 48.

Rich, A. 1979. *On Lies, Secrets and Silence*. New York: W. W. Norton.

Roberts, H. 1981. "Some of the Boys Won't Play Any More: The Impact of Feminism on Sociology". *Men's Studies Modified*. Edited by D. Spender. New York: Pergamon Press.

Rogers, S. 1978. "Woman's Place: A Critical Review of Anthropological Theory". *Comparative Studies in Society and History* 20.

Rohrlich-Leavitt, R., B. Sykes, and A. Weatherford. 1975. "Aboriginal Women: Male and Female Anthropological Perspectives". *Toward an Anthropology of Women*. Edited by R. R. Reiter. New York: Monthly Review Press.

Rorty, R. 1979. *Philosophy and the Mirror of Nature*. Princeton, N.J.: Princeton University Press.

Rosaldo, M. Z. 1980. "The Use and Abuse of Anthropology: Reflections on Feminism and Cross-Cultural Understanding". *Signs: Journal of Women in Culture and Society* 5.

Rosaldo, M. Z., and L. Lamphere, eds. 1974. *Woman, Culture and Society*. Stanford, Calif.: Stanford University Press.

Rose, H. 1983. "Hand, Brain and Heart: A Feminist Epistemology for the Natural Sciences". *Signs: Journal of Women in Culture and Society* 9, no. 1.

———. 1988. "Beyond Masculinist Realities: A Feminist Epistemology for the Sciences". *Feminist Approaches to Science*. Edited by R. Bleier. New York: Pergamon Press.

Rose, S., ed. 1982. *Against Biological Determinism*. The Dialectics of Biology Group. New York: Allison & Busby.

Rossi, A. S. 1964. "Who Wants Women Scientists?" *Women and the Scientific Professions: The MIT Symposium on American Women in Science and Engineering*. Edited by J. A. Mattfeld and C. G. Van Aken. Cambridge, Mass.: MIT Press.

Rossiter, M. 1982A. "Fair Enough?" *Isis* 72.

———. 1982B. *Women Scientists in America: Struggles and Strategies to 1940*. Baltimore: Johns Hopkins University Press.

Rowbatham, S. 1979. "The Women's Movement and Organizing for Socialism". *Beyond the Fragments: Feminism and the Making of Socialism*. Edited by S. Rowbatham, L. Segal, and H. Wainwright. London: Merlin.

Rowbatham, S., L. Segal, and H. Wainwright, eds. 1979. *Beyond the Fragments: Feminism and the Making of Socialism.* London: Merlin.

Rowell, T. 1972. *Social Behavior of Monkeys.* Baltimore: Penguin.

———. 1974. "The Concept of Social Dominance". *Behavioral Biology* 11.

Rubin, G. 1975. "The Traffic in Women: Notes on the 'Political Economy' of Sex". *Toward an Anthropology of Women.* Edited by R. R. Reiter. New York: Monthly Review Press.

Ruddick, S. 1980. "Maternal Thinking". *Feminist Studies* 6, no. 2.

———. 1984. "Preservative Love and Military Destruction". *Mothering, Essays in Feminist Theory.* Edited by J. Trebilcot. Totowa, N.J.: Rowman & Allenheld.

Ruddick, S., and P. Daniels, eds. 1977. *Working it Out: 23 Women Writers, Artists, Scientists, and Scholars Talk About Their Lives and Work.* New York: Pantheon Books.

Ruse, M. 1973. *The Philosophy of Biology.* London: Hutchinson.

———. 1979. *Sociobiology: Sense or Nonsense?* Hingham, Mass.: Kluwer.

———. 1981. *Is Science Sexist?* Dordrecht: D. Reidel.

Russell, B. 1905. "On Denoting". *Mind* 14. Reprinted in *Readings in Philosophical Analysis.* Edited by H. Feigl and W. Sellars. New York: Appleton-Century-Crofts, 1949.

Ruth, S. 1981. "Methodocracy, Misogyny and Bad Faith: The Response of Philosophy". *Men's Studies Modified.* Edited by D. Spender. New York: Pergamon Press.

Sacks, K. 1976. "State Bias and Women's Status". *American Anthropologist* 78.

———. 1979. *Sisters and Wives: The Past and Future of Sexual Equality.* Westport, Conn.: Greenwood Press.

Sanday, P. 1981. *Female Power and Male Dominance: On the Origins of Sexual Inequality.* New York: Cambridge University Press.

Sargent, L., ed. 1981. *Women and Revolution.* Boston: South End Press.

Sassen, G. 1980. "Success Anxiety in Women: A Constructivist Interpretation of Its Sources and Its Significance". *Harvard Educational Review* 50.

Sayers, J. 1982. *Biological Politics.* New York: Tavistock.

Scheman, N. 1983. "Individualism and the Objects of Psychology". *Discovering Reality: Feminist Perspectives on Epistemology, Metaphysics, Methodology, and Philosophy of Science.* Edited by S. Harding and M. Hintikka. Dordrecht: D. Reidel.

Schilpp, P. A., ed. 1963. *The Philosophy of Rudolf Carnap.* La Salle, Ill.: Open Court.

Schuldenfrei, R. 1972. "Quine in Perspective". *Journal of Philosophy* 69, no. 1.

Scientific Manpower Commission, AAAS. 1975. *Professional Women and Minorities: A Manpower Data Resource Service* (pamphlet). Washington, D.C.: American Association for the Advancement of Science.

Scott, J. W. 1988. *Gender and the Politics of History.* New York: Columbia University Press.

Scott, J. W., and L. A. Tilly. 1978. *Women, Work and the Family*. New York: Holt, Rinehart and Winston. Republished 1987 by Methuen.

Segerstrale, U. 1986. "Colleagues in Conflict: An 'In Vivo' Analysis of the Sociobiology Controversy". *Biology and Philosophy* 1, no. 1.

Shafer, A., and M. Gray. 1981. "Sex and Mathematics". *Science* 211.

Sharp, F. C. 1950. *Good and Ill Will*. Chicago: University of Chicago Press.

Shea, W., and J. King-Farlow, eds. 1976. *Contemporary Issues in Political Philosophy*. New York: Science History Publications.

Shebar, W. 1987. "In Quest of Quine". *Harvard Magazine* 90, no. 2.

Sherman, J. 1978. *Sex-related Cognitive Differences: An Essay on Theory and Evidence*. Springfield, Ill.: Charles Thomas.

———. 1980. "Mathematics, Spatial Visualization, and Related Factors: Changes in Girls and Boys, Grades 8 – 11". *Journal of Educational Psychology* 72.

Sherman, J. and E. T. Beck. 1979. *The Prism of Sex: Essays in the Sociology of Knowledge*. Madison: University of Wisconsin.

Sherman, J., and E. Fennema. 1979. "Distribution of Spatial Visualization and Mathematical Problem Solving Scores: A Test of Stafford's X-Linked Hypothesis". *Psychology of Women Quarterly* 6.

Shields, S. 1975. "Functionalism, Darwinism, and the Psychology of Women: A Study in Social Myth". *American Psychologist* 30.

Showalter, E. 1977. *A Literature of Their Own: British Women Novelists from Bronte to Lessing*. Princeton, N.J.: Princeton University Press.

Sicherman, B., E. Monter, J. W. Scott, and K. K. Sklar. 1980. *Recent United States Scholarship on the History of Women*. Washington, D.C.: American Historical Association.

Signs: Journal of Women in Culture and Society. 1975 – present. Chicago: University of Chicago Press.

Simpson, E. L. 1974. "Moral Development Research: A Case of Scientific Cultural Bias". *Human Development* 17.

Slocum, S. 1975. "Woman the Gatherer". *Toward an Anthropology of Women*. Edited by R. R. Reiter. New York: Monthly Review Press.

Smart, C., and B. Smart, eds. 1978. *Women, Sexuality and Social Control*. London: Routledge & Kegan Paul.

Smith, D. 1974. "Women's Perspective as a Radical Critique of Sociology". *Sociological Inquiry* 44.

———. 1977. "Some Implications of a Sociology for Women". *Woman in a Man-Made World*. Edited by N. Glazer and H. Waehrer. Chicago: Rand McNally.

———. 1979. "A Sociology for Women". *The Prism of Sex: Essays in the Sociology of Knowledge*. Edited by J. Sherman and E. T. Beck. Madison: University of Wisconsin.

———. 1981. "The Experienced World as Problematic: A Feminist Method". Sorokin Lecture. Saskatoon: University of Saskatchewan.

Smith, D. E., and S. J. David, eds. 1975. *Women Look at Psychiatry*. Vancouver: Press Gang.

Smith, G. 1964. *Help Wanted—Female: A Study of Demand and Supply in a Local Job Market for Women.* New Brunswick, N.J.: Rutgers University, Institute of Management and Labor Relations.

Smith-Rosenberg, C. 1985. *Disorderly Conduct: Visions of Gender in Victorian America.* New York: Oxford University Press.

Sober, E., and R. C. Lewontin. 1982. "Artifact, Cause, and Genetic Selection". *Philosophy of Science* 49.

Sociobiology Study Group of Science for the People. 1976. "Sociobiology—Another Biological Determinism". *BioScience* 26, no. 3.

Spelman, E. V. 1982. "Woman as Body: Ancient and Contemporary Views". *Feminist Studies* 8, no. 1.

———. 1983. "Aristotle and the Politicization of the Soul". *Discovering Reality: Feminist Perspectives on Epistemology, Metaphysics, Methodology, and Philosophy of Science.* Edited by S. Harding and M. Hintikka. Dordrecht: D. Reidel.

Spender, D. 1980. *Man Made Language.* London: Routledge & Kegan Paul.

———, ed. 1981. *Men's Studies Modified.* New York: Pergamon Press.

Stack, C. B., M. D. Caufield, V. Estes, S. Landes, K. Larson, P. Johnson, J. Rake, and J. Shirek. 1975. "Review Essay in Anthropology". *Signs: Journal of Women in Culture and Society* 1.

Standish, L. 1982. "Women, Work, and the Scientific Enterprise". *Science for the People* 14.

Star, S. L. 1979. "Sex Differences and the Dichotomization of the Brain: Methods, Limits, and Problems in Research on Consciousness". *Genes and Gender II: Pitfalls in Research on Sex and Gender.* Edited by R. Hubbard and M. Lowe. New York: Gordian Press.

Steady, F. C. 1981. *Black Women Cross-Culturally.* Cambridge: Schenkman.

Strathern, M. 1972. *Women in Between: Female Roles in a Male World.* London: Seminar Press.

———. 1981. "No Nature, No Culture". *Nature, Culture and Gender.* Edited by C. P. MacCormack and M. Strathern. Cambridge: Cambridge University Press.

Tabet, P. 1982. "Hands, Tools and Weapons". *Feminist Issues* 2.

Tanner, N. 1981. *On Becoming Human.* Cambridge: Cambridge University Press.

Tanner, N., and A. Zihlman. 1976. "Women in Evolution. Part I: Innovation and Selection in Human Origins". *Signs: Journal of Women in Culture and Society* 1.

Tarski, A. 1956. *Logic, Semantics, Metamathematics.* London: Oxford University Press.

Tavris, C., and C. Offir. 1977. *The Longest War: Sex Differences in Perspective.* New York: Harcourt, Brace and Jovanovich.

Technology Review (MIT). 1984. Special issue on Women in Science, November/December.

Tiger, L., and R. Fox. 1971. *The Imperial Animal.* New York: Holt, Rinehart and Winston.

Tobach, E., and B. Rosoff, eds. 1978. *Genes and Gender I: First in a Series on Hereditarianism and Women.* New York: Gordian.

Traweek, S. 1984. "High Energy Physics: A Male Preserve". *Technology Review* (MIT), November/December.

———. 1987. *Particle Physics Culture: Buying Time and Taking Space.* Forthcoming.

Trebilcot, J., ed. 1984. *Mothering: Essays in Feminist Theory.* Totowa, N.J.: Rowman & Allenheld.

Trivers, R. 1972. "Parental Investment and Sexual Selection". *Sexual Selection and the Descent of Man.* Edited by B. Campbell. Chicago, Ill.: Aldine.

Tuchman, G. 1980. "Discriminating Science". *Social Policy* 11, no. 1.

van den Berghe, P. L. 1980. "Sociobiology: Several Views." *BioScience* 31.

van den Berghe, P. L., and D. Barash. 1977. "Inclusive Fitness and Human Family Structure". *American Anthropologist* 79.

Verrall, R. 1979. "Sociobiology: The Instincts in Our Genes". *Spearhead* 127.

Vetter, B. M. 1973 "The Outlook for Women in Science". *Science Teacher* 40.

———. 1976. "Women in the Natural Sciences". *Signs: Journal of Women's Culture and Society* 1, no. 3, pt. 1.

Vetterling-Braggin, M., F. Elliston, and J. English, eds. 1977. *Feminism and Philosophy.* Totowa, N.J.: Littlefield, Adams.

Vicinus, M., ed. 1972. *Suffer and Be Still.* Bloomington: Indiana University Press.

———, ed. 1977. *A Widening Sphere.* Bloomington: Indiana University Press.

Volpe, J. 1989. "Stroud and the Significance of Skepticism". Forthcoming.

Waddington, C. H. 1975. "Mindless Societies". *The New York Review of Books,* August 7. Reprinted in 1978 in *The Sociobiology Debate.* Edited by A. L. Caplan. New York: Harper & Row.

Wade, N. 1976. "Sociobiology: Troubled Birth for a New Discipline". *Science* 191.

———. 1977. *The Ultimate Experiment: Man-Made Evolution.* New York: Walker.

Walker, B. M. 1981. "Psychology and Feminism—If You Can't Beat Them, Join Them". *Men's Studies Modified.* Edited by D. Spender. New York: Pergamon Press.

Walsh, M. R. 1982. "The Quirls of a Woman's Brain". *Biological Woman—The Convenient Myth.* Edited by R. Hubbard, M. S. Henifin, and B. Fried. Cambridge: Schenkman.

Wartofsky, M. W. 1968. *Conceptual Foundations of Scientific Thought.* New York: Macmillan.

Washburn, S. L. 1960. "Tools and Human Evolution". *Scientific American* 203.

———. 1978. "What We Can't Learn about People from Apes". *Human Nature,* November.

Washburn, S., and C. S. Lancaster. 1976. "The Evolution of Hunting". *Kala-*

hari Hunter-Gatherers. Edited by R. B. Lee and I. DeVore. Cambridge: Harvard University Press.

Weisstein, N. 1982. "Adventures of a Woman in Science". *Biological Woman—The Convenient Myth*. Edited by R. Hubbard, M. S. Henifin, and B. Fried. Cambridge: Schenkman.

Whitbeck, C. 1973. "Theories of Sex Difference". *The Philosophical Forum* 5, nos. 1 and 2.

———. 1983. "Feminism and Dualism". Paper delivered at the After the Second Sex Conference, Philadelphia, 1983.

———. 1984. "A Different Reality: Feminist Ontology". *Beyond Domination*. Edited by C. Gould. Totowa, N.J.: Rowman & Allenheld.

Wilson, E. O. 1975A. *Sociobiology: The New Synthesis*. Cambridge: Harvard University Press.

———. 1975B. "For Sociobiology". *New York Review of Books*, December 11.

———. 1978A. *On Human Nature*. Cambridge: Harvard University Press.

———. 1978B. "Academic Vigilantism and the Political Significance of Sociobiology". *BioScience* 26, no. 3.

Wittgenstein, L. 1968. *Philosophical Investigations*. Translated by G. E. M. Anscombe. New York: Macmillan.

Wolpe, A. 1978. "Education and the Sexual Division of Labor". *Feminism and Materialism*. London: Routledge & Kegan Paul.

Woolgar, S. 1982. "Laboratory Studies: A Comment on the State of the Art". *Social Studies of Science* 12.

"Work in Progress". The Stone Center for Developmental Services and Studies. 1982 – present. Edited by J. Hall. Wellesley, Mass.: Wellesley College.

Wuketits, F. 1986. "Evolution as a Cognition Process: Towards an Evolutionary Epistemology". *Biology and Philosophy* 1, no. 2.

Yerkes, R. 1943. *Chimpanzees*. New Haven: Yale University Press.

Young, I. 1979. "Socialist Feminism and the Limits of Dual Systems Theory". *Socialist Review* 50 – 51.

Zihlman, A. 1978. "Women in Evolution: Subsistence and Social Organization among Early Hominids". *Signs: Journal of Women in Culture and Society* 4, no. 1.

———. 1981. "Women as Shapers of the Human Adaptation". *Woman the Gatherer*. Edited by F. Dahlberg. New Haven: Yale University Press.

———. 1985. "Gathering Stories for Hunting Human Nature". *Feminist Studies* 11.

Zukav, G. 1979. *The Dancing Wu Li Masters*. New York: William Morrow.

Index

Addelson, K., 146, 147, 163, 164, 321nn.
16, 24; cognitive authority, 10, 137,
139–45, 148, 160, 321n.18, 326n.53,
332n.107, 339n.1; epistemology of science and sociology, 139–45, 168–70,
180–84; metaphysics and cognitive authority, 94, 141–46, 148, 166–68,
339n.13; science communities, divisions
in cognitive labor, authority, and
prestige in, 32, 138–40, 168–75, 231–
32; science communities and social/
political context, 139–45, 322n.27
Aggression, male: assumption of
universality, 147, 152, 201, 206–12,
228–34; as genetically determined, 147,
152, 201; as hormonally determined,
194–96; and scientific ability, 194–96,
201
Analytic/synthetic distinction, 45–46; implication of its demise, 91–94, 115,
118, 237, 251–52, 356n.200; and
"physics question" in feminist science
criticism, 92, 251–52, 335n.42; Quine's
challenge to, 90–94, 334n.33
Androcentrism, 189–90, 359n.34; androcentric methodologies, 90–93, 206–12;
in anthropology, 191, 193, 201, 206–
22; and autonomy of science, 234–44;
consequences for content of science, 31,
188–212, 232–34 (*see also* Feminist
science criticism); as culturally deter-

mined bias and not subject to empirical
controls, 238–44; in developmental psychology, 191–93; and empiricist
accounts of science, 32–33, 186–89,
205, 211–12, 222–34, 261–75, 280–
82, 291–99; and good science/bad
science distinction, 188–90, 193, 197,
200–206, 211–12, 232–34, 249–54;
and individualism, 32–33, 233–34,
261–75, 280–92, 291–99; in "man, the
hunter" theory, 205–12, 232; and objectivity, 249–54, 300–317; as political,
204–5, 221–22, 227–30, 232–34; in
research into sex differences, 193–205;
social and historical relativity of, 189–
90, 359n.34; in social sciences, 191–93;
348nn. 24, 26, 27, 29, 30; in
traditional frameworks, 29–31. *See also*
Feminist science criticism
Animal sociology: androcentrism in, 201,
206–12, 228–30, 232–34;
anthropomorphism in, 228–30, 232–
34; male dominance, assumption of,
206–12; and politics, 221–22, 227–30,
232–34; relevance to human behavior
and sociology, 206, 208–12, 221–22,
228–30, 232–33. *See also* Sociobiology
Anthropology, androcentrism in, 191,
193, 201, 206–12, 348n.24. *See also*
"Man, the hunter" theory
Anthropomorphism, in scientific models,

389

3818